OUT OF THE IMMORTAL NIGHT

Samuel E. Loveman, 1906

OUT OF THE IMMORTAL NIGHT

SELECTED WORKS OF SAMUEL LOVEMAN

Edited by S. T. Joshi and David E. Schultz

Second Edition, Revised and Augmented

Hippocampus Press
───────────
New York

Copyright © 2004, 2021 by Hippocampus Press
Introduction and editorial matter copyright © 2004, 2021
by S. T. Joshi and David E. Schultz.

Published by Hippocampus Press
P.O. Box 641, New York, NY 10156.
www.hippocampuspress.com

All rights reserved.
No part of this work may be reproduced in any form or by any means without the written permission of the publisher.

Select unpublished texts by Samuel Loveman have been published by permission of the John Hay Library, Brown University. "Conversations with Sam" and "For Samuel Loveman" copyright © 2021 by Thomas J. Hubschman. Photographs by Walker Evans are © Walker Evans Archive, The Metropolitan Museum of Art, and used by permission. Ink sketch of Samuel Loveman on p. 378, credit: Hart Crane Papers, Rare Book & Manuscript Library, Columbia University in the City of New York. Interview with Sam Loveman by John Unterecker (1962) credit: *Impressions of Hart Crane*, Oral History Archives at Columbia, Rare Book & Manuscript Library, Columbia University in the City of New York.

Cover illustration from a drawing by William Sommer (1867–1949) in *The Sphinx* by Samuel Loveman (W. Paul Cook, 1944). Frontispiece photograph from *Cartoons* 1, No. 4 (November 1906): 30.

Cover design by Daniel V. Sauer, dansauerdesign.com
Hippocampus Press logo designed by Anastasia Damianakos.

Second Revised Edition
3 5 7 9 8 6 4 2

ISBN 978-1-61498-277-7 paperback
ISBN 978-1-61498-278-4 e-book

Contents

Introduction 13

I. Poetry 39

Poems (1911) 41
  In Pierrot's Garden 41
  Ode to Ceres 42
  Fra Angelico 43
  Song 44
  To P. G. 45
  Lines 46
  A Twenty-second Birthday 46

The Hermaphrodite and Other Poems (1936) 49
  The Hermaphrodite 49
  River Pattern 67
  Will o' the Wisp 68
  Steener Haakonson Dances 69
  Dream Song 69
  Heckscher Building 70
  Euphorion 70
  Agathon 70
  Arcesilaus 71
  Lineage 71
  For a Book of Poems 71
  Ascension 72
  Thomas Holley Chivers 72
  The Ramapos 73
  Oscar Wilde 73
  John Clare in a Madhouse 74
  The Minstrel 75
  The Chopin-Player 75
  A Dedication 76
  Vice 76
  Transience 76
  Dolore 77
  Bacchanale 77
  To Simone's 78
  Ad Fratrem 78
  Isolation 78

Remonstrance	79
Proteus	79
A Voyage	79
Legend	80
The Return	80
Memoralia	81
Forest of Rhododendron	81
Understanding	82
Ecce Homo	82
Ariel	83
Visitor	83
Inarticulate	83
Madison Square	84
Contrast	84
Invocation	84
Song	85
Harbour	85
Admonition	85
Foes	86
Limbo	86
Interlude	86
Gates Mills	87
Wasteland	87
Amy Levy	87
Forest Hill	88
Andenkung	88
Dream of Spring	88
Finis	88
A Georgia Garden	89
Palingenesis	89
Belated Love	89
Nostalgia	90
Becalmed	90
Mutation	90
Dirge	91
To Dionysus	91
To Apollo	92
Quatrains	93
Poppies	93
Forgotten Poets	94
Space	94
Music	94

  Simeon Solomon 94
   Aftermath 94
A Chinese Pavilion 95
Ben De Casseres in Camden 97
Terminus 98
UNCOLLECTED POEMS 99
 A Poet 99
 A Sonnet: Lethe 99
 The Birth of Fear 99
 Pierced 100
 Be Thou a Jew! 100
 A Lily 100
 Lost Youth 101
 Avalon 101
 Hope 102
 The Old Cobbler 102
 Shadow-Land 103
 The Song Unsung 103
 Ship of Dreams 103
 The Birth of Poesy 104
 On Lost Friendship 104
 Peccavi 105
 The Plaint of Bygone Loves 105
 Eventide 106
  I. Sunset 106
  II. Twilight 107
  III. Night 107
 David Gray 107
 De Profundis 108
 Ode to Homer 108
 An Epitaph 109
 Quatrains 109
 To Alfred Noyes, Oversea 110
 Michael Scott's Wooing 110
 Prologue to Arcadia 111
 Two Poems for Book Marks 112
 Thomas Dermody 114
 Debs in Prison 115
 Resurgam 118
 Shadow-Love 119
 Euthanasia 119

A Burden 119
A Departure 120
W. E. 120
On the Passing of Youth 121
A Triumph in Eternity 124
Talent 126
[Untitled] 126
[Untitled] 126
Adventure 127
Epilogue 128
In Sepulcretis 128
Saturday Evening 128
A Letter to G—— K—— 129
Ernest Nelson 131
Heldenleben 131
Winter 131
To Satan 132
Christmas—1923 133
Genesis 133
Night Piece (Forest Hill) 134
Monolith 134
Oscar Redivivus 134
Unfulfilled 135
Unfulfilled [Alternative] 135
To Mr. Theobald 135
To George Kirk on His 27th Birthday 136
Music 136
My Tribute 136
Vigil 137
To a Child 137
The Dead King 138
Kin 138
Episode 139
Rescue 139
Transit 139
The Abyss 140
Times Square 140
Metropolitan Museum 141
The Faithful 141
An Admonition to the Ladies 142
For the Chelsea Book Shop [I] 142
For the Chelsea Book Shop [II] 143

Nepenthe 143
Quatrain 144
Reliquiae 144
Spring at El Retiro 145
Versailles 145
[Untitled] 145
The Goal 146
[Untitled] 146
Phryne 146
[Prologue to *Circe*] 147
Illicit 147
Dowager 148
John Clare in 1864 148

II. DRAMA 149
   Oedipus at Colonus 149
   Belshazzar 153
   Nero 155
   Varden 157
   Narcisse 160
   Arcady 163
   Scene from "The Duchess Tragedy" 166
   A Scene for *King Lear* 169
   A Scene for *Macbeth* 175
   The Sphinx: A Conversation 178

III. TRANSLATIONS 197
A Song of Chamisso's 197
Twenty-four Translations from Heine 197
Catullus 208
Translations from Baudelaire 209
   La Musique 209
   Parfum Exotique 209
   Horreur Sympathique 210
   De Profundis Clamavi 210
   La Beauté 211
   Causerie 211
   Chant d'Automne 212
   Le Couvercle 213
   Le Chat 213
   La Fontaine de Sang 214
   Sonnet d'Automne 214
   Ciel Brouillé 215
   Les Chats 215

Translations from Verlaine 216
    Sagesse 216
    Bruxelles 216
    Romances sans Paroles 217
    Il Bacio 217
    La Bonne Chanson 217
    Vert 218
    Sappho 218
Sonnet: After Leconte de Lisle 219
God's Work 220

IV. FICTION **221**
Antenor 221
A Ruined Paradise 221
The One Who Did Penance 223
The Faun 225
The Departed 232
The Dog 234
Ferris Thone 237
An Impression 240
A Hopeless Love 241
The One Who Found Pity 250
Christmas-Eve with Sherlock Holmes 253

V. NONFICTION **257**
Tips from the Hobo 257
By the Way 258
Cleveland Notes 259
Ballads 259
George Herbert 262
Charles Lamb 262
Notes and Reviews 264
Notes and Reviews 266
George Meredith 268
Amateur Poetry 270
Critic's Letter 272
Notes and Review 272
The Cleveland Amateur Press Club Comes to Life 278
Cleveland Club Notes 278
Mr. Sterling and Minor Poets 279
A Keats Discovery 279
Comment 281
Comment 281

Bureau of Critics 283
Official Criticism: Bureau of Critics 286
Modern Poetry (An Exorcism) 289
Ernest Nelson: In Memoriam... 290
Comment... 291
A Note [to *Twenty-one Letters of Ambrose Bierce*] 292
Preface [to Oelenschlaeger's *Hakon Yarl*, translated by George Borrow]........293
Bureau of Critics 295
A Convention Address..296
A Foreword 297
The Book of Life 298
A Preface [to *The Fear*]... 300
Edna Hyde: A Preface... 300
Foreword [to *Poppies and Mandragora*] 301
Preface [to *The Man from Genoa*] 302
Hubert Crackanthorpe: A Realist of the Nineties........................303
Marcel Proust..310
Literature and Dry-Rot 312
The Theatrical Season 314
[Untitled] 316
A Letter on Hart Crane..316
Collecting Curious Books 319
A Conversation with Ambrose Bierce 321
A Holiday Post-Card... 322
The Coast of Bohemia 323
A Whittier Discovery.. 325
Books in Summer...326
A Sea-Coal Fire 328
New York Dynamics..330
Forth from La Mancha 332
Boswell Redivivus.. 333
A Feast of Charles Lamb 335
We Break the Silence..336
Literature and Life..338
Back to La Mancha...339
Under the Mistletoe 341
An Unedited Anthology 342
Books That Talk 344
Where Do They Go To?... 345
A Holiday Party... 347
Forgotten Books 349
Why We Read 350

Charles Dickens and Christmas 351
Howard Phillips Lovecraft 352
Lovecraft as Conversationalist 356
Introduction [to *Dead Letters Sent and Other Poems*] 359
From a Diary 360
Preface [to *The Hart Crane Voyages*] 369
Of Gold and Sawdust 372

APPENDIX 375
Interview with Sam Loveman, *by John Unterecker* 377
Conversations with Sam, *by Thomas J. Hubschman* 407
For Samuel Loveman, *by Thomas J. Hubschman* 471
Samuel Loveman, *by Harry Edwin Martin* 472
My Friend, Samuel Loveman, *by Rheinhart Kleiner* 473
A Scene for "King Lear" by Way of Introduction, *by Harry Edwin Martin* 477
Editor's Note to "A Scene for Macbeth", *by H. P. Lovecraft* 478
Rhymes and Reactions, *by George Sterling* 479
Preface [to *The Hermaphrodite*], *by Benjamin De Casseres* 480
[Review of *The Hermaphrodite and Other Poems*], *by Ernest A. Edkins* 481
[Review of *The Hermaphrodite and Other Poems*], *by William Rose Benét* 486

BIBLIOGRAPHY 487

INDEX OF POETRY TITLES 505

INDEX OF FIRST LINES 511

ILLUSTRATIONS
Samuel E. Loveman, 1906 2
Silhouette of Samuel Loveman cut on 25 March 1925 24
Samuel Loveman circa 1965, from *In Search of Hart Crane* 36
Drawing of Loveman by H. P. Lovecraft 38
Hart Crane and Samuel Loveman, 1929, by Walker Evans 376
Samuel Loveman, as drawn by Hart Crane 380
Samuel Loveman, c. 1929, ("Flight") by Walker Evans 398
Loveman's bookplate 486

INTRODUCTION

At first glance it might be thought that Samuel E. Loveman (1887–1976) was a mere hanger-on of the great. A correspondent of (briefly) Charles Algernon Swinburne (1837–1909), Ambrose Bierce (1842–1914?), and George Sterling (1869–1926), and a close friend of H. P. Lovecraft (1890–1937), Clark Ashton Smith (1893–1961), and Hart Crane (1899–1932), Loveman could easily be dismissed as a literary dilettante whose own accomplishments seem meager when juxtaposed to those of his associates. If this is so, it is in large part because Loveman made little effort to put himself forth as a literary figure in his own right. More diffident than even Lovecraft in approaching professional markets for his work, and adhering to standards of poetic style and diction that, with the advent of Modernism in the 1920s, consigned his exquisitely crafted verse to the margins of literature, Loveman seemed content to appear in amateur and small press venues. So careless was Loveman of preserving his work that his friend Lovecraft would urge him to recite his poems *viva voce* so that Lovecraft could transcribe them and tenuously preserve them for posterity. Loveman's two slim volumes of poetry, the first no more than a privately printed pamphlet, comprise less than half of his known output of verse, and it has taken the effort of several scholars, poring through crumbling amateur journals of nearly a century ago, to resurrect a number of forgotten poetic jewels. Loveman made no effort whatever to collect his scattered short stories, essays, and prose-poems.

Loveman's biography, pieced together from a multiplicity of sources, in the end remains fragmentary and episodic. He was born on 14 January 1887. The first thirty-seven years of his life were spent largely in Cleveland, and in many ways he retained emotional and literary ties to that metropolis. His literary awakening occurred at an early age: in 1902, according to a brief memoir by his fellow-Clevelander Harry E. Martin,[1] he joined the National Amateur Press Association (NAPA), although no publications with his work prior to 1905 have been found. In that year, howev-

---

1. Harry E. Martin, "Samuel Loveman," *National Times* No. 1 (June 1921): [3].

er, a number of Loveman's poems appeared in amateur journals, and he also issued what appears to have been a pamphlet or one-shot magazine called *Dedication,* containing two poems, "David, King of Israel" and "The Witch of En-dor." Regrettably, no copies of this publication have come to light, and its contents must be adduced only from a lengthy review of it (probably by Nelson G. Morton, then chairman of the NAPA's Bureau of Critics) in the *National Amateur* for March 1906. The review describes the poems as "recitals in the verse of Biblical incidents, with slight imaginative additions." The first poem "portrays the anxiety of David for Absalom and his grief over his son's death";[2] the second is not described by the reviewer, but is presumably a retelling of the celebrated encounter of Saul with the Witch of En-dor and her raising of the spirit of Samuel, as described in 1 Samuel 28:3f. Loveman contributed poems prolifically to the amateur press in the period 1905–10, especially to Martin's *Sprite* and other local papers. In "A Convention Address" (1923), he speaks warmly of the influence of amateurdom upon his life:

> I remember my entry into Amateur Journalism as though nothing else had intervened in all those years. I remember the papers that flooded my mails. I remember the shiver of delight with which I beheld my first contribution, a poem, and I remember my first convention, when, for the sheer ecstasy of anticipation, I could not sleep for two weeks ahead, awaiting the glorious event. I remember [Warren J.] Brodie's boyishness, [Tim] Thrift's idealism, . . . [John S.] Ziegler, the then-philosopher, [Alfred V.] Fingulin, impulsive and warm-hearted, [Richard R.] Kevern, and [William] Feather and [W. J.] Kostir—and these things that I remember, I assure myself can never be forgotten, for they have entered into the making of whatever has been worth while in my life, whatever has been vital, sincere, artistic and strengthening, in an otherwise no very successful literary career. For Amateur Journalism gave to me at that crucial period, what it has given to so many others, what we hope it will continue to give to so many an impulse and a defined incentive for keeping a flame in the torch, a light to go by, in an age almost hopelessly money-mad or material.

2. "N.A.P.A. Official Criticism by Bureau of Critics," *National Amateur* 28, No. 4 (March 1906): 4.

These words are strikingly in accord with those of another shy, bookish, introspective writer who found in amateurdom exactly the literary and personal encouragement he needed at a critical stage of his life—H. P. Lovecraft, who in "What Amateurdom and I Have Done for Each Other" (1921) declares that "With the advent of the United [Amateur Press Association] I obtained a renewed will to live; a renewed sense of existence as other than a superfluous weight; and found a sphere in which I could feel that my efforts were not wholly futile."[3]

In 1908 Loveman took a much bolder step toward establishing a place in the wider literary world when he wrote to Ambrose Bierce. Specifically, he sent his poem "In Pierrot's Garden" (first published in the amateur journal *Cartoons* for November 1907 and winner of the NAPA's laureate award for poetry the next year) to Bierce in care of the *Cosmopolitan*, under the impression that Bierce worked in an editorial capacity for that Hearst magazine and would be in a position to consider its publication there. As Bierce told Loveman in his reply (17 October 1908),[4] he was merely a regular contributor to and not an editor of *Cosmopolitan*, so he did not think he could do anything with the poem, although he spoke of its "excellence." Some months later Bierce wrote that he was planning to include "Pierrot" in his own monthly column, but in May 1905, before the poem could be published, Bierce had severed relations with *Cosmopolitan*. At that point Bierce began an unsystematic attempt to secure publication of "Pierrot" in one of the major magazines of the period. Loveman had already noted that some of his poems had been rejected by *Harper's* because they "lacked the modern note,"[5] and Bierce forthwith garnered rejections of "Pierrot" from *Everybody's Magazine*, *Atlantic Monthly*, *Harper's*, and apparently some other magazines. In this procedure Bierce was consciously reprising his years-long attempt to find berth for his pupil George Sterling's "A Wine of Wizardry," which after being rejected by as many as a dozen periodicals finally was published in *Cosmopolitan* (Sep-

3. *Collected Essays* (New York: Hippocampus Press, 2004), 1.273.
4. For Bierce's letters to Loveman, see *Twenty-one Letters of Ambrose Bierce* (Cleveland: George Kirk, 1922; rpt. West Warwick, RI: Necronomicon Press, 1991). Loveman's letters to Bierce survive in ms. in the Stanford University Library.
5. Loveman to Bierce, 20 October 1908.

tember 1907). Bierce seemed to amuse himself with the notion that the leading magazine editors of the nation could not recognize true poetry when they saw it, and he frankly used Sterling's and Loveman's work as test cases to confirm his theories on editorial obtuseness.

Loveman actually met Bierce in New York in September 1913, a few months before Bierce disappeared in Mexico,[6] but Bierce's interest in Loveman's work could hardly have justified the latter in stating, many years later, that he was a "protégé" of Bierce.[7] Bierce did perform one simple function that would prove significant: he put Loveman in touch with George Sterling. Sterling himself was a protégé of Bierce, and the latter quickly recognized that the two younger poets were both devoted to older standards in poetry, stretching back to the early Romantics (Keats, Shelley, Coleridge) up to Swinburne. In 1909 Bierce sent "Pierrot" to Sterling, who announced that it was "poetry clear through"[8]—high praise indeed, given Sterling's devotion to what he called "pure poetry," or poetry whose sole function was the expression of beauty and not the propagation of social, political, or moral lessons. Sterling remained a somewhat sporadic correspondent with Loveman, but he always spoke warmly of Loveman's poetic work; as early as 1913 he wrote to him: "Yes, Sam, you are a poet, a true poet, and a poet showing promise of being at least the equal of any person writing verse in this generation. And in such faith I am most firmly established."[9] It was exactly at this time that Sterling put Loveman in touch with his own protégé, Clark Ashton Smith, resulting in a rich relationship that would last the better part of both poets' lives.[10]

Loveman's own literary career, however, was not advancing in any

---

6. Loveman to Sterling, 14 February 1925 (ms., Huntington Library and Art Gallery, San Marino, CA [hereafter abbreviated HL]).
7. Loveman to Carol Smith, 25 January 1970 (ms., John Hay Library, Brown University [hereafter abbreviated JHL]).
8. Sterling to Bierce, 12 October 1909 (ms., New York Public Library [hereafter abbreviated NYPL]).
9. Sterling to Loveman, 8 May 1913 (ms., HL).
10. The joint correspondence of Loveman and Clark Ashton Smith (his letters to Loveman are at the Bancroft Library, University of California, Berkeley) has been published by Hippocampus Press (2021) as *Born under Saturn*.

significant way. Harry E. Martin states that Loveman left the NAPA in 1910. The next year he issued the first of his two volumes of poetry, a 24-page pamphlet entitled simply Poems, published in Cleveland at his own expense. He sent the book to Bierce, who urged him to send it to H. L. Mencken for review in the Smart Set, but whether Loveman did so is unknown. No publications by Loveman for the next six years have been located. Martin speaks of Loveman being employed as a "cost accountant," and Loveman himself noted to Smith in the summer of 1915 that the added burden of tending to his ailing father resulted in "twelve to fifteen hours of hard labour [a day], mental & physical."[11] Loveman's father Marcus, who had been born in Hungary, died 27 December 1915, thereby easing one aspect of the physical burden but probably not assuaging the mental burden appreciably. Around this time Loveman began work on a novel called *Philip Heather*, a chapter of which he sent to Sterling and Clark Ashton Smith, but it came to nothing and apparently does not survive.

In 1917 Loveman rejoined amateurdom, enrolling in both the NAPA and the UAPA. H. P. Lovecraft prided himself on the fact that it was he who had persuaded Loveman to reenter the amateur movement.[12] Lovecraft had stumbled upon Loveman's early amateur verse and had written a poem about him as early as 1915, "To Samuel Loveman, Esquire, on His Poetry and Drama, Writ in the Elizabethan Style" (*Dowdell's Bearcat*, December 1915); at that time he was not merely unaware of Loveman's whereabouts, he also was uncertain whether Loveman was alive. Two years later, he somehow (perhaps through a Clevelander like Harry E. Martin or William J. Dowdell) established epistolary contact with Loveman. In his memoir (1948), Loveman wryly describes the gist of Lovecraft's first letter: "Was I alive or dead? Would I write to him if I were still in the land of the living?" The correspondence between Lovecraft and Loveman must have been both voluminous and fascinating, but little is extant: only seven letters

11. Loveman to Clark Ashton Smith, 12 August 1915, *Born under Saturn* 51–2.
12. Lovecraft to Rheinhart Kleiner, 8 November 1917; *Letters to Rheinhart Kleiner and Others* (New York: Hippocampus Press, 2020) 93.

and three postcards on Lovecraft's side,[13] and only a few scraps on Loveman's, which survive only because Lovecraft used the versos of them for rough drafts of stories or essays.[14]

Although Loveman would later come to have mixed feelings about Lovecraft, there is no question the Providence writer was taken with the Clevelander, both for his erudition in the obscure byways of literature (in 1919 he notes admiringly that Loveman "has a vast library of rare first editions and other treasures precious to the bibliophile's heart"[15]) and for his refined aestheticism. To such a degree had Loveman entered Lovecraft's imagination that he served as the protagonist, or at least the trigger, of three of Lovecraft's weird tales of the period: "The Statement of Randolph Carter" (December 1919), an almost literal transcript of a dream in which Lovecraft (cited in the story as Randolph Carter) watches Loveman (cited as Harley Warren) enter a centuried crypt but not emerge; "Nyarlathotep" (December 1920), which was inspired by a dream in which Loveman tells Lovecraft, "Don't fail to see Nyarlathotep if he comes to Providence. He is horrible—horrible beyond anything you can imagine—but wonderful. He haunts one for hours afterward. I am still shuddering at what he showed"[16]; and "Hypnos" (May 1922), dedicated to "S. L.," the protagonist of which is an aesthete and enthusiast of Greek antiquity, much like Loveman himself. One suspects that Loveman was exactly the sort of person Lovecraft, at this stage of his life, wanted to be—learned, bookish, poetically gifted, and almost excessively sensitive to both the beauties and the tragedies of life and literature.

---

13. They are included in *Letters to Maurice W. Moe and Others*, ed. David E. Schultz and S. T. Joshi (New York: Hippocampus Press, 2018).

14. In "Lovecraft as a Conversationalist" (1958) Loveman states that he owns "500 folio pages" of Lovecraft's letters. He had purchased Lovecraft's letters to Frank Belknap Long, now in the possession of the John Hay Library of Brown University, Providence, R.I.

15. Lovecraft to the Gallomo, 11 December 1919; in *Letters to Alfred Galpin*, ed. S. T. Joshi and David E. Schultz (New York: Hippocampus Press, 2003), 64.

16. Lovecraft to Rheinhart Kleiner, 14 December 1920; *Letters to Rheinhart Kleiner and Others* 174.

In "A Letter on Hart Crane" (1933) Loveman states that he first met Hart Crane in 1919, but this appears to be an error, and Crane's biographers agree that the two did not meet until 1921, when they ran into each other at Laukhuff's bookstore in Cleveland. Loveman had been drafted in the summer of 1918 and spent the next year and a half at Camp Gordon, Georgia. His life there was not happy, as he suffered both from "bronchial trouble that put me in the hospital in the army"[17] as well as heart trouble; his bad eyes had prevented him from being sent overseas. Upon his return to Cleveland he apparently was unable to return to his job as an accountant, and seems to have been unemployed for some years. The young Crane was immediately taken with Loveman, although temperamentally they differed significantly, Crane being emotionally open, flamboyant, and an enthusiast of literary Modernism while Loveman was shy, reserved, hypersensitive, and devoted to the literature of a century or more ago. Crane speaks affectionately of "my classic, puritan, inhibited friend Sam Loveman."[18] Loveman introduced Crane to the artist William Sommer, and they began developing a cadre of like-minded artists and writers in Cleveland, including William Lescaze (later an internationally known architect), Edward Lazare (who would briefly mingle with the Lovecraft circle in New York in 1924–25 and would later become a longtime editor of *American Book-Prices Current*), and others. Crane biographer John Unterecker speaks of Loveman as "perhaps Hart's most faithful friend,"[19] and he not only would take care of Crane's ailing mother, Grace, after Crane's early death, but then also become Crane's literary executor after Grace's death in 1947.

Loveman's separate worlds—the worlds of amateur journalism and weird fiction, represented by Lovecraft, and the world of the aesthetic avant-garde, represented by Crane and his associates—would meet for the first, but not the last, time in the spring and summer of 1922. Sonia H. Greene, the dynamic Russian Jewess who had met Lovecraft at an

17. Loveman to Clark Ashton Smith, [August 1920] *Born under Saturn* 257.
18. Hart Crane to Gorham Munson, [c. 18 June 1922]; *The Letters of Hart Crane 1916–1932*, ed. Brom Weber (New York: Hermitage House, 1952), 91.
19. John Unterecker, *Voyager: A Life of Hart Crane* (New York: Farrar, Straus & Giroux, 1969), 17.

amateur journalism convention in 1921, clearly wished to see more of him (they would marry in 1924). She managed to persuade both him and Loveman to come to New York for a visit, although for Loveman it was at least in part a working vacation, as he sought to make contacts among New York booksellers. This "convention of freaks & exotics"[20] gathered on 6–12 April and included such figures as James F. Morton, Rheinhart Kleiner, Everett McNeil, Arthur Leeds, Frank Belknap Long, and other members of what would become the Kalem Club of 1924–26, but in many ways Loveman and Lovecraft were the stars of the show. Two months before meeting him, Lovecraft painted a portrait of Loveman that would remain an accurate depiction of this sensitive soul:

> Loveman himself is a romantic figure, about whose poverty, sufferings, genius, and divine melancholy one might write a moving volume. He is today almost destitute—has been forced to sell some of his treasured books, including rare incunabulae extending back to 1482—yet will not accept the loan of a farthing. He is one step in advance of his beloved vagabonds and bohemians—for he has pride, honour, and character. A glorious pagan—and a Jew by race.[21]

Loveman's own first impression of New York is expressed piquantly in a letter to Smith:

> It was one continual round of museums, theatres and sight-seeing—without a chance for employment—and I got home minus about ten pounds with enough cynicism to start a cyanide factory, and eyes that were full of forfeited sleep. It's a hell of a fine place, but the people are impossible. The women paint like hetaira's, one and all. The men carry canes. Both sexes lead poodles and bulls, although it would better become them to raise families and trundle baby-carriages.[22]

Loveman was not at this time successful in securing employment in New York, so he returned to Cleveland. Lovecraft was, however, hot

---

20. Lovecraft to Rheinhart Kleiner, 21 September 1921; *Letters to Rheinhart Kleiner and Otheres* 192.
21. Lovecraft to Frank Belknap Long, 8 February 1922; *Selected Letters* (Sauk City, WI: Arkham House, 1965–76), 1.166.
22. Loveman to Clark Ashton Smith, n.d. *Born under Saturn* 316–17.

on his trail, for after another visit to New York in July he boarded a train to Cleveland, arriving there on 30 July and remaining until 15 August. His purpose was to meet not only Loveman but also his young correspondent Alfred Galpin (1901–1983), who had struck up a friendship with Loveman and decided to spend the summer with him. It was in this way that Lovecraft first became acquainted with Hart Crane and the rest of his circle. Indeed, Lovecraft felt somewhat embarrassed that he seemed to be the center of attention:

> It gave me a novel sensation to be "lionised" so much beyond my deserts by men as able as the painter Summers [*sic*], Loveman, Galpin, &c. I met some new figures—Crane the poet, Lazar [*sic*], an ambitious young literary student now in the army, & a delightful young fellow named Carroll Lawrence, who writes weird stories & wants to see all of mine.[23]

Lovecraft paid the Crane circle the unusual tribute of writing a free-verse poem, "Plaster-All" (a play on Crane's poem "Pastorale," *Dial*, October 1921), supplying an impressionistic account of his Cleveland visit in general and of Loveman in particular. (Steven J. Mariconda is, however, correct in believing that the narrator of the poem is Crane himself.)

> Soon I met and succeeded
> In surrounding myself
> With a few of the intelligentsia
> That Cleveland affords.
> Loveman, Sommer, Lescaze, Hatfield, Guenther. . . .
> But Loveman
> Left the fold early—pity, yes!
> I might have made much of him,
> In spite of his Hebraism,
> Which (sibilantly whispered)
> I did not recognize,
> Even on my mother's hearsay—

---

23. Lovecraft to Lillian D. Clark, 9 August 1922, *Letters to Family and Family Friends*, ed. S. T. Joshi and David E. Schultz (New York: Hippocampus Press, 2020), 54.

> But there was much of the rebel,
> Inborn and instinctive,
> (As in all Jews)
> In Loveman.
> And so, after a perfectly wild argument
> With him one lovely night, late July,
> With the syringas in full blossom
> On 115th Street,
> We parted
> To meet no more—at least as friends.[24]

Loveman's literary career was at last progressing to some degree. He had begun his exotic prose drama, *The Sphinx*, in 1918,[25] working sporadically on it for the next several years. In February 1921 he started his best-known poem, *The Hermaphrodite*.[26] It is not clear when this work was finished, but Lovecraft appears to have read the complete poem (also the complete *Sphinx*) in April 1922. He also published three issues of his little magazine, *The Saturnian* (June–July [1920], August–September [1920], and March 1922). In the first issue he had promised to publish a lengthy appreciation of both the poetry and the artwork of Clark Ashton Smith but failed to carry out the promise. He did, however, publish in the third issue his twenty-four translations from Heinrich Heine, on which he had been at work since at least 1909,[27] along with superb translations from Baudelaire and Verlaine. In the summer of 1922 another Cleveland friend, the bookseller George Kirk (1898–1962), issued his one and only book publication, Loveman's edition of *Twenty-one Letters of Ambrose Bierce*. This slim booklet is perhaps more impressive for its typography and design than for its contents, for Bierce's letters to Loveman are quite insubstantial. H. L. Mencken was being perhaps only a bit too harsh when he wrote in a brief review: "The result was a polite exchange of

---

24. *The Ancient Track: Complete Poetical Works* (New York: Hippocampus Press, 2013), 255.
25. Loveman to Clark Ashton Smith, 4 February 1918, *Born under Saturn* 105.
26. Loveman to Clark Ashton Smith, [c. 12 February 1921], *Born under Saturn* 290.
27. See Loveman to Bierce, 18 May 1909 and [27 July 1909].

letters, but there is scarcely a word in any of them that justifies printing them. To them the editor prefixes a bombastic preface containing some gratuitous and nonsensical criticism of Hergesheimer and Cabell."[28]

It was at this time that an amusing contretemps over Loveman's poetry roiled the amateur press for well over a year. In an unsigned review of the first issue of Sonia Greene's *Rainbow* (October 1921), Lovecraft waxed eloquent about Loveman's "The Triumph in Eternity," writing:

> Samuel Loveman is the last of the Hellenes—a golden god of the elder world fallen upon pygmies. Genius of the most poignant authenticity is his, opening in his mind a diamond-paned window which looks out clearly upon rarefied realms of dreams and scenes of immortal beauty seldom and dimly glimpsed by the modern age.[29]

But the poem's expression of certain pagan and possibly anti-Christian sentiments aroused the stodgy amateur critic Michael Oscar White, who in a critical article on Loveman criticized Lovecraft's review (although White was unaware of his authorship of it) for praising a poet whose "insincere misanthropic" views taint his work, and whose use of pagan gods is not only antiquated but sacrilegious; remarking specifically of "A Triumph in Eternity," he wrote: "In anyone but an amateur poet with an amateur perception of things held sacred in a Christian country the whole piece would be considered blasphemous."[30] This excursion into fatuity elicited some predictable responses from Loveman's partisans, including Galpin and Long, both of whom wrote vitriolic attacks on White.[31] Lovecraft himself replied with a certain understated cynicism in "In the Editor's Study" (*Conservative*, July 1923), while Loveman himself stayed entirely above the fray.

---

28. Mencken, "Confidences," *Smart Set* 70, No. 1 (January 1923): 142.
29. [H. P. Lovecraft], "*Rainbow* Called Best First Issue," *National Amateur* 44, No. 4 (March 1922): 44; rpt. in *Collected Essays* 1.310–11.
30. "Poets of Amateur Journalism: III. Samuel Loveman," *Oracle* 3, No. 4 (December 1922): 12–17.
31. Galpin, "A Critic of Poetry," *Oracle* 4, No. 2 (August 1923): 8–10; Long, "An Amateur Humorist," *Conservative* No. 12 (March 1923): 2–5.

Silhouette of Samuel Loveman cut on 25 March 1925 in New York City with others of the Kalem Club by E. J. Perry, a popular silhouettist in the early 20th century

Sometime in 1923 Loveman had apparently secured a job at Eglin's, a leading bookstore in Cleveland, but by November of that year he had lost the position.[32] As a result, when Hart Crane moved to New York in August 1924, Loveman followed him the following month, thinking his chances of finding a job in New York no worse than in Cleveland. Just prior to leaving, he and Don Bregenzer had assembled an anthology of essays on James Branch Cabell, *A Round-Table in Poictesme*, published by the Colophon Club of Cleveland. Evidently Loveman had gotten over his initial hostility to Cabell to the point of saying that "comparatively little has been done in appreciation of the life-long sacrifice and assiduity of James Branch Cabell to creative literature."[33] In any event, Loveman was this time successful in securing employment in the book trade: Dauber & Pine, booksellers, at Fifth Avenue and 12th Street, hired him to a position he retained into the 1930s.

Of Loveman's multifarious meetings with both the "Lovecraft circle" and the "Crane circle" during 1924–26 it is difficult to speak in small compass. Perhaps the most pungent occasions were when the two groups—specifically, Lovecraft and Crane—encountered each other, as they did a surprising number of times. Crane's letter of the fall of 1924 is well known: "Miss Sonia Green[e] and her piping-voiced husband, Howard Lovecraft . . ., kept Sam traipsing around the slums and wharf streets until four this morning looking for Colonial specimens of architecture, and until Sam tells me he groaned with fatigue and begged for the subway!"[34] A later comment is no less piquant:

> Sam, as I wrote before, has been working in a bookstore. For nearly two weeks I didn't see him at all. Then last Saturday I called on him at his shop and invited him over for Sunday evening. He brought that queer Lovecraft person with him, so we had no particularly intimate conversation. Just as well, of course, as I am sure they would have been the same disparagements of everything and almost everybody, as usual.

32. Hart Crane to Elizabeth Belden Hart, 10 November 1923; *Letters of Hart Crane and His Family*, ed. Thomas S. W. Lewis (New York: Columbia University Press, 1974), 229.
33. Loveman and Bregenzer, "A Foreword," *A Round-Table in Poictesme* (Cleveland: Colophon Club, 1924), ix.
34. Crane to Grace Crane, 14 September 1924; *Letters of Hart Crane 1916–1932* 187.

He isn't getting along any better with his boss than he did with Eglin in Cleveland, and despite my reminding him of this and other examples of the past he still feels himself the eternal martyr and longs for his bed and home, his mending and home-washed laundry and home cooked food.[35]

Loveman at this time was pursuing an interest in the American writer Edgar Saltus (1855–1921), a once-popular but now forgotten writer of cynical society novels and eccentric works such as *Imperial Purple* (1892), a series of evocative prose-poems on the Roman emperors. Loveman once declared to Smith that he had "undivided respect" for only four American writers—Smith himself, George Sterling, Saltus, and (oddly) Sherwood Anderson.[36] He pursued his Saltus interest for years, getting in touch with Saltus's widow, Marie, and writing an entire monograph on the author. Although Lovecraft states that this monograph was actually scheduled for publication by Brentano's,[37] it never appeared and does not appear to survive; all Loveman had to show for his efforts was a collection of the poems by Edgar and Marie Saltus, *Poppies and Mandragora* (1926), to which he contributed a brief preface. Crane scoffed at Loveman's interest in Saltus,[38] and Mencken is probably right in declaring that of all Saltus's books

> only "Imperial Purple" holds up. A certain fine glow is still in it; it has gusto if not profundity; Saltus's worst faults do not damage it appreciably. I find myself, indeed, agreeing thoroughly with the literary judgment of Dr. [Warren G.] Harding. "Imperial Purple" remains Saltus's best book. It remains, also, alas, his only good one![39]

---

35. Crane to Grace Crane, 14 October 1924; *Letters of Hart Crane and His Family* 354.
36. Loveman to Smith, [13 October 1920], *Born under Saturn* 274.
37. Lovecraft to Lillian D. Clark, 24–27 October 1925, *Letters to Family and Family Friends*, 472. The book initially was to be published by the Centaur Press of Philadelphia (Lovecraft to Edward H. Cole, 24 February 1925, *Letters to Alfred Galpin and Others*, ed. S. T. Joshi and David E. Schultz (New York: Hippocampus Press, 2020) 57.
38. See Crane to Gorham Munson, Thanksgiving 1922; *The Letters of Hart Crane 1916–1932*, 91.
39. Mencken, "Edgar Saltus," *Prejudices: Fifth Series* (New York: Knopf, 1926), 282.

Otherwise, Loveman was contributing poetry sporadically to the amateur press, although so far as is known he published only two original poems in 1927, none in 1928, two in 1929, and none in 1930 and 1931. W. Paul Cook issued *The Hermaphrodite* as a slim pamphlet in 1926, as one of the first publications of his Recluse Press. Loveman also contributed a lively essay on the *fin-de-siècle* British writer Hubert Crackanthorpe to Cook's one-shot magazine, *The Recluse*.[40]

Loveman's activities in the later 1920s are not entirely clear. He continued to live in New York and work in the book business, and his association with Crane flourished. Lovecraft's departure from New York and return to Providence in 1926 by no means ended their relationship, and Loveman not only met Lovecraft frequently in Providence or Boston on book-hunting trips, but he did Lovecraft the somewhat dubious favor of putting him in touch with such revision clients as Zealia Bishop and Adolphe de Castro. No correspondence to or from Lovecraft (or, for that matter, to Smith) for this period appears to survive. In early 1928 Loveman became the proprietor of the Rowfant Book Shop at 165 William Street.

In 1932 Loveman helped to establish the literary magazine *Trend*, and although he is listed on the editorial board for only the first issue (March–April–May 1932), he contributed poems, essays, and reviews to the first several issues. At last, in 1936, a significant collection of his poems appeared: *The Hermaphrodite and Other Poems*, issued by the Caxton Press of Caldwell, Idaho. It contains 72 poems, or well under half his extant corpus of poetic work, and it is not clear that it featured all his best work. In particular, it included none of his poetic dramas, certainly a striking phase of his writing. Some of the poems had appeared in Hyman Bradofsky's amateur journal, *The Californian*, for Summer 1935.

For Loveman's later career there is little evidence. Sterling had died in 1926, Crane in 1932, Lovecraft in 1937. Loveman later told John Unterecker that Crane was "the best friend I ever had . . . the most charming, the

---

40. In a letter to his aunt, Lillian D. Clark (6 August 1925), Lovecraft speaks of reading the first chapter of Loveman's Civil War novel *Thracia Deane* (*Letters to Family and Family Friends* 332). This work does not survive.

most *alive* human being that life has ever given me, barring none."⁴¹ It may well be that the deaths of these colleagues had something to do with the drying up of Loveman's own literary voice. He wrote several memoirs of Crane, most of them saying much the same thing. In 1935 he established the Bodley Book Shop, a mail order book business,⁴² and under the imprint of the Bodley Press he published three books in the late 1940s, including Brom Weber's *Hart Crane: A Biographical and Critical Study* (1948). W. Paul Cook finally issued *The Sphinx* in a limited edition in 1944. Loveman continued to work in the book business in New York into an advanced age, including such venues as the Gotham Book Mart; he also established his own bookstore, which was discontinued a few years before his death.⁴³

In the later 1940s Loveman reestablished contact with Sonia Greene, who thought she had divorced Lovecraft in 1929 and married Dr. Nathaniel Davis in 1935. In their letters (surviving at the John Hay Library) there is much discussion of Lovecraft's anti-Semitism—something that was apparently a revelation to Loveman. The matter seemed to fester in Loveman's mind; although his first two memoirs, "Howard Phillips Lovecraft" (1948) and "Lovecraft as a Conversationalist" (1958), are on the whole respectful (although in the latter he refers tartly to Lovecraft's letters as "verbal vomit"), Loveman's resentment at what he believed to be Lovecraft's hypocrisy flared out unexpectedly late in life. In the brief memoir "Of Gold and Sawdust" (1975) he writes bitterly of his years with Lovecraft in New York:

> What I did not realize (or know) was that he was an arrant anti-Semite who concealed his smouldering hatred of me because of my taint of Jewish ancestry. It would be impossible for me to describe the smug, cloaked hypocrisy of H. P. L. . . . Lovecraft had a hypocritical streak to him that few were able to recognize.⁴⁴

---

41. Unterecker, *Voyager* 771.
42. See Rheinhart Kleiner, "My Friend, Samuel Loveman," *Aonian* 3, No. 3 (Autumn 1945): 244.
43. Obituary, *New York Times* (18 May 1976): 18.
44. *The Occult Lovecraft* (Saddle River, NJ: Gerry de la Ree, 1975) 22.

It would take a volume of commentary to explain the fallacies in Loveman's position; all we can do is express sympathy that his later years were marred with misplaced hatred. And yet, his aesthetic sensibility never fell into abeyance; a month or so before his death he wrote his last poem, "John Clare in 1864," one of several poems about the British poet he championed; and it is difficult not to read in the final stanza an awareness of his own imminent departure from this life:

> John Clare stares up, his dull eyes bright.
> Someday I'll follow in his flight.

Samuel Loveman died on 14 May 1976, at the Jewish Home and Hospital for the Aged. He published relatively little poetry in the last forty years of his life, and it has taken more than four subsequent decades for his work to be resurrected, chiefly as ancillary to Lovecraft's. But Loveman's work deserves study and appreciation on its own, for it is scarcely to be doubted that he possessed poetic gifts of a high order.

Poetry as delicate and ethereal as Loveman's is difficult to analyze, although its general features are evident: precision in metre and diction, an exhaustive use of Graeco-Roman myth to focus on concerns of universal significance, a refined, at times *recherché* lyricism that occasionally crosses over into obscurity, and a keen sensitivity to the smallest nuances of aesthetic and emotional resonance. There is a sense that Loveman, at least in his early verse, derived greater inspiration from art than from life, as witness his odes to Dionysus, Apollo, and Ceres (pure evocations of Greek myths with little attempt to draw out their broader implications or contemporary relevance) and his many poems on other poets (Shelley, John Clare, Thomas Holley Chivers, Oscar Wilde) or artists (Fra Angelico, Chopin). This, indeed, was the focus of a somewhat harsh but not entirely unjust comment by Hart Crane:

> . . . I see literature as very closely related to life,—its essence, in fact. But for Sam, all art is a refuge *away* from life,—and as long as he scorns or fears life (as he does) he is witheld [sic] from just so much of the deeper content and value of books, pictures and music. He sometimes

talks about them in terms as naive as an auctioneer would use. Yet he is instinctively so fine and generous that I will always love and pity him, however much my admiration is curtailed.[45]

It was, perhaps, exactly this quality of seeking "refuge *away* from life" that caused such writers as Sterling, Smith, and Lovecraft to admire Loveman's poetry, for their own work in many ways tended in just that direction.

Crane's comment highlights the chief disjunction in aesthetic sensibility between a poet like Loveman and the literary Modernists who emerged in the course of the 1920s. There is no doubt that Loveman, like Sterling, Smith, and Lovecraft, looked backward rather than forward; his worship of ancient Greek life and culture is fully in accord with the temperaments of such poets as Swinburne, Ernest Dowson, and other poets of the later nineteenth century. What he thought of the Modernists is made abundantly clear in his hostile snarl, "Modern Poetry (An Exorcism)." To say, however, that Loveman looked backward rather than forward is not a criticism; in poetry it is not necessarily a virtue to be up-to-date. Clearly Loveman still found an ample fund of vitality not only in the standard metrical schemes of English verse but also in the classical heritage that so many poets, from the Elizabethans onward, drew upon for inspiration. His own fidelity to Greece is frequently expressed, perhaps no more poignantly than in "Lineage." "Bacchanale" is another paean to antiquity; its dedication to the teetotaler Lovecraft may seem anomalous until we reflect that the wine of Bacchus is, for Loveman, merely a synecdoche for the more spacious, unbridled life that he envisioned to be possible under a pagan rather than a Christian sensibility.

This contrast between paganism and Christianity can be said to be at least one major strand in Loveman's greatest poem, *The Hermaphrodite*. What the Hermaphrodite—offspring of Hermes and Aphrodite, and endowed with both male and female genitals (although Loveman says nothing about this aspect of his protagonist)—represents is the pagan beauty and youth that classical civilization embodies in its literature, its art, and its morality. There has scarcely been a more poignant lament at the passing of antiquity than in the lines of Loveman's narrator:

45. Crane to Grace Crane, 23 September 1924; *The Letters of Hart Crane, 1916–1932* 191.

> I murmured: "For three thousand years
> Is that tale done, yet bitter tears
> Come to me now—to clasp and close
> The delicate ecstasy of those
> That vanished through no fault of mine."

Loveman states plainly that the advent of Christianity—and specifically the Christian emphasis on sin and punishment—effected a cataclysmic moral change that destroyed the pagan lightheartedness of the classical world:

> "[. . .] But One there was,
> Since thy long sleep had come to pass,
> Who drove the antique fiery mirth
> Forth from this mute and dreaming earth;
> Who, crowned with thorns and soft as air,
> Bade the Elysian world despair;
> Hopeless and bitter, dusk and brief,
> With great eyes brooding on his grief,
> And vast heart burdened by such things,
> Unknown to thy imaginings;—
> He conjured Hell!"

There is a pervasive, aching sense of lost beauty that makes *The Hermaphrodite* inexpressibly plangent and overridingly melancholy. George Sterling, in a letter written only two weeks before his death, wrote that it "is truly a remarkable poem, as uniquely beautiful as anything written in my own lifetime."[46]

We have seen that Michael Oscar White had criticized the purportedly anti-Christian sentiments of Loveman's "A Triumph in Eternity." It is a bit difficult to penetrate the meaning of this opaque poem, but Loveman makes clear in a letter to Sterling that the poem at least partly reflected a hostility to Christianity: "it doesn't quite breathe my 'sentiments' as regards my religion, for I am nearly an atheist."[47] More

---

46. Sterling to Loveman, 5 November 1926 (ms., HL).

47. Loveman to George Sterling, 23 January 191[6] (ms., HL). At this time the poem was called "A Triumph of Anarchy."

straightforward is "To Satan" (first published in Lovecraft's *Conservative*), which portrays Satan as a Prometheus figure seeking to liberate humanity from the "tyrant" God.

It would be unfair to Loveman to suggest that all or even most of his poems are, as it were, second-order creations—derived from other works of art rather than from "life," however that may be defined. His touching elegies to departed friends—from as early as "To P. G.," and moving on through "Ernest Nelson" (a member of the Crane circle and a co-worker with William Sommer at Otis Lithography in Cleveland),[48] to the soldier immortalized in "W. E.," no doubt an army buddy in Georgia—exhibit a poignancy born of real emotion. Later poems, such as "River Pattern" and "Ben de Casseres in Camden," similarly find poetic substance in life rather than in literature, although the latter is a tribute not only to the eccentric poet and critic who wrote prefaces to Loveman's *Hermaphrodite* (1926) and *Hermaphrodite and Other Poems* (1936), but also to Walt Whitman, who by this time Loveman had come to admire as a rebel battling against American bourgeois conformity.

A temperament like Loveman's was not often given to whimsy, but "An Admonition to the Ladies" (a poem written in reply to one by Rheinhart Kleiner) shows him to be not lacking in self-deprecating wit. "Oscar Redivivus" is one of several poems written by the Lovecraft circle upon the untimely death of the beloved cat of a neighbor of George Kirk. Loveman pays Lovecraft himself a fine tribute in "To Mr. Theobald," showing keen awareness that Lovecraft's return to the colonial haven of his native Providence was essential to his mental equilibrium. Loveman's friend George Kirk also inspired several poems, not only to himself ("A Letter to G—— K——") but to his Chelsea Book Shop.

It is in Loveman's verse dramas that he shows most clearly another side of his personality—his devotion to the Elizabethans. If, as a lyric poet, he is a child of the *fin de siècle*, evoking the delicate aestheticism of Wilde and Pater, as a dramatist he draws upon Shakespeare and, through him, to Greek tragedy. As early as 1909 he was announcing to Bierce:

---

48. Unterecker, *Voyager* 229.

> I suppose it is a rather gigantic scheme for a fellow of my inexperience to assume, but it involves in epic form, nothing less than the entire Oresteia of the Greeks, and as I have it, commencing with a prologue of old Saturn in which he emphasises on fate, etc., then turning to the murder of Agamemnon by Clytemnestra and the subsequent sorrows brought upon Orestes. My plan is to go in strongly on the old Hellenic idea of Destiny and to make this palpable characteristic assume predominant proportions throughout the meaning of the tragic tale.[49]

This grandiose plan was jettisoned very early on, but "Oedipus at Colonus"—not in any sense a translation of Sophocles' play, but a depiction of Oedipus' death through a Shakespearean lens, as he expresses world-weary sentiments more in tune with Macbeth or Lear than with a Greek protagonist—is one of the notable contributions to *Poems* (1911). It is no surprise that *King Lear* and *Macbeth* appear to have been Loveman's favorite Shakespeare plays, and both his "additions" to them constitute (as Lovecraft wrote in an editor's note to the latter) "a notable achievement in the annals of archaic imitation." His "Scene from 'The Duchess Tragedy'" is a purported extract from a fictitious Elizabethan drama.

The Sphinx, though in prose, constitutes "pure poetry" as much as anything in Loveman's entire corpus. As with *The Hermaphrodite*, it could be said that a religious conflict (or, perhaps more accurately, contrast) is at the heart of this drama: the three chief figures—a Greek, a Hebrew, and an Egyptian—speak of their different gods and, by implication, of the differing perceptions of the world and attitudes to life represented by these three great civilizations. Unusually in Loveman's generally chaste work, sexual imagery is abundant in the work, and there, if anywhere, we perhaps gain an inkling of his homosexual orientation, as when the Greek Hermes is told of "the perilous love of men for women, of their blossomy breasts." But this is an element of both his personal life and his work that Loveman designedly understated, and it emerges in the rest of his work only by implication—as in, say, the nearly total absence of love poems directed to women. As for *The Sphinx*,

---

49. Loveman to Bierce, 15 March 1909.

Lovecraft was correct in deeming it "a poisonous flower grown in Syrian marshes where the Orontes winds down to the sea from Antioch."[50]

Loveman's other work in prose also requires some discussion. He himself noted that "my prose is labored and I know it,"[51] but he was being highly unjust to himself. Elsewhere, in disputing the amateur writer Richard R. Kevern's scorn of "highfalutin" prose, Loveman presents a stirring defense of poetic prose that manifestly applies to much of his own work:

> Has Mr. Kevern read Jeremy Taylor, Browne, Bunyan, and Pater? Can he trace the degeneration of the "splendid and terrible" arsenal of Dryden's prose down to that of our own parsimonious twilight of snivelling, drivelling manikins? And is he aware that our best prose is undergoing what [Theodore] Watts-Dunton has rationally defined as the Renaissance of Wonder; a period in which the bottomless barrier between prose and poetry is described as becoming less defined from the hackneyed strictures of that slough of affected classicism, the Georgian Era? We believe not.[52]

Loveman contributed critical commentary to the amateur press from as early as 1907 to the 1920s; and if some of these pieces betray several of his crotchets and idiosyncrasies, they remain shrewd and perspicacious in dissecting the failings of the amateur writing of the period.

There is also much substance in his surviving short fiction. Such tales as "The Faun" and "The Man Who Found Pity" are again wondrous re-creations of classical Greece, but whereas the former seems little more than a playful, even flippant, tale of gods and demigods, the latter—more an allegory or parable than a story—displays, in spite of Loveman's avowed anti-Christian ethos, the authentically Christian notion of *agape*, or love inspired by empathy with another's lot. The touching love story "The One Who Did Penance" is also heavily allegor-

---

50. Lovecraft to Maurice W. Moe, 18 May 1922; *Letters to Maurice Moe and Others* 85.
51. Loveman to Sterling, 5 May 1915 (ms., HL).
52. "Notes and Reviews," *Buckeye* 1, No. 2 (January 1908): 1–2.

ical. "A Hopeless Love" is a piquant historical tale set in medieval France, with the poet François Villon as a character. "Ferris Thone," perhaps the only extant story of Loveman's to be set in the contemporary world, seems patently autobiographical, dealing with a man born of a Jewish mother, who served in the Army who subsequently took to writing poetry in the manner of Poe and Baudelaire. (The fact that the narrative proves to deal with an avowedly fictitious character does not lessen the obvious similarities to Loveman's own heritage, circumstances, and literary inclinations.)

If these stories, along with *The Sphinx*, most exaltedly embody Loveman's ideal of poetic prose, his other prose work—much of it, in the form of essays and reviews, not consciously written in a prose-poetic idiom—has numerous points of merit. Loveman's sensitivity to fine shades of emotion allows him to probe into the psyches of friends like Crane and Lovecraft in such a way that his memoirs become far more than mere recollections of external events. Crane was probably correct in believing that Loveman's critical judgment was not to be trusted, as his exaggerated fondness for Edgar Saltus attests; and Mencken is correct in his dismissal of Loveman's brief discussion of Bierce in the preface to *Twenty-one Letters*. Although his harsh review of Ludwig Lewisohn's *Expression in America* ("Literature and Dry-rot") makes some telling points, it also seems to reveal a blanket disapproval of all contemporary writing that does not augur well for Loveman's critical judiciousness. His best purely critical essay is probably his lengthy study of Hubert Crackanthorpe, although one would not suppose that this author's tales of social realism would find much of an echo in Loveman's own temperament. It is a pity that he did not write the critical evaluation of Clark Ashton Smith that he had long promised, for both in temperament and in their literary work the two men seemed remarkably, even uncannily, attuned to each other.

But Loveman truly shines in the piquant mini-essays he wrote for various catalogues for the bookshops for which he worked—Dauber & Pine and the Bodley Book Shop, from the 1920s into the 1940s. Here Loveman's fascination with the obscurer corners of English, American, and foreign literature come to the fore, revealing him to be a "bookman" in the best sense of the term.

Samuel Loveman circa 1965, from In Search of Hart Crane *(1966), Leo Hurwitz, dir.*

If Samuel Loveman is destined to be remembered chiefly as a member of the Lovecraft and Crane circles, then his variegated work shows that he deserves at least passing attention in his own right. Aside from Smith, he was the best poet among Lovecraft's associates, and far superior to Lovecraft himself. *The Hermaphrodite* and *The Sphinx* deserve to live as much as Smith's *The Hashish-Eater* or Lovecraft's *Fungi from Yuggoth* or Donald Wandrei's *Sonnets of the Midnight Hours*, and any number of his other poems, prose-poems, stories, and essays can take their place with the finest productions of Frank Belknap Long, Rheinhart Kleiner, or Alfred Galpin. The paucity of biographical information on Loveman may render him an enigmatic, even inscrutable figure, but as a prototype of the sensitive, eternally youthful lyric poet he will always command attention. A Shelley or a Chatterton placed unceremoniously in the concrete megalopolis of New York, he managed to preserve his aesthetic sensibility by retreating into an imaginative realm of his own making, where pagan gods, fauns, and satyrs gamboled as they had done two millennia before. In his slender but substantial literary output he himself became a faun who would lead us back to the classical world from which he drew so much artistic sustenance:

> But come, I have never grown old, and if you but hearken
>   My song shall bring you release.
> Far, far from these faces, these eyes that shiver and darken . . .
>   I can take you back to Greece.

Samuel Loveman's work will never gain a wide audience, but there is much truth in the prediction he made to the interviewer Thomas J. Hubschman in the 1960s: "It is just possible that someone will rediscover me."

—S. T. JOSHI

A Note on This Edition

This edition includes all known poems, verse translations, and verse and prose dramas by Samuel Loveman, with a selection of short stories and essays. The editors do not claim to have located all works by Loveman, since he was notoriously lax in preserving his published and unpublished writings, and no known bibliography of his work exists. This volume has been assembled largely by combing exhaustively through major collections of amateur journals, notably at the New York Public Library. Some texts derive from handwritten transcriptions made by H. P. Lovecraft, now in the John Hay Library of Brown University.

Among the poems, the works in *Poems* (1911) and *The Hermaphrodite and Other Poems* (1936) are presented as they appear in the respective volumes, with some modifications. In *Poems*, "Ode to Dionysus" and "Dirge" are excluded, as these appeared in *The Hermaphrodite and Other Poems* in revised form. We have, however, preserved the longer (five-section) version of "In Pierrot's Garden" from the earlier volume, as its appearance in the later book is in four sections only. "Oedipus at Colonus," in *Poems*, has been transferred to the section of verse dramas.

The uncollected poems are presented in chronological order, usually by date of publication, as in most cases date of composition is not known. At the end of this sequence are poems of uncertain date, all previously unpublished.

Among the fiction and prose-poems, "The Dog" is an unpublished manuscript found among Loveman's letters to Clark Ashton Smith. Part of the second page of the text is mutilated, rendering some words illegible.

Drawing by H. P. Lovecraft, inscribed "Saml Loveman, E/q^r. by H: Lovecraft Gent 20th Septr 1724."

The book concludes with two substantial and previously unpublished interviews, one by John Unterecker (conducted in 1962, presumably in the course of his research on his biography of Hart Crane) and one by Thomas J. Hubschman, conducted a short time later.

Douglas A. Anderson provided much of the bibliographic information contained in the bibliography. We are grateful to Douglas A. Anderson, William Groveman, Mara Kirk Hart, Mike Horvat, Derrick Hussey, Christopher O'Brien, Juha-Mata Rajala, Jordan Douglas Smith, and David Tribby for providing some of the texts used in this volume and additional bibliographic information. The Library of Amateur Journalism at the University of Wisconsin–Madison, Special Collections, yielded many of the pieces new to this revised edition. Several previously unpublished poems have been abstracted from Hubschman's interview.

—S.T.J. AND D.E.S.

I. Poetry

Poems (1911)

In Pierrot's Garden

I

There's a lark that's drunken with the daedal moon,
    And I sing to the shy-fledged singer;
Lonesomest thing in the world but one,
    He bids me wait and linger.

Hush, little brother, your heart is fire,
    Hush, little one and forget;
He will not tarry, but wings him higher,
    And my eyes are wet, are wet.

II

This is the way the moon comes up
    From under the glimmering fallow fields;
First but the rim of a silver cup,
    Where the farthest twilight primrose yields

Her earthly beauty up;
And now where the deep light winks abrim,
    You can see it flutter and fail for breath,
And a single star falls rapt and dim—
    I call it Death.

III

These are my moths, a brooding slumber
    Falls from their painted placid wings,
The shifting dusk is white with their number,
    They stir to the song one sings.

Into the heart of a poppy they hover,
    Out of the purple starlit night;
Ah, they are gone now, poppy and lover—
    I am their short delight.

IV

Do you hear it?—my bubbling nightingale,
    With a thousand notes to a single trill;
The moon and the stars are passion-pale,
    Listen they must at will.

Such a world of ache, such an ancient wrong,
    I have tried to fathom it all forsooth;
But the deep night covers the singer and song,
    And youth, it cries—youth—youth!

V

I wonder what the night can hold
    Beyond the sea-blue sloping boughs,
The heart of all the west is gold,
    I wonder why it glows.

My thoughts lie heavy on my eyes,
    I have so many dreams to dream,
So many little fantasies,
    To solve and scheme.

They creep upon me unawares,
    They flutter in and out my brain,
Each one finds housing in my prayers,
    I hold them free from stain.

Ode to Ceres

I

Sweet Mother, saffron-haired and argent-eyed,
    That holdst four seasons in thy mellowing hand;
Foison and plenty on thy measur'd side,
    Wisdom and warmth at thy uncurbed command;
That with braced breath at dusky-veined eve,
    Stirrest the furrow and the winnowing wain,
        What time with fragrant finger thou let'st fall,
Soft-shining from the pressure of thy sieve,
    A dew ambrosial—
    Bow thy dim head, withhold thy golden rain.

II

Not aegis-bearing Jove with gulfy might,
    Nor great-eyed Juno, deathless and divine,
Hold half the grace, kind Mother, half the light,
    Enkindled in the splendour of thy sign;
Our fallows coucht with oxen serve thy haste,
    Consume them not but lend thy pitying heart;
        Fountful thy wheaten measure, choose our seed,
And when the north with reedy rein lays waste
    Moist hill and ample mart,
        Shelter us with thy azure robe at need.

III

O love divine! O deep immortal grief!
    Still dost thou yearn for Enna's dewy fields?
Thine, thine the rapture whence each budding leaf
    Bespeaks the favour that thy blest bed yields.
O Mother, great bright Mother, let thy light
    Shine on us with the wisdom of thy girth,
Clip close our sheaves, o'erbrim our fruitful herd
Sacred and silver-bright,
    And make and purge with thy most-weighty word,
    The rich divinity of this swart earth.

Fra Angelico
(1387–1455)

This is a babe Angelico painted,
    Red chubby cheeks and the daintiest nose,
A flaxen poll that the years have sainted,
    Yet somehow, it glows.

You see the budding lips half pursed,
    It seems but yesterday they smiled,
Acanthus-like i' the gold dispersed,
    Eyes bluely mild.

Where the sleeve's frail hem slips down and under,
    Ah, what a miracle of hands!
Not the slightest swerve to make a blunder,
    Superb it stands.

Did you hold it perchance to your heart encrusted,
    You, Angelico (Fra by grace),
Till its spacious wisdom bloomed and dusted,
    Some barren place?

Or, did it creep unawares to your portal,
    Weed-overgrown and gray in part,
Then with a bound purge clean immortal,
    Some ancient smart?

Ah, Angelico, life is deeper
    Than ours the poet's hand can plumb,
Bent that a birthright wakes the sleeper,
    Why, we know not, dumb.

Only feel that in spite of the metals,
    Dross and the manifold slag that grows,
Somewhere beneath it with perfect petals,
    Slumbers a rose.

Lippi would rim it in lucent letter,
    Sandro bejewelled with easy grace,
But you, Angelico, saw it all better—
    A perfect face.

Song

Blossoms, blossoms, pink and white
    Under the silver boughs;
What is it, reason or delight,
    Who knows, who knows?
But your eased burden lies
In our empty melodies.

To P. G.

There lies a nook in the imminence of night,
Flooded with fire and dew, all lost delight,
Things that the iron world chose to forget,
There in the pendulous azure dusk are set;
And grief that brimm'd itself to joy and wrought
Happiness in the aching vast of thought,
Faces that glimmering quiet acquiesce,
Knowing the end as barren bitterness,
Anguishing all, yet by the ebbed stars,
Still'd to the peace that neither makes nor mars.
This paradise, you see, is none of mine,
I rail at all things, human and divine,
Half faun, half satyr—shyer than those broods
That flit above your moonlit mountain woods;
Confess me neither, dub me what you will,
Ixion sleepless, Tartarus baleless, nill!
I miss your ministry, your patient laws,
Impelling purposes and divine saws,
Gusty in none but golden everywhere,
Autumn that spurs the subduance of the year.
Wiser than misty Spring whose violet
Plays Ariel to the delicate woods and wet,
Or Summer, poppy-bound with sultry fire,
Ruining glitter, wandering feet that tire.
You, who would fathom better things in me
Than the dull moan of bowed humanity,
Who glimpse the beauty that my aims would strive,
The winged spirit and the darkling gyve,
Unutterable loveliness and love,
Life trembling lest her bliss of wonder move,
And in the veined marble of my rhyme,
See the unwinnowing temper hued by time;
I take my cue, and in your equal trust,
Shapen a roseal splendour from the dust.

July 31, 1911.

Lines

I know no light beyond the night,
    I see no star to pierce the star,
But still'd and windless in my sight,
    There pass the dreams that once were fair.

Oh! to have known and lost all this,
    The brimming youth, the joy to reap,
And in its stead a transient bliss,
    To drift in unforgetting sleep.

April 20, 1911.

To toil with fools, to drudge with slaves
    And keep above them giant-wise;
To know the world is full of knaves,
    Yet deem it but one's miseries.

Heine, thy spirit I invoke,
    Blood of one blood, our race divine,
Invest me with thy glittering yoke,
    Poison me with thy fairy wine.

Give me to know the world as 't is,
    Bereft of joy and bitter-bare,
And leave me in my dreams but this,
    The gift of beauty everywhere.

May 30, 1911.

A Twenty-second Birthday

One last sweet look at boyhood's fledgling gleam,
A mutinous onset on the rapt sea-marge;
I must not falter in my destin'd dream,
I must not tarry for the day is large.
So much defected, so much to redeem,

The sleep that circles in our wearied eyes,
The love that clutches at old memories,
How can I grasp it all, the subtle scheme?
Only the beauty of the fluttering light
That each divining loveliness forbears,
This, lest oblivion creep upon and smite
Our nature with the sanctity of tears—
Blind, groping children of inevitable night,
That spins its fabric on our inverse prayers.

The Hermaphrodite and Other Poems (1936)

The Hermaphrodite

Out of the deep, immortal night
Came to me the Hermaphrodite,
Moonlight-breasted, pale, antique,
He spoke to me in deathless Greek:
"Brother of mine, it has been thus
Since I came forth from Anthemus.
Before the Satyrs' gate of gold
I stood with wingèd eyes grown bold,
Fire on my lips, music, light—
The unfathomable Hermaphrodite.
'Whither goest thou—whence?' they prayed.
Then to their laurelled priests I said:
'Behold me, who of gods am wrought,
Burning desire and profound thought;
I, where the star-brimmed evening falls,
Would follow my folk, the Bacchanals,
To Phrixæ, then to Sybaris,
Where their still-flowery worship is,
Then on and on to Pergamon,
A marble city in the sun.
Long have I tarried, yet to me cries
The flame that follows the flame that dies;
I pass—but worship me, hold me still,
Body and soul inseparable. . . .'"

I asked: "Didst thou then find thy bliss
In Phrixæ or at Sybaris?"

He moaned, "Not there . . . not there! I found
A god arisen, blithe and crowned,

Beautiful, on a fadeless plinth
Of poppy-flowers and hyacinth;
And as I passed the city wall
One on a tower began to call:
'Lo! an impostor comes to us,
The Lydian Dionysius,
Bound as with vines, his eyelids gold,
Godlike and marvellous to behold.
Beware! The sculptured cities dim
That sang and bowed and burned for him,
They, that in shadowy, silver spring
Uprose with mothlike murmuring
To obscure lust, to inverse night,
They knew him . . . this Hermaphrodite!"'
I said: "He lied unto them then.
For thou hast ever been to men
That which with unsustained despair
They seek, but find not anywhere;
The supreme loveliness that lies
In all men's souls, on all men's eyes!"

He cried: "There was no rest for me,
I could not bear their mockery;
So, in the sapphire-coloured day,
I passed my lonely antique way
With halcyon feet by seas of rose,
Against whose foam the ilex grows,
To Nyssa, where with golden strings
Bacchus his laden leopard flings.
Crying and drunk with secret dread
Lest joy be disinherited,
Upon the temple steps they fall,
God, Mænad, Faun, and Bacchanal;
Vases and urns that on their brink
Once lured each loveliness to drink,
Vine-leaves and laurel, ivy, grapes,
Over their still, enamoured shapes—

But in the moonlight, green and cold,
The world seemed suddenly grown old. . . ."

I questioned: "Was it ever young
Save in the songs that men have sung?"

"Listen!" he murmured, "then there came
 A remote voice that called a name:
'Bacchus, awake, awake!' it said,
'The whole world mourns these doomed or dead;
Take up thy burden, wild and sweet,
Tyrannic joy on flowerlike feet;
Arouse thy brethren from their dreams,
The low moon pales, Orion gleams;
Bid thy Bacchantes, white and still,
The wine cups from their beakers fill;
Thy Fauns stir from their rose-hung bed
That slumber in the dawning red—
O passionate, wayward, loving son,
Make thou thy way to Pergamon!'"

I said: "Good fortune favoured thee,
For thou didst join their company."

He answered: "Yes, but in that space
A light fell on the fair god's face.
'Evoë! Evoë!' he cried. 'Again
Truth fires our lips, wine floods our brain—
Come with me ere your souls grow dim!'
The young Fauns laughed, 'We go with him!'
One sang and danced, while one, half mute,
Blew music on an ivory flute;
The Mænads in the crimson glow
Called: 'Come with us—go whither we go!
This day we leave with stainèd faces,
Forever, our ancestral places;
If with much grief thine eyes are wet,
Do as we do . . . forgive, forget. . . .'

And shivering, swaying, crying on,
I followed them to Pergamon!"

"Like the fine purple Bacchic frieze
In our museum, where one sees
That pagan, vinous rout!" I cried,
"And there thou passest wonder-eyed;
Something that earth could not annul,
Lonely and brief and beautiful,
Yet saddened, O Hermaphrodite!"

Tears glistened in his eyes like light;
Then with a pale hand poisèd, he
Said in archaic melody:
"Before the luminous city wall
Bacchus spoke: 'Hearken to me, all!
In my youth, lovelier than the day,
I wandered o'er Ionia;
Here, outcast, mutable, and graven,
They spurned me who besought them haven,
But I, who glimmered many a spring,
Violet-wreathed in wayfaring,
Drunken with wine and beauty yet,
In all those years could not forget. . . .
Don yourselves robes of pallid lawn
And enter in their gates at dawn,
But underneath your veilèd dress
Divinely leave your nakedness,
And still upon your hooded hair
Bind the dim cirque of vine-leaves there.
When in the marble streets I cry
The name my mother knew me by,
Then shall you lose all fear and cast
Mantle and raiment free at last;
But to the wintry hearts of men
Something long lost shall come again,
And one shall give the cry that thrills

The Mænads in their clustered hills,
Strange joys and weeping betwixt laughter,
Ere, with my thyrse, I follow after...."

"Mankind," I said, "O lovely friend,
Is hopeless in the bitter end,
Hast thou not heard of two that died,
One poisoned and one crucified,
And still another, who with blood
Forswore his life to brotherhood?
Their name is legion in the wind,
Betrayed, misunderstood, maligned,
But they sleep well—the ones who bled,
Mysteriously comforted,
Or those, that even in derision
Pursued one hope and saw one vision.
And thou, beloved Hellenic face,
Carven of coloured dreams and grace,
Surely beneath the fervid sun
Thou foundest joy in Pergamon?"

"O no! no! no!" he answered, "There
I found a dreamless sepulchre
In a chryselephantine house,
Oblivion after my carouse,
But not forever.... The tale is told
On urns and saffron altars old,
Where mouth meets mouth, and grave boys make
Soft melody on lyres that ache
In the elusive marble still,
Charred, broken, yet imperishable!
Thou, too, hast seen them...."

                        I nodded on.

"At dawn we entered Pergamon:
But in a tower against the sky
A watchman cried: 'Whence pass ye by?

Speak! if for good or ill it be. . . .'
And one said: 'Priests to Cybele,
Sombre and vowed against the sun,
We seek her shrine in Sarpedon.
There, in Lycia, we are told
Men worship her even as of old,
There, turreted by forests deep,
The elder gods in exile sleep,
Row beside row, uplift in space,
With stars upon each placid face,
Dreaming before their lustrous spheres
The happiness that once was theirs.
Thither we go, but here we would
Take counsel with our brotherhood.'
Then to the city azure-walled
He swung his lamp of emerald:
'Pass on—pass on, O holy men!
I, that am eld, remember when
On such an eve, in such a flame,
Bacchus from farthest Phrygia came.
Lo, on that very spot are ye
Where the god stood in ecstasy!
Alas! we knew it not that night,
But ere the morrow came a blight,
Duress and famine, pale and bold,
Bare silences in every fold,
Save in the vineyards—there alone
The grapes hung purple, every one,
And from each laden stem there fell
Wine, gushing as a miracle,
When in a reddened mist unseen
The cry came: "Drink! here have I been!"
But if one drank—the gods forbid!
That thing became a Bassarid,
Ravening in the drooping feast,
Cry of a bird, soul of a beast;
Until in all the city wide

There was no heart unpacified.
Only before Apollo's shrine,
From the lit mouth there came forth wine,
Wine and more wine—and yet more ills;
But far upon the terrene hills,
Beneath the moonlight one arose
And said: "Too long have we been foes;
The moaning and the madness past,
Let holiness return at last. . . ."' "

I mused: "The frenzy that one sees,
Or reads of in Euripides,
Is like. Of Agavè, who slew
Her son, not knowing what she knew;
And on Cithæron, wild and dim,
The horror took her, even as him;
I felt it once . . . but thou, my friend,
Didst not partake of such an end!"

He answered: "I, who had been shy,
Laughed with their joy, wept with their cry,
Knew this alone, in me was come
Rapture a long time tranced and dumb;
Beneath the vine-leaves and my dress
Burned still a hidden loveliness,
As a flower sways in sleep and night,
So shook I, the Hermaphrodite. . . .
Then in the blinding dædal dawn
The god cried 'Eleutherion!'"

"His signal for the crew?" I asked.

He said: "No longer were we masked.
In me a madness rose and fell,
Beauty and lust made visible.
At the god's beck, at the god's side,
Where whoso drank was deified,
And by the wine-press, circling round,

The Mænads whirled without a sound.
Flowers on their breasts, grapes in their hair,
But from each mouth a wild despair;
Yet secret—for we dared not cry,
Lest the still city waken by,
And underneath the serene sun
They slay us ere our task be done...."

"Glaucon," I said, "of Æacus,
Writes that in Glisas there came thus
At evening in the slanted light
A naked youth, a stricken wight,
And far as islets in mid-sea,
Followed him bands of minstrelsy.
Then he, compassionate and bowed,
'O beautiful ghosts,' called forth aloud,
'Abide with me!' But uttering cries,
They fled to ghastly melodies...."

"He saw my brethren flee," he said,
"And some they buried with the dead.
Others in pillared colonnade
They scourged and crucified and flayed!"

I murmured: "For three thousand years
Is that tale done, yet bitter tears
Come to me now—to clasp and close
The delicate ecstasy of those
That vanished by no fault of mine.
Radiant, remote, these friends of thine,
So long ago! Another says
That in Pieria many days
The vintage through an autumn mist
Shone purple amid amethyst,
While in their vines one eve of gold
The tortured god walked as of old,
Bacchus, no doubt."

He swayed in grief:
"They perished through my misbelief.
A young priest in the temple called:
'Lo you! this city is enthralled!
From Asia, in the wine-red dawn,
These revellers come hither drawn.
Be not misled, though their god wear
Light in his Dionysian hair.
Flushed are their garlands, poison-scent,
Sanguineous is their blandishment;
From Pythia, enaisled and riven,
Strangely exalted were they driven;
But by each lintel, coloured flame,
Whithersoever their feet came,
In every city, dim and deep,
Waked from a lotus-lidded sleep,
Men laughed, fought, wept, with hearts afire,
Snared by the music of their lyre . . .
Back to your portals—fast there, pray
Until this curse be passed away!'
They hearkened to him. I, the least—
I, O my brother, slew their priest!"

"And yet," I said, "thy hands are white,
Not bloody, O Hermaphrodite!
Innocent are those eyes that keep
Vigil, a thousand years asleep.
It may be in the peakèd earth
Some dream found agonizing birth,
Until, intestine, there was wrought
The vision prophesying thought—
Beauty is thine, and pagan praise,
Forgotten in these evil days,
When life's a hideous thing at best,
And better rid!"

He beat his breast:

"O horror! horror! I heard a cry,
'For that one slain, their host must die!
Be merciless! Be to their ease
Colossal winged Eumenides!
Blind and convulse, torment, assault,
Redden the dayspring's golden vault,
So they remember!' This was their token:
Beautiful bodies, white and broken,
Fauns that still held the cup of drouth
Pressed wearily pale mouth to mouth,
Bacchant and Satyr, chill in death,
The Mænads moaning a last breath,
Their spears with arbute-blossoms pied,
Plunged in each stark and bleeding side;
But those that fled wailed as the leaves
Some vast autumnal spirit grieves,
When in the nadir, sick with light,
A ponderous wind proclaims the night. . . .
I only—I, whom none forgave,
They buried living in a grave,
Swathed me in silver talc and thrust,
Saying, 'Here ends thy frozen lust!
Though thou shouldst in the mystic night
Awaken, O Hermaphrodite,
Æons and æons passed and gone,
Unheeded by no mortal one,
And hear a cry from burning lips:
"Come with us to our painted ships,
Come with us who have loved thee ever";
Thou shalt abide inurned forever. . . .'
O brother—I, who loved the sun,
They left me to oblivion!"
"Not that!" I sadly interposed,
"Say rather thy fleet house was closed,
The lights were veiled, the vestments hid,
And dusk fell on thy pyramid;
But life, unleashed with misery,

Ceased not in turmoil over thee,
Prophets were stoned while evil fed,
Mute pestilence inherited,
The wise made ensign to the knave,
Beauty a jest, with truth a slave,
And if, among the multitude
One arose fearlessly and good,
They swept him recreant from their sight,
As thou, beloved Hermaphrodite!"

He said: "Upon me, stilled of moan,
Lay the first silence I had known
Since long ago in Anthemus
The goddess whispered: 'Born to us
Mild gods that gave thee birth, a flower—
Sundering sorrows mark thine hour!
Thou shalt appear in many places,
Love shalt thou love, but not fair faces,
Yet before each soul must thou falter,
And seek a still diviner altar;
Fierier, fiercer, shalt thou give
Thy piteous, brave prerogative,
Forewarn, forget, remember, stay
The inevitable, narrowing day,
Unbare to Love's infuriate might
Thy bosom and thy limbs of light,
Then under starred and moon-hung skies
Bow pale-cheeked to men's blasphemies. . . .'
But in my heart there seemed to creep
Something of marble, more of sleep;
Dust on the eyelids, fringed and low,
And on the mouth, curved like a bow,
And on the breasts where no breath stirred,
To flutter like a Grecian bird;
But in the silence my lips spake
And said: 'I died for Beauty's sake;
I perished so that men might give,

Strange, fleeting, poignant, fugitive,
Voice to their vision';—all things else,
Save silence weaving miracles,
I had forgotten. Under me
The dead lay still eternally,
With masks of gold, with leaves of bronze,
The pallidest of myrmidons,
Where low and lordly slept the same;
But not my spirit, drenched in flame,
Was vanquished. Overhead
Something moaned long rememberèd,
The sound of water that abides,
Refluent with the curving tides,
Clasped and caressed me as a gem
Effaced upon a diadem. . . .
It was the sea! Where dusk had been,
The water filtered blue and green;
Then I began to cry and stir,
Unveiled in fronds of gossamer,
And called my mother's name aloud,
Lightless in her liquescent shroud.
But where the dolphins of the deep
Passed me on azure chasms of sleep,
I felt the imminent years that bring
The tyrannous leash, the broken wing,
Till white upon my whitening grave
Swung me the low, sequestered wave;
Sibilant, sheer, and huge to cover,
Exultant, the disdaining lover.
But in the flower-heavy bounds,
Memory and memory of sounds,
Music that fell from lyres long-passed
Came with the sleep that comes at last,
Drifted and blown and unsubdued,
To all our lonely brotherhood
That waits the cry none cares to give,
Heartening the perishèd to live,

As I then hearkened, marble-pale,
Omniscient to the phantom wail,
Unbroken in the silence."

                    "Death was this,
No snowlike metamorphosis,"
I vouchsafed to him, "Hadst thou lain
Until upon this earth again
The golden age delirious
Her shawms and cymbals rang to us—
The whole of heaven filled with birds,
Leaping articulate to words,
Had joined thee then. But One there was,
Since thy long sleep had come to pass,
Who drove the antique fiery mirth
Forth from this mute and dreaming earth;
Who, crowned with thorns and soft as air,
Bade the Elysian world despair;
Hopeless and bitter, dusk and brief,
With great eyes brooding on his grief,
And vast heart burdened by such things,
Unknown to thy imaginings;—
He conjured Hell!"

                    He said: "Not these,
But up the level, jacinth seas
Something I could not still nor stay
Brought me into the light of day;
A galley, oared and Cyprian-green,
On waters traced with topaz keen,
By islands in the evening light,
Wine-coloured or with malachite,
A world from shards and chaos grown,
Unlike the wonder I had known;
Cities of opal, halls of jade,
Pinnacle, tower, balustrade,
Where, in the blue and crystal dawn,
One hand aloft and one withdrawn,

The people gathered to me thence,
Strangely, in all my eminence,
And whispered, 'Shall we worship him?
Behold! our other gods are dim.
Hath he not beauty? Where shall we
Find ever his supremacy?
Comes he from Sardis, hath he way
From flower-fragrant Syria?
Those elder gods that men have made
Are gray and old and disarrayed;
But he that to this image prays,
And to those lips his own mouth lays,
And to those eyes o'erbrimmed with wine
Treads the year's vintage for his shrine,
Or where the sleepy garlands fall
Over the purple pedestal,
From the still-locked, ambrosial hair
Where violets and jonquils fare,
Down to the hyacinthine limbs,
By tears of joy, by chaunt of hymns,
Takes to his soul the Bacchic riot—
Never again shall he be quiet,
But in his brain there shall be ever
The violence and joy of fever,
Colour and perfume, sound and sight,
And a great world fulfilled with light;
A noise of singing, a cry, a sway,
Shelterless through the blinded day;
This is our new god, this is he
Who gives us immortality!
O ye, that fear the night to follow,
Dead is our Zeus, dead is Apollo;
There was a silence and a wind
That perished with their dreaming kind,
A suspiration of our faith
Crying to each transfigured wraith;
But here is he that comes again,

Beauty, in guise of man to men,
Clear, alternate, unveiled to view,
Hidden by none but free to sue
As a god greatly!' They worshipped me,
Beatific in my sovranty,
And to this ancient heart of mine
Libation poured from urns of wine;
By day and night in the lulled streets
They drank upon their marble seats;
The milk-white oxen bound with bays
Entered from steepy mountain ways,
While on the pavements, pale and still,
The vintage ran, a rosy rill,
And where the red horizons are
I heard a revel from afar,
But could not break and dared not stir
To where the drunken minstrels were;
Where lowly in an April sky
Blossoms and branches fluttered by,
With grapes uptossed and garments rent,
And joy in the whole firmament."

"Their world," I said, "was darkling night
Until thou cam'st, Hermaphrodite;
Somewhere thy heart grew great, I think,
To liberate our souls by drink,
Even as on thy pagan tresses
Men yearned in sleep for thy caresses,
Or from their beakers drank to slake
The thirst that made their fury wake,
But by the first divine oblation
Kindled to love an incantation,
Unquenched since then."

                        He nodded slowly:
"My way was ever dim and lowly.
At night and by the torches' fall

I glimpsed their moving Bacchanal,
Saw in the shadows lit and drear
The ghost of Bacchus hover near,
Then heard the shrill procession cry,
'We, that were slaughtered once, draw nigh!
Peace dost thou seek and joy to bind,
Thou, that art kith and of our kind;
But never to this dancing mirth,
And never on the wild green earth,
And never under natal sun
Shalt thou find rest, O wearied One;
Deeper than the descending sea
Is grown thy immortality,
More solitary than the stone
That marks the city Pergamon,
Or the disquiet star that moves
Alone forever, and unloved, loves!'"

"This was a frenzy of thy brain;
There are no spectres, is no stain,
But what we make of good or ill
Holds us in fantasy until
We deem it such," I comforted.

He bowed his moonlit, pagan head:
"There was a murmur in their flight
That made more luminous the night;
A long breath and an endless wail
That gathered in the burning gale;
But far beyond the city's length
They swept, mænadic in their strength,
And farther in their molten troth,
Shadeless or like a faint-veined moth,
Where delicate domes and legion spires
Kindled and shook as waves with lyres,
Each one a crimson fire to trace
In the last light on the last face,
I saw them pass and disappear,

The roseal host, their charioteer . . .
Then by my side from everywhere
The city's folk assembled there,
With hands upheld as though to pray
All night, divinely into day,
From lips that once again dared speak
In lovely, dead, enamoured Greek,
Each bringing for my marble thirst
Flagons to break and grapes to burst;
And now it seemed as though, a stone,
I tried to stir—I strove to moan,
While the calm eyelids, curved to cling,
Trembled as if awakening,
And saw the crescent moon that spills
Silver upon the hollow hills,
And heard one voice above them all,
Crying: 'The city is to fall!
This is an evil god that stays
Upon our temple's precinct ways;
Not to the new-starred age came thus
The vine-girt Dionysius,
Nor where the youths and maidens sing,
Stooped he to flame and ruining.
Beautiful was this god and tender,
Whose footfall loosed Olympian splendour,
Where on the golden hair were set
Windflowers for a coronet.
And never in those dusk eyes broods
The fury of the multitudes,
Nor on the petalled mouth dares stray
The lightning's quick, revengeful ray. . . .'"

I said: "O never should it be
Twice to endure this agony;
Even as when, in light steeped thus,
Rain ravages the Caucasus,
Or on the cleft Hydaspian walls

Thunder with sleet and darkness falls;
But in some garden green, where deep
Hours shine and glitter and fall asleep,
White and eternal, mild and still,
When evening comes with stars that fill
Night with her prescience—thou shalt stand
With the gold apple in thy hand,
And on that crocus-coloured brow
Cherish the truth men disavow
In all the insatiate lust and strife
Of restless movement and roaring life,
Burning a beacon to deliver,
Beauty, to hands that stone the giver
Or slay the soul."

        He dreamed a space:
"In all the press I saw one face,
I saw one face alone that drew
Mine, as the sunlight drinks the dew,
Mine, as when in the domed night glows
A fiery star on fierier snows;
Brief as the curvèd evening wind
When the horned ivory moon swings blind,
And faint nectareous roses each
Climb to the sun they dare not reach. . . .
I heard him cry with eyes of light,
'Be frozen, O Hermaphrodite!
May to thy veiled and living veins,
Whither this fever floods and rains,
Nothing but chill and silence come;
Let now thy singing lips grow dumb.
Henceforth be marble and be free,
Save in thine antique agony,
When in this bitter, murmuring gyve
Thou dreamest that thou still dost live.
Yet ere the votive music fades
By far blue seas and quiet glades,

Faint and yet fainter hope shall dart
Possessive to thy sleepless heart;
Loveliest thou of those that found
Life broken, futile and unsound,
That in thine ageless searching saw
Flower-meshed change and fettered law,
And in the wayward weft of feet
Passed fearlessly and bright, but fleet.
Close, marble lids, on gentian eyes,
Wiser than those that made thee wise;
Cease, silken breasts, to moan and stir,
Beauty takes back a dream to her,
Fragile and shining, pale and proud,
Beyond the vigil of the crowd,
To the utmost, endless, inset shrine
Where all things are, and all divine.'"
He paused, he smiled, he faced the night
And faded, the Hermaphrodite.

River Pattern

All night the Mississippi on the banks
Hangs to the shelving shore. Eyes that peer forth
Fashion the emerald bayous, fringe the sweep
Of molten silt and copper-coloured slime,
Or where the runnel perseveres to gray,
Caress each inlet and curve the spectral tides
Slow to their solvent fury. If you could span
Its unslaked entry where the lapping mouth
Rivets the gulf that takes profoundly blue
The spokes and islets flaked with dawn and light,
Your gaze would find a long and level way,
Up the wide liquid roadside to the north,
From where the moss with silken streamers spun,
Covers the wine-red sheen against the sky,
Covers the green of cliffs, the yellow hills

Past terraced towns and roof-tops lost in trees,
Of cities and spires of cities that decline
And straggle into farms.
                      Winds lighten and flare
And run the clean length of the river bed,
Blowing the saffron smoke that hides the sun;
Elms, alders, willows, profiled each to each,
Strike silhouette against an early gold;
The cumuli of rose turn pale and fade,
Plucked like a sistrum in gigantic hands,
Blanched whiter by the emptiness of space.
Space everywhere, in heaven and on earth,
With all of heaven hanging on to earth,
And in between the two a core of fire.

Will o' the Wisp

The golden visit of the sun
    Is yours, and the moon's spying;
I know a place where waters run
    And flowers bloom undying.
Comfort yourself in this green wood,
With dreams of peace and drowsihood.

I shall be shepherd in the hills,
    When skies are black with danger;
When in your heart that joy fulfills
    To which my grief is stranger.
Beneath what sunken plummets shine,
This joy of yours, this grief of mine.

I am the dust and spark at night,
    Your evanescent dancer;
Behold me limned with eyes of light,
    Your question and my answer.
But if the darkness quench the star
Find me where deeper waters are.

Steener Haakonson Dances

I saw a dancer dancing on a mesh
    Of stars and moonlight in a night half gone;
Of honey-coloured marble turned to flesh—
    But dancing all alone.

Ere ever in my world of dreams there came
    Division of the darkness and the sun;
This was myself, another leaping flame,
    My dancing but begun.

To see him shadowed on a bridge of gold,
    Shadowed and figured in the fire and light;
I, haunted by a pagan world grown old,
    I follow in his flight.

Follow, for of all things restless I am he,
    Unstable and unwilling to the end;
Molten and marble, peace and ecstasy,
    That the gods break or bend.

Dream Song

Byron's soul was mire,
    Goethe's heart was ice;
But mine is a fire
    From Paradise.

Joy without a grief,
    Songs without words,
As beautiful and brief
    As are singing birds.

I, who loved the light
    Where silence dwells,
Heard in the night
    The sound of bells.

For hours and hours
  On the still deep,
Came the odour of flowers,
  Came the colour of sleep.

What should one who tries
  To dream the world away—
But to close his eyes
  For a better day?

Heckscher Building

The golden cock in the golden night,
  He crows while the people sleep,
But ever the golden stars alight
  And fall in the golden deep.

Yellow and topaz, amber-pale,
  The day begins anew—
I am the one who could not scale
  Those lonelier peaks of blue.

Euphorion

Once, with the south wind and the swallow,
  A stranger to your door there came;
And I, the rapt son of Apollo,
  Kindled again the golden flame.

You will forget ere your day closes,
  The joys that come, the loves that die;
But never the vine-leaves and the roses . . .
  Never the one immortal cry!

Agathon

There shall be music in the night,
  Libation made, and love confest;

Yet he, before the morning light,
> His heart shall grow the bitterest.

Yet ere his laurel wreath be shrunken,
> He shall steal out before the rest,

Far from the revel, shrill and drunken,
> And from the stranger-woman's breast.

Arcesilaus

Never again shall I come to you in Spring divinely drunken
> The god who came to you;

With the lore of Greece on my lips and eyelids sunken,
> Heavy with dreaming, too.

O beautiful! I sang as a bird that sings—as a bird that sings its fill,
> While crescent Summer wakes;

With laughter and love, with the joy of singing until
> The burning heart of it breaks.

Lineage

I would be back in Lesbos when the Spring begins to break,
> And the Grecian daylight pales;

And something should return to me that long ago was Greek,
> With the singing nightingales.

A thousand years they held me, and a thousand years they bound me,
> While they strove to make me speak;

But ever when the lovely Spring came back again it found me
> In all things still a Greek.

For a Book of Poems

The nightingales that sang in their Asian garden
> Are mute, and the Tyrian dreams

No longer of sultry wines that made him their warden,
> Drifting in dyed triremes.

. . . . .

But come, I have never grown old, and if you but hearken
    My song shall bring you release;
Far, far from these faces, these eyes that shiver and darken . . .
    I can take you back to Greece.

Ascension

The rain came down on Easter Day and Jesus bared His head;
"The world is full of misery . . . I go to Heaven," He said.
"I, who pass to meet the Father, am His sole-begotten Son,
But bring the little children near and let His will be done."

The little children circled close and sang: "Stay, Jesus, stay!"
They piped their treble voices in the rain on Easter Day;
But Jesus drew His mantle fringed with violet and red,
"Come follow me to Heaven, little children," Jesus said.

Thomas Holley Chivers

(*Buried at Decatur, Georgia*)

Beneath these pines and lucent skies,
    Forgotten, save by those that know,
The loneliest Immortal lies—
    A poet and the friend of Poe.

Somewhere on Heaven's chancel floor,
    Where wandering stars and orbits meet
So high, it dared no longer soar,
    His song rose marvellously sweet.

He sang of Heaven ere twilight fell,
    Of cherubim and seraphim,
And in the radiance visible,
    Their loneliness crept over him.

Something half-alien and remote,
    A sense of gold on lips athrong,
And from that perilous lyric throat,
    The wonder of celestial song.

And he who uttered in his mood
> The music of the stars and sun,
Lies here as any mortal would,
> A serf to long oblivion.

The Ramapos

Ivy grows wild among the hills,
> The laurel is Apollo's,
A garden takes the daffodils,
> And violets the hollows.

Crown yourself with the stars at night,
> Let this your heart be graven:
Sorrow comes ever with delight
> And finds no better haven.

Oscar Wilde

He lived within a golden house,
With grapes and vine-leaves on his brows,
> A slave to Beauty thrall'd;
His eyes were deeper than the sea,
His lips were spoken melody,
> His soul an emerald.

The dryads and the fauns of old
Came to him from their wood of gold,
> Each by his vision led;
And one by one he heard them cry,
"Wouldst thou for Truth or Beauty die?"
> "For both," he laughing said.

But baser than the night that is,
There came to him his Nemesis,
> Crowned with black nenuphars;
And in the elder evening hurl'd,
He saw the ruins of his world,
> The ashes of his stars.

There, in the pagan darkness, he
Felt his own radiant agony,
    And heard the gods affirm;
"That which thou soughtest shalt thou find:
Beauty, a breath of wandering wind,
    Dust, and the drowsy worm."

John Clare in a Madhouse

I am a dreamer in the world,
And by mischance come hither hurled,
    Out of the coloured skies;
For in mine eyes there still appears
This ecstasy of joy and tears
That saw the silver-linkèd spheres
    And shone in paradise.

Against the sunset light there came,
Flame with the utterance of flame,
    The Muses as of old;
But once their grieving voices spoke
And love that in me slept awoke
To take their many-flowered yoke
    And splendours manifold.

Unto those crystal souls in bliss,
I, who am least, crave only this:
    Light within radiant light;
Such pity that unceasing brings
Immortal tears for mortal things,
Yet not without Thy roseal wings
    To scale the vault of night.

No wisdom that this heart may leaven,
Before the burning host of heaven,
    Or in this joy divine,
Dares, from Thy empyrean gaze,
Pluck forth the mystery of days

Unblinded by the fixèd rays,
    That from Thy scarred face shine.

O blessed glory of the dew,
Into whose depth such beauty flew,
    That from one soul there came
No judgment but, like love, there fell
The gnomèd azure of this shell;
And sandalled thence invisible,
    Life, like a singing flame.

Within these lowly hands that hold
This measure of pure gems and gold,
    I make the stars my thrall,
Only, beyond the world's pale brim,
The angels and the seraphim
Listen, and with strange faces hymn
    Their beauty over all.

The Minstrel

I was a harp untouched by fingers
    Until the wandering minstrel came;
Behold, he said, within me lingers
    Still the authentic, staunchless flame.

And struck me half in jest and vision,
    Poignant, unsearchable and sweet;
Then cast me from him in derision,
    Broken and jangled at his feet.

The Chopin-Player

As I sit in this room with half a shiver,
    The night begins in rain;
And I think of two, by the ancient river,
    With one who loved in vain.

    . . . . .

And hear from the self same lips repeating,
    A brief and bitter cry,
Of one, who passed as still and fleeting
    And hopelessly as I.

A Dedication

If, in the Æschylean night
    You lift the curtains of despair,
And see within a world of light,
    The face of Beauty everywhere—

My love, observe me then, a flame,
    Deep, deep in shattered chaos flung;
Without a hope, without an aim,
    Save yours, for whom these songs were sung.

Vice

Bronze, in the green, inverted night,
    Forth to his lust, so one supposes;
Eros, turned an hermaphrodite,
    Shivers beneath his phallic roses.

But lightly past Ionian seas,
    Blown in an iridescent hour,
Phædrus meets Alcibiades—
    Two faces, each a poisoned flower.

Transience

I shall walk to Dover when the blackbirds fly,
    In a heaven blue and wide;
But I shall see before me to the hour I die,
    The one who walks beside.

And hearken to the joy I know full well,
    That could not come to stay—

Falling as the apple blossoms fell,
    Once, in the month of May.

Dolore

Back to the fountain runs the flame,
    Back to the joy returns each grief;
Beauty, unhousell'd, pleads the shame
    That cries our misbelief.

Look, in the silver night and see,
    Once as the wise men saw of yore—
A radiance in the agony
    That wisdom ever bore.

Bacchanale

(*To H. P. Lovecraft*)

A flagon is filled for the vintage guest,
    The grapes are crushed at the brim;
The young lord loosens his loric vest,
Violets bound on his brow and breast—
    And the revel is all for him,
    The revel is all for him.

There, where the orchards fire and smoulder,
    Agavè dances around;
Arm to white arm and shoulder to shoulder,
Naked Pentheus leaps to enfold her—
    But the Mænads make no sound,
    The Mænads make no sound.

In Mysia, a low wind shakes and sighs,
    An oarsman calls to his crew;
There is a cry the dead man cries,
Once, ere the darkness fills his eyes—
    With a knife that his mother drew,
    A knife that his mother drew.

To Simone's

As we came up the little steep street of signs,
    There was a clash of cymbals, a cry in Greek;
And forth from the figs, the grapes, the drench of wines,
    A voice began to speak.

"Worship me, though the last worshipper be gone,
    Save, where in Atlantidean islands still,
The Bacchants stir their limbs beneath the sun,
    The old rites to fulfill.

"Where, to the margin of music sung beside urns,
    A flute-player pipes in accents sweet but strange,
And dreams of an age that not once more returns—
    Changing, as all things change!"

So shivering in the constellated night,
    Measureless, lonely, mailed in radiant air,
The beautiful, swift and wingèd voice took flight—
    But not the old despair.

Ad Fratrem

So bade my brother when he passed away:
Not flowers nor any transitory things,
Nor light, where for one moment a bird sings,
Then flies away with a vain flap of wings;
Not these upon my body shall you lay
(So bade my brother when he passed away)—
But some immortal substance which shall stand
Time and his granite feet, his granite hand.

Isolation

I shall go back to my life of dreams,
    To my life of dreams and bury me deeper;
And nothing in all the world, it seems,
    Shall waken again the sleeper.

. . . . .
Save when the poignant Summer flies,
    And in all of heaven's azure hollow,
Faint voices call . . . I shall arise,
    And mutely and blindly follow.

Remonstrance

I that am Beauty's slave,
    Drunk as a moth with light,
How shall I bear to have
    These eyelids filled with night?

The heart of me a sun,
    The soul of me a star—
O cheap oblivion,
    To make and then to mar!

Proteus

Proteus of Sparta came to Troy to thieve,
    Spy, mercenary, pander—what you will;
Sleek-mouthed and oval-faced he heard men grieve,
    Half-hidden in the hollow of a hill.

Heard Helen's laughter, Hector's stalwart moan,
    Cassandra crying as a wave or wind;
Then deafer than a mountain turned to stone,
    Tiresias' curse on all of humankind.

A Voyage

Eurydamus of Crete, with his beaked green ships
    In the Grecian night set sail;
With Theron the flower, whose Cyprian lips
    Laughed at their elder's wail.

Past Argolis, past a sea they sought
    That never Grecian knew;

Writes one, they hated, and one, they fought,
    And one, they loved and slew.

Legend

Caught in a web of silver hail, then blown
    Shimmering into Pylos, the green spars
Of Hieron's golden ship stood in her zone,
    The masthead lit with stars.

Leaertes enters first, then Helion,
    Then Phædrus, lover of both, beloved by each;
Not long are these to see the burning sun,
    Save on this tragic beach.

A wind at moonrise fills the orange sail,
    The rowers chant. A mute from Daulis throws
Sweet sandal perfume. Night begins to pale
    And every rower rows.

But whence or whither? In Plato you shall find
    Phædrus retaken from a brothel's blight;
Concerning those he loved, we too are blind,
    And on the rest hangs night.

The Return

Look for me at dusk when the lights begin to burn,
    But be sure you keep the old familiar chair;
For out upon the threshold where your golden hearts will turn,
    I shall be waiting there.

With the same smile of old and the trusting hand,
    And the lonely, lucent eyes;
Only take me close ere I vanish where I stand,
    Lest I leave but memories.

Hold me and cleave to me close—O so true!
    For at dawn is when dreams must fade,
And a shadow has come to stay with you,
    Where never a shadow has stayed.

Memoralia

Here, in the room as darkness falls,
    Faces are pressed against the pane;
The night without is shrill with calls,
    And oh—the boys are back again!

"Open the door—we've come!" they cry,
    Some that are scarcely dust and light,
And they that fared so brave to die,
    Pass in from the tempestuous night.

Tucker and Osborn, blithe as gold,
    Miller, with Keats-like radiant face....
And suddenly the room grows cold,
    Shadows are these that take their place.

For phantom are the eyes that shine,
    Hands I would clasp, souls I would keep;
Yet this immortal hour is mine,
    That takes them from eternal sleep.

Forest of Rhododendron

The leaves were silver in the wood
    When day began to pale and turn;
The core of beauty where we stood
    Burned as the day began to burn.

And lightened and shook me as a feather,
    Poised, while the storm takes breath to start—
On roads that always come together,
    And paths that always lead apart.

Understanding

You knew this thing as we two sat together,
    Friends without friends and alien as your doom,
'Scaped from the leash that held us both in tether,
    Exquisite souls but broken on fate's loom;
Till I, who whispered guardedly at first,
    Of refluent water's flow and shining sun,
Of youngsters, bathing where a great wave burst,
    And of the gulls returning one by one—

Heard your close, tremulous heart-beat at my side,
    And saw your lips made passionate and wise,
As in your gaze beneficent and deep,
    A light that caught my speech ere the word died,
Kindled immortally with mortal eyes,
    The pagan heart of me that woke from sleep.

Ecce Homo

I am a withered chaff tossed by the wind,
And starward flung to heaven's august decree
Yet saving my memorial misery,
The loneliest of lonely humankind;
A thing of fate, forever unresigned,
With paradisal splendour in mine eyes,
Yet ever barred from lucent paradise,
And ever seeking what I dare not find.

Fool's golden and ashen hopes! had I but known
This cup was mine to drink—so bright and broken,
To founder on the veiling marge of years—
I had not ventured forth secure and lone,
Nor in the sudden night to leave us broken,
Precipitate, the memory of tears.

Ariel

I was born a singing bird,
    Honey-mouthed, golden-wise;
In my music some have heard
    Elfin melodies.

If they snared me, if they caught me,
    I could never sing again,
Of the pity men have taught me,
    For the souls of men.

Visitor

I, who came from a wandering star,
    And fell to a moody earth;
Carried my radiance from afar,
    My pity and my mirth.

Sang for a season, lived my days,
    A lonely, unsought thing;
To follow forever the violet ways
    That vanish with the Spring.

Inarticulate

O to be with gods, to shout the golden tumult
    Out in the golden day!
I, the broken-hearted clerk, the broken dreamer,
    Without a thing to say.

But stumbling in the darkness found a symbol
    That veiled the god from sight,
And kissed the fringes of his raiment in the darkness . . .
    Apollo, pale with light.

Madison Square

Leaves shine and flicker on the walk,
    Loafers are we this hour of ease;
I bend my head and idly talk,
    Even as one who dreams and sees,

Deep through infinity enskyed,
    A heaven beyond this blue that pales;
So once another poet cried
    Singing of wine and nightingales.

Contrast

The great immortal poets
    They pass the lowly by;
Their music is a torrent,
    And mine is but a cry.

Theirs is a world of rapture,
    The largesse of the sun—
I stir the perfumed darkness
    Around oblivion.

Invocation

A moth's wing beats the feathered night,
    The thin new moon hangs breathless there;
Come, bring your music for delight,
    Then pause upon the outward stair.

There was a fire that lit your brain,
    A fever in your heart, a riot;
Never shall this be so again,
    But where you are, let there be quiet.

Song

In the Spring of the year, in the silver rain,
    When petal by petal the blossoms fall,
The robins begin to mate again,
    But the heart forgets not all.

For within the budding flowers and leaves,
    A spirit of joy awakens and stays;
But the soul of grief remembers and grieves,
    All her lonely and alien days.

Harbour

Below were ships and then the bay,
    And in this heart that beat your will,
Something that silence would not say,
    That joy could never kill.

Stars blew and glittered pale and white,
    A wind arose and roared at dawn;
I was desire—I was delight,
    Long after you were gone.

Admonition

Fever and heartache, joy and grief,
    Take pause, for the change must come;
Beautiful songs so frail and brief
    From beautiful lips long dumb.

Fasten your heart to the cherry-bough
    That touches the light and wakes;
All that is dark and secret now
    Will end when the blossom breaks.

Foes

I shall build a palace with a wall around it,
    Deep, deep and hidden from the ravelling wind;
To no one in the world shall I ever say I found it,
    Not one of humankind.

Butterflies and moths are there and flowers with golden anthers,
    Luminous by moonlight and stained with fire by day;
But deep within my forest are leopards, panthers—
    With music all the way.

Limbo

There was a moth that took the flame at even
    Against the sunset sky;
And saw with wings that covered half of heaven
    A vaster butterfly.

So far within the moonlight fluttered deeper
    The wings that could not scale;
A night that takes the dreamer and the sleeper
    And all brief things that fail.

Interlude

Kings of the Nile that lie in painted wood,
    Blue and vermilion, gold with staring eyes;
They sleep the sleep that only dead things could,
    Yet never were their quiet souls more wise;

Than mine, in whom this passion stirs and shakes,
    Bared of an ancient love that burns and strives,
Even as a long dead sleeper who awakes
    To perish for another thousand lives.

Gates Mills

Starlit and blue
    The sheepfolds lie;
And staring through,
    One meets the sky.

The river straying
    Cuts runnels deep;
The hounds are baying
    In their sleep.

On perfumed boughs
    The leaves lie stark;
Light in your house,
    In my world—dark.

Wasteland

Black hulls, black spars against the darkness lie;
A wind between the marshes and the sky
Shivers, and as the silence is, am I.

The stars that sang at morning sing no more;
There is no beat upon this surfless shore—
I stand alone who stood not so before.

Amy Levy

Something within her like a fever,
    Cried: "Forth . . . this love is thine to seek!"
And so she left her kin forever,
    By shore and temples that were Greek.

And passed with singing in her faring,
    Alone, immutably apart;
Till night fell on her soul despairing,
    And night upon her Sapphic heart.

Forest Hill

He, with his dying eyes said: All is well,
    And in a faded vision saw again,
        Sun, stars, and wind, a silver twilight, rain;
And once before the charnel darkness fell,

Three on a hillside in midsummer deep,
    Beheld the moths fly, heard the robins call,
        While from a Phidian heaven over all,
The gods of Greece bent over him in sleep.

Andenkung

(*For William Sommer*)

Bill, when the eastern moon hangs low,
    And honey-coloured windows shine;
I'll come to you with eyes aglow,
    A ghost that haunts the Brandywine.

And hear you cry out clear and bold:
    "Sam!" ere the purple darkness grows;
Till all your valley brims with gold,
    And gold is on your orchard boughs.

Dream of Spring

The petals in the soft May wind,
They hear the voice of Summer call,
They leave their parent bough behind.

And to the perfumed night each brings
The transiency of flowers that fall—
Dreaming the dream of broken things.

Finis

The wingèd petals of roses,
    Silver and gray and white,

They fall with the day that closes,
    They fall in the soundless night.

If one had a heart like flame,
    If one had a soul like light,
The end would be still the same:
    Good night, it would be—Good night!

A Georgia Garden

Here in this valley blue with mist,
    Wild Autumn holds her painted riot,
Alone she keeps her maddened tryst,
    Ere Winter finds her pale and quiet.

And in this muted heart of mine,
    Something awakens ever after—
From lips half-drunken with her wine,
    An echo of her pagan laughter.

Palingenesis

Swift to elude and to evade,
    The phantom years drew each apart;
When, deeper than the rest essayed,
    The last blind veil fell from my heart.

I came with music wild and fleet,
    As flowers bend I bowed to change;
Till something in my heart grew sweet
    And something in my soul grew strange.

Belated Love

That fool am I to whom love came,
    Not as the soft wind comes at last,
But something terrible with flame,
    Lighted and stricken in the blast.

. . . . .

With all the universe in bliss,
    Close and yet closer grew despair;
Till I, before the dim abyss,
    Found emptiness and ruin there.

Nostalgia

On a day of azure in the golden Spring
Along a road of Georgia, I went a-wayfaring;
With eyes that sought the heavens but saw them not for tears,
In memory of memories for the forgotten years.

Beyond the heaven's cresset, beyond the mountain's rim,
Larks fluttered in the zenith as the eyes grew dim;
With half a world of wonder but in the heart a cry—
On a road of Georgia I felt that I must die.

Becalmed

At Andre's in the soft Spring night,
    The windows open to the Square;
And soft and delicate and light,
    A gray mist hovers everywhere.

And keeps me in its toil. I take
    The pool whereon its veil is thrust,
Far, far to some still bitterer lake
    That turns the dead sea fruit to dust.

Mutation

I was once in fever
    With my heart at riot;
But there came the touch of marble
    And my heart grew quiet.

Marble on marble
    And snow on snow;

Not to reawaken
> With the selfsame woe.

Yet what if one should shiver
> And know the sign? ...
O Love, O Love!
> That fate is mine.

Dirge

Close thine eyes, the night is come,
> Leave the world's desire;
Kiss thy love ere thou lie dumb,
> Let none thy smart inquire,
Fame and fortune are but lies,
Dross beside thy mistress' eyes.

Reap thy sowing, thou hast need
> Of its decaying measure;
Time will pluck it at his heed,
> Grant it all his leisure.
All thy glories are but one,
Night and deep oblivion.

Wrap thy sheet about thy head,
> Think thee pleasant dreams;
All is done that hath been said,
> Life is what it seems.
Though thy sorrow held the sea,
Lasting sleep awaiteth thee.

To Dionysus

O thou, from whose pale brow the vine leaves fall,
> Into thy beaker brimmed with Attic wine,
At whose behest the hoofèd Pan does call,
> Across the curvèd pathway where thy shrine
Lies warded deep in arbute-boughs that stall

Linkt faun and satyr, nymph and bacchanal;
    Methinks I saw thee wind thy lovely way,
    Into the forest scarce at break of day,
Heard the shrill fluting of thy myriads,
And glimpsed thy dusky shepherd lads
    Purse their soft lips to pray.

Hither came Psyche, Cupid by her side,
    I heard them whisper virginal sweet vows;
She pluckt an azure blossom, dewy-eyed,
    He bent to kiss her lips beneath the boughs,
        His pinions fluttering wide.
Hither came silver Dian from the rest,
    To pledge her maidenhood before thy shrine,
She, with a glory on each budding breast,
    Rosy and half divine.
And all the faun-folk, pouting lips awry,
    Entered the old Ephesian solitude,
Lingered a still space, then with half a cry,
    Vanished into the wood.

O fairer than the garlands on thy brow!
    O sweeter than the lips that press thine own;
    I will forsake all chances of renown,
And bear me gentle suppliance to thy vow.
Yet, make me thine, and by forgotten rills,
    Down quiet fallows into shadowy deeps,
    Where Love his ivied thryrse unheeding keeps,
        And Time suns aimlessly—
Be mine the night that laps the lonely hills,
    The sleep that hinges on eternity.

To Apollo

There is a moaning o'er Sicilian ways,
    Of gods forgotten and still-haunted shrines,
Poseidon in the silver darkness strays,
    And Psyche for her kissèd Eros pines;

But where the stars their clarion fires uproll,
Apollo sits communing with his soul,
And to the ruined and emblazoned leaves,
    With bright and burning dole,
Weeps, as a god in bitterness who grieves.

O golden head! O splendour veil'd and brief!
    Pinions of moonlight and immortal tears!
Strange lords have ta'en thy song in unbelief,
    And o'er thy quenchèd hope enthroned them peers.
Yet one shall come with mouth and heart aflame,
Pleading eternal Beauty in thy name,
But with the world discrowned and men denied,
    With hush'd, memorial fame,
Shall lay him down enamoured at thy side.

For we are they who 'mid their sorrows vast,
    Drunken with Beauty and consuming awe,
Have brooded on those glories that are past,
    Rapt in thy pagan and prophetic law;
I, too, with quiet voice and eyes alight,
Shall pass into the many-storied night,
My chalice broken, blinded by the sun—
    To fare from all men's sight,
Dreaming and deathless in oblivion.

Quatrains

Poppies

Ere men can pluck you stem by stem,
    Comes Death, a sleep-impelling snare;
Once only does she beckon them,
    With ministrations of despair.

Forgotten Poets

Brothers, who passed before me, one by one,
    Within mine eyes the selfsame visions shine;
I, too, shall perish with as little done,
    And in the hushèd darkness leave no sign.

Space

Dawn, shimmering like a boundless rose,
    Dislimns her raptures from afar;
But only night in anguish knows
    The loneliness of star to star.

Music

A dream of music in the long, long night;
    What is it that joys and moans and changes?
Laughter, golden-mouthed, and dim delight—
    And time that fades and estranges.

Simeon Solomon

Blake, who beheld the stars beyond the sun,
    Heard in a lighted crypt the angels sing;
But madness came with grief to Simeon,
    Who perished broken in the evening.

Aftermath

Deep in the moonlight—Oh, so deep and quiet!
    Fury came by, a lighted Bacchanal;
With cries and clangour and with leafy riot—
    While I, in silence, followed after all.

A Chinese Pavilion

1

Li Ho Chan in the sunset's gleam,
Murmurs, "Life is an opium dream.

"Drugged or drunk were the gods that blew
"This world on their lacquered pipe of dew.

"That wrought in the poppy's coloured deep,
"Laughter and love and an endless sleep!"

Li Ho Chan descries from afar
The yellow moon and the evening star.

2

I am a fan embroidered by Ming in the month of the nightingale,
With petals of tranquil roses that drift and fall in the sea-blue sky,
With a youth who pleads and a maid who listens forever to his tale—
They love and they know not why.

But Ming with her almond eyes and her heart of dew is dead long years,
She who wrought me and taught me my beauty—then crept away to die.
Yet the soul of my gossamer silk remembers and shivers again with tears,
At her one heart-broken cry.

3

At night the azure flowers unfold,
    Each on their swaying stems,
Their dream is of a world of gold,
    Strange kings and orient gems.

And whoso, in the moonlit night,
    Finds rapture in their scent,
His soul becomes a chrysolite,
    His heart grows somnolent.

He to their nacred bloom shall fall,
    And o'er their petals bend,
A spirit grown imperial,
    But lonely to the end.

4

Fu Chu of Yen came back to his village at dawn,
    "Where have you been, O Fu?" the old men say,
"We that were young have grown silver—ah! long agone,
    "And our eldest have crept away!"

"I have been for an hour," said Fu, "with the sleepers of Yee,
    "I have drunk of their wine and hearkened enchanted song,
"Their eyes are of amber, their lips are as melody,
    "Yet I tarried not overlong."

And he says not a word as he sits with unshed tears,
    Fu Chu, the mortal, returned to die with his kind;
But he holds his head as one who listens and hears
    The temple bells in the wind.

5

A wind in the jade-green grasses
That shivers and passes;

The swallows that, nesting, call
In the almond-blossom's fall—

I know their passionate cry
As they vanish to die.

6

I am Li Sun who threw my net in the haunted sea,
    In the haunted sea by the dragon castle of old,
And out of the emerald deep there came in my net to me
    A marvellous sight to behold.

Fishes of lilac and violet, silver and bronze and gold,
    With faces of human ken and with yellow hair,
And some spoke soft and cajoling, and some were sweet and bold,
    But each had a strange despair.

So that after a moment's space my madness and horror grew,
    And I flung my obscene burden far in the foam,
And a sonorous wind came out of the sea and a tempest blew
    As I turned my dazed way home.

BEN DE CASSERES IN CAMDEN

(*"I left Philadelphia at 3:30 a.m., and woke up in the early morning on Walt Whitman's doorstep in Mickle Street, Camden."*)
                                                  —B. DE C.

Stars splinter the night, the moon rides high,
And under the moon I see all Camden lie,
Blue and pervasive, pale as the orient deep,
When in the dusk that unrolls, the colours sleep.
Behold me, a wastrel god, dislimned of my might,
Not as a mortal but as a god on a height,
Who hears the loosed footstep, feels the lash that falls,
A Titan still in whose vast, penumbral halls,
Where the least tread is thunder, the faintest moan,
Mountain toppling on mountain, once here and gone,
Is gone, gone forever.   Walt, are you there within?
They have taken your rotting tenement, gutted thin,
Forth under quiet skies over fields that were
Beautiful, when you roamed a wanderer,
Daft, dionysiac, drunk to your riotous fill—
But listen, Walt, they keep you a prisoner still,
Meshed in their books and mortised within each brain,
Come out, be with us, be one of us again,
Damn some, hang others, crucify most!
                                      You shall see
A world grown sick and disheartened, not as we
Who drank to it—you at Pfaff's, I at Joe's,

Worshipping each his own particular woes,
You, Eros, I Cypris—each in his own way forever,
The unrelenting, ever-resistless fever,
That which besieges us, Sapphic and bitter-sweet,
But O, with what broken shards to lie at our feet,
Cruelly twisted and marred!
                            You knew from the first,
The solitude that is brackish and evil with thirst:
Barrier beyond barrier with walls that face still more odds
And behind the veil that is always veiled—the gods!
In the blue air at Paumanok where breakers roam,
Starlit and huddled into sleeping foam,
One with myself, you laughed at the carrion crew,
A bubble their cosmos, a figment their faith—you knew!
Only to me there came in an ultimate hour,
One as a flower that sleeps within a flower;
Another caressed by a suicidal wind,
A singing Greek in a world that would not mind;
All else negation and violent summons, the sweep
Of wisdom that ends in pathos, in horror and sleep,
But never for long in Lethe. . . .
                            Hail to you, Walt—
Rest and sleep well in your tightly-lidded vault;
Here, in the early day, in the golden sun,
Camden forgets you, much as the others have done.

Terminus

Here we are come to a place where Summer ends,
    Beautiful still in her ruinous azure day;
With laurel and roses between us, O friend of friends!
    But not the revel and music along the way.

I, with a heart led deeper and deeper by fate,
    And you, the riddle, who did not question why—
Now we can see in a world made desolate,
    The broken column under a Grecian sky.

Uncollected Poems

A Poet
(*Dedicated to Frank Honeywell*)

                    He is
A rising star, ascending in the blue
And studded firmament of Fame. Glad Wit,
Companion to a strict and chosen few,
Doth favor him. Philosophy doth glide
From off his ever ready pen, as rain
From verdure green. And like the sun, his torch
Illuminates the Poet's Page, and casts
A glamour o'er the reign of Poesy.

A Sonnet: Lethe

Could I but drink a draught, however small,
Of thy dark waters gushing forth below,
And drinking deep, forget the pain and woe
And misery, that has hung as a pall
O'er my spirit; forget stern Duty's call,
And live in but the present—life would be
Eternal bliss until Eternity;
The past, a dense, impenetrable wall,
And Love, the future, chastened, holy love,
Uplifting life to unalloyed delight—
As bright as Venus, shining clear, above,
A ray of purity in darkest night.
But thoughts are vain, 'twill never be, I know,
But thus—the weaving Fates have willed it so.

The Birth of Fear

A man is but the Pendulum of Fate,
    Swung back and forth at a tremendous rate;

Repenting oft, when dreaded Death draws near,
    He learns the first time "what it is to fear."

Pierced

Cupid grasped his bow one day,
    Ready for two hearts;
Spied a man and maid at bay,
    Fired the fatal darts.

To interfere was all in vain;
    Man and maid were wed:
Affection blossomed in their train;
    They followed where love led.

Be Thou a Jew!

Be thou a Jew! Let oppressors scoff
And jeer who will. But be thou steadfast,
And thy firm faith shall be to thee a shield,
Impenetrable and invincible,
Against thine enemies.

                Be thou a Jew!
Thy people are the Chosen Ones, for God
Will ever champion the cause of Right;
And though storms of adversity compel
Thy faith to waver, hold thy grasp—
For brighter, better days are yet to come.

A Lily

A blossom dropped from God's domain
Fell in a world of rack and pain,
Its lovelight shed a lustre bright,
Transformed a world of deadly night
Into a world of dazzling light—
So beautiful the bloom.

A Sinner spied the flower one day,
Repented from his evil way:
And so the flower blooms and glows
As chaste and pure as winter snows
Upon the Sinner's tomb.

Lost Youth

Old remembrances, how sweet?
    Distant from all toil and sorrow,
Lighten all the cares we meet,
    Make us better on the morrow.

Ah, it all comes back to me,
    Days of happiness and pain,
But I *know*, the Joys of Youth
    Never will return again!

Avalon

I can not think it that the souls of all
We know and love must perish with the form,
Even as leaves, fast driven by a gust
Of hurtling wind, down through the desolate boughs,
To rot with yellow age in stagnant heaps.
A good life is not ended with the grave,
But by the Maker's will lives ever on,
Amid the glory of a brighter sphere.

Far where the sea-gull wings its lonesome flight,
Beyond the shimmer of the hazy skies,
With clouds rose-flecked and seas pale green,
There lieth a land—if land it may be called,
For in the gray haze it doth come and go,
Now scintillant and radiant in the light
Of early morn, now vague and blue amid
The shadows of the sombre night—and men

Call this fair land, the land of Avalon.
I see it now before me as I gaze . . .
The pearly breakers and steep cliffs sky high,
With stretching glimpses of the pleasant vales,
Dark, wooded heights, and over-head a sky
Blent with the hues of amethyst and gold.
And even as I gaze, the sun of light,
Glinting the lapping waves with threads of fire,
Descends, and sable shadows dusk and creep
Along the shining shore, until the giddy mist
Blinds sea and land in fetters, silvery white,
Transfixes one last molten gleam, and then
Blots out this wondrous land of Avalon.

Hope

The rose is dead, the leaf is sere,
The bough is bent and desolate:
Still sings my heart a song o' cheer,
That melts the bitterness and drear,
    And bids me wait.

The Old Cobbler

Still he sits and pegs away,
In the twilight of his life,
Shadows come—the sky turns gray,
But he heeds not stress nor strife.

His old gray head is bent and low,
But he murmurs with a smile,
"Soon the sun will come, and glow,
Just a while, Lord—just a while."

Shadow-Land
(*To a Memory*)

There where the azure skies
Dip into ocean's blue—
(Ah, Love, if thou but knew)
    Shadow-land lies.

Throstle and nightingale,
Roses that bud and blow,
Dream-ships that sail and sail,
All in the golden glow.

Purple the mists that rise,
Balmy the winds that woo—
(Ah, Love, if thou but knew)
    Shadow-land lies.

The Song Unsung

Sweeter than all the honeyed sweets,
Than the sky-lark on the wing,
Sweeter than thy heart's pulsing beats,
Is the song I long to sing.

The dripping wine doth music make,
And the gold hath a winning ring,
Sweet as they are—none would I take,
For the song I long to sing.

Ship of Dreams

Over the silent mere it drifts,
Far through the purple dusk and night,
Into the depths and foaming rifts,
Leaving a wake of pallid light.

Fantastic shadows come and go,
Vanishing in the amber sea;
Wraiths shimmer from the shallop's bow,
And beck and point and whisper to me.

Over the western rim it dips,
Parting a glint, a gleam of gold:
Breeze-born a song from deathless lips
And all the world is bitter cold.

The Birth of Poesy

Lo—from the lapping sea, there rose a star,
In shimmering radiance; and casting far
And near a flood of dazzling, silver light,
As it flashed slowly into darkest night.

Then, there arose a sound both strange and sweet,
As breezes rippling through a field of wheat;
And then there came the rosy flush of morn
A brighter day, for Poesy was born.

On Lost Friendship

Friendship! thou mighty crown of love's devotion!
    Ah! hand in hand we went long years ago;
Now, buried in that vast tumult'ous ocean
    Of a lost past, still dost a glamour throw.

Thou wert my friend, I placed my trust in thee;
    Rememb'rest thou, the compact we two made?
'Twas to be kept until Eternity,
    And woe betide the one that ever strayed.

I loved thee—yea, thou wert my very life;
    But Fate will ever interfere in Love;
We sorrowed both, in hours of pain and strife,
    And nearer, ever dearer bonds we wove.

But came the day when Envy broke her bounds,
    Came to distress, disrupt a life so fair;
And as a slave pursued by hellish hounds,
    Thou wentest far away—I know not where.

The world grew dark to me, I felt a chill
    Sweep over Earth and Sky—but all alone
I faced Temptation; conquered by my will;
    Threw all my dice anew, and lo—I won.

Peccavi

Night had come, and o'er the moor,
Black and chilling, stormed the wind,
Wailing ever in its cry,
Echoing my dreary sigh,
"God forgive me—I have sinned."

But the storm died to a calm,
And I heard a voice from heav'n,
Come from depths afar,
Falling, as a radiant star—
"Cleanse thyself—thou art forgiven."

The Plaint of Bygone Loves

Lord! how they loved in a wanton way
    Aude, Saille, Isoude and Genevere,
Loved with the heat of an eager day,
Laughed and wept and I still can hear
    The might of their mirth as they crept away—

(Mother of pain! here are worms below.
Up from our lips red roses grow.)

And some fared forth to a bitter death;
    The golden haired Pasiphae
Got her hence with the sigh of an inward breath,

Far to the shift of the utmost sea;
    Cried loud to the purple tides, and saith,

(Mother of pain! here are worms below.
Up from our lips red roses grow.)

The Lesbian Sappho passion drove,
    Headed the lure of the fostered form,
And the crimson gold of its whitless wave,
Speeded her love-lorn burthen home;
    Shroud unto shroud, ye may hear her rave,

(Mother of pain! here are worms below.
Up from our lips red roses grow.)

Liker the youth tides come again,
    As the olden golden wine hot love;
Gone—they have strayed with the falling rain,
Yet comes the cry from weald and grove,
    Sorrowful silence of stealth and stain,

(Mother of pain! here are worms below.
Up from our lips red roses grow.)

Eventide

I. Sunset

A purple mist o'er-shadows all the vale,
The sunset's crimson flush dies to a glow,
The shepherd-lad long since has told his tale,
The husband-man departed from his flail,
And wended home with ponderous steps and slow.

II. Twilight

A thousand shadows darken yonder hill,
Evanishing amid the golden afterglow,
And plashing drowzily, the little rill
Keeps ever softly murmuring, until
The voices of the night chant soft and low.

III. Night

There on the lonely moor, storm-swept and bleak,
A blot against the monotone of gray,
The gibbet with its burthen gives a creak—
And then the night comes on with wail and shriek,
And a wan-white moon struggling on its way.

David Gray

The very dusk seems shrined in silver here,
    White as his own fair soul, the glimmering hills
    Sleep their fast silent sleep, and Luggie rills
Its endless way through glen and mead and weir,
And here, by the sedges which he held most dear,
    Love let us pause; perchance his spirit strays
    Even now above the daisied turf, and lays
Its stress upon us, gently unaustere
In an eternal resurrection—yea,
    His deep eyes, wearied of their mortal might,
    Sought an abounding peace, and closed their sight
From earthliness, and on a sunless day,
    Found their heart-brother* sorrow-wise of pain,
        In hope that life and kin-ship come again.

*Keats

De Profundis

I am the surge and the song of the sea where the tides sweep along to
    their refluent sleep,
Bitter and grey from the dawn to the dusk and the pitiless shadows that
    waver and weep.
I am the voice of the deep.

Faint and ephemeral, up from the whispering darkness, the sleep-slaying
    silence of sight,
Whither and wherefore the quavering cries and the glimmering lips
    wrought for death and delight—
Of these, the song and the sorrow the pain and the pleasaunce, the fear
    of an unknown night.

I am the rift of the shelterless sea and the trend of the foam at its
    incoming neap,
The soft summer seed that ye sow with a shift and the wild winter
    whin that ye flail and ye reap,
I am the voice of the deep.

Ode to Homer

Though who dost hold in thine eternal hands
    Life's little dust; thou to whose sovereign eyes,
Time and all things are but as symphonies
    Bound in implacable bands;

Give me thy blessing, this an hour's span
    Of holy hospice, from whose sundering tongue
The dust of Helen once stirred to perfect song—
    Ravished the lips of Pan.

For hast though not seen Agamemnon, he,
    King of all kings and brooding emperies,
Laid low perforce, by one fair woman's kiss
    To cheap mortality?

Hast though not heard the Syrens, subtly-wise,
    On fabulous isles and promontories sing
Their craven hearts away in worshipping
    A tranc'd sacrifice?

O hold me thine, and let the Thracian sea,
    Purple beyond the sunset's utmost verge,
Come to my heart and with an infinite surge,
    Kindle another Odyssey.

An Epitaph

Heere beneath this marble lyes,
A little Babe with closed eyes:
Ere the gawdie Worlde co'd wake it,
Th' shining Ones themselves did take it;
Pray you passe it not, but set
On the turfe one violet.

Quatrains

I

Up from the night that rounds earth's sovereign steep,
    I heard the wailing of a babe unborn;
Hush—hush! thy sorrows are not many—sleep!
    Life slays the pitiful with slight and scorn.

II

Such a world of wonder lies,
In a baby's deep, blue eyes;
Could I fathom it—why then,
The Golden Age might come again.

III

Little sophist, sweetly-wise,
    Glints askance mid yellow hair,
Bids me make the moody skies—
    Blue and fair.

To Alfred Noyes, Oversea

Ere half my youth had flowered and broken
    To boyish shapes and words athrong,
The Muses with a graver token
    Gave me their gift of song.

And as a boy's brain fires and quickens
    Before the breath of lasting life,
Ere the man's heart within him thickens
    To stress and strife,

I saw all things and knew them Beauty,
    Unfair, I held them slight to scorn,
And all my heart divined its duty,
    One sweet May morn;

To sing, outsing the stars—what meeter,
    I durst but try, and trying, fail—
And in my dreams there crept the sweeter
    Still summer's nightingale.

Michael Scott's Wooing

A Fragment

O Michael Scott is a-wooing gone
    Ere the westering wind blew free,
And he's ta'en his heart's fast friend, Sir John,
    To bear him company.

Sweet, sweet the scent of the winnow'd whin,
    And the freshened furrow green,
But Michael's blood leapt hot within
    At his manhood's dole and teen.

They have spied the hut on the sandy shore,
    And the flickering light within;
He's clencht baeth hands with a curse and swore,
    "This night shall be sweet wi' sin!"

"By the power of darkness vast as the deep
    Whence none can fathom to span,
May never a bone in my body sleep,
    An I luve her not more than man!"

"O Michael Scott forbear thine oath,
    Ere the foul fiend prompt his will!"
Sae loud, loud laught he, "Friend, in sooth,
    This deed shall work me nae ill."

He's gar'd the moon stand still i' the lift,
    He's gar'd the stars burn dim,
And twice and thrice from the night's sheer rift,
    The foul fiend beckoned him.

And now from the slowly opened door,
    Came Janet, the woodman's daughter,
And her arms beat at her bosom's core,
    As she sped to the wide waste water.

"Janet, Janet, my bride ye maun be,
    O luve me or else I die!"
She's turned her face to the moonlit sea
    And claspt her hands with a cry.

PROLOGUE TO ARCADIA

[Spoken by a Faun]

Gentles and Ladies, and it please you list,
Our love shall prove no simple casuist.
Consider then within this bound there lies
Undreamed-of Titans and their emperies.
Whose golden eyes were kindled by the sun
Ere thro' this earth unendless life begun.
Their power yours, but yet more winged wise,
To bear the burden of our patient sighs.
Pan is the hero, from his garden-fane,
We've brought him hither to rehearse again.

How on a girdled mead shy Psyche stood,
And one might trace her amorous-running blood.
How Pan through the interspersed leaves would kiss,
The exceeding object of his doting bliss.
And peering through the purple vine he lays,
Upon her head a crown of chrysoprase;
But she—being tryst to Cupid's plan—doth see
Him from the hillock on the grassy lea,
And in a sudden flings her heady swain
Into a bed of roses thick with rain.
Shy ivory minx! his imprecations bear,
The stillness of that honey-laden air;
And there he lays 'mid thorn and bursting briar,
Unquenched yet unconsumed by wild desire,
Until some naked faun in pity bent,
Shall free him from his scorn'd predicament,
Or nymph or dryad straying thro' the wood,
Shall yield him an enslaved maidenhood.
You've heard our amour, yet your eager eyes,
Betray the soft flame of their sympathies:
Such idle dreams are ours best to amend,
If you such thrifty measures would attend.
Do we please?—smile, our ready service bears,
No deeper than the worship of your peers.
Our folk are all assembled, hither bent,
To give you one day's summer merriment.

Richard Fotheringay, 1664.

Two Poems for Book Marks

I

In Florence, under morning skies,
    In lands far lovelier than these;
Carved in Carrara, mute there lies,
    A tyrant of the Medicis.

And on this tomb in that far place,
    Are Pan and Fauns in revel met,
But blown along the mightier base,
    Children in veined violet.

For this was he, who, ere he died,
    Called to his servitor and said:
"Perish with me my desolate pride,
    Had I but gone where wisdom led.

"What men divine, what men decree,
    That which is wise alone is good;
Brothers of one great dream are we,
    Who dares deny that brotherhood?"

O you, who hold me in your hand,
    And on these classic pages dream,
Whether by Homer's lordliest strand,
    Or Plato's golden Academe;

Know: the immortal lonely soul,
    That seeks but love and sees but light,
Finds this alone, when goal to goal,
    Falls, as it must, eternal night.

II

When you sit down to read a book,
    And straight before your eyes there stand,
The lighted gates where you may look
    Far into an enchanted land;

And hear the elfin voices sing,
    And see their wonder-haunted eyes,
Or where the silver lark takes wing,
    Follow them into paradise—

Be sure you greet this charmed host,
    That with the years so soon must part;

Yet ah, take those you love the most,
    And press them closer to your heart!

Thomas Dermody
1775–1802

Thus died the poet Dermody: I, Gray,
Sat by his bedside all the dreary day,
But when the dusk with muted silver came,
He called me softly, quickly by my name,
"Gray, don't you see them?" "What?" I asked and caught
His hands that trembling to my own besought.
"Oberon and his frolic, færy glee,
Luring me hence with perilous minstrelsy.
O! let me go, for I must be seen
In the white moonshine by their moon-white queen;
I beg you, Gray!" I held his swaying head,
Pitiful, hollowed cheeks that plainly read
Passionate ruin, unpermitted ill,
Breaking against the too-exceeding will,
As night to chaos. "Hush!" I said, "and sleep,
Or take this sweet drowsed opiate that will creep
In all the healing channels of the heart,
And sudden lucidness of dew impart."
"No, never, never!" moaned he. "Gray, I think,
Life gives us only bitterness to drink,
And I must be forgotten with the dead,
In unsunned darkness miserably led,
Dust grieving dust, imperishable flame,
Plighted to the unknowing whence I came,
A mock, a scorn to living memory,
Unfixed with bright damnation when I die,
Or like some frozen and abandoned world,
Perish in sleepless wonder, tempest-hurled;
Ere one has lived, reflected—to forget.
O Gray, Gray, Gray! I hadn't half-tried yet!"
I turned away. "Read me," he whispered soft,

"The passage (I forget by whom) that oft
We conned together, writ in olden time,
Yet murmurous with the luxury of rhyme,
I fain would sleep on't."
      So I slowly read,
"Sithen the soule is love apparailed,
 And lyf been noght withouten joye and lyte,
Beseemeth beste ere cometh grete nighte,
A litel pacience and eek gentilnesse,
That thou in Hevene y-fare no wit the lesse;
For certein, as the sclendre aungels hence,
Geten hem blisse in mankinde's innocence,
So by ther swete purveyance shal you see,
Love that transfigureth Eternitie."

I lifted eyes from reading but it seemed,
A lustrous joy bent on him as he dreamed,
That from its sunken and tempestuous sign
Hung inmost and invisibly divine.
"Tom, do you sleep?" I urged and vaguely bent;
No stir, no sigh! I knew he was content.

DEbs iN PRisoN

"Peradventure ye pronounce this sentence on me with a greater fear than I receive it."
      —GIORDANO BRUNO

1

Mother, that in the Asian sapphire dawn,
 First spoke the word that made my dead soul flame,
Here, on this height and from the world withdrawn,
 I, who alone dare cry your missive name,
Your prophet and your lighted hierophant,
 I, as of old, rejected in derision,
  Forgotten, outcast, spurned of all mankind,
 Yet in this heart your love and in these eyes your vision,
And on these lips your agonizing chant,
  Unblinded by oppression lead the blind.

2

As in a dream I see your cohorts pass,
    Maimed, chained and trodden, fastened each to each,
Even ere the violet way to Athens was,
    In soft communion and inebriate speech;
For these are yours that since the world began,
    Beheld the stars beyond their molten day's sunsetting,
        With light, with splendour and with pity hallowed,
    But for the past oblivion and forgetting;
Who saw the godhead not in god, but man—
        "Brother!" they called and trustingly I followed.

3

And in the night and by the western sea,
    Your sons assemble once again to speak,
Jesus, and he from Ossawatamie,
    Bruno and Casement and the deathless Greek;
Each for the naked, the despoiled, abhorred,
    Each the eternal truth in many places,
        Haltered and manacled and crucified,
    They, with transfigured gold upon their palms and faces,
They, with the tenderness that knew no sword,
        Proclaim their faith in which they lived and died.

4

"No peace—no peace for us!" their voices cry,
    "How can we rest with souls that grieve and burn?
Beneath this clear, star-haunted, silver sky,
    Your kin, O Mother, find no place to turn!"
And He, the ashen-faced, with lonely eyes,
    Speaks: "Once again my orient word is passed and broken,
        On ghastly fanes my love is sacrificed;
    I, who between two thieves once gave my token,
Am scourged and fettered by their deadly lies,
        And in the name of tyranny called Christ!"

5

And one says, with the moonlight on his face,
    "My name I have forgotten long ago,
Nor what my deed, nor whence my dwelling-place,
    And why I suffered—ah! but this I know,
That somewhere, bound with vine-leaves in the Spring,
    And in my hand the flowering thyrsus ever,
        Beneath a green pine in a blossomy glen,
    I heard a matin voice cry, Follow me forever!
And I who followed without murmuring,
        Heard always in my ear the cry of men!"

6

Another murmurs: "I am newly come,
    With lips that still bear plumèd ecstasy;
Brothers, mine was no alien martyrdom,
    For as they led me forth at dawn to die,
While I, the living, communed with the dead,
        Not yet were in the Celtic night the stars arisen,
        But I—I heard their holy voices sing,
    And Joy came to me as I wept in prison,
Came to me even as I perishèd—
        Joy for each pitiablest, human thing."

7

One rises with a face of suffering,
    Beautiful as a god with golden hair,
Austerely saying: "I am Louis Lingg,
    I am the priest whose gospel was despair,
We, on that terrible eve forever gone,
        Draped with the anarch red your fleeting altar,
            We dared—O holy Mother—even we;
    Lied on and spied on, never once to cease or falter,
And I, who perished without word or moan,
        I cry aloud your name, O Liberty!"

8

I see them in the broken moonlight throng,
    Their mystery and radiance as they fade;
I hear strange speech and amphionic song,
    And I, too, face the darkness unafraid.
Within these walls, before these hostile bars,
    Far from the many-tinted lucent morns of heaven,
        They break and prison that which is divine—
    Forgive these, that have never yet forgiven,
Who see not in the paling night the stars,
    Nor in their souls what I have seen in mine.

9

Until the brotherhood of man is come,
    And all that wrong is righted for the weak;
Until those mouths by tyranny made dumb,
    Give utterance to the word they fain would speak;
Until with healing and with human wings,
    By reed and trumpet blown beyond their power,
        Love everlasting, hearkens to our ken;
    Until your voice, O Liberty, proclaims that hour—
Ransom and light for your divinest things!
    I stay imprisoned with my fellow-men.

Resurgam

When I am dust blown by the wind,
    And in the night—above, below,
I see the stirring of my kind,
    And hearken to their dying woe—

I shall awaken once again,
    Pale and disquiet, riven deep,
But in my bitterness will fain
    Turn to oblivion and sleep.

Shadow-Love

I lay at last in my resting-place,
Earth to the earth on my mouldering face,
And all the years were of peace that fell
Under their span invisible.

Then one beside spoke plainingly,
"A root has fastened the mouth of me,
And I fain would stir and be wise again,
But my heart is dust, and my lips are rain!"

Then I—I bent to her murmuring side,
And pledged her my love thro' the still night-tide,
But her heart was dust, and so I crept
Back to my resting-place and slept.

Euthanasia

The west wind ere the morning came
    Turned all the heaven to mist and fire,
And in the tremulous dawn a flame
    That saw the embodied stars expire.

I, too, shall perish and stand confest,
    With lifted finger and wearied head;
So bright and bitter yet fain to rest—
    A hopeless soul to the happy dead.

A Burden

Cleis, the daughter of Sappho, she sat by a twilit sea,
And her heart was bitter, bitter, with passionate memory.

The ilex leaned like a shadow into the violet foam,
The doves called one to another out of the evening gloom.

A moon rose great over Lesbos, lowly and honey-pale,
And into the wounded silence, there shivered a nightingale.

But Cleis, the daughter of Sappho, she wist not what it might be,
For her heart was bitter, bitter, with passionate memory.

A Departure

At evening in the moonlight on the regimental street,
The boys fare forth together and they march with golden feet,
The road's a path of silver and all heaven is lit with stars—
O friends of mine and souls I knew that vanish to the wars!

Each with musket at right-shoulder and the ghostly crescent pack—
"Goodbye, old man—good luck to you—here's hoping you come back!"
But something makes you shiver with the pathos of the sight—
A loneliness that takes one as they pass into the night.

W. E.

Brother and bunkmate, old friend Epe,
They tell me you have gone to sleep;
Soul of crystal, heart of dew,
And one of the few—one of the few.

But wherever you may be,
Don't awake for reveille,
Take another hour abed,
That's the privilege of the dead.

See the lights flare, hear the call:
"Rifles—side-arms—one and all!"
As of old lie still and sleep;
Good old Epe—ah, good old Epe!

On the Passing of Youth

"Però trascorro a quando mi svegliai
    e dico ch'un splendor mi squarciò 'l velo
    del sonno, e un chiamar: 'Surgi: che fai?'"
                        —DANTE.

    I am he who came
A thing of wonder, a breath of flame,
With questing heart unsought, unscaled,
But for the something that within me wailed.
I was the poised wind that urges
The moon-beached, moaning surges,
A soul intagliate, unshriven,
That knew no place but heaven;
My lips unvised, my joy fulfilled,
Ere ever sorrow thrilled.
Not mine—not mine to feel
Life's pitiablest broken at their wheel,
Only about me stirr'd
Voices of dreams unheard,
Legional strays of laden wings,
Enchanted, dew-like things,
Crying, "Thou goest?—ah! not yet,
Lest we—we too forget,
This lucent, linked, tranquil star,
The lighted eyes, the lips oracular."

    And I said:
"Ere my crystalline youth be withered,
And I pass hence,
Sole in my penitence;
Ere I be dim,
To sun and seraphim,
Having read Joy's pagan missal,
Fire-lighted, paradisal,
Seen in the compass'd night,
As a star, as a light,

Once—ah! but once in state,
Regal and passionate,
With hearts like molten dew,
Antique Apollo and his burning crew;
Ere to Time's hued abysm,
I fling my staff, my chrism,
And lonely on life's portals,
Abide like other mortals—
I, too, must trace,
As a wind shifting ways,
I, too must wend,
Light within darkness to the veiled end!"

    Where the tremulous dawning towers,
One came to me with flowers;
Violet-crowned and sapphire-eyed,
With wings unutterably wide;
Shone on her brow the rays
Of leaping chrysoprase;
Beautiful, august, with perilous, flashing feet,
And face divinely sweet;
Calling, "Come thou with me,
Not in austerity,
Nor with faint, broken hands that wage
At misery's ceaseless heritage,
But by quick plumes of fiery wings,
Desire for aureate wanderings,
Unresting hope, disquiet way,
Light beyond light, day beyond day,
In all thy solitary soul,
The irreconcilable goal.
Bear with me in thy laughing, April years,
Golden delight of golden tears,
My way alone shalt then endure,
The immortal, radiant vesiture,
The prophetic, still, responsive cry,

That in the whole world finds ecstasy,
Beauty and wonder, terror-deep,
And in the end a sudden, healing sleep."

    I am he who departed,
Baffled and bitter-hearted;
Dreamer and dream of many habitations,
Torn from those white, Elysian stations,
The soul of me disorb'd and sent
Divinely into banishment;
Unprofitable, wandering, vagrant still,
Inalienably mutable;
Chance-borne, yet shaken by the power
Of each enduring hour,
Beyond the stars, beyond the sun,
Into their bright oblivion,
Then lost in unascending spheres,
Save to all grief, save to submissive tears.
Only amid those darkling places,
Shine argent wings and burning faces,
"Thou, too, O Brother—thou too," they cry,
"Hast gazed on Beauty and must die,
The lips that fade, the love that flies,
The inexorable memories,
That mystery hoarded and apart,
In thy secretest, lyric heart;
Yet once—yet once ere thou dost go,
With weary-paced steps and slow,
Ere bowed and trodden in derision
Thou see'st the one, the unblinded vision,
And where the stars of morning sing,
Weep'st in estranged remembering—
Gather thy luminous mantle on this height,
And pass into the night."

A Triumph in Eternity

"L' angoscia de le genti
  che son qua giù, nel viso mi dipinge
  quella pietà che tu per tema senti."
                              —DANTE.

There rose from dreaming in a hueless spring,
  A wind that gathered every silken flower,
And all its breath was fire and ruining,
  And all its might fulfillment of a power,
Darkness, destruction, and the void that flings
Thunder of night and imminence of wings;
And I, the sleeper, panged with indecision,
  Of clasped joy and radiated fears,
Heard naught beyond the moaning of my vision,
  Beyond the present bitterness of years.

And from their riven pomp and sundered dust
  Arose imperial in their print of flame
Œdipus, Agamemnon ever just,
  And hoar Tiresias wearily the same;
Beautiful souls, unquenched dooms of men,
Crying, "Who calls us from our anarch ken?
Is it the night hath ta'en your hope immortal,
  O miserablest of earth's unwary ones?
None gaze upon this adamantine portal,
  Unblinded by the sapphire-lighted suns!"

And all those human seers that burned of old,
  Soft-voiced, pleading, passionately mild,
With eyes illumined and with hearts of gold,
  Uprose in desolation and undefiled;
But o'er the pendulous and living night,
A spark upon the haunted deep, a light
Of wonder in their interlunar prison,
  With thorns for joy and enmity for love,
Came he whom men have called divine and risen,
  Ensandall'd and predestin'd from above.

For in his eyes the light of faith was gone,
    And in his heart had hope long perished,
A wind that withered 'mid the stars at dawn,
    Dismantled pity and eternal dread:
No lonelier soul in chaos moaned than he,
Since from that hour of central agony,
By heaven's implicate and unknown wonder,
    Of radiant fury 'gainst all humankind,
He bared his soul alone to fire and thunder,
    In the ancestral darkness of the blind.

Only about him lingered yet the ghosts
    Of little children loved and sung of yore,
Pellucid phantoms aureoled in hosts,
    Bewildered sprites that sought his hand once more;
But sought in vain, for in his kindred eyes
Lay broken vows and lustered memories.
Fain to forget and fain be unbeholden
    To mutability of alien years,
The flame above his head was bright and golden,
    But on his cheek the savouring of tears.

Yet still he dreamed his hope would be fulfilled,
    And in the furrowed night, august and pale,
The frozen heart of him again was thrilled
    By light of stars to mankind's piercing wail;
To waken once again now still and furl'd,
The pagan beauty of another world,
Ere eld had made it gray, ere grief could follow,
    To blot the lucency and hush the dream,
The music of that god which was Apollo,
    The time elysian and the joy supreme.

But even as he ponder'd in the vast
    And moaning wrack of sere oblivion,
A voice cried, "O my sovran Son! at last
    Our perishable splendour lies undone;
We had not pity to our aim aligned,

But built our structure in the darkness blind,
Thou with thy dreams and I my might of making,
    In fealty to noble faiths and trust,
Better a ruin, rather the forsaking,
    Than bitterness that burnishes in dust!"

Still plots the Son 'mid heaven's reflecting peace,
    Still chides the Master from eternity,
And truths that burn and ills that may not cease,
    Are graven as in fire on all that be;
Alas! for joy that promises no less,
For hope that ends in barren hopelessness,
Yet for this comfort that finds strength assurance,
    Betwixt such lampless and such mystic foes,
The souls of us are pacified in durance,
    By sleep that waits with darkness and repose.

                      1916

Talent

Dante saw hell, an opal lit with ice,
    And heaven, the loneliness of love long flown;
I, who have neither hell nor paradise,
    Breathe speech and beauty into hearts of stone.

[Untitled]

He said: This is the city . . . . here have we,
    Pestilent hell, arisen in irisen towers;
And I: There comes to me the scent of flowers,
    In a forgotten temple by the sea.

[Untitled]

Within my little plot of light,
    I sang of Heaven, but far and wide,

The shadows and the wings of night,
    Came close to me at eventide.

For in the darkness known by few,
    One handed me a wine-cup deep;
And I, who loved the light, drank too,
    In bitterness and scorn, of sleep.

Adventure

Oh, 'tis I that would be a pirate bold,
    Moustachio'd, fierce, and fair;
With a glistering cutlass, pieces of gold,
    And a head of raven hair.

I would range the seas and the azure isles
    That becalm the tropic foam,
For my soul is sick of the dullard's wiles,
    And the ministering cares of home.

And my men should be men in a world of men,
    Such sprites of dew and flame,
Who have chafed at their bonds and once again
    Would return from whence they came.

And our barque we should call *The Dead Man's Skull*,
    A thing of fear in the night;
Our scuppers with rubies and diamonds full,
    And our prow ablaze with light.

But at last 'neath a yellow lotos moon,
    By the ribb'd and shelving shore,
I should bury my treasure all too soon,
    I should dream, but set sail no more.

Yet my lonely eyes would turn to the sea,
    Where my moonlight galleons lay,
And my heart should be fill'd with the mystery
    That bids me be on and away.

For 'tis I that had been a pirate bold,
    Moustachio'd, fierce, and fair,
With a glistering cutlass, pieces of gold,
    And a head of raven hair.

Epilogue

Now with wings furled and the long storm over,
    Comes to me the Viking, comes the flame;
Once again the wild blood calls the rover,
    To rest is sloth and shame.

The hulks are black, the wind is soft and daring,
    The night is still and deep;
Oh, fine it were to be for ever faring,
    But better 'tis to sleep.

In Sepulcretis

They have brought Lawrence back from France with flowers,
    Lawrence, who loved men's souls, the sun, the rain,
Who wrote: My friend I count the very hours,
    Until we meet again. . . .

Buried him, close among an alien breed,
    Lawrence, the pagan, whom no creed enticed. . . .
But carven on the headstone one may read:
    Thy Servant, Jesus Christ.

Saturday Evening

The beggars in the night and rain,
    Along the pavement slink and whine;
Good times (they say) and will come again,
    But oh! their miseries are mine.

And something leaps to me with crying,
    To me, in tears of pity yet. . . .
A word that fell from lips undying,
    Upon the mount called Olivet.

A Letter to G—— K——

Here, in the night, are winds that cry and keep
Their frozen clangor on the wall of sleep;
Autumn, in pyramidal splendour pales,
But in her heart the joy it is that fails
And fades. Not all her sun, rain, wrath, her cries,
The red lustration of a soul that dies
Uncherished and regretful, still'd in bronze,
Under the year's immortal gonfalons—
Dare keep her with us. To her clarion call
Is whispered moaning the confessional
That precedes Winter, when by way and flood,
Steals as a doom, the whiter brotherhood,
Unshriving and unshriven with a speech,
Deeper than heartache in the depth of each,
Alone, yet muted.
    O my dearest friend!
Never the day that does not reach an end.
Never yet in the wild symphonic din,
But there came subtlier the cry within:
Give up . . . give over!
    I am he who said:
Until this disquiet heart be quieted;
Until upon these eyes, this lyric brain,
Not even a winged vestige shall remain,
Save the one prophesying voice that spells
Rebellion for this nethermost of hells;
Protest against the blind, the dumb, the driven,
Beggar'd on earth yet still denied their heaven;
Not until thither as a torch at tryst,
There perish in my soul the mutinist,
Shall I be silenced!
    I have heard it told,
Of a vast tower of perfume and of gold;
About a wayfarer as in a dream,
Who saw the molten spire and windows gleam,

Heard cry a voice in the enchanted night,
From lips like music, laughter and delight;
Something that pealed: Enter! for here at feast,
Thou, that of mankind art accounted least,
Shalt as a god sit, strange, imperial, lone,
Tremulous and sublunar on thy throne . . .
And entered in huge silence, but at dawn,
One who beside him stood, cried: Now, begone!
A shadow art thou henceforth, even as these
That wrought so cruelly thy destinies—
Call thyself Pity, ever after!

I

Must be that wayfarer until I die;
Shall seek, and always seeking, never find
Wisdom in hearts, beauty in eyes stone-blind,
Then pass to one who passed before me. . . . He,
Who so loved life, who so loved liberty,
That all the darkness in eternal space
Shone golden on us with his godlike face,
In still, saturnian largess.
We remain,
Never to know his druid self again;
Nor on the water's perilous rise and fall,
To hear soft-brimm'd, that voice of voices call
Lines from the sonnets he so loved to speak,
Shakespere, Stagnelius, or some purple Greek,
Who sang to lyres by the Ionian sea,
Forgotten, save by him alone. But we,
When spring begins out Dover-way, shall find
The butterflies again upon the wind,
And see in all the blue sky, pink and white,
The apple-blossoms in their downward flight,
Hearken the birds upon the boughs that bend,
To sing the song that only Spring shall end,
And hear his soul, the cry in flowers and leaves,
Love me—but love me not, who pines and grieves!

Ernest Nelson

One who sought his soul in a life that joyed in faring,
    Stellar-eyed and golden-haired and dim with light;
He hailed the few he loved and undespairing,
    Passed bravely into night.

Between the song and silence shown the lifted finger,
    Luminous and lovely among the gods afar;
Signal to signal for still another singer,
    On still a lonelier star.

Heldenleben

(*For George Kirk*)

The boys who did not choose to fight—
    So long it is—so long ago!
Still, in the solitary night,
    There comes to me their endless woe.

For always, keen and bright, there thrills
    The vigil of my friends in pain—
Clark, a deserter to the hills,
    And Cross, a bullet in his brain.

Winter

(*For Howard P. Lovecraft*)

When, in the night on hill and hillside shaken,
    The wind in darkness wailed;
I remembered Miller, whom death had overtaken,
    So early when he failed.

Unhurt and undillusioned by the life that bound him,
    Yet could not bid him stay—
Even as the snow that fell all night and found him,
    White, in a whiter day.

To Satan

"Tu tires ton pardon de l'éternal martyre,
Infligé sans relâche aux coeurs ambitieux."
       —BAUDELAIRE.

    To H. P. L.

When, mid the hyacinth deep that girds the sky,
  You saw, O Brother, ere your eyes grew dim,
  In wrath and loneliness the sight of Him,
Amid His bow'd and litten hierarchy:
Heard songs that fell from lips half-strange with years,
  Outcast and ruin'd, beautiful in flame,
    You—with the lost among the damned few,
    The fallen rebel crew—
  Hearing the flattery that fawned His name,
Turn'd back to hell a face that shone with tears.

Did you not at the sunken portals wait,
  And where the golden estuaries fell,
  Gazing at heav'n before the glow of hell,
Stretch forth your hand to where the tyrant sate?
With the first cry that shook th' enslaved world,
  Swift, silver, clarion, Lo! I make you free,
    Free as the winds and as the waters are,
    Sons of the morning-star!
  O souls of mine, I give you liberty—
No withering hate into the darkness hurl'd!

Not from those spaces charm'd to dusk and rose,
  Nor in the scarves with light and music pent,
  Came the soft wail of disillusionment,
But lower than the lowliest in their woes,
The trodden and the dispossess'd of fate;
  These, brooding in a quiet flash of tears,
    By stars that to the massive night are graven,
    Recall'd their austere haven
  The sorrow and the bitterness of years,
Conceiv'd in ruin and embalm'd in hate!

And now shall men no longer fear and dread!
    For heav'n is shattered, faded is the host,
      That without pity judg'd the tortur'd lost,
And radiantly parcell'd forth the dead.
See! where your molten throne uprears in night
    The legions gleam, the drowsy vultures wing;
        That which first met your plaintive, human eyes,
        Ev'n that, is paradise. . . .
    At last, my Brother, the awakening!
Ere dawn appears, a perfect chrysolite.

Christmas—1923

As I went through the rain and wind
    The beggar-men by twos and threes
They bowed and murmured: "Sir, be kind
    Unto our mighty miseries."

And I, whose brain was never quiet,
    I saw, eternal to their call,
Heart-ache and penury and riot,
    With Death the master of it all.

Genesis

Half the world was chaos,
    In the golden deep;
God blew on the waters,
    And murmured: Let them sleep.

Blew upon the daybreak,
    And hid within His wings;
Men awoke in sorrow
    At the memory of things.

Night Piece (Forest Hill)

The moon climbs over the garden wall,
The petals of roses begin to fall;
And nothing in the deep night knows
My trouble—save this ruined rose;

That shivered as the petals went,
Perishing in the firmament.
I give the cry that a poet gave:
"Be brave, my heart—but not too brave."

Monolith

I would make the thing I love,
    Remote, estranged, apart;
And yet it is the thing I love,
    That shares another's heart.

I would be the charmed wind
    That hears the long wave moan—
O, bitterness! each to its kind,
    With one who loves alone.

Oscar Redivivus

Oscar, when your eyes of light
Face the vast abyss of night,
And on ghostly stairs you crawl,
In your paradisal hall,
Take a lighted doorway where
A sign reads: "Chelsea Bookshop here";
Enter, if you care to play,
Sleep by night and dream by day,
Tarry till your eyes grow dim,
And you meet the feline Him,
While He hears where shadows fall,
Your immortal catterwawl.

Unfulfilled

Bend close and listen: Long ago,
    One lived as I, a Greek;
His heart was flame, his head was snow,
    He loved, but dared not speak.

O foolish fates! this one was loth,
    And loved a third unkind;
So now as then, the dust of both
    Blows idly in the wind.

Unfulfilled [Alternative]

Bend close and listen: long ago,
One loved as I, a Greek;
His heart was flame, his lips were snow,
He loved but dared not speak.

O foolish fate! the second loth
Loved still a third, unkind;
So now, as then, the dust of both
Blows idly in the wind.

To Mr. Theobald

(*Upon His Return to Providence*)

In Providence at fringèd eve
    Old Theobald takes his cap and cane,
And where the antique shadows weave,
    Dreams his Colonial dreams again.

Sees the pale periwigs that pass
    Pause delicately by, then fare
Past balustrades that shine like glass
    To seek his eighteenth century there.

Dream, Theobald—close your tired eyes,
  Forget the ruder world around;
Only these by-gone folks were wise,
  Only the vanquish'd world was sound.

Hold them an instant if you will,
  Shadows of perfume, light and flowers—
We never knew their grace until
  You, by your genius, made them ours!

To George Kirk on His 27th Birthday

Still do I hear where hillside winds are shaken,
  When the long daylight ends;
From one whose lips shall never re-awaken:
  "Be friends, and always friends."

Friend, to one friend—we only and none other,
  This lustrous vigil keep—
The memory of our violet-laden brother,
  Bound fast in Roman sleep.

Music

When I stood in mid-heaven,
  Among the wingèd host,
My face with joy was riven,
  Mine eyes with starlight crost.

Oblivious of the hours,
  Sang the immortal crew;
Songs lovelier than flowers,
  And lovelier than dew.

My Tribute

Brave, pitiful, loyal, suffering, true,
Was Hazel Adams. I, who only knew

Her radiance for the briefness of an hour,
Yet marvelled at the light of all that day:
  Place here before her dust a single flower,
And pass—as all things pass—upon my way.

Vigil

I in the night heard
A voice that stirred
The darkness with a word.

Saying: "Arise!
Brother, be wise,
Open thy dear, dead eyes."

O brave! O brave!
That me to save
Wouldst stir the secret grave.

And the old lust
Sang to my dust:
"Waken at once, thou must."

But I, dreaming, slept,
Heard naught except
One, who beside me slept.

To a Child

I

The stars are adrift in the breathless night,
    And the silken winds are furled;
And it's you and I for our heart's delight
    Must sail to the end of the world.

For life is a jest or the bitter truth,
    And it isn't best to awake;
So we're off again—to youth, to youth—
    All for your lovely sake.

II

This is our tinted ship of dreams that never
    The winds pursue;
All it needs is a kiss to move the lever
    Manned by a faery crew.

Into the dusky night half sped and shaken
    For dewy hours,
I pluck a star from the sea, and lest you waken,
    Cover you deep with flowers.

III

All the world's a golden flower;
    All the dawn's a rose;
Lark and threstle, bird and bower,
    Bid it to unclose.

All your life is like this petal
    That the winds would woo.
See—I hold it lest it settle
    In a drop of dew!

The Dead King

So still he seemed, so still he lay,
    A King of Lethe, blanched and pale,
Oblivious of his mortal day,
    And to the women's piercing wail.

But when the murmuring had ceased,
    When grief to grief had broken low,
I, who had loved him not the least,
    I bent to kiss his royal brow.

Kin

When you lie below in darkness and in duress
    And you hear the young spring call

Then shall come to you far lovelier than loveliness
    The pity of it all.

And your eyes shall see their confines ere they darken,
    But your heart must show no dread,
For across the lowly spaces you shall hearken,
    The dead men call the dead.

Episode

Three friends had I, spake Socrates,
    A subtle thing, a soul of fire,
And one beloved by both of these:
    A knave, a rogue, a cheat, a liar.

Whom loved you, Master, best of these?
    Whom held you closest to desire—
The soul of flame? Quoth Socrates,
    The knave, the rogue, the cheat, the liar.

Rescue

Lucent was the twilight
    And ivory the dark,
When forth upon the fringed rain
    There rode a shining spark.

Cup of Troy or Holy Grail,
    How was I to tell?
But O, the little difference
    That cast me out of Hell!

Transit

Over the western rim it slips,
    Parting a glint, a gleam of gold,
Breeze-borne a song from deathless lips—
    And all the world is bitter cold.

The Abyss

Where, in the frore Atlantic, peaked and hurled,
One world is tumbled on another world,
Blue over green, green over white, then scaled
Gradation to another color paled,
Mounted and molten, each one clasped to spurn
An ecstasy that overleaps to burn,
But dares not, dares not!

                    Ice, ice everywhere—
Here, in this room and in this heart, the spear
Within, without— something that clings so deep,
Not Spring, a bitterer solstice— no, nor sleep,
Dare ever leave me, ever cast weight hence,
In desperate and driven penitence.

I cry: "Give way, it hurts!"

                    If only once
Into the gray-veined crystal of this sconce,
The frozen, shattered, derelict beauty felt,
A rosy ichor pierce its way to melt . . .
Well, what?—why nothing! Even as I speak,
The abyss that some philosopher, a Greek,
Inhabitant of Chios, Attic-born,
Haunter of silences, himself half-torn
Between the blunder that negation moves
In its own starred and interlineal grooves,
Writes of in fear and trembling

                          Takes me. . . .

Times Square

    The boys of Times Square,
With beautiful, ruined faces,
Stand in the golden twilight,
Holding a net for their prey;

Some to be blackmailed and robbed,
Some to be beaten or murdered,
Each to his harried fate;
While in the dusk of the subways,
Deep in the calyx of night,
Pale, unkempt, yellow-haired,
Adhesive and aching for love,
Three thousand miles from Montmartre,
Apart and exiled from Paris,
Stand the brothers of Paul Verlaine,
Awaiting their Arthur Rimbaud.

Metropolitan Museum

Rose-colored in its firmament of clay,
    Admired by many for an ovalled grace,
Spring smiles with Rodin on this Autumn day,
    And on the golden rondure of the face.

"Beautiful are the curves of lip and cheek,
    And beautiful the world itself, I guess,"
Says Helen: "I, who dare not speak,
    Reflect the body's hidden bitterness."

The Faithful

Come, Jesus, be this night my guest,
    And walk the rainy streets with me,
With halt, and maimed, and dispossessed
    That rot along the Bowery.

    . . . . .

Bring them your pity vast and deep,
    Take each one to your gentle side—
These are the poor who could not sleep
    The night that you were crucified.

An Admonition to the Ladies

Ladies, when at night you close
    Deaf ears to each piner,
Take your heed to none of those,
    But to Rheinhart Kleiner;
He that loved you all his life,
Dared take none of you to wife.

But when evening shadows slouch,
    And the night is luring,
Never by his virgin couch,
    Naked and assuring;
If his spirit takes not fire,
Something's wrong, or I'm a liar.

For the Chelsea Book Shop [I]

Walk into Chelsea where each street
    Climbs down to take a tug or wherry;
Never a rose-tree shall you meet,
    Never a lilac near the ferry.

By slip and spar and silhouette
    The ancient ghosts cling each together;
The city streets are damp and wet—
    They vow 'tis only fine Spring weather.

Yet when the winter, vast and pale,
    Beckons with snow and wind at riot;
They seek a shelter from the gale
    Within your realm of books and quiet.

And see your shelves stand row on row,
    And hear the world move by with laughter—
More than the living ever know,
    The wisdom of the dead knows after.

For the Chelsea Book Shop [II]

The night is over Chelsea Town,
    But far below the houses lie;
Mute, mute is all the city grown,
    Stiller than silence now, am I,

Who saw the yellow moon that climbs
    To flood the purple, Attic night;
Then gave the cry of ancient times,
    Half ecstasy and half delight.

Come with me now, as one believes
    That when the dawn begins to stir
The birds must sing among the leaves,
    While hedges break with lavender.

And heed no more the city's ache,
    Than he who sang the age of gold,
Within a heart that needs must break
    Seeing the tired world turn old.

Nepenthe

    "Then opened I my mouth, and behold, he reached me a full cup which was full, as it were of water, but the colour of it was like fire."
    —ESDRAS.

Out of the night exhaled in sleep and tears
Of weariest and unprofitable years,
A voice calls, lonelier than humanity,
"O brother, brother, wouldst thou cease to be?
Hast thou borne all things murmurless, bound even
Irradiant lips to earth, as hope to Heav'n?
Know thou, that mine enamoured crystals hold
Silence, far lovelier than antique gold;
Whispering wonders of high-curvèd seas,
Imagined ivory dew serene as these;

Pervasive azure of yon trackless space,
Imperishable peace of tranquil days.
In my lit eyes and o'er my moonlight breasts,
Only annihilation trembling rests,
And of the spark whence all my jewels burn
Life reconceives its casual, ghostly turn.
As bart'rer I in hope, nor faith to limn,
And yet within this goblet's raining brim,
If thou but knew it, thrice-dissolved there lies
Communicable sleep from memories."

So I, pang'd with an ache that never shows,
Oblivious wisdom or divine Repose,
Drink to forget—but ah! Who knows, who knows?

Quatrain

Life is a pearl that with the sea
    Some glimmering joy divides;
But mine—ah, mine is memory
    That knows her bitter tides.

Reliquiae

A little white lady who lived apart,
    She fell in love in a wintry year:
With blossoms and branches over her heart,
    And a grief too great to bear.

So, fiercer the maenad-fury grew,
    And sudden the helpless, tortured one—
There was nothing in all the world to do,
    But to die as the others had done.

Spring at El Retiro

Spring comes this way on bud and briar,
    With birds that wing in sun and light;
And deep within her dreaming fire,
    She yearns again for space and flight.

Hold her, O master and her lover,
    Keep her beside you all her years;
Blue as the bluest sky above her,
    Her eyes are often filled with tears.

Versailles

In old Versailles the days that fare
    Are as the leaves that flutter by,
And loiter on the golden air
    In old Versailles.

When all that faded host draws nigh,
    A phantom smiles in deep despair,
Then turns to weeping with a cry.

And still by terraced fountain there,
    The Queen, who does not live nor die—
Shivers at beauty everywhere,
    In old Versailles.

[Untitled]

I dreamed I had a pocket book,
Filled far and deep as eye could look,
And everywhere I went to buy
The merchants yelled: Her comes the guy,
Who thinks in brass and spends in gold,
Just collar him and knock him cold—
    Then I awoke,
    Dead broke.

The Goal

Beautiful was the byway,
    I took it with a song;
And there upon the highway,
    I shouted to the throng:

"With laughter and with pity,
    I can snare your hearts of stone...."
So I entered in their city,
    But I entered all alone.

[Untitled]

The lanes are drifted white with snow,
'Twist vale and hill the windows glow,
    Red in the rosy light;
O be it joy or be it grief,
The faded or the fallen leaf,
For all things beautiful and brief
    We bid good cheer this night.

Phryne

"A Courtesan of Ancient Greece"—Bullfinch

Under the rain-reflected light,
Phryne solicits for the night;
Not for desire, nor for delight.

But for the money that she sees,
To keep her when the sidewalks freeze,
On nights as terrible as these.

Then, to her eyes that mist and grope,
There comes the iridescent hope
Of flowers on an Attic slope.

Where on a marble fane were flung
Roses, where roses always hung
Before a face forever young.

And in a temple by the sea,
Men worshipped that which may not be
Ever again a mystery.

Take her or leave her—give no sign
That what she is was once divine;
Who seeks your level now, and mine.

[Prologue to *Circe*]

Forth from the deep, the Odyssey in blue
Dancers and players have we come to you.
Where from an island ringed in light and gold
We tell a story many times retold.

Close but your eyes and open them to be
Flung from a doomed ship in the wind-logged sea.
Before these serried cliffs that hold with guile
Circe, enchantress of a magic isle.

Illicit

The apple blossoms drift apart
And strew the way to Dover.
Something has come into my heart—
I follow as your lover.

If you could guess, if you could trace
The secret that I cover,
I should be alien all my days,
And nevermore your lover.

Dowager

Encased in rouge, a rhythm gone astray,
She dines at André's, tabled at my right;
Listening and half inert, I turn away;
It rains without, a rainy summer night.

She drools and dribbles chicanery and guile,
Tartuffe and Pecksniff feminized by wits;
I choose an entrée with a winning smile,
And slowly tear her tawdry soul to bits.

John Clare in 1864

Here, in the shadows of the creek,
Sits Clare, the gentlest of the weak.

Across the tethered portico,
The shadows come, the shadows go.

He sees the blue skies overhead,
But at his feet the flowers are dead.

Once only are his eyes alight,
An effort less of lark in flight.

John Clare stares up, his dull eyes bright.
Someday I'll follow in his flight.

II. Drama

Oedipus at Colonus

"Who rose like shadows between man and God."
          —SHELLEY.

 Oedipus: Who comes?
 Antigone: Haemon, my lord.
 Oedipus: Make fast the door.
There's terror in the barren wind tonight,
Our privacy's unsur'd.
 Haemon: Not as a foe—
 Oedipus: But like the cormorant and musing owl
That feign a prayer in slaying. Hence away!
There are no kin where beggary sits scant
And suffers for a pittance.
 Antigone: A true friend,
Whose heart stood ever on the fallen side
And privileged the losing. He brings news,
Good news, we trust, to make ill fortune sweet.
 Oedipus: But quick, or ere our ruined thoughts forget.
 Haemon: O good my Lord, the princes both are slain,
Fall'n in a quarrel fostered by the king;
The eldest lies unburied.
 Antigone: Patience, Gods!
Lest I lose hope. This is the flaw that coils
Our searching patent. Oh! he weeps not yet,
But stirr'd by the extremity of ache,
Holds the dew scathless.
 Oedipus: Something there cracks within!
 Haemon: Courage, good friends, for of the moving kind,
These are but bolts that shoot invisibly.
 Oedipus: Girl, has thou fed them yet?
 Antigone: My Lord, my Lord!

Oedipus: The poor, the poor, that with unvised mouths,
The piteous air importunate and load.
I would have 'em all, all fed.
 Antigone: He only hears.
Pledges that follow like the sweet south wind
And leave no wake in peering. Father, father!
O grief-recounted heart that bleeds to fix
A finger on earth's cheapened misery.
Poor seared eyes!
 Oedipus: Let me be filial censor.
Swear, there are no more honest men i' the world,
Swear, that the best of us will err, lie, thieve,
Throttle the mother's milk, convent such crime
And serious depredation of regard,
That heaven stooping to the lips of hell,
Breathe dross'd and vary-hued. Swear, swear, swear!
 Antigone: Still!
You drift on passion's sea, that bears a host
Of wrecks precipitate and viewless craft.
Take trust and anchor, all things work to good,
We cease not to believe in miracles.
 Oedipus: How? how? we shall have cause for joy full soon,
Sorrow comes after. Let there be all things said
And nothing done. Look you, I am not vile,
Only incapable of making good
Half-blown offenses and their chariest truths.
O monstrous! monstrous! I that feel, fawn, feed,
To call my brother clod to the dull earth,
And tread him as we do the brooded worm.
I am well paid—well paid, I say! no need
To bare myself to the annealing wind
And beg for penitence a wintry shift,
The quick confusion of our bitter bliss
Signs chaos into surety again—
I shall sleep the long night out at last.
 Antigone: No! No!
Not yet! I'm all alone in the world.

Oedipus: Soft, soft!
The little children call me from the dark,
Eteocles and Polynices—sons all,
I held them dandled at my naked knee,
And suckt fond kisses from their cherub lips,
But none of them would come, none to help bear,
My whole world's weight of leaden misery.
 Antigone: Stay quenchless, eyes, until we weep our fill,
My lord, I did not leave you, I—I came.
 Oedipus: The mist between us works a deadly bar!
I would see sweet eyes, know many numerous things,
And let graced wit my madness overblaze.
Comfort me, comfort me!
 Antigone: I do, but O!
My heart's top-heavy.
 Oedipus: Steep it in molten brine.
And let there be a new dependency
To green quarled serpents. Beggar thy loveliness!
Thy soul's the cistern, at the bottom lies
Their golden custom's vital esquiry.
Alas! alas! I am so wretched, wretched—
The end discrowns our need.
 Antigone: Sigh, hush, and sleep.
What use to war with gods?
 Oedipus: With my spent power,
And from my degradation's dying stamp,
What though I reck their fleecy thunderous hail,
I curse—I curse—
 Antigone: Woe's me! leave it unsaid.
 Oedipus: The butterfly that scaped the crawling stage!
Be as thou ever wast, best of thy kind,
Kiss me—I face the dark—what, what, what, what!
It breaks—

                  Dies.

 Haemon: Our jove-like souls are instruments
That quaver sometime in their playing. Rest,
Life's but a moment's space of wilderment,

Set in a sudden darkness. There's the sway
That profits by no fortune.
  Antigone: Done's the dream.
I close thine eyes, I smooth thy stricken brow,
Tenderly, gods, the fault was not his own.
  Haemon: Where now, Antigone?
  Antigone: To Thebes, my lord.
  Haemon: The king gainsays all kindness in his mood,
His heart of stone derides that flawless gem
That burns in freezing. Measure your life with mine,
I mean the intent, and let our fortunes be
One and commingled. It may hap that both
Shall find some purpose meet.
  Antigone: My duty first.
The falcon we have strook deserves perforce
Such pity that the clouded heart can give.
We yoke our sorrows to the midnight stars,
And take their weight in silver.
  Haemon: Ah, not so.
To dare the omnipotence of the Gods,
And leap within their golden graciousness,
This were most nobly done. But where the vow,
Lessens itself upon the deeded heart,
Were it not wise, think you, Antigone,
To rear and love self first?
  Antigone: My hand alone
Must pile the laurel on his unbalmed corse,
And kiss the ghastly death-dew from his eyes.
I were not woman else.
  Haemon: Then hear the truth.
Our father's edict harbours instant death,
With no more pity than the viewless air,
That slays with kissing honey.
  Antigone: O just Gods!
Make me unalterable to the end.
Not fire, nor famine, and the halter's scourge,
Swerve my set cause, but when the work is done,
Give my grief rein to mourn the dear departed,

And dew their noble memory in tears.
Lie low! lie sweet! others have done the same,
That drew not half the penance, summ'd not all
Commitment on their head, but as it is,
We thank the smiling Gods.
  Haemon: Then take me with thee,
And come what may, I'll follow in thy steps,
The sea runs on forever.
  Antigone: Like our souls,
That ebb and break. I go alone, my Lord.
Farewell, farewell.
  Haemon: Love speed you.

Belshazzar

Persons Represented:

BELSHAZZAR, King of Babylon.
FANES AND BARAS, Counsellors.
QUEEN.
SINGER.
DANIEL, A Hebrew Captive.
Nobles, Wives, Attendants, Dancers, etc.

  Singer, sings:
White gleams the lotus-flower, gliding along,
Timbrel and silvery harp, chant thee a song,
Idly the breezes blow, dallying the while,
There met I thee, my Love, where flows the Nile.

  Chorus
Come Love, come Love, press thy rosy lips to mine,
  Skies of sapphire vague and far,
  Tremulous the evening star,
Come Love, come Love, press thy rosy lips to mine.

Blue the sky above, pearly the foam,
Soft is the river's flow to waft thee home,
Idly the breezes blow, dallying the while,
There met I thee, my Love, where flows the Nile.

Chorus

    Belshazzar: The weightiest bag of gold, be thine, sweet singer,
Say you not so, my lords—no bird at dawn,
Singing amid the day-break's flaming fire,
Ere sang a song one half so sweet.
    Baras (throws a bag at the singer's feet): My lords!
Do you all follow suit, and give the lark
His due—see—I have given my choicest pearls,
My rings of sardius and chrysolite,
The purest hues of opal, amethyst,
To compensate this muse.
    The revellers shower their gifts at the singer.
    Belshazzar: Drink! let us drink to Astareth and Baal,
To these fair houris in our embraces.
Drink! and in the glorious revelry,
The long carouse, forget the somber night,
Forget the woe and wretchedness on earth,
And live content, to bask in radiant light!
    All: Drink!
    Belshazzar (caressing the Queen): In truth, thou art a queen, my
        gem divine,
Thy ebon hair, thy dusky eyes, thy cheeks
That out-rival the asphodel in hue
Of purity. I would—
    Gazes terror-stricken at the wall.
        See—yonder wall—
The hand outstretched—my lords, I am undone—
    Queen: Nay, Lord, be not afraid, 'tis naught. I know
Of one who can interpret this, and who
Shall change thy fear to joy. Send for the seer,
This Daniel from Judea.
    All: Send for him!
    A messenger leaves.
    Fanes: Aye, I have heard of this young man,
The wonders that he works—
    All: Aye!
    Enter Daniel.

Belshazzar: Art thou he
Whom men call Daniel? This very night
There hath appeared upon the farthest wall,
A writing whereof I know naught. Therefore
Have I called thee to tell me of its import,
Vast treasures, all at thy command, shall be
Thine if thou canst tell.
    Daniel: O mighty king!
I care not for thy vaunting gifts—thy wine,
Give these to servile hands, but not to mine.
Great God left thee thy kingdom rich in spoil,
Begotten by thy father—by his toil;
But thou hast sinned, bowed down to gods of gold,
And in thy greatness waxed exceeding bold;
Thou hast not heeded thine own father's fall,
Thus says the writing on the wall:
    Points to the wall and reads:
"M'ne, God hath numbered thy kingdom and made an end of it.
T'kel, Thou hast been weighed in the balance and found wanting.
P'ress, Thy kingdom hath been divided, and is given to the Medes and
    Persians."
    Belshazzar bows his head.

Nero

    SCENE.—Rome. The balcony of the palace, overlooking burning Rome. Enter Nero, Poppaea, his wife, and nobles.

    Nero: 'Tis just begun, my lords—ah, what a sight—
But Beauty is of Terror born, therefore
I, Lucius Domitius Nero,
Grand-son of the far-famed Germanicus,
Vow to the Gods a thousand sesterces,
An ye see not a wond'rous scene tonight.
    Poppaea: Good lord—and shall we not be favored with
An ode, such as the Gods delight to hear,
Composed by Thee, Olympus-born? Nay—nay,
Refuse us not.

Nero: Refuse thee, Love?
I would as lief refuse—myself! Ha! Ha!
My wit is efflorescent as my wine,
Ye Gods! it cheereth, doth it not, my Lords?
    Lords: Aye—to be sure!
    Nero: Now night with sable pall approacheth fast,
Where are the gods these Christian dogs bow to?
See! how the seething flames begin to rise,
And lick the lowly hovels, till the curs,
Encompassed in the mighty crash that falls,
Shriek out the torments of a damned soul—
Ah—let them scream—'tis music to my ears!
See how they fall upon their knees and pray,
Pouring their utmost anguish out to Him
They deem a god—'tis all in vain howe'er,
My legions have I counseled, not to give
A drop of respite to their cursed souls . . .
What chant is that I hear, that rises, ebbs,
And falls amid the tumult of the din . . .
Ah—this is Art—but Art so glorified
That all the common rabble term it Death.
Now gentle Poppaea, my ode . . .
    (*He takes his harp from an attendant and sings.*)
    O MUSE, INSPIRE WITHIN MY SOUL
    A SONG OF HEART-FELT PRAISE
    TO THEE . . .
    (*He gasps and falls back.*)
I would retire, my lords, the air grows faint,
These hot, oppressive vapors do diffuse
A poison, not unlike the deadly breath
Of some secretive herb—come let us hence.
    (*They retire.*)

NOTE—I have endeavored in the foregoing dramatic poem, fragmentary as it is, to correctly picture my idea of Nero's character and disposition. Nero, I believe, had the soul of an aesthete—a lover of the sublime and beautiful. This, I have tried to portray. Whether I have succeeded or not, remains for the reader to decide.   S. E. L.

Varden

A TRAGEDY

"The best in this kind are but shadows."—Shakespeare.

VARDEN, a dreamer.
LADY MARGARET, a bride.
SIR RALPH, her husband.
GILES, an old servant.
Guests, Servants and Other Attendants.

SCENE—A Room In The Castle. Enter Giles And Varden.

Giles: These be great goings-on today Master Varden.
Varden: Aye, the dead are dancing with their shadows.
Giles: I ha' seen my Lady, and a wonderous sight it is. Hath a fine purple smock beribbed wi' posies, yet goodly and gracious she gazed upon me and withal seemed exceedingly happy—
Varden: On the lea's down edge, where the old prickle-bush trends to the sweep o' the sea—know'st it, man?
Giles: Yea now, that I do.
Varden: I found them there at sunset—nay, tell him not I told thee—but I would there were a beginning to all things; my head is aweary thinking on 't.
Giles: Whom saw ye?
Varden:
    Yet held her thus, and thus he clipt her lips,
    And ever the night-sea's mist besmirched the headland,
    And sought the sheer verge where the gibing weeds
    Scud softly to the breaking moat below,
    Until they twain were driven back to shelter,
    And I crept hence.
Giles: (*Aside*) He's daft as usual.   (*Exit*).
Varden:
           This is the fire
    Doth brast upon me i' the night. A sea
    Of asper fire it is, and on the rim,

    Doth slumber Proserpine with cowled barb,
    For in her sleep she sings, and with her song
    There comes unto my heart an old, old pain.... (*He weeps*)
    Ah me, but Hesper shineth on the mere,
    A flood of silver phantasy it is.
    The woof whereof is love; for I have seen
    The meadow hills break with enflowered bloom
    When my maid trips along the dim alure,
    To brush with sprightly besom, hands outstretcht,
    The cobwebs from a dewy moon. At morn
    Her fierce, red lips cleave unto mine, and ever
    Her hair smells soft of basil, calamus,
    And nard... Ah! she is come, our Lady of Pain,
    Gripes me with yearning breath and tumbled hair—
    Gone? gone when I would but yield. Lo, the puit
    Is yesty with the tides of night—yea night;
    The frost-weed and the helle-bore keep court
    At dusk they say; I'll deftly pluck them both,
    Pluck them, until I press their amorous blood
    For timely dower. (*Enter* LADY MARGARET.)
              Good e'en to thee fair lady.
Lady Margaret: Yea, so to you sir.
Varden: Thou art comely, thou.
Lady Margaret: But let me pass.
Varden: Bide thee content with me.
    No blowzy winds shall rough their scorn upon thee;
    Sequestered, sheltered in mine idle arms,
    Thou shalt play Helen, I thy Paris—sweet!
Lady Margaret: Out upon thee for an ill-mannered fellow!
Varden: Come thou with me—.   (*He approaches her*)
Lady Margaret: Husband—Sir Ralph! O—oh!
(*He carries her away. Exeunt. Enter* SIR RALPH *and* GILES).
Sir Ralph:
    Methought I heard her cry 'Sir Ralph!' and then,
    A muffled piteous sob brake forth. I'll seek.
    Her tiring-woman—Christ! this hath unnerved me.
Giles: I with you sir, in comfort.   (*Exeunt.*)

(*Re-enter Varden, half supporting Lady Margaret. A knife is in her breast.*)

Varden: I ha' murdered her!

Lady Margaret: Break—break, my heart! Oh—oh—　　　(*Dies*).

Varden: Ah—she is dead. (*He bends down to her*).
　　I loathe thee—loathe—thee—hence!
(*He spurns her with his foot.*)
　　Nay then, I love the; thou art so fair in death. . . .
　　　　　　　　　　(*He stoops as though to kiss her.*)
　　I'll wake her not; she hath that in her eyes
　　Betokening immortality.
　　Life's but a moment's space of wilderment,
　　Set in a sudden darkness. I ken the babe
　　Upon its glimmering threshold, and then—then all's
　　Immutable. I'll have done with it. See—
(*He draws the blade from her body.*)
　　Aye—aye, but to lie underfoot and feel
　　Spring, summer, autumn—winter, pass like dreams
　　Immeasureless above one; hear the seed,
　　Spaced by the singing ploughman, crack to life
　　I' the utter clod—God! but it stifles me—

Sir Ralph: (*from without*)—Heard you not voices?

Giles (*and others*): Marry, but we did!

Varden: I must make shift of it before the night
Falls on me—
　　　　　So—(*Stabs himself*)

Sir Ralph: Unbar the door there!

Varden: Dreams—dreams—and always dreams, I would there were
An end to't . . . (*Dies*)

(*They burst the door open. Enter Sir Ralph, Giles, and others.*)

Sir Ralph:　　　　　O woeful sight!

Narcisse

Dedication
To
Irving MacDonald SinClair

My dear SinClair:

In remembrance of the few happy hours we spent together on your last visit here, allow me to inscribe this little drama. Perhaps in the reading of it you will readily understand that its one dominant keynote is a steady, unswerving optimism. At any rate, I have only attempted to express in the rather too-mature philosophy of my Narcisse, what Browning in his supremely lovely characterization of Pippa intimated with a consummation comparable only to the childlike faith and sincerity of Shakespeare's Perdita:

> "I will pass each and see their happiness,
> And envy none—being just as great, no doubt."

Believe me to be,
    Sincerely your friend,
        S. L.

Cleveland, October 10, 1907.

Persons Represented

NARCISSE, a Peasant Girl.
FATHER JOHN, the Parish Priest.
BRISAC, an Escaped Prisoner.
JULES, a Captain.
Gendarmes.

SCENE.—A peasant cottage on Christmas eve. Narcisse before the window.

Narcisse: Ah, what a night: one scarce can see the way
For snow and darkness. Spar and gable seem
A world of under-shadows wrought to whim
Some stolid Titan's fantasy ... now to bed,
And lest the fire die low, I'll thresh it up
To an existence—warmth for me I say,
And happiness, in all the winter's stress,

This goodly Christmas eve.
Why, but the veriest wretch's at heart a king,
Housed under four staunch walls, a lusty blaze—
Marble or mortar hearth, it matters not,
As little pleasure as beseems their need,
Christ's mercy on them all!
The city, squalor, sin, unloveliness,
Yoked to its utmost core—I pity all—
Would take them in my single, lonely heart,
For succor and repentance—if needs be,
For the imperfect blossom, yet unfolded,
In each God-given soul.
                (*A knock without*)
Yes, yes—enter!
                (*Enter Father John*)
You, Father John, on such a night as this?
    Father John: I do but see my lambs safe in their fold,
Lest ill befall them. Our wolves are fierce and wild,
They roam these heather moorlands famished quite.
Hast thou no fear, my child?
    Narcisse: None, father, none!
    Father John: Thy lips are ruddy like forgotten wine . . .
Ah youth—youth! time and tide are naught to thee—
But I must go; the hour's exceeding late.
    Narcisse: Good night, Father!
    Father John: Peace and good-will on earth . . .   (*Exit*)
    Narcisse: Dear old man . . . how it snows. Across the moor
Shines his light, Jacques. Now glimmer—glimmer, then
Extinguished to the night; not though until
Its shine has softened—shed a gentle lustre,
On all the blackness nigh interminable.
Now Michel's light . . . sleep-time is come for all,
And all the day's toil ended.
                (*Unfastens her hair*)
                Can it be
This round o' life-love leads to things insensate—
Night-time and an eternal sleep perchance,

Or say . . . like Spring's blown chrysalis
Disperse all heart-fears?—But I'll take the latter,
Life-everlasting, call it if you will—
God's sunshine and deep peace.
Yet I should pray that with the day's toil ended,
My heart remain unshrivelled—tempered so
With life's illimitable sacrifices,
Let what befall me, so it be not night
And pressing darkness, all old things
Retain their new-perfected beatitude.
And though my little presence do not stir
The potent planets from their blinding courses,
I am a part of all i' the world's set creed—
Must make and yet unmake . . .
     (*A knock without*)
         Ah, Father John,
Thy way was none o' the best . . . returned to bide
The storm's insistence—yes, I come—
     (*Opens the door. Enter Brisac*)
         A stranger!
 Brisac: Lass—lass! the snow is deep, my way is far—
The gendarmes seek me. Hide me for the love
Of our Lord Christ this Christmas eve . . .
 Narcisse: For the love
Of our Lord Christ . . . in here—
     (*Hides him*)
        O mother—mother!
     (*A knock without*)
Ah, the gendarmes . . . (*Slightly opens the door*)
     You, Pierre Chabot?
     (*Enter Jules and gendarmes*)
     Messieurs!
 Jules: A beastly storm! Pierre Chabot . . . now i' faith,
I envy him the lass. These Provence maids,
Swart-haired and lily-cheeked—eh girl, what say you?—
     (*Attempts to kiss her*)
 Narcisse: Oh fie, Monsieur—

     (*Repulses him laughingly*)
 Jules: How now! she'll give me none.
Pierre Chabot gets them all. Come—come! I say
Hymettus ne'er knew better sweets. So—so—
     (*Kisses her*)
 Narcisse (aside): It burns my soul!
 Jules (and gendarmes):   Ha! Ha! Ha!
         But now to business.
We seek one Brisac, scaped today from prison,
Traced to the upper country where the larches
Grow rank and thickest. Know you aught?—
 Narcisse: Monsieur!
This night, but scarce a short hour since, there came
A knock upon my door, impatient like,
A thinking it . . . stept soft and oped it space-wise—
Let in a man, Monsieur—but such a man!
His hair hung like the mist one sees o' nights,
Matted and stark, bare-fallen to the breast
All eft and bloody . . . so I screamed, Monsieur,
And he—he fled to Vigny . . .
 Jules: Vigny, men!
Ah there, good night, wench—
 Narcisse: Yes, yes—yes! to Vigny . . .
    (*Exit Jules and gendarmes*)
(*She falls into a chair and buries her face in her hands. Brisac steps from his hiding place.*)
 Brisac: Lass—lass!
 Narcisse (sobbing violently): My first lie, Monsieur, my first lie . . .

Arcady

 Master of Revelers: Green shawes, and wheresoe'er ye go, glad light
Of many shining hills and singing seas,
Speed ye with smitten songs and bright-eyed mirth,
Sunlit with gold and roses garlanded;
And all the wide hills bear the distant din
Unto the silent mesh of field and flowerage,

To re-awake with silver pipe and reed,
Cephissus and his Echo fast asleep.
>   *Chorus:* Yea, over the hills where the green leaves lie,
>   Steeped in the gold of a summer sun;
Where the shadows that flit with the sea's soft sigh
>   Girdle the crests of Calydon;
And the long line surf beats the shingle by,
Ere it slips to the hasp of a white weft spun.
Yea, over the hills where the day and the dusk
>   Creep to an arm of the merging sea;
Where the first faint buds slip their bitter husk
>   To the ache of an ancient melody;
And over the swale a drift of musk
Comes to the breath of things that be.
Speed we and heed we the glimmering dawn,
>   For Love seeks its death at the dearth of a day;
Silenus' head falls to the feet of the Faun,
>   And he laughs with a leer in his drunken way;
Cries out an oath, and the litten lawn
Echoes a lilt to the old beast's bray.
Come let us hence, God and Mænad,
>   Unto far woodland and rivers that run;
Glad with the fill of a love that is glad,
>   Brave with the fervor and fire of the sun.
>   *Cybele:* The great Gods gave us sweet unrestfulness,
Passion-played hearts and pool-deep eyes for love,
Clear carven limbs and wondrous wealth of hair,
Wherefore to speak soft words and blandishment.
>   *Chorus:* So it has been since the morning sea
>   Came, and bespreading the waste, sang love;
So it shall be to eternity,
>   Labor and life for the Gods above.
Labor and life and the love therein—
>   When ye have wept the stain lies clear;
Heart of the heart and the soul within,
>   Naught have ye now to fear.
>   *Pan:* I shall pipe such plaints as float

From Calypso's song-swept throat;
Lyric silver, love and fear,
Tithe and guerdon, smile and tear;
Hope begirt with deep flame flowers,
Love beloved of sanguine bowers;
Every sweet a song may prove,
Honeyed from Hymettus' trove,
Wilder yea, and fair by far,
Than the Sirens' voices are.

 Cybele: I meet thee Pan by the silver rill,
  Where the reefs and the rushes that border the stream
Slip up to the rim of the purple hill,
And melt in the wake of a dream.
Through the sun-flecked paths and the freighted vines,
  Where the wild grape hangs in the breeze soft blown,
And the ivy twines and intertwines,
There we wove thee a wreath for thy throne.
I met thee Pan in the covert hid,
  And thy reed played a tune to the lisp of the rain;
Right blithe danced Nymph and Bassarid,
To the lilt of thy Bacchanal strain.

 Marsyas: Ah, speech and song are as one tender strife!
 Chorus: Soothly they kindle hot blood in our ears,
Bright beacon lights unto dim devious ways,
Or star-shine to an hollow wilderness;
Breme winds they cozen down to mellowness,
Harsh nights as soft refulgence blown afar.

 Marsyas: And none like these our Master-singer trills.
 Chorus: Nay none, for in them doth he sift his soul,
The essence of all things devout and fair—
What wonder then that they be beautiful?

 Pan: By the three high Gods, but ye flatter me.
 Chorus: Lo, the dawn quickeneth in an amber fire,
And Ilion's purple towers trail into mist;
Shadow and shine gold girt with swift desire,
Wake into wells of blissful amethyst.

 Marsyas: Topmost the marsh mist rises into fire;

Let us away lest Zeus aureate
Blind us with his dire splendor.
    Chorus: Let us go.
    Pan: Where away the day dreams,
Flashes into far beams,
Affluent and gold gleams,
    Love for thee and me;
Let us bide the bright side,
Cross the cleaving night tide,
Part the past a might wide,
    Deem it our decree.
But a day we wait here,
Listen, laugh, and mate here,
Not unknowing fate drear,
    Mute the mystery;
Like the laving lillies,
When the night astill is,
Drink the crystal chalice,
    Cross the summer sea.

Scene from "The Duchess Tragedy"

The Duchess, Ghismond, plots with her paramour Ricardo, to slay her just and virtuous husband, the Duke of Venice.

    Ricardo: Your Grace—
    Duchess: O stay, Ricardo.
    Ricardo: Please you, Lady.
    Duchess: What makes thee such a blushful visitant?
The dignity that providence o'errules
Doth dispossess thy favor in our stead.
I shall draw him best thus.   (*aside*)
    Ricardo: The imperfection
That makes us lowly makes timid too,
You are kind, Madam.
    Duchess: Imperfection—ay!
We count a man imperfect when the gods
Distract with virtue violent perfections.

Why who shall feign it when our betters make
Evil commodities of priced dreams?
Ha! I have drawn blood from my nether lip—
And still it bleeds! They say blood staunches blood,
And with a golden flux heals piteous means.
Does thine equivocate its heartlessness?
    Ricardo: You move me, Madam, but whereto l know not.
    Duchess: Yet I do frown—see. So congealed ice,
Sucks from the glitter of the frozen air
A chargeable foison. Must I plead
And dare you be defective. I'm in a fever.
Quench me, Ricardo!
    Ricardo: You pleasure me for certain.
I am undone if I but answer once
Contrary to example. Have pity, Lady.
    Duchess: Art thou ambitious; does thy purpose burn
Similitude to stars, and vaunting breath,
Conceive the dream that binds thee fast to earth?
    Ricardo: I am as others are, most gracious Lady.
    Duchess: We shall affect to make thee different.
Hark ye! my Lord is in our way—
    Ricardo: What then?
    Duchess: Here, kiss me lest I burn! Strange my joy,
That trebles with unmodulated voice,
The sheerest frenzy to its purposes!
When we would rid us vermin from our path,
Poor little atoms in this night of pitch,
Do we use kissing honey? This shaken gem,
Being flaw'd within its heaven's flaming glass,
Will it still serve my needs? Our comfort blows
Extremity to sport. I'll tell thee what,
This must be done most quickly.
    Ricardo: Bless us, that's murder!
I have been taught to think on an hereafter
To grace my soul.
    Duchess: Five-pence will buy us a villain.
Kindle thy courage from the flame within me.

O my conscience, it is nought! Better we have
The confidence that with unvaled balm
Endures its own vexation. Hold me close,
Thus—when the deed cements our twinning souls,
Thou shalt be lord in's place.
    Ricardo: I halt in this,
But my ambition reaches such a height,
It will not sleep.
    Duchess: Why, that's the immortal part
That will not sleep! When this is done and subject
Within the counsel of our better sense,
We shall swear opportunely, call it most good.
And make the image of our coloured past
Contrive a heavenly future. Once strike the need,
The motive then is thine. Ah! let me live.
Dost thou fear fortune blinded?
    Ricardo: So it clamour
Against the gate of prescience and with mettle
Unlock the key contentment.
    Duchess: Think it then.
For by such means the dead forsake their graves.
Fathomless purpose, undishonour'd sleep,
To reign on us accursed who still live.
Oh, that we two had been a linked brand,
Pluckt from the general hollows of vast Hell!
    Ricardo: Nothing more, Madam?
    Duchess: Ay, of deadlier thought,
That holds us breathless where a tangled gulf
O'erleaps this precipice of instant depth.
Thus, and no more. We must bethink ourself
Clearly the marshal of a leiger way
To firm-set purpose—
    Ricardo: Hark!
    Duchess: Some one knocks. Go!
No word of this.   [*Exit* Ricardo.
          O God, make me pure air!
Toss this unprimed ache and passionate heart

Atop some pendant peak whence I may view
Common existences and purportless floods
Whilst mine be bared to thunder. Let me range
To perdurous conception of high fate,
Not madness, on my soul not final madness—
But absolute office. [*Exit*]

A Scene for *King Lear*

"No man, even if he had the mind to do it, would now dare to write like Shakespeare."

—WALTER RALEIGH, Shakespeare.

A forest adjoining the British camp near Dover. Enter an OFFICER *and* FOOL, *prisoner.*

Officer: Hadst thou as many lives as hath thy god Momus, so shouldst thou still hang, hang, hang! Hast thou no fear, Fool? Bethink thee well what it means. There shall be no more jesting at large. Wit shall be toothsome and commissive, yea, we must even take an injunction on downright sadness when her loyal scullion lies dead and bleaching. Where's thy Master, Fool?

Fool: Before thee, knave.

Officer: Ha! that shall we soon know.

Fool: Then wouldst thou steal knowledge from thy betters. An oath! an oath! a very oath! Here's one who dares rob the poor of their only patrimony! I would that I were Justice, blind-folded and with a torch in my right hand!

Officer: How then, worm?

Fool: Thou shouldst be i' the dark no longer, knave. Why, thou mightest even set fire to Justice herself, taking upon thee the burden of honorable office.

Officer: This is the rinsing of a jest. (*Strikes him.*)

Fool: Knave, strike me but once again and thou shalt see—

Officer: What, sirrah Fool? Be quick!—what shall I see?

Fool: A pair o' blows, knave.
Had you more wit and I more sense,
Either of us were evidence.

We that are serfs to that slut Wisdom grow wise by association. I give thee the nuncio thereof, but thou hast that which no one hath ever had heretofore.

Officer: What have I, Fool?

Fool: Thyself, knave. Dost thou deny it, Jerkin?

> O many a tale hath been jest,
> > And much it is over-wise,
>
> But the truth that is ever veriest
> > Was bred by the mother of lies.

No, faith, either thou art mouldy Satanas or the god Mercury with an ivory caduceus. Thou hast a stench, man; by my folly, thou art putrescence itself. It will take more than the riddle of riddling Erebus to solve thy salutant darkness.

Officer: Sirrah Fool, take thy fill o' the sweet sun, pray thy prayers and reckon thy last reckonings, for whither thou goest is there none of this. Thou shalt swing free and high under the branches of this leafy oak, but for the present do we bind thee fast. (*Ties him to a tree.*) What ho! bravado, hast thou content? Thy grievances are now but as naught, be assured!

Fool: Ay di me! Here's weeping in April weather.

(*sings*)

> The fire in the mist
> > And the horned star,
>
> O come, if you list
> > And follow afar.

> In the streaming rain
> > And the still-blown wind,
>
> Ere we grieve again,
> > False hearts will prove kind.

> Down pride, up wit!
> > Our straw, our rags!
>
> Here shall we sit
> > While the mad world wags.

> Thy wither'd corse
> > Must we lay i' the dew,
>
> For blind remorse
> > Hath slain us too.

(*Enter* LEAR *and* CORDELIA, *prisoners, escorted by Captain and soldiers.*)

Officer: His Majesty, as I draw living breath,
And with the lady, Queen of France, Cordelia.

Fool: O nuncle, nuncle, that thy servant should have come to this! I am pinioned hand and foot—I, that once had wings to fly and strength to cleave as any unjessed falcon!

Lear: How! have they snared thee too, my jewel?

Cordelia: Chide not!
Thou know'st that heat brings nothing to our cause!
Rather it may be that our miseries,
Finding a surfeit on their barren height,
Will speedily descend.

Captain (to Officer): What is thy purpose?

Officer: Hanging. I pr'ythee thine.

Captain: Listen— (*He whispers to him.*)

Lear: Not that!
Let the poor fool go free! Thwart me with bonds,
Consume me in a scourge of thousand fires,
The ecstasy of hate and tyranny,
And I'll not whimper at one word or deed,
But only let our aimless pleasures go
That served our happier hours. O! that this venom
Should pierce the crystal hearts of those that loved
And cherish'd most our hope and royalty!

Captain: Quiet, old man! thou canst not help one jot.

Fool: Hast thou no more authority left, nuncle? I fear not death, I, so that it be six feet i' the good mould and my purple swathe of kingliness around me,

Wi' potbellied Joan at my side,
My bonny, bonny, grewsome bride—

but in the wide air with no certain foothold, I do dread it worse than thou dost thy two evil daughters. Nuncle, nuncle, they unfasten me to perform their office! Canst thou not put in thy sole word of intermission? I beg thee, do! do! and do! else I am undone.

Officer: Up with thee, pleasantry! Thou art as light
As zephyr in a hurling thunderstorm,
And e'en as brave!

Lear: O boy, dost thou not see?
We are bound and vised and shackl'd as thyself,
And tho' my tongue should bid the sea to ebb,
And spatter heaven with a new list of stars,
The evidence were fruitless. (*To Cordelia.*) Turn thy head,
Sweet soul, there's that to come thou must not see;
Thou'st had thy share o' minister'd bitterness,
And what's to follow is not for thy kind;
Thou must be safely fended from all grief,
Aye, safely fended!

Captain (to Officer): Pray you then, be quick!
There's much yet to be done; thou know'st the end.

Lear: Cheerly, my heart! We two shall yet i' the sun
Sit by the garden wall and side by side,
Tell witless tales together.

Officer: So—so—so!

Fool: O Lear! there's something within me that would fain cry out but will not! Thou wert not thus in the days of old when I stood thee in stead of better things. Art thou deaf, nuncle? Hast thou made incision of the black poppy? Had it but never been so!

    The yellow, yellow leaf,
        For love and I must sever,
    With up joy and down grief
        And bitter-sweet forever!

There shall be henceforth no more laughter—none, none, none! Pray for me, nuncle, lest I die unshriven! (*Dies.*)

Captain: Nobly i' faith!

Officer: Now must thou make good speed.
The old king hath suspicions, but the lady
Recks not her froward fate nor what's to follow.
Be politic and hasty. What ensues
Depends on our progression, and if snipt,
To betterment of service. I have long'd
For such advancement these last twenty years,
And buoyed myself to preference and hope,
Only to grasp at bright and empty gold,
Mere pittance for the valour of my chance.

I'll give thee such assistance as thou need'st,
But deem it best thou tak'st the lady first—
Quickly!
  Captain (to Cordelia): The light that from this welkin pours
Dazzles the eyes. I pray you let me be
Minister to your comfort. (*Blindfolds her.*)
  Lear: O no! no!
Thou shalt as soon tear from the giant girth
Of this wild oak that haunts the quiet sky
A branch that cleaves there moaning, as from me
This new-found joy, this treasure! Let us be!
We, that have but discover'd a strange world,
Would find a little happiness therein.
Let us depart, and if thou dost, why then,
Thy sleep shall be as sweet as that which hangs
Droop-lidded from the dewy cherubim!
Come! come! Make haste.
  Cordelia: Whither, O good my Lord?
My sight is mask'd and darken'd.
  Lear: Where thou wilt,
So that it be away, away from men,
And I to follow always at thy side,
Grieve in thy grief and joy upon thy joy,
And be slave forever and forever!
  Officer: Unless we hasten in our desperate work,
Reprieve may come, or change of mind perchance,
And all our golden hopes be flown or vaded.
  (*To a Soldier*)
Hold the old dotard graybeard!
  Lear: Loose me, dog!
Eyes, ears, and all, sense mischief!
  Cordelia: O my Lord!
Here's evil done to me!
  Lear: O this is monstrous!
Injustice on injustice even till heaven
Turn into ruth her bitter mockery,
And cry aghast! This my flesh, my blood,

Sweetened unto me by adversity,
And vested in these flaw'd and bleeding years!
Let be, I say, let be!
    Soldier: He tops my strength.
Help, comrades, help!
    Lear: Down! down! and haddest thou
Forges of iron, nets of puissant steel,
And overhead a bloody catapult,
Thou shouldst not hold me thus against my will!
Cordelia!   (*Escapes.*)
    They that would keep me from thee now,
Must reckon with a stronger thing than hate!
    Cordelia: Patience, above all else—   (*Dies.*)
    Lear: See! see! brave heart!
Thou fear'st to ope thine eyes lest that thou view
Miscreant lips and furtive threat'ning brows.
'Tis I that take thee, I that press thee close,
Not soon to leave thee, no!
    Captain: She's dead, my Lord!
    Lear: And all my hope is dead! Thy poniard, villain!
    (*Stabs him.*)
    Captain: Eternal darkness take me—   (*Dies.*)
    Lear: Too late! too late!
And I shall rest now never— O—
    (*Exit bearing Cordelia.*)
    Soldier: His anguish
Tears at my heart.
    Officer: I have heard such a cry,
Given at night by the conspiring winds,
An hour ere moonrise. Come, we'll follow close,
But what will happen, no man of us knows.
    (*Exeunt.*)

A Scene for *Macbeth*

The Scene
(Act V)

Dunsinane. A Room in the Castle. Enter a DOCTOR OF PHYSIC *and a* WAITING-GENTLEWOMAN.

Doctor: How does the queen?

Gentlewoman: Ill indeed. Her frenzy will not leave her in peace, but she wanders from hall to hall and from chamber to chamber. Yea, betimes in a fever, she cries out as one suddenly mad.

Doctor: Seems not a visit from the king to affect her?

Gentlewoman: Most strangely so, for thereafter she falls a-brooding to herself and will sit for hours and smile subtly as one with a secret. Anon, her malady transpiring again, she becomes malign and shapens herself a monstrous dagger in the air or imprecates an invisible influence. I am greatly concerned, doctor, for she grows weaker.

Doctor: And aptly. Does she partake of nourishment?

Gentlewoman: None, or nearly none; for when her hand would bear a morsel from the plate to her lips, she becomes suddenly transfixed and with eyes glassed and woefully staring, suspends her intention. I have observed this day by day and with the same effect. It is truly pitiful.

Doctor: Aye, aye! The soul starves the body, yet life will have an end even under sufferance.

Gentlewoman: What betokens the stir without the castle? The queen seems utterly oblivious to the clamour.

Doctor: The king marches against Malcolm this very night. There are those what hold him impregnable as fate, and yet there are others that sternly construe different.

Gentlewoman: Heaven help us all!

Doctor: Even so. Look you—she comes.

Enter LADY MACBETH *leaning on the arms of two* ATTENDANTS. LADIES *following.*

Gentlewoman: Be seated, gracious madam.

Lady Macbeth: Lights! more lights—
And yet more lights! Conspiracy's afoot
That keeps the world in darkness!

Gentlewoman: Lights for the queen!
What ho—a brace of lights!
Doctor: How does your highness?
The night without is bleak and piercing cold,
But here is warmth and comfort.
Lady Macbeth: Where's my lord,
That I am mewed and prison'd as a sprite,
Midway 'twixt heaven and chaos?
Doctor: Madam, the king
Makes haste this night to Birnam, where at dawn
He holds forth battle 'gainst the risen foe,
Who now advances by twenty stalwart leagues.
Heaven speed the right!
Lady Macbeth: O! I am sick—sick—sick!
Think you that brain is mad, which in its deep,
Forever sees the wings of horror brood,
And lists her speechless fury? I have fears,
Monstrous as night, more terrible than death,
Unpitying as hate, within whose bounds
I am held a most unwilling prisoner!
Doctor: Madam, I have a vial in my chest,
Compact of drowzy flowers and orient herbs,
Sweet to the taste and perfum'd to the smell,
That takes, as 'twere, the senses in its foil,
And by one draught, with poppied certitude,
Gives rest to crying nerves, surcease from thought,
And patient, easeful dreams.
Lady Macbeth: No sleep! no sleep!
If I should syllable that which is seal'd,
And in my slavish senses utter out,
What else were secret as the deep, deep sea—
No more—I pray you, cease!
Doctor: (*Aside*) Poor, perilous soul!
That tosses on what oceans of despair,
Unsighted, save by night and ravenous winds,
To the sea's waste and turmoil.

Enter SEYTON.
    Gentlewoman: Seyton, madam.
    Seyton: I bear a message from our noble king.
He bids me swear his love and fealty,
And by that wifely virtue and true faith,
Which you have ever dowered in the past,
Begs, that until this final essay fall,
You grant him patience. Even now, his host,
With banners flying, bright and unsheath'd swords,
Hearts uppermost and as one man to men,
Gather in strength their march on Birnam wood,
To make their common cause a victory.
    Lady Macbeth: Where is the lady of the Thane of Fife?
What did you to her nurslings?
    Seyton: On my soul,
And as I hope for bliss in paradise,
Partaking of that golden beatitude,
And purg'd of my most mortal dross and sin,
I had no bearing on 't!
    Lady Macbeth: Here's where it hurts!
O little baby hands that pluck me close,
Poor wandering atoms in this night of pitch—
Fordone, fordone, fordone!
                                                          (*She weeps.*)

    Doctor: Most gentle sir,
Our gracious queen is much distraught today.
I pray you speed unto the noble king,
Who, with his burden's weight of war and joust,
Recks not the import of her drooping health,
And bring him hither.
    Seyton: Certainly.
    Gentlewoman: O see!
    Doctor: Ladies, the queen—she faints!
    Lady Macbeth: My lord Macbeth—
    Gentlewoman: She, in her anguish, calls the king. O madam.
What is it you desire?

Lady Macbeth: Pardon, pardon—
Pity and sleep!

(*Dies.*)

Gentlewoman: Alas! the queen is dead.
O woe within the walls of Dunsinane!
   Doctor: Cease—wring no hands—let be all outward grief,
All vain remand for nature's only fee,
Her heart hath on this instant still'd its beat.
Else I would say, that in the redd'ning storm,
A fledgling bird found hid its nest at eve,
And bode content from faring. Gently then,
I that am different shall go grieve with men.

(*Exeunt.*)

The Sphinx: A Conversation

To
W. PAUL COOK
and to the memory of
HOWARD P. LOVECRAFT

Il ne faut pas dire cela. C'est une idée très dangereuse. C'est une idée qui vient des écoles d'Alexandrie où on enseigne la philosophie grecque. Et les Grecs sont des gentils. Ils ne sont pas même circoncis.— OSCAR WILDE.

SCENE:—The edge of a desert. THE SPHINX awakens and blows her conch of ivory. MEMNON answers with a tumultuous, golden cry from his enchanted slumber. The CHIMAERA, circling aloft, shakes her wings of lapis. In the desert the blue-eyed BASILISK counts her endless tasks on a chain of flashing emeralds. The three SATRAPS who lie naked before the SPHINX, prostrate themselves at her feet. They are HERMES the Greek, EPHRAIM the Hebrew, and HATHOR the Egyptian.
   The Three: What is thy desire, O Sphinx? Thou knowest we are thine, body and soul, forever!
   The Sphinx (with a shiver of her bronze wings): I desire, but what I desire I know not. In Ethiopia mine eyes were once freighted with a terrible dream. I slept. When I re-opened them there lay on my breasts a

strange, flower-faced youth who whispered maleficent things to me and clung to my lips, beseeching me to tell him my secret. But I dared not—ah, I dared not!

The Three: Wherefore not, O Sphinx? Why didst thou not disclose thy secret?

The Sphinx (she moans and her eyes become iridescent): In Carchedonia the wasted young King came to me with his treasure of sapphires, chrysolites, amethysts, opals, beryls, terebinths, topazes, and male rubies. Likewise with him came the incestuous Suffete of Epirus. And when they saw me they hated one another so that their venom knew no bounds. But I had prefigured that whatsoever might transpire these two evil souls were mine, and in the morning I found them dead at my feet.

The Three: Wonderful, that this should happen, O Sphinx.

The Sphinx: At Colchis the snowy elders came to me by moonlight with their staves of satyrion. And they wept bitterly, crying, Woe be upon us! Our young men and our youths have forsaken their women and lie in effeminacy together. Some have dyed their hair with saffron; some have painted their lips with vermilion and their eyes with antimony. They drink the infamous Gnidian wine and on their brows are bound chaplets of vine-leaves and violets. When we spoke to them they arose from their porphyry benches with flagons of silver and jeered at our anger. When we departed they postured and mocked at our wrinkled eld. And I said, Bring your young men and your youths hither. So they came to me crowned with red roses, their bodies veiled only with thinnest veils of hyacinth. Yet even as they gazed at me they became men with the desires of men and casting their diaphanous coverings before them, abode with me all that marvellous night. In the yellow dawn they went their way.

The Three: We too, O mighty Sphinx, have ministered devoutly to Love in our several ways. Yet we found it all too brief and bitter saving our unquenchable passion for thee.

The Sphinx: Tell me thereof, since I profit by all men's tales. Through the papyrus-leaves I see the world but I am almost forgotten and men already say that I grow old. Yet listen! In my heart there is still the burden of wild joys and the antique pageantry of an elder existence. I have been beloved of the black Antinous. Together we drank the violet wine of the gods—together we swore everlasting fealty. Serapion has fondled me with his scarlet python, yet was I fearless of its venom. I seduced Iolaus before ever the comely nymphs from his Titan-lover, Hercules!

The First (in a woman's voice): I am Hermes a Greek. Of mine early youth I know little save that my father, a beautiful Apollonian, and my mother, a loathly Scythian, perished in their unholy love for one another. When I outgrew my boyhood I was taken by the priests of Heliotis who bore amongst them the flame of innermost Beauty. Ah, what happiness was ours! But after a time there came to us a stranger, a Cappadocian, clad in a purple vestment with hair the color of heliochrysus. And after he had dwelt among us for a space he ascended the vast pylon to Antares and in a voice of thunder bade us instantly desist lest our eternal souls perish even as our mortal bodies. His master was Heraclitus, a wise man of the Ephesians. For he spoke to us of the perilous love of men for women, of their blossomy breasts, and of the madness that possesses all mankind in the fulfillment of this monstrous, unknown love.

The Sphinx: Monstrous? Yet thou dost love me!

The First: O Sphinx, my brethren were distraught and on that very night, we separated forever. And I took with me Herodian, a fair Lacedæmonian youth, wandering in such wise until we came to Corinth.

The Sphinx (poisonously): Ah . . . my sister, the Lamia, lives in Corinth with her paramour Lycius! She lives in a house of Numidian ivory with portals of black sardonyx and a pavement of constellated gold. Her pools are pure chalcedony and her labyrinth is lighted by a single chrysoberyl. Her chariot is drawn by two Nysæan tigers with eyes like Attic emeralds. Each night veiled, white eidolons enter her chamber with sweet voices, sinful gestures and subtle perfumes. These are the beings that concert with my sister to do evil. Our father she turned into a winged phantom that haunts Cenchreas, our mother she stifled with a monstrous word that is known only to the malignant divinities of the Massagetæ, and me—O horror! horror!—(*She weeps violently*) But let her beware! for happiness is alone a gift of the gods. It is for this reason that I withhold the consummation of my terrible revenge. It is for this alone that I refrain and meditate. . . .

The First: In Corinth, the youth Herodian dissembled with me and became enamoured of the courtezan, Rhodope. As we entered the carved Gate of Satyrs at eve, a woman came unto us drawn in a litter who cried, Is it thus, Lord of my Desire, that thou enterest the white city of Corinth? I am she, beloved of Charaxos in Naukratis—Rhodope. As others serve gold until their hidden desires turn wan and ashen, even so have I served and dedicated myself to the delicate altar of Love. Hast thou wandered over many lands in search of pleasure? Art thou minded to forget the turmoil of this mad life? Behold, my Lord, the lotus-flower that trembles on my silver breasts! Now when the Youth heard her speech he became sick with desire and against my heed entered her litter. But I beheld him no more for I sailed overseas in a pirate-galley along the sea-coast of Phœnicia to the city of Tyre.

The Sphinx (dreamily): I, also, have been to Tyre. At dawn the Tyrian girls pass through the marble streets with their amphoræ of red wine, the fishermen follow, bearing on their shoulders columnar vases of gem-coloured tunny, and the merchants ply their wares by sweet cries from hollow lotus-pipes. At wharves, the dusk-eyed mariners embark with strange songs in their ships of gopher, yet their hearts are eternally beholden to the many gods that are luminously gilded on the tall mast-heads. Above the city are the hanging gardens and in their cavernous haunts are quiet groves that hold forever the Spring's lost nightingales. It is here that Dagon, Lord of the Assyrians, wooed me. He wooed me by flattery and false caresses, even as Dionysus, the golden-haired wine-god of Phrygia, and I bore with him patiently even as I did with the Greek in all my mighty hate. But after a thousand years I spoke to him subtly and with a honeyed tongue. What seekest thou, Lord of Assyria? I am made faint by thy continual embraces, yet have I nothing that is thine. And he made answer, fawning upon me, Beautiful one, I crave thy virginity.... (*She utters a falsetto scream*) He desired my virginity....

The First: O wretch! Thou shouldst have slain him utterly. He deserved annihilation!

The Sphinx (indignantly): But he did not possess me; I remain inviolate; I shall always be a maid.

The First: As I knelt before the shrine to Herè in the Temple of Apollo, a youth drew near me in violet raiment with a silver pomegranate in his hand saying, This signifies that thou art henceforth favoured of fortune. Arise, our king bids thee come to him. So I arose astonished and followed, but in the market-place the blonde Heteirai gathered before us and plucked at the hem of my stained garment saying, Hire us for one night's pleasure, sweet voluptuate. But for one night's pleasure hire us and let the price be thine own. Thou shalt find between our rosy breasts a haven for all the world's bitterness and if thou be so disposed to take us unto thee we shall serve as an unflickering torch or a sibilant flame. Who knows—ah, who knows? For we, who have loved overmuch would fain at last find peace in the crystal of our world-wearied and passionate hearts. O! take us unto thee—take us unto thee! And I cried at last in sudden anger, Hence! I will have none of you! I hate you! I despise you! O most unnatural beings!

The Sphinx (with sophisticated laughter): How he loathes womankind! Can it be? . . .

The Second (whispering into her ear): The Greeks are a race of effeminates. Bacchus was a monster, Apollo a beautiful hermaphrodite, and Ganymede a curled servant of the lust of great Zeus. It is all one with their kind. They . . .

The Sphinx (she checks her immoderate mirth): Be quiet! He may overhear thee and take offense. Let him deliver the rest of his tale. Proceed, O Greek, with the relation of thy wanderings.

The First: As we entered the palace of ivory and cornaline the king himself descended from his throne in a garment of Laconian purple figured with vipers of gold. And his catamites and lascivious youths ran toward me and would have taken me evilly but their master cried, Hold, slaves!—this is my guest! Then we knew one another for it was none else than our wanderer, the yellow-haired Cappadocian, who had estranged us of old among the priesthood of Heliotis. And in great dread I bowed low and would have swooned in my amazement but he embraced me and said kindly, Have no fear but abide with me for I have come into my kingdom. Thou shalt show me the flame of innermost Beauty that perished with thy brethren of Heliotis. These which thou seeëst know only the love that is gross and vile and earthly, but I am minded to become supernally wise in thy great wisdom of love. Let me partake of thy knowledge.

The Sphinx: Many men have sought Beauty. Euryanax, the lovely son of Iacchus, set sail from Zacinthus in a bronze galley with his comrades, one blue dawn. Ah, whither goest thou faring? cried the bearded Ionians. Abide with us, O Youth, and we shall make thee king of all this ancient realm. Yet he heeded them not and their cries were futile and unavailing. And after many days they came with their torches at dusk to a moon-white isle in the Asian sea of Symë, whereon my beautiful, pallid mother abode in a palace of green alabaster with her lordly minions of evil. He sought Beauty.... (*She laughs softly*) He sought Beauty.... (*Her mirth becomes louder*) He sought Beauty.... (*She screams*) He found ashen corruption, hideous putrefaction, charnel Death!

The First: I was the last of my kin. I should have taught him my secret, O Sphinx, but there came and beleaguered our city the Hebrew, this Ephraim, with his circumcised legions and their great, thewed women. They did that which is unutterable ... they did ...

The Sphinx: Faugh ... faugh ... an abomination! Thou tellest the truth?

The Second: He lies, O Sphinx!

The First: I swear it. They slew the Cappadocian and flung him body and raiment to the jackals. I alone fled into the desert.

The Second: Let *me* tell my tale. I have a tale which the kings of Edom sat in their scarlet chambers to hear. They sat before blue crystals in which they foresaw the beginning and end of the world. Their wives were the daughters of Lilith, who played marvellous music on silver dulcimers. But they were serpents in the guise of red-lipped women and when I had ceased, they moaned and shivered and beating their shadowy wings, crept away. The kings of Edom alone remained to sing my praise and murmur their holy enchantments. Let me tell the tale I told them, O Sphinx!

The First (with a shriek): If he says aught of me in despite, I shall slay him!

The Sphinx: Peace, children of Love!

The First: O Sphinx, this man did me a great wrong!

The Sphinx (with grave somnolence): In my youth I came to the land of Larymna near the emerald city of Thronium. And a leper, sinuous and evil, fawned before me by the wayside, saying, O fair Monster, I was once a king of this very city of Thronium. Here I am now, the gust of every wind and immortally in exile. Let me follow thee and enter, for I crave my one vengeance on this folk! Then my breasts hardened with lust and I answered, Dost thou promise me payment even this very night? ...

The First (with little screams of joy): He promised thee ... he promised thee ... say that he promised thee, O Sphinx?

The Sphinx (shaking her head): He was a magian of the elder world. With lofty, lunar wings he took the siderite stair to the throne of Courtesans; then, over all the mute and sleeping city he cast a spell. The inhabitants turned in their slumber and cursed the ancient, secret gods. Ah, but his vengeance was imperious and sweet! He bade them love one another. Their love turned to despair ... their despair to fury ... then ...

The Second: What happened, O Sphinx?

The Sphinx (tragically): They slew!

The Second (with a gesture of deprecation): Mine is no tale of revenge. I am Ephraim a Hebrew. As I herded my father's sheep in the vale of Shinar there came a caravan of fifty men on camels and Medic horses by moonlight. And the chief whose name was Javan, a Midianite, brought me to his tent with many courtesies saying, O youth, we go to Erech and Accad in Calneh and thence to Jerusalem. Lo! our number has been decimated by an attack of the Chemmitæ who drew their swords and slew three-score of our horsemen in a lonely mountain-pass of Haran. Three-score, O youth—but we tarried not for vengeance, nor did we abide even though our hearts burned as torches within us. We are merchants to the king's own self—to Ahab, who sits on a violet throne with his spouse Jezebel in their chryselephantine palace in Jerusalem. We bear for him cassia, styrax and nard, frankincense, ledanum and cinnamon. We come newly from the Greek city of Sinope whither we went in quest of pearls, but alas! the robber hordes had despoiled the city and slaughtered all save the elders who starve in their houses of heliotropium. From Jerusalem we go to Tyre, thence to Egypt. ...

The Sphinx (whispering to herself): These Hebrews are a strange and avaricious folk but their love is powerful, mysterious, consuming. I have never been beloved by any save this one. He swears madly that he will forsake even his vast and loathsome God, whom no one has ever seen ... whom they dare not mention aloud ... who teaches infinite procreation without lust ... (*She draws her breath sharply*) ... for love of me!

The Second: So I left my master's sheep alone at night in the vale of Shinar and followed them dreaming to Jerusalem. What might have befallen me had my heart been content with shepherding, I knew not. As we entered the city of God, the boys and flute-players, mimicking Bacchus of the Greeks, came from the king's palace led by golden leopards. Priests of the temple of Solomon, painted and mutilated, descended from their blue chariots beating cymbals of pale bronze. The male dancers with wild cries of acclamation, scattered leaves of laurel and ivy with roses, through all the streets of the great city. This was their welcome to us and my heart sang as with a thousand harps. But our chief, Javan, admonished me gravely saying, Guard thine eye, O youth, for these are enticements of evil. We go presently to seek an audience with the king, who mayhap will reward us well for our perilous venture.

The Sphinx: This reminds me of my entry into the pagan city of Tritæ, a town in Phocis. The priests of Cybele ascended their tower of chrysolite when they beheld my approach with an assembly of lovers, eunuchs and effeminates. And their youngest, Diomede a Megalopolitan, held up his gemmed hand with a shrill cry, Enter, O Sphinx—but enter at thy peril! We know thee well, aye—and they that know thee not have heard of thee. Thy loves are adulteries, thine orisons hate and venom, thy passion, death. Thou, too, shalt die ere dawn; such is our decree. We can snare thee with a single ray of moonlight. We can suffocate thee with delirious perfumes, stupefy thee with the music of human lyres, madden thee with aphrodisiacal wines whose vintage is frenzy and whose aftermath is death. We have citadels, palaces, porticoes, temples and obelisks, wrought of cobalt marbles and lighted with asiatic jewels, that reach heaven and vanish into annihilation. Gaze but at them, touch them, desire them—nay, worship them—and thou perishest forever! We have waited for thee long ... how long we dare not say ... thou comest by reason of our consummate magic.... Welcome, O Sphinx! I laughed at them in scorn and entered with my host. But no sooner were we in the city than their sorceries began. My eunuchs became abominable creatures with gigantic phalluses of black ivory; pitifully, they besought me to slay them. My effeminates multiplied into panting serpents that sang and sorrowed and wailed—into scorpions with cinctures of soft and poisonous flowers, weeping and lamenting as they crawled from my sight. My lovers grew luminous and disappeared imploringly into light and resonance. I alone ...

The First (eagerly): Thou alone, O Sphinx! Thou alone ...

The Sphinx: I cried, in a voice of thunder and fury, the one word with which my archaic mother, the Unknown, made me immortal ten-thousand years ago by the abysmal Nile! But the city, and the people in the city, have been forgotten ever since. The fools and the wise men are dust in the desert. I remain.

The First (with beguiling subtlety): What word made thee immortal, O Sphinx?

The Sphinx (she speaks quickly but cautiously): I have forgotten it. This also happened long ago in my youth. Besides . . . I have always been mistrustful of those that I love. (*In an undertone*) This beautiful, treacherous Greek will betray me. . . . I must encompass his ruin.

The Second: Before my lodging a strange man caught my robe and embraced me, whispering into mine ear, O Youth, this folk are idolaters of their women. They worship an idol on their altar which they call Ascheria, but I beheld the same figure named Aphrodite in the land of the Lydian Greeks. It has eyes of sapphire, lips of vermilion, breasts of jasper, wings of onyx, limbs of basalt and extremities of clay. Thrice a year at the new moon, their priests, veiled in silken vestments, with basins, ewers, chalices and crotals of light gold, prostrate themselves before it, beseeching the secret of Beauty. But the mouth of their mockery god is everlastingly sealed. I have that secret, O Youth! There is no living soul in the city of Jerusalem who has it but me. I found it written on an ivory scroll with letters of stibium in the archives of the wanton prefect at Alexandria. . . .

The First (with a cry of rage): He means me . . . now, I know that he means me! Heed him not, O Sphinx! By my love I swear that my brethren were the priests of Heliotis. I have never been to Jerusalem. This man is a perjurer . . . no Hebrew, but a Samaritan . . . and the Samaritans always lie. The Judæans crucify them on vertiginous pillars in their hills and before their temples. . . . O Sphinx! give me justice and reparation, else I shall go mad!

The Sphinx (unconcernedly): If he utters a falsehood, wherefore shouldst thou be troubled? If he speaks the truth, thou canst hate! (*Austerely to the Second*) Why did he accost thee?

The Second (with his eyes on the First): I shudder to tell thee. He was a Greek. I followed him into a grove before a shrine to the beautiful god Tammuz, wrought of ophite and ebony, with nipples and genitals of gold. From a phial of crystal, he scattered an offering of green aromatics and spoke to me in a voice like ineffable music. He was enamoured of me. I repulsed him and called aloud to my one, omnipotent God. He became violent. He cried out a strange name—one Aristippus of Cyrene. O Sphinx . . . he sought to seduce me!

The First (terrified): Not I ... nay, O Sphinx, not I! It was my young brother who is a sandalled neophyte to the epicene priests of Byblis. Their simars are of dyed silk, painted indigo-blue with swallows and pyramids; their girdles are writhing, yellow serpents, which they loosen only to those that they passionately love. But I remained in Tyre with the Cappadocian, whither this lying Hebrew followed.... (*Turns accusingly to the Second*) Didst thou not come to Tyre? Didst thou not slay the Cappadocian? He dares not deny his guilt! O Sphinx ... how could he forswear what I affirm? ... his hands are immortally reddened with blood! Ah ... only to remember!

The Sphinx (decisively to herself): It is even as I had suspected ... the Greek must perish! Now, am I resolved, lest his colossal cunning also suffer me evil. But the Israelite ...

The Second (uninterrupted): He cursed me as I fled. Together with my companions and our chief Javan, I entered the palace of the king. And Ahab sat beneath a dais of silver on a milk-white peristyle, paven with agate, and sculptured with glittering friezes of satyrs, fauns, griffins, harpies, lemures, apes and peacocks in Assyrian gold. His beard was powdered with lilac, his face shone with perfumed benzoin, his lips were coloured with scarlet pigment, he smiled perpetually and nodded his head elusively, as though in continual dread....

The Sphinx (confidingly): It is the fashion of kings to live in secret fear. Some tremble in avarice and covetousness over their treasure, some in hatred of their mercenaries, still others for retribution of their terrible injustices. But the dread of Ion, an emperor of Heliopolis, surpassed all of these. He feared Death! And he summoned his wise men and sages, the hierarchs and patriarchs of the city to his side saying, Lo! that which I dread is none other than the common enemy to mankind. Make me a god! Make me immortal lest I perish before my time! I would live forever! ... And they murmured one to another, He would live forever! He would live until Time itself empties into Eternity! He would become a god ... but we dare not even comprehend his desires! Alas! how can an emperor of the Sun take equal stature among the radiant gods? It is rumored that Apollo is wondrously malignant ... did he not flay Marsyas? ... did he not vanquish Hyperion? And one cried above the rest, I know! There is a monster, half an immortal herself, who alone can vouchsafe us wisdom. Call the Sphinx.... So they sent their obedient runners, smeared with oil and honey, east and west, north and south, until they found me at last in the court of the mad king of the Lestrygonians....

The First: What was his madness, O Sphinx?

The Sphinx: Love had crazed him! He became an enchanter! He read the obscene books of Elephantis, he sought the nomad lore of Hemitheon the Sybarite, he sang the burning hymns of Philænis ... to know any of these is to become violently contaminated with their insidious madness. The walls of his chamber were built of multi-coloured metals depicting the Bacchanalia of Scylas, the inspired son of Ariapithes. Even as in life, the green leaves murmured on their branches in the marble wind, and the Mænads, with hair unbound and filleted, shouted, Evoë! Evoë! He summoned the shades of Helen of Troy, Thomyris the Scythian, Pasithea the Cypriote ... halcyon-breasted, immortal-souled and unconsumed, they came to him with hearts of ice and prophetic lips from their remote habitation in Hades. But I knew that his end was near! The messengers of Ion found me and as they drew close cried feverishly, O Sphinx! we beseech thee to return with us to Heliopolis! Save that thy mighty wisdom grant him intercession, our royal master must perish as pitifully as ourselves. He craves to be a god! Our votaries have consulted the sun, but in vain. Seventy, beautiful, virgin youths appeared before the lidded oracle of Mars on the silver hypostyle of Papremis, but their prayers remained unanswered. They were torn to pieces by the fury of the populace....

The First (he repeats with compassion): Seventy, beautiful, virgin youths torn to pieces!

The Sphinx: And I said to them sternly, What profit have I from your master, the Emperor of the Sun? If I make him a god he will spurn me. Alexander of Macedon did so in Ecbatana, and from that moment his ungratefulness turned my heart to stone. Ere the strange madness of this king comes to an end, I shall have learned that which Sotades the Mantinæan preached on a summer's day to his disciples in the wilderness near Sycion. The secret perished with them, yet this king still holds it. Last evening, he spoke lasciviously to the moon. His eyes dilated, his brow glistened, his dalmatic grew white with fulgurance. From the abysses of heaven came music and laughter, then a voice that cried long in the silence. He names it Nemesis! It is his purpose tonight to invoke each of the multitude of stars and call them separately by name. He calls to them in their æons of loneliness, and star by star they respond. But there is one that will not answer. It is the orb Arcturus, who follows his own way blindly and wilfully alone in the vast interstellar night. To hear what this mad king will say to him is why I wait.... I shall continue to wait, for he *must* answer!

The Third (he makes a mystic sign): What a strange tale! She tells of a mad king who held converse with other worlds! Mother of Ptah! I fear.

The First (valiantly): I have no dread, why then, shouldst thou? The heavens are blind, dumb and uncharted ... the god that made them is banished or dead!

The Sphinx: They fondled my sphered breasts ... they knelt at my feet of brass. I hearkened to them. O beautiful beast! O magnificent Sphinx! they implored, Sleep shall be perpetually forsworn from our wearied eyelids, oblivion from our poppied senses, if we return without thee. Hear us, O Sphinx! What follows, we swear is the truth. In his wanderings over the blossomy land of Phæacia, our king came with his curved barque to the fabulous treasure-house of Thone the Egyptian. It rose in a peristyle of iris, on a hill of olives, within sight of the tranquil, azure sea. At his side there fared with him his companion, a noble Scherian, the youth Rhexenor. When they unbarred the door they beheld by their torches, a sight that not the gods have ever seen ... to the lintel of bronze, to the roof of cedar ... fire, moonlight, and dew, that flashed, smouldered and faded.... O Sphinx! it was filled with a treasure of amethysts, rubies, jacinths, diamonds, and emeralds!

The First (to the Third): They lied to her. Think you, the gods would have tolerated a theft? They would have stricken them blind or dead.

The Sphinx: With guile, they continued: The Phæacians were eaters of the lotus. At dusk they chapleted themselves with garlands of that flower, and reclining dreamily before their slim cressets, gazed with lustrous eyes at the Bithynian mariners of our king. Unperceived, with his companion the Scherian, he bore the jewels away ... they extinguished their torches ... the mariners sat at their oars. As the Phæacians sang wantonly of love to the music of their myriad lyres, they rowed slowly afar in the night. That treasure they conveyed to our city. There it abides, O Sphinx! It is thine if thou but come with us! And I answered relenting, Have patience, this once! Take yourselves wine and slaves with hyacinth bodies, drink deep of Lethe and love till dawn. This mad king will speak and I am resolved to depart with you. You promise me this treasure? ... They swore the oaths of their fathers and I believed them profoundly.... I believed them.... (*She appears to sleep*)

The Third (to the First): I burn, yet I am cold. I would that I had my raiment. Her eyes are ominous and cruel. A terrible misfortune awaits me, I fear!

The First: Soft! it may be that she will disclose the mad king's secret. I also am troubled. Her intentions are to slay me. When it darkens we shall go hence together ... hearest thou? Thy beauty is like that of my god Apollo who wanders homelessly in exile. He was first seen in Caria, then by the purple sea at Inarime, again as a shepherd in Argolis. Some knew him by the light in his hair, others by his great and solitary grief. When they discovered his identity, he departed. Ah ... perchance thou art even he, and I, thy priest, shall take thee in sanctuary and worship thee again as of old. But beware of the Hebrew ... he swore vengeance on me, once at Jerusalem, afterward in Tyre. Yet I carry a charm, an image of the three-fold gods, that I procured from a vendor, a prophet in Canopus ... behold! (*He shows him the figures*)

The Third (he gives a cry of recognition): It is they. These are the gods that I served as an acolyte at Meroë! O happiness!

The First: Even so.... (*He places a sibilant finger to his lips*) She begins again....

The Sphinx: At nightfall he entered the adytum with his attendants. The blue sarcophagi of gods and kings stood by in colossal repose. Their mummies were swathed in linen and their eyes were rimmed with gold. I followed him step by step and crouched in silence at his side. He called the stars beginning with Alioth, the youth of Heaven, and star by star they pealed their answer to him in the enchanted night. Some wept and cursed, others sang hymns and pæans to peace and annihilation. Altogether they wailed, As it is with us even so shall it be with you. There is naught in space but darkness and desolation and the cry of the everlasting, immemorial dead. Lord, if thou hast power, slay us! And the mad king answered, I dare not! Your creator still lives! And they spoke in unison, Thou canst, O Lord! He that wrought us is long since departed. Why dost thou withhold thy mercy? Have we not followed thy behest in all things? Then he spake with a shrill cry, There is a traitor amongst you, one who has despited me in all things and remains silent!

Arcturus! Arcturus! They moaned, Speak to him, O Brother, for he has promised us oblivion. Hast thou not also desired peace and nonentity? Behold, it is ours and thine if thou but pay thy reckoning to him. O Brother, speak! Arcturus! Arcturus!

The First: At last, we shall learn the secret!

The Second: Why do I fear?

The Sphinx: A Hand came forth from heaven and plucked him! A Voice cried, I am still a greater one than thou! He vanished before me!

The First (with a gesture of despair): I shall never know the secret of Sotades the Mantinæan!

The Third: It is better not to know any secret! Too much wisdom beats darkly into the soul.

The Sphinx: At dawn, we departed for Heliopolis. . . .

The First: Didst thou give the king his immortality, O Sphinx?

The Sphinx (shaking her head): In Anthemus they worshipped me for a god. On their streets of cinnebar they bound me with cyclamen and violets, with hyacinths and wild-flowers, crying and singing at the top of their voices, Abide with us! Abide with us, O Sphinx! A thousand years ago our reverent soothsayers prophesied thy coming. In the meantime there appeared impostors . . . the Theban Sphinx with wings of mercury and eyes of doom . . . Arcesilaus of Cypris in the guise of a beautiful adolescent . . . the Lamia!

The First (eagerly): Thy sister, O Sphinx!

The Sphinx (suddenly darting at him with her talons): Thou spy and emissary! They stoned her from the gates of the city. Had I been there, I should have counselled her death! Hast thou, then, followed me into the desert for this? . . . *(Aside)* He serves my sister, the Lamia!

The First: O Sphinx, I bleed!

The Sphinx (resuming her monotone): In Cleone the inhabitants came forth with rods of myrtle, smiling and beseeching me with words of flattery to enter the gates of their city. And I answered, O fearful folk, wherefore do ye carry rods in your hands? O strange creature, they cried, we have discovered that which is most akin to pleasure . . . behold us! They struck at one another until they bled. I dared look at them no longer since I, too, was filled with a great desire to do likewise. . . .

The First: The flagellants! In Dindymus they emasculate themselves and pray obscenely to a huge phallus of gold. In Samothrace . . .

The Sphinx: I passed on.

The Second: At the side of Ahab I beheld Jezebel, painted, with her hair in towers. . . .

The First: Forbear thy spilth, O Jew!

The Sphinx: In the full moon there came to us a stripling crowned with acanthus leaves, who bowed before me saying, O Sphinx, our king is dead and his folk await not many leagues hence to slay thee. And I asked, O youth, why dost thou betray them? For love of thee, O Sphinx, he answered, for very love of thee. And I said to him, For this shalt thou partake of my love. Then my servants compounded a drink, perfumed and poisoned, in sultry chalices carven for the drunken Greeks at Troy. And I instructed them saying, When mine enemies cry long and shrilly for wine, let them drink of these . . . in the first lies thirst, in the second madness, in the third death.

The Third: O merciful Sphinx!

The Sphinx (sagely): I showed no mercy. They drank thrice. . . .

The First: But the stripling, O Sphinx!

The Sphinx: Him I loved and made king. But he forsook me and betrayed me for a monster in his own kingdom . . . seven heads, seven breasts, seven mouths . . . but no heart! (*She screams suddenly*) O infamy!

The Second (he begins, resolutely): When Ahab had drunken his wine and the musicians and dancers had charmed him into deep slumber, desire came to Jezebel . . . her breasts shivered with silver, her eyes became laden by iniquitous and terrible longings, she spake in her unspeakable lust, O young Hebrew, O lovelier than our priests to Adonis, at last dost thou hearken unto me. In Napthali I sought for thee and in Manasseh, but wheresoever my messengers tarried, even thence hadst thou departed. So I summoned thy master to me saying, These many years hast thou held in thy heart hatred and despite for me and mine. I, O Javan, could have wished it otherwise. Behold! in my coffers are webs and fabrics and filaments, dyed yellow and beryl and ivory by the Nubians in our realm. These are thine. I can whisper into the ear of the king's tetrarch, Hipponicus, a blonde sophist of Idrias, who will petition to his master that thou be made merchant over all merchants to Egypt, Babylon, Mysia, Samaria, and Ampe, even to the uttermost ends of the earth. All this can I do—but thou, thou, O Javan—canst thou not do likewise even for me? Thou shalt bring to me Ephraim, the Hebrew youth, who shepherds his father's flocks by night in the vale of Shinar ... thou shalt bring him to me, I say, lest this heart sting and perish if he have not his quick desire of me! But if thou dost deny me this, then hearken! I shall bespeak the king when he descends to feast with his prophets, his dancers, his eunuchs, and his clamorous concubines. Ere they pour him wine from his red vases shall I say, O my dread Lord, here is one in thy presence who sought me outrageously for his lust by night—yea, O King, even as I lay in my sealed chamber, prostrate at prayer! Then shall he cry aloud, Who did this unto thee and unto us, O Jezebel? Though his face be the countenance of a young god, yet shall he perish athirst and charred in his unassuaged desire! Who shall I say but thee, O Javan, the Midianite?

The Sphinx: Thou shouldst have cast her forth ... cast her forth to the dogs!

The Second: I said unto her, O Jezebel, my master Javan the Midianite is my surety and first must I seek counsel of him. Yet that night we departed for Tyre, thence to Egypt. ...

The Sphinx: She would have beguiled thee while her spouse, the king of the Hebrews, slept; made thee her slave with wine, perfume, incense, and somber, motionless lusts ... then slain thee! I know ... how well I know! The queen of Thasos, Erythera, had a palace coloured blue like moonlight, set apart on a field from the city. At night there came to her many lovers in their beaked green ships with the golden head of Clymene figured hugely on their prows. They came to her with love from Imbros and Lada and from the flaming city of vintages near Myrrhene. Each night I lay solitary in her courtyard below and laughed until the tears glittered as dew on my disquiet face. At dawn she appeared before her window and called down to me, O Sphinx, behold these, the princes from Imbros and Lada who have drunken deep of my wine, and Diodorus of Myrrhene, who hath covertly unveiled the nacred flowers of my breasts and in his fury embraced me ... do thou slay the three lest they despoil thee of my love!

The First (curiously): How, O Sphinx? We knew not that thy loves were other than men!

The Sphinx: That is hidden in my heart. ... (*She gazes at him piercingly*) I slew. But there drew near me from the holy city of Eleusis a delicate lord in a panther-skin with clusters of grapes on his brow and in his hand a spear topped with ivy-leaves and crocus-flowers. I stirred slowly from my reveries and said, Whence come ye and whither go ye, O youth from afar. And he answered, O Sphinx, my name I know not, but meseems that of old there was on my lips a great cry as of joy, and in my heart a ravening light and flame as of gardens and citadels. In Naxos I remember naught save the crystalline sky and a great host that followed my chariot, drunken and tinted, with pipes, hautboys and timbrels, carrying beakers of rosy wine.

The First: I have heard of this. There was a strange god who came dancing through the world . . . his way was madness, O Sphinx!

The Sphinx: Thou hast not heard all. The multitude that attended this god, everywhere adorned the curved pilasters of their temples with pyramidal festoons of grapes, with the leaves and tendrils and blossoms, so that men seeing them made a vintage thereof to snare and gladden the hearts of their kind. I followed them to Pythia, they drew me with them to Pergamon. . . .

The First: O Paphian Hermaphrodite . . . (*He begins to weep*) O the long, long sleep on the weaving night! That was the city where the strange god disappeared. My brothers, the priests of Heliotis, worship him even to this day. The Persians and the brown Cypriotes have carved him out of peach-coloured marble in the secret crypts and recesses of their holy shrines, but his real self lies in a quiet sea that laps the remote Cassiterides, in a casket quarried by the green Tritons who guard him day and night. Thou knewest this not, O Sphinx?

The Sphinx (with hatred): Have a care, O Greek, I know everything! They slew him because *he* slew. They loved one another until this god came with his lyre and besought them to follow him alone to his riotous, rose-hung temple in far-away Crete. He slew their priest. . . .

The First (with a cry): No, no, no! This was a beautiful god, a merciful god, a god filled with love like light! Ah, the image of divine beauty!

The Sphinx: They came into the city veiled and hooded and silent, in the guise of priests to Cybele. But behold, no sooner were they within the sacred precincts than they flung themselves naked, uplifting gilt flagons, brandishing peaked thyrses, maiming and violating their silver youths . . . this I beheld with mine own eyes.

The Third: O dreadful folk!

The Sphinx: I perceived it from my mount before the temple to Daphne. Thy god (*nodding to the First*) slew their priest! He was buried alive and swathed in talc, then painted with the most accursed sign of his wanton, viny crew. Whosoever would find him must slay me first. O Greek, thou hast lied. (*Her talons draw close to him*) Thou hast lied from the beginning, but I shall no longer withhold my anger from thee.

The First (with a scream): O Sphinx, I dare not die!

The Sphinx (gazes at him fixedly): Thou hast known my sister ... thou hast been beloved by my sister, the Lamia! ... It is she who hath sent thee unto me! Mine eyes are bared to thy treason.

The First: It is true, O Sphinx, but I repent me and love thee alone—thee alone ... but do not slay me! I have a secret. . . .

The Sphinx: Ah ... but *my* secret thou shalt never know!

The Second: This was the beautiful strange god that the Greek swore me his oaths by in the grove to Tammuz! (*He beats his breast with both hands*) I have never been the same since; I shall never be the same again, O Sphinx! Revenge—I beseech thee!

The Sphinx: Come close ... still closer. . . . (*She draws him slowly to her*) He seduced thee ... the truth, O Hebrew ... thou must tell me the truth! He did unto thee evil in the grove to Tammuz, in the sacrificial garden before the figure of the Syrian god in his shrine ... he did unto thee ... evil!

The Second (shielding his face with both hands): Not in Jerusalem, O Sphinx, but in Tyre. He followed me thither with oaths and protestations and with him was Herodian, the fair Lacedæmonian youth. . . .

The Sphinx (softly): Thou hast also lied. . . . Thou shalt also die! Thou, too, didst plot against me. Thou hast known my sister, the Lamia. . . .

The Second: Once only, O Sphinx, in Corinth!

The Sphinx (she opens wide her bronze wings, her eyes dilate, her breath becomes audible): Ai! Ai! Ai! Ai!

The Third: Be merciful, O Sphinx!

The Sphinx: Silence. Thou shalt remain.

The First: Not death, O Sphinx!

The Second (cringing): Suffer thy servant to live! I can take thee with me to Nineveh, richer than all royal Tarshish, where the treasure of the priest Pagiel is stored. Once thither, thou canst bear this gold away with thee. . . . O beautiful gold ... O riches beyond the dreams of vast avarice ... it is all thine, O Sphinx!

The Sphinx (her gigantic laughter re-echoes in the pagan night): I have been betrayed by love ... once again have I been betrayed by love!

The First and Second (in unison): Help us, O Lamia! We perish beneath the wings of thy sister, the Sphinx! (*Their screams are heard, first loudly, then fainter, as she enfolds and crushes them*)

The Sphinx (to the Third): Dost thou love me, O my last lover?

The Third: Thou knowest I am thine, body and soul forever, O Sphinx!

The Sphinx (benignantly): Come, then, let us go forth together into Egypt.

>A curtain of dust and darkness
>descends and covers the scene.

III. Translations

A Song of Chamisso's

Roses soon to follow,
    All so fair and fleet;
Swallow mating swallow—
    And the world is sweet.

Summer-roses burning,
    Swallows . . . love at last!
And my youth returning,
    Fain forgets the past.

Twenty-four Translations from Heine

A Prefatory Note

With Heine, poetry was mostly a matter of passionately exalted lyricism, but his translators, new and old, seemed to have divined something vastly and variously different. Mr. Louis Untermeyer, the latest, for instance, approaches him with all the conception of a Ulyssean galley-maker. The dawn is blue and radiant, the material is chryselephantine—true enough—but his restive craft will not reach Ithaca, hardly. In his hands the marvelous music of "Die Lotusblume," a thing of opal and iris, becomes unreal and metronymic. It is not thus that great poets are translated, nor is it thus that great poetry is ever written. More than one translator and his translation have foundered under the too-liberal interpretation of literalism.

    The following four and twenty versions owe their inception, as part of an unfilled volume, to the mythical Mr. Ambrose Bierce. Peace to the nobility of his memory! Whether he perished in murderous old Mexico, or closed his eyes placidly under the incantation of South American skies—as his last, unpublished letter to the writer seems to indicate—matters little enough. The scribbler who prophesied that Ambrose Bierce would one day ascend Mount Horeb and forget to return, spake the truth, truly. And still the legend grows. The late Mr. Howells, we see, has already included "An Occurrence at Owl Creek," [sic] among his "best American Stories." Others will follow. There will be books of biography and books of criticism. No doubt, there will be much adulation. But we—somewhere between Hesper and the swinging Pliads—faintly discern the leonine, white head and the kindly, human eyes. It is there that he belongs—it is there that we place him. *Atque in perpetuum, frater, ave atque vale!*

1

By a wizard moon in an elfin wood,
    The faery-folk passed by me singing;
And I peered across to their phantom rood
    Where I heard horns blowing and bells a-ringing.

For I saw the gossamer steeds they rode,
    And I glimps'd the glitter of gold and vair,
As they flashed on high to their blue abode,
    Swan-circled in the enchanted air.

And the queen sped by me—aye, the queen!
    With her sea-green eyes and her airy laughter;
So I wondered at length what it all could mean—
    Was there death to come, or a new love after?

2

On her hand a lamp lies gleaming,
    In her breast a mighty flame;
Where the golden youth lies dreaming,
    Psyche hovers, red with shame.

Blushes as she overtakes him,
    Fain she would not, yet must see,
And her ecstasy awakes him,
    For the god turns but to flee.

Eighteen-hundred years of travail,
    Years of passionate redress—
Still the lady tries to cavil
    Over Cupid's nakedness.

3

Shadow-love and shadow-kisses,
    Shadow-life—O sweet, sweet, sweet!
Did you think that all your blisses
    Would not fail and fleet?

Those we love and fain would cherish
    Vanish like the dreamful past,
And the heart itself must perish
    And the eyelids close at last.

4

Death comes—now I can say with pleasure,
    That which my pride forbade me say:
    For you alone—by night, by day,
This heart of mine beat out its measure.

They bear my coffin in their keeping,
    Lower me—O almighty peace!
    But you, beloved, will not cease
To mourn me, ever weeping, weeping.

You wring your pretty hands and languish;
    Take comfort, dear—that is the fate
    Of all things good and true and great—
The bitter end is always anguish.

5

Three holy Kings came from the East,
    And asked in each town aidance:
Which is the way to Bethlehem,
    Beloved youths and maidens?

The young and the old they knew it not,
    The Kings passed on together;
They followed a certain golden star,
    Set in the azure weather.

The star hung over Joseph's house,
    The bells began a-ringing;
The oxen lowed, the children cried,
    The three Kings entered singing.

6

They loved one another but neither
    Would utter their still desire;
Enemies they together,
    With hearts that were hot as fire.

They parted pale and harried,
    'T was only in dreams they met;
The two are dead and buried,
    But neither knows it as yet.

7

A pine stands bare and lonely,
    North, on a flaw-blown height;
He slumbers, shrouded only
    In ice and snow and night.

And dreams of a palm in anguish,
    From the utmost morning-land,
Lonely and left to languish
    On leagues of burning sand.

8

Out of my infinite woe
    I make my little songs;
    That flutter away in throngs,
As to her heart they go.

Each with a burden or sigh,
    Enters her gracious ears,
    But departs again with tears,
And will not tell me why.

9

Death is the cool sweet night, they say,
And life but the breath of a sultry day;
It darkens and sleep has come desired—
The day has made me tired.

Over my bed thro' the tree-tops pale,
I hear the song of a nightingale;
She sings, she sings of love and laughter,
I listen but the tears come after.

10

The world is so sweet
    And the sky is so blue,
The roses are drunken
    With dreamless dew—
Yet I would be at rest
On some dead love's breast.

11

The roses bud and blossom,
    And wither on the heath;
They bud and blossom and wither
    And that's the way of death.

I know this and all my pleasure
    Loses its love and zest;
My heart is so bright and witty,
    And yet it bleeds in my breast.

12

A star falls out of the heavens,
    Into the lonely night!
That is the star of Venus,
    That falls before my sight.

The leaves and the apple-blossoms
    Descend from their parent tree!
And suddenly comes the south-wind,
    That stirs them to ecstasy.

The swan sits on the water,
    And mirrors herself in the wave,
And softly she sings but softer,
    And finds her watery grave.

So still it is, so darkling!
    The leaves and blossoms are fled,
The swan with her song is silent,
    The star is ashen and dead.

13

With her shadows vast and dreary,
    Comes the wicked night we dread;
And our souls are sick and weary,
    As we gaze astonished.

You grow old but I grow older,
    Flowery spring is long departed.
You grow cold but I grow colder,
    Comes the winter, bitter-hearted.

Ah, the end is mud and mire!
    Never more love's hopeful breath;
Still there lingers a desire,
    After life and loving—death.

14

The lotus-flower closes
    Her heart to the sun's delight,
Bereft and bowed she reposes,
    And dreaming, waits for the night.

The moon is her crowned lover,
    He shines on her lowly place,
And only to him above her,
    She bares her flower-like face.

She blows and glows and quivers,
    And stares and gazes above;
She sighs and moans and shivers,
    For love and the woes of love.

15

My songs, my songs are poison'd,
    How could it be otherwise?
You have poured your glowing venom
    Into their melodies.

My songs, my songs are poison'd,
    How could it be otherwise?
My heart holds many serpents
    And your sweet eyes.

16

There was a king of olden,
    His heart was heavy, his head was gray;
Only his crown was golden,
    But he took him a wife one day.

There was a standard-bearer,
    Red were his lips and his eyes were keen;
Night and day he drew near her,
    This young and gracious queen.

And the song that a few still cherish?
    So sweet the chime, the rhyme thereof!
Both of them had to perish,
    For their beautiful, hopeless love.

17

The good king Wiswamitra
    Finds life a burden now,
In peril and in warfare,
    He seeks Wasishta's cow.

O good king Wiswamitra,
    Why what an ox art thou,
That thou so blindly strivest
    After a scurvy cow.

18

They tortured me with their whimsies,
    They wrought me a thing of fate,
Some with their love and longing,
    And others with their hate.

My bread they dipped in poison,
    Drugged what I drank and ate,
Some with their love and longing,
    And others with their hate.

But she, the last, triumphant,
    Mercilessly elate,
She drugged me not with longing,
    Nor poisoned me with hate.

19

Within my breast there sits a woe
    That breaks my heart with thronging,
And where I sit and where I go,
    It will not cease from longing.

It leads me where my loved one sighs,
    Far from unrest and fever,
But when I see her holy eyes,
    I flee her side forever.

Though I ascend the highest hill
    That holds all heaven in keeping,
There's loneliness that takes me still—
    And blind desire and weeping.

20

The lady sleeps in her chamber,
    The moonlight shivers by;
And a ringing begins and a singing,
    Of a waltzer's melody.

"I shall look out of the window,
    And see what awakens me."
A shadow stands among shadows,
    And fiddles unceasingly.

"You promised to dance with me living,
    You broke your vow to wed:
Tonight they dance in the graveyard,
    Come forth, and dance with the dead!"

She falters not but she follows,
    Over the lighted way;
She, with the dancing shadow,
    Who fiddles as dead men may.

He fiddles and sways and dances,
    And claps each rattling bone,
The dead stand by in the moonlight
    And nod their heads and groan.

21

She was a flash and he was a thief,
They loved each other beyond belief.
When he called her his little grafter,
She threw herself down in laughter.

Their day passed by in joy and pleasure,
At night she lay on his breast, a treasure.

When they flung him in prison just after,
She stood at the window in laughter.

He sent her a letter, "O come to me,
If only you knew my misery,
I call to each lonely rafter—"
She shook her head in laughter.

At six in the morning they hung him,
At seven o'clock unstrung him;
But at eight or not long after,
She drank red wine in laughter.

22

The yellow leaves are falling,
    One can feel stark Autumn's breath;
Ah, everything sweet and enthralling
    Soon finds a way to death.

On wood and on hill there faces
    The sunset's flying gleam;
Summer it is, that embraces
    Perishing Beauty's dream.

For something within me flutters,
    Something that may not weep;
Despair, heart-broken that utters
    The memory that would sleep.

And I—I parted from her,
    Yet knew that she must die;
I was the passing Summer,
    She was its plaintive cry.

23

O my sweet love, when to the grave
    Your sightless way I follow,

I shall not hear the voices rave,
    But creep into your hollow.

And kiss and enfold and press you close,
    So still, so cold and forsaken!
But in the burden of my woes,
    Pray that we never awaken.

The dead shall arise at midnight lone,
    And dance in their cerements lighted;
But hidden beneath our vault of stone,
    We two shall be reunited.

The dead shall arise at judgement-day,
    Each to his hell or heaven;
But clinging together, we two shall stay,
    Immortal and unforgiven.

24

I am the princess Ilse,
    And I live at Ilsenstein,
O come with me to my palace,
    And you shall be only mine.

I would bathe your head and eyelids,
    Out of my legion springs,
And your woe shall be forgotten,
    Loneliest of human things.

Over my snow-white shoulders,
    And by my ivory side,
You shall love to the world's end,
    Whatever the woe betide.

And I shall love you and kiss you,
    And love you and kiss you again,
As I did to the emperor Heinrich,
    That princeliest of men.

The dead are dead forever,
    And only the living live,
But I am youth and beauty,
    Eternal the joy I give.

Come to my palace with me,
    To my crystalline throne,
The ladies and knights are dancing,
    But we shall dance alone.

The silken trains are sweeping,
    And spurs are fleet in the hall,
The dwarves have awakened from sleeping,
    You can hear them cry and call.

And only my arms shall enfold you,
    And only your lips shall know
What I did to the emperor Heinrich,
    When he heard his trumpets blow.

Catullus

CI

Over many lands and many seas I come,
To commune, Brother, with thine ashes dumb;
And with such rites that love would have us pay,
Vainly, since youth and beauty pass away,
To take thy memory in our rifted heart,
And once again to mourn thee ere we part.
So this for thee, our love and rue and tears,
'Mid all the graven solitude of years;
Friend, spirit, comrade—more than plaint can tell!
Hail, Brother, and forever fare thee well.

LXXXV

I hate and love. You ask how this can be?
I know not, but I feel it burning me.

Translations from Baudelaire

La Musique

Music, that bears me oft times as the sea!
    Toward my pale silver star,
Under a heaven of haze and ecstasy
    My sail I set afar.

Breast forward and the divine lungs inflated,
    A pennon in the wind,
I climb the ridge of foam accumulated,
    Which night veils dim and blind.

I sense vibrating in me the repulsion,
    The vessel's agonies;
The prescient wind, the tempest, its convulsion

    Upon the immense abyss
Lulls me.... At other times, calm, mirrored there,
    Behold my great despair.

Parfum Exotique

When, with eyes closed, a sultry autumn night,
I breathe the odor of thy vehement breast,
I see myself upon strange beaches rest,
Dazzled and charmed in the unsetting light;

A slothful isle favoured in nature's sight,
With monstrous trees and fruits of savour blest,
Lithe-bodied men in vigorous behest,
And women, candid-eyed as chrysolite.

Led by the odor toward that lovely clime,
I see a port with sails and masts that wait,
Still wearied by the billows' endless chime,

Where hangs the perfume of green tamarinds,
That touch the sky and sense or soul inflate,
To blend the mariners' song upon the winds.

Horreur Sympathique

Out of this strange and livid shell,
Tormented like a doom on me,
What thoughts that in your void soul dwell,
Descend? . . . . Reply: "Debauchery."

Avid and still insatiable
Of the obscuring mystery,
Never yet, as for Ovid, fell
That Latin paradise to me.

I am torn as the carrion are,
Into your mire is my esteem!
Your darkness, vast, without a gleam,

Is the dim hearse that holds my star;
Yours is the spark reflected from
That hell of hells from which I come.

De Profundis Clamavi

I implore thy pity, Thou, the unique adored,
The bottom of the abyss my heart is buried,
A world deject with the horizon harried,
That swims in night where horror is the lord;

A sun that holds no heart for six months hovers,
Ere darkness falls, and emptiness and dearth;
A place more naked than the polar earth;
No beasts, no streams, no luminous green for lovers!

But not in me this deed to mankind cries,
The frigid hatred of this sun of ice,
Nor the immense night that ancient chaos brings;

I fear the fate of many wretched things,
That dread immersion to a stupid sun,
Even as much as in oblivion.

La Beauté

Beauty am I, O mortals, dreamed in stone!
My breasts to which all men are bruised and bound,
Await, so that the poet's love be crowned,
Mute as the earth, eternal and alone.

I throne in azure like a sphinx asleep;
A heart of snow with pallor of the swans;
I hate that passionate striving which is man's;
Nor ever do I laugh, nor ever weep.

The poets, bowed before my spheral station,
This monument that only dawn discovers,
Consume their days in singing and oblation;

For I can fascinate these docile lovers,
By mirrors that reflect all things more fair:
Mine eyes, my large eyes radiant with despair!

Causerie

Thou art a sky of autumn, clear and rose!
But in my blood a sadness like the sea
Is leashed in flowing by these lips morose,
Bitter with ooze of poignant memory.

Thy sinuous hand glides on my swooning breast;
That, which it seeks, love, is a place unfit,
Where fang and tooth of woman found behest.
Seek not my heart; the brutes have eaten it.

My heart's a mansion by the mob opprest;
They drink, they slay, they hale me by the hair! . . . .
. . . . A perfume swims upon thy naked breast.

O beauty, scourge, and deeper than despair!
With eyes of fire, lustrous as at thy feasts,
Calcine these tatters left me by the beasts!

Chant d'Automne

Ere long we plunge benumbed into the pall;
Farewell, boon splendour, of our summer's breath!
I hear with dread the clashing funeral
Of leaves on pavements in the court of death.

Winter, there came into my life, and dolor,
Hatred and horror, obdurate toil with cries,
And like the sun in emptinesses polar,
This heart of mine grew stagnant blood and ice.

I saw and shuddered, secret by the grave,
A scaffold risen, heard the footfalls soundless;
And in my soul as on that architrave,
Fell the same blows, unwearied and boundless.

To me, it seemed as if in sleep, like noises,
Of a vast coffin wrought within a mart......
For what?.... To pass the night; autumnal voices!
That cry mysterious sounds and then depart!

———————————

I love your weary eyes of luminous green,
Mild beauty! Bitter is this day to me;
And not your love, nor hearth where I have been,
Comforts me, nor the star that lights the sea.

Yet for the scorpion-grass, that silken mother,
Even for evil by an ingrate done,
Lover or sister, or for such another,
There is wild autumn with the setting sun.

Cease work! The tomb attend; for it remembers!
Ah, leave me with my face poised to your gaze,
There to lament for summer, pale with embers,
When, in this lost year, shine the yellow rays.

Le Couvercle

Whatever land be his, in places wan,
Under a clime of fire or suns aslant,
Servant to Jesus, Cythera's courtezan,
Gilt Croesus or the saddened mendicant.

Citizen, rustic, scholar, vagabond, he
Of a frail mind, attentive or remiss,
Man suffers terror by his agony,
And trembling, eyes the self-same sheer abyss.

Above, the Sky! a suffocating wall,
Beneath, a room where song and laughter fall,
Where every player tramples bloody grounds.

The drunkard's dread, hope of the eremite;
The Sky! a cover to this pot of night,
Where vast and transient Humankind abounds.

Le Chat

Lie, lovely cat, the idol of the wise;
Here, let your paws and talons settle,
And let me plunge into your glorious eyes,
Those eyes of agate and of metal.

When with my fingers I caress at leisure
Your quivering head and flanks elastic,
And to my hand, inebriate with pleasure,
There palpitates your body plastic,

I see my wife in very soul. Her gaze,
Is yours, O amiable beast,
Profound and frigid, as a whip that flays;

And from the feet as from the breast,
A subtle air, a dangerous perfume,
Floats negligently in the room.

La Fontaine de Sang

It seems my blood runs ever on and urges,
Even as a fountain to some rhythmic sighing;
I know full well the murmur of the surges,
But never have I understood its crying.

Across a city, walled and closed, it pilots,
Transfiguring the earth to watered islets,
And satiates the thirst and moan of all,
Until this life is coloured roseal.

I, who demand so much insidious drink,
To numb the hideous day that never dies;
Wine that makes subtlier the lighted eyes!

I, who have sought in love, oblivion's brink,
And not a bed for idleness to rest;
Bestow this cup upon the cruellest!

Sonnet d'Automne

They say, these crystal eyes, so clear and mute:
"For thee, strange love, why needs my soul disguises?"
Be fair and silent. This, my heart despises,
All save the candour of the antique brute.

Nor will it bare the secret of the devil,
To thee who art the somnolence of nights!
Nor this black legend in the flame that writes;
I hate all grief, the spirit does me evil!

Let us love calmly. Love in his retreat,
Obscure and ambushed, bends his deadly bow;
The snare of his old arsenal I know:

Crime, horror and folly! . . . . O pale Marguerite!
Like me, thou art the sun's autumnal glow,
O my so white, O my so frigid Marguerite!

Ciel Brouillé

They say your gaze is of a cloud enthralled;
Your eye mysterious (blue gray, emerald?),
Alternate tender, dreaming, cruel, driven,
Reflects the indolence of pallid heaven.

You summon the white dawn, tepid and veiled,
Yours is the fount where hearts are ensorcelled,
Convulsed in evil by an unknown ache,
When sleeping nerves to agony awake.

For you, at times, are like the sun that lies on
The lighted mist of a late year's horizon;
Resplendent as a drooping world in rain,
That falls from stars of ecstasy and pain.

O dangerous woman! O seductive skies!
You, I adore, your sorrow and your lies;
That wound is mine, implacable and lost,
From joy as sharp as steel and keen as frost.

Les Chats

Those fiery loves and they who wisdom carry,
Enamoured and alike in their ripe season,
The cats, so puissant and void of treason,
Even as these, are chill and sedentary.

Friends to all learning and to deep delight,
Silence they seek and horror of the gloom;
Erebus holds them frozen in his might,
And curbs in bondage what would else consume.

They crouch in dreams of noble attitudes,
Great sphinxes lengthened where the desert broods,
Enslaved in reveries none dare surmise;

Their fecund loins are filled with magic flashes,
With gleams of gold among the somber ashes,
Emblazoned vaguely in their mystic eyes.

Translations from Verlaine

Sagesse

A heaven is over these houses,
    So blue, so calm!
The tree, that above them drowses,
    Sways like a palm.

A bell, in the clearest azure,
    Placidly rings;
A bird in the leaves for pleasure,
    Warbles and sings.

My God, my God, life about me,
    Is so filled with pity;
This tumult I hear from without me,
    Ascends from the city!

.... What have you done, who are chidden
    To weep for the truth;
Tell me, where have you hidden
    Your beautiful youth?

Bruxelles

The flight is pink and green
    Of the hills and lowly fences,
    The lighting of lamps commences,
Confused are things that were seen.

The hollow is gold that brings,
    A placid stain on the leaves
    Of the trees where still there grieves
One bird that feebly sings.

Sad with the soul of despair
    Each semblance of autumn seems,
    And my languors are troubled with dreams
That cradle themselves in the air.

Romances sans Paroles

The shadow of trees in the hazy river
  Dies like the mists that shiver,
While in the air amid pale boughs above,
  Mute dove complains to dove.

How long, O traveller, in that ghastly guerdon,
  Thou mirrorest thy burden,
How sadly weeping in the loftiest trees,
  Thy hope is drowned, as these.

Il Bacio

Kiss! rose-red hollyhock in the garden of caresses!
  Fiery accompaniment on the piano's keys,
  Burden of love long sung by burning souls like these,
Voiced like an archangel to the languor of charmeresses!

Sonorous, clear and gracious Kiss, O Kiss divine!
  Voluptuous deliverant, drunken, indescribable!
  Hail! He who stoops to drink thy cup adorable,
Arises dazed and drowned from such felicitous wine.

Like the vintage of Rhine and like that lovely music of old,
  Thou consolest and drowsest. All sorrows to thy endearment
  Expire and tremble on each fold of thy purple cerement
..... How noblier sung by Goethe or Will, in lines of gold.

I, who am naught, the piteous singer of Paris, come after,
  And proffer these flowers, this innocent children's verse:
  Be kind, for the love I hold that these mutinous lips disperse;
To one who knows thee, O Kiss, alight on her mouth in laughter.

La Bonne Chanson

The moon of snow
Shines in the wood;
From every bough
Thin voices brood
That the green sprays cover....

O my dear lover.

The pool at our feet
Profoundly traces
The silhouette
Of the willow that faces
The bleak wind's power....

Muse on: it is the hour.

A vast and far
Content is given,
And where we are
Descends from heaven
An irised star, a flower....

It is the exquisite hour.

Vert

Behold the fruits, the flowers, the leaves, the branches,
    And then my heart which no one else shall hold,
Tear it not with your hands, their white that blanches,
    But take to your eyes the lover, submissive yet bold.

I come to you once again all secret and bleeding
    With the icy wind of dawn congealed to my face,
Suffering, wan, at your feet I repose here pleading,
    And in dreams of joy beseech a moment's grace.

On your young breast let but my head sustain there,
    Sonorous still from faded kisses and woes;
Let it, until the tempest is passed, remain there,
    And sleeping a little, dream, while you repose.

Sappho

Furious, with sunken eyes and rigid breasts,
Sappho, the languor of desire excited,
Roams, a she-wolf, on shores where no man rests.

She dreams of Phaon, forgets the altar lighted,
And seeing not her bitter tears in scorn,
She tears her hair, even as a flower is torn.

Then she evokes in torments without number,
Those times in which pure, radiant and white,
Her loves sang to her each remembering night,
Virginal souls, that long since crept to slumber.

Then knowing herself corrupt and poor, she bends,
And in the waters of La Moire she springs. . . .
And heaven, a light that shivers the darkness flings;
Thus has the pale Selene avenged the Friends.

Sonnet: After Leconte de Lisle

(For Alfred Galpin)

Ecclesiastes said: Better a dog that lives
Than a dead lion. Save to drink and eat,
Life is a flame and smoke. The world still thrives,
But emptiness pervades the tomb's deceit.

In ancient nights under the austere skies,
Upon his tower as from a mount alone,
In silence, with his ever-peering eyes,
So dreamed he on his elephantine throne.

Old sun-lover, who gave his anguished cry:
Unending death, that too, is but a lie,
Happy the man who leaps engulfed in strife!

But I, forever listening in dismay,
Hear only the immortal hideous day,
And the long roaring of eternal life.

God's Work

(*After Rainer Maria Rilke*)

Workers are we: masters, disciples, pages,
    And build you, O you high and mighty nave.
Then sometime comes a stranger down the ages,
Who shows us shivering in each soul that rages,
    A newer and a nobler architrave.

We rise to where the scaffold sways unshaken,
    And in our hand the hammer finds release;
The stars are on our faces as we waken,
They shine as though they, too, had overtaken
    The wind that followed you from overseas.

There is a hail of many hammers driven,
    And from the hills we hear a clang afar;
Only at evening under evening star,
We see your giant contour, vast and riven.
    O God, how great you are!

IV. Fiction

Antenor

Antenor of Samosata is buried here, who loved some one who loved still another. Foolish fates! the two lie side by side with a wind that blows day and night through a grove of olives from the Ionian sea.

A Ruined Paradise

It was dusk when Worth and I paddled our way stiffly against the sluggish current of the Lustral. Over our head the huge poppies bent half to the other side emitting that peculiar odor (even for poppies) which Worth in an extensive treatise on "erotic" botany has since termed "despairing," but which he disclaims having ever experienced before or since, the occasion I am about to relate. Unlike the *Religieuse* of Harding, the calyx held an infinitesimal number of purple and yellow spickles. When one brushed against the stem ever so lightly a distinct chatter became audible among their fibrous tendons. The perpetual recurrence in the variety of perfumes and again, the growing height of the species, became noticeably apparent with the narrowing of the stream.

Here, where a sudden turn of matted growth arrested the main stem of the weir, we plied our energies with renewed assurance. By an almost human docility the skiff, strangled and choking in the golden filth that submerged her brass bow and threatened the body itself, drove hardily through the proximity of an hundred yards. Then we stopped, before us an about us one wall of flaming flowerage and impassable undergrowth.

Worth, with his usual excitableness, became uneasy. "We have missed the main stream—we have missed the main stream," he repeated, "and now must bear the consequences. A night in the miasma and poison of this pool would suffice for an after-life of ill-health. I feel it already." He shivered.

"True," I replied, "but let us find an outlet." It had occurred to me that I caught a whiff of fresh water as we entered the reaches of the

Lustral below. Faint and far it seemed, but easily assented to by nostrils overburdened with the narcotic along the banks. If this then were the case, by the blindest mischance or perversity, we had stumbled into one of the many winding inlets that the Lustral is known to inhabit in the extreme rainy season. I stated my view to Worth. Unquestionably, this monstrous rack of foliage found little sustenance during drouth. We had overlapped the channel by not more than a score of miles, but with slight help from the listless-enough current our journey might be retraced by early dawn.

He gazed at me drowzily, but vouchsafed no answer. As I pored over the chart I caught him looking at me with what seemed little short of a leer in his usually placid laughter-loving countenance. As I have said, the air became momentarily heavier with the breath of those vague, unlovely, pendulous things that hovered audibly in the surrounding gloom. Once or twice I found myself muttering unintelligibly as the mist rising in soft clouds from the phosphorescent depth below entered into my eyes, into my throat, and into my head, choking all utterance. Worth lay at the bottom in a thick, breathless stupor. It must have been shortly after this that I relapsed into unconsciousness, and yet I remember reasoning dimly with myself in an inconsiderate way, that the best part of life was one's propensity for dreaming it away. In a delirium that made itself lucid by the sheer idea of Self becoming inanimate, Oblivion (in a word) seemed cognizably vaster than Eternity.

Kill—kill—kill, sounded incessantly in my ears. My temples bounded to bursting and I had dim dreams of being quenched by the remorseless hand of some shadowless Titan, whose golden eyes were kindled by the sun before ever earth, fire, or water, took imminent fashioning. What then, was the slender shuttle that wove the fabric of such an agonizing impossibility? I opened my eyes. Worth lay before me with his tongue lolling out of his mouth. Relaxing for a moment he uttered a string of obscenities— Worth, the cleanest-minded man it has been my fortune to meet with! "Stop!" I commanded. He cursed me again—God! such oaths that left his boyish lips. Enraged, yet with a sudden impassionate madness that I have myself perceived working in the venomous malice of habitual opium users, I drew my clasp-knife and in a trice whipped it across his frothing lips.

"Murcheson!" he screamed, "O Murcheson, what have you *done?*"
I had completely severed his tongue from his mouth....

* * * * *

Our relief party found us the next morning and we were duly separated. Worth recovered, as later events have shown—but not his speech. The "Organica" bids fair to make him a giant among scientists. Censure him as one naturally will in his controversy with Herr Bauer—a discerning student will find him negligible only in his (to me) old faults—an overweening desire to excite notoriety and the usual febrile hastiness. We have never met each other since.

The One Who Did Penance

There was a Man who repented him of his sin and he came to the Woman who had sinned with him, and he said to her: "Lo! what is passed is passed; I shall sin with thee no more. Do thou as thou likest, but I go out into the world as the white flame of an inspiration, a spark to that light of holiness which may peradventure yet win me a place in innermost Heaven forever."

And the woman bared her garment that was the color of hyacinth and showed her carven breasts enticingly.

"Behold," she said, "are these not fair enough for thee? Am I not all rose and alabaster, and were not my lips likest to poppies in the summer fields?

"Gave I not thee all manner of strange delight and saidest thou not we should grow old in love together?"

And he gazed at her sorrowfully and answered: "Thou art all of this, and thou hast been good to me in thy way. Yet ever in the heart of our joy do I hear a voice that cries: Thou art chosen but thou heedest not. Still art thou chosen, and My word will yet lead thee forth triumphing among mankind. Would thou keep me with thee against my will?"

Then the woman laughed scornfully and cried: "Fool, the joy of Life lies in the forgetting, else hadst thou perished for fear long ago. Thinkest thou that the world will hail thee as prophet and succor thee in their innocent credulity? But go thy way, for thou shalt indeed know the truth in the end if to thy enduring folly there is an end."

And he left her and passed into foreign parts attired in the simple gray garb of a holy man. And he preached his word to all that were concerned, but his prayer fell as rain in a sea of dust, for the world had long ago wearied of its prophets and their homily of moaning wisdom.

And after a time he came to a land which was riotous with wickedness, with a vice made gilded and pleasurable for the inhabitants.

And he said to them: "Why do you sin?"

And they answered: "Because we fear Death and the sleep that knoweth no waking. We strive to forget that our end is night and oblivion."

And he rebuked them sternly crying: "Alas! for ye! Know ye not what cometh hereafter? Have ye no fear of Hell and of eternal torment?"

And they laughed at him, saying: "Not we, nay! Ask of the subtle and discerning worm which is our uninvited guest!"

But he was silent and pondered over their intent.

Then they said to him beguilingly: "Come, be one of us. What profits it that thou waylay palsied old with thy hoary word of an uncertain god? Take thee a chaplet of vine leaves and a garment of violet cloth. We have a yellow liquor in goblets of scarlet chalcedony and honey sweeter than was ever fabled of old. Our women are blood and ivory, and of these thou mayest have any for thy delectation. We have need of thee, therefore be of our company."

So he was persuaded, and abiding with them partook of their ways.

And it chanced after a while that the Woman also repented, and seeking the Man came at last to the folk with whom he abided. For she had hidden her beauty and her vanity and departed with her sin.

And when she halted at the gates of the city the watchman cried to her: "Thou must not enter, for here is the plague newly come. Seven have I buried this hour and still they fall as thick as flies to a honey-pot. Got knows, which of us will go next—not I!"

And she answered: "Open, for I come in mercy."

And he opened the gates wide to see what manner of person so dared to brave death. And he said to her: "Surely, thou art mad to enter in the face of this peril."

And she answered him: "I have no fear save of God."

So she passed into the city and ministered that night and for many nights to the sick and dying. For the dead multiplied and there seemed no abatement to the destruction.

And there came to her one day a painted eunuch who cried out in a shrill voice: "The King of Pleasure is sick! The King of Pleasure is sick unto death! Wilt thou not come and minister to the King of Pleasure? Whosoever cureth him shall have what he wills, even to the word's desire, which is the treasure of gold and emeralds beneath the foundations of this marvelous city. But make haste! make haste! make haste!

And she said: "Take me to thy master."

And when she perceived him she knew that it was the Man who had loved her in the past, and she said: "Dost thou not know me?"

And he answered: "Elsewhere have I seen thee, but I dare not think on what occasion. Mayhap, it was at a better time of life than this."

And she gave a little cry, saying: "Thou didst know me of old and I returned thy love!"

Then he knew her and wept, crying: "Hast thou come to single me out in my wretchedness? Behold, I am King of Pleasure who must die even as other folk. Oh! but while it was dawn I feasted and drank deep!"

And the Woman said sadly: "But thou didst plight thy service to God. Where was thy Conscience?"

And he answered her wildly: "Thou shalt find my conscience after I die; thou shalt find it, I swear!" And so saying, he closed his eyes and lay stark in death.

Then the Woman bade the mutes take the body and divest him of his raiment. And she wept when he lay before her, for behold! there was no part of him that was not seared with torture and agonized with mutilation.

And she kissed his mouth and cried aloud in her grief, saying: "Would that thou hadst stayed in thy lesser sin, O my Love, and I in my happier unrepentance!"

The Faun

(*In Memoriam: Morris Longstreet Miller*)

After his hopeless love for Syrinx, Pan sickened and it seemed that he would die. He sat all day long among the yellow reeds by the river-bed and would not be comforted. In the red dawn the Nymphs tripped down the thymy slopes of Mænelos and danced on the dewy sward. At mid-day the Dryads appeared from their ancient abodes in their gossamer raiment and sang to him of the life of the trees and of the wind that impelled the green leaves of the great branches to give forth sustenance to their august parent. And in the heart of sunset the Mænads came over the purple hills from Thrace with their winy locks and their inarticulate cries and passionate gestures. But Pan sat oblivious even to this, so that at last the disheartened wood-folk left him to perish alone.

Then a young Faun with pink face and pointed ears who loved him crept up to him and said, "Pan, Pan, is there nought that will make thee well and blithe again as of old?"

And Pan answered him disconsolately, "Nothing, little Faun. I shall lie here and dream until I fall asleep and I shall never awaken again. Run away, therefore, and play among thy friends. Thou hast no soul and dost not understand. Thou canst not die, little Faun, thou art an immortal."

Then the little Faun who had no soul sought himself a nook and began to weep. And he wept until the Hybla Bees buzzed into his ear and asked of him, "Wherefore dost thou weep, little Faun? We know a spot in the golden sun where wan orchids and silver moon-flowers grow as high as thy head—aye, even above it. Come with us and they shall love thee even as we do, little Faun."

And the Faun answered, "How can I play with you when Pan is sick and there is nothing in the world that will cure him?" And he wept again, rocking his head in his hands as all Fauns do when they grieve.

Then they buzzed one among the other until the eldest cried, "Our knowledge is so slight and our burden so heavy; yet we love thee and would fain be of service to thee. Go to the old Satyr who teaches his grandchildren in a glen among the hills and tell him of thy plight. Assuredly, he will help thee, but if he deal with thee in any manner otherwise, tell him he found our honey sweet under Attic skies and give him this portion for remembrance. He is deep in wisdom, little Faun, for he was once a servant to the elder Gods. Take heart and go to him quickly."

And the Faun came to the old Satyr whom he found teaching his sprightly young grandchildren the secret lore of nature in a hollow glen among the lonely hills.

And he said to him shyly, "Old Satyr, I have brought thee honey from the Hybla Bees, who bid me remind thee of their services to thee in years that are past."

And the old Satyr, whose eyes were bleared and whose voice was high and thin, cried out, "From the Hybla Bees! Ask what thou wilt, little Faun, for I dare not refuse thee!"

But when the Faun had made his desire known the old Satyr knitted his shaggy brow and shook his wise head. "I know many things," he said, "I know what the silken buds say when they lie sheathed in their long sleep and awaken wonderingly into the brief ecstasy of Spring. I can tell thee the despairing cry of the leaves to their tree when they fall to the earth in the wild Autumn. Wouldst thou know what it is? 'Mother,' they cry, 'we perish, perish!' I know many things, little Faun, but the marvelous mystery of Life and Death—that I do not know."

Then the Faun turned to leave and the tears welled into his placid eyes. But the old Satyr cried out to him, "Hold, there is one even wiser than myself. It is the Centaur who lives in a vale of Thessaly and he is older than I am by a thousand years. He is the last of the Centaurs and when he dies there will be none left of his kind. But go to him only at the full of the moon. All the day he slumbers but at night the memory of his perished race awakens his woe and he cries aloud for an end to his immortality. The stars hear him and shiver and the ruby-eyed Lapithae moan for fear in the eternity of their subterranean darkness. But in the morning he prays to Zeus for forgiveness and falls quietly asleep."

"He wishes to die?" asked the Faun.

"Yea," nodded the Satyr sagely, "but he must live until the Gods themselves are mightily dissolved, and the Gods are deathless, as thou dost well know. I, myself, have never wearied of my long life. Hast thou of thine, perchance, little Faun?"

"Never!" cried the Faun with a shudder and a look of fear that shone in his eyes. "How dreadful, when one should ask to live forever!"

Then the old Satyr pranced with his slender goat's-feet on the turf and screamed aloud for sheer joy. His young brood, who had returned from the neighboring wood, clustered about with coronals of ivy and arbutus, beseeching him to return straightway to his task. So he bade him prosper and the Faun departed.

After many days the Faun came to the dwelling-place of the Centaur in a vale of Thessaly. And as soon as it was darkness the stars began to shiver and the ruby-eyed Lapithae to moan and presently the Centaur appeared against the great, full moon. And he stood there for a space and then cried out in a piercing voice, "Is there no one to help me? Am I to endure my fate until all things cease to be? Verily, I shall slay myself. I shall drink of the blood-colored venom that bubbles forth from the spring on the sand of Phrygia. I shall gaze into the blue Scythian crystal at Arginusæ or cry aloud that dread name to the divine oracle of Dodona, either of which means certain death. O! O! O! intolerable that one should live forever!"

But when he perceived the Faun he called to him not unkindly, saying, "Hast thou brought me a vial of saffron Nepenthe, little Faun, or one of the seven scarlet Poppies of Oblivion? For either would I give thee all of mine ancient, useless wisdom!"

And the Faun answered, "I know nothing of these but would have thee tell me of a remedy for the great god Pan who has forsaken his pipe and his rustic mirth while he sits despondently among the reeds by the river-side. I have come from a long distance, father Centaur."

Then the Centaur closed his eyes and held up his head to the moon. And he remained there motionless like an arabesque of bronze against the purple night or like a figure of hewn basalt, save for the tears that still glistened strangely on his face.

At last he said dreamily and with a voice of music, "I know, how well I know! At the mouth of Hades sits Persephone and with her are the violet-eyed daughters of Celeus—Callidice, Cleisidice, Demo, and Callithoe. She sits there from dawn to dusk unwearied and on her lips is the entire burden of Hades which is despair. When she smiles the dead become instantly hopeful and ply their tasks with renewed assurance, but when she weeps their bitterness gives vent to hate and scorn and it knows no bounds thereof. On her brow is the white lotus-flower and around her girdle are bound the seven scarlet Poppies of Oblivion. And when she sees thee she will cry for news from the outer world. Then must thou answer her, 'Thy mother, Ceres, yearns for thee as of old and swears to meet thee at Eleusis not many months hence.' And when thou hast told her this she will weep and grant thee a single boon. Be wary and wise, little Faun. Thou must ask her for one of the seven scarlet Poppies of Oblivion. And she will beseech thee softly to choose the lotus-flower instead, but persist in thy choice and when thou hast it in thy hand place it nearest thy heart, for only Pan must crush the Poppy of Oblivion."

Then the Faun thanked him and prepared to leave. But the Centaur cried out after him, "On thy life, beware of the Harpies! They have the white breasts and honey-sweet faces of women, but their souls are an abomination. Beware of them, little Faun!"

And at the end of the third day the Faun came to the mouth of Hades, where, even as the Centaur had foretold, there sat Persephone, and with her were the violet-eyed daughters of Celeus who ministered unto her day and night. But when he approached, the Harpies who hovered over them came to him with a monstrous whirr of wings. Their breasts were shapen like chalices of ivory and their faces honey-sweet but their bodies were feathered as terrible, winged things. Yet their voices were full of guile and they cried, "Welcome, Lord, welcome! Our sweet sister, the Chimaera, has a silver isle that hangs pendulous in the blue mist between heaven and earth. It has a shrine of clear jacinth and in the forest are pools hollowed out of green porphyry. At one end crouches our mother, the eternal Sphinx, who has four eyes of sapphires and six wings of beaten gold. Her ebon lids are unclosed but she slumbers a million years ere she awakens once. Our father was a beautiful Eidolon from Tartessus who slew all the pale kings of Bythnia. He slew them with his love which is even deadlier than hate. Yet he, himself, was in turn vanquished by the leprous priests of Cybele who whispered an evil incantation and snared him at twilight in an emerald. Come with us, Lord, come! Only from us shalt thou gain what all men vainly and sorrowfully covet, the desire of immortal Beauty. The world is grown old and overburdened but we never change. Ah, come! come!"

But when they saw that the Faun paid no heed to their wiles they grew enraged and threatened him, crying, "Ai! Ai! Ai! How we lied to thee! Not a word of our tale was the truth! Our false sister, the Chimaera, has no silver isle that hangs pendulous in the blue mist between heaven and earth. Our mother, the deadly Lydian Basilisk, engendered us, and not the eternal Sphinx. We would tear thee to pieces if we had thee within our grasp, but we shall bide our time and wait. We shall bide our time! Ai! Ai! Ai!"

And when they were silent Persephone held up her hand wearily and said, "What news, O Stranger, hast thou brought us from the far, outer world?"

And the Faun made haste to answer, "Thy mother, Ceres, yearns for thee as of old and swears to meet thee at Eleusis not many months hence."

Then she, who had wept and bemoaned the sorrows of all other mortals, wept over her own. And she cried, "Then I am not utterly forsaken! Then I shall once again know the mother-heart! O Enna, Enna, a long time ago!"

And when she had grown calm she turned to the Faun and said, "What is the boon thou seekest from us? I perceive thou art still of the living and it may be we can serve thee in good stead."

And after the Faun had made his request she said softly and with a smile, "Wouldst thou not leifer have the lotus-flower which is heavy with dreams or a kiss from my mouth that is incarnate with all desire and moulded to all supreme beauty?"

But when the Faun had persisted in his choice, she plucked from her girdle one of the seven scarlet Poppies of Oblivion. And she said, "Guard it well. Thou hast that which is desired by the quick even as with the dead. Farewell."

Then the Faun made good speed homeward. But when he drew near the dwelling-place of the Centaur it was strangely silent and he found no trace of the weariest immortal. Yet as he stood under an aspen tree he heard the leaves murmur one to another.

"What does he seek?" asked one.

"He seeks the Centaur," answered the second.

"Ah!" sighed the third, "if he only knew!"

"What dost thou mean, brother?" rustled the leaves in unison.

"Under the long grasses a little further beyond us, lies the good, wise Centaur, slain by his own hand. Last night I heard him grieve louder than ever before. The stars shivered so violently that the largest fell terror-stricken from their inwrought mantle of the sky. The ruby-eyed Lapithae moaned for fear until their voices ascended into a mighty shriek. Suddenly there came a vast silence and at dawn I spied his dead body where it lies even now. Look, brothers!"

So the Faun who had never seen a perished thing crept timidly to the spot where the Centaur had chosen for his last rest. There he lay with his eyes large and open, staring at the great, full moon as though forever entranced, and on his white breast was the cruel, red wound that still bled drop by drop with his life's blood. And when the Faun had gazed at him a moment he gave a pitiful scream and holding his hands over his eyes fled forever from the accursed place.

And in the glen among the hills he found the old Satyr at his ancient task, for though his brood made but scant progress, their preceptor never despaired. And when the Faun had told him his tale the old Satyr beamed graciously and said, "Thou art indeed one after mine own heart. Come to me when thou hast leisure and I shall disclose unto thee my profoundest secret, such that I would not reveal even to these, my nearest of kin. Truly, thou hast found favour in my sight, little Faun!"

Then the Faun nodded his happy head and made him a promise. And when he had done this he bade the old Satyr adieu and left him still at his endless task in the peaceful evening light.

And as he drew near the river-side he saw Pan as of old, yet so frail that he seemed but a shadow of his former self. About him were grouped the wood-folk who whispered among themselves, "Is it possible that he can survive another day? Surely it is only a maleficent sprite that now tenants this empty and useless house."

And when he saw the Faun the great god Pan smiled wanly but durst not speak. Then the Faun kissed his master and drew from his breast the scarlet Poppy of Oblivion. "Pan! Pan!" he cried joyously, "crush it against thy heart for it cures all ills. I have gone to the mouth of Hades, I have seen the Harpies and spoken to Persephone, and I have grieved over the good, wise Centaur. Crush it against thy heart and be well again, Pan!"

And after Pan had followed the Faun's behest, he said, "I shall live again. I shall live to love thee, little Faun. From this day henceforth, hast thou a soul. Thou shalt know good and evil, joy and grief, holy and unholy wisdom, and someday I shall whisper the world's divine secret into thine ear. I alone know what it is. I alone dare tell thee."

Then the wood-folk foregathered in festivity. The Nymphs came with their cymbals and tambourines, the Satyrs with their antique viols, the Sylvans with their harps, and even the blonde Nereids with their vari-coloured shells from the green sea. The Mænads chaunted their pagan hymns and Silenus himself rode thither on an ass with a flask at his lips and vine-leaves in his hair. But the little Faun was happiest for he lay awake in his covert all that night and in the crimson dawn fell fast into a dreamless sleep.

Do you ask how I know of this . . . . of Pan, the Hybla Bees, the Satyr, the Centaur, the Harpies, of Persephone, and of the nearly-human Faun? Ah, gentlest of friends! The dust of me has blown for a thousand years in withering exile. I, too, was once of Arcadia.

The Departed

When the good Man died, they bore him to the graveyard by the blue sea, where a single ilex leans forever into the still, white, foam. And ere they consigned all that was mortal of him to the earth, each paid their tribute unto him.

And one said, "His years were few but blameless!"

"A kindly soul!" vouchsafed another.

"Nay," cried a third, "a martyr and a saint!"

And they condoled with one another and comforted themselves by weeping.

Then they were aware of a woman who stood veiled and apart and with her were seven that seemed servants.

And she came forward and said to them, "Lo! I, too, am here."

And they asked of her, "Who then art thou?"

And she answered them, "My name is Secrecy and these are my seven handmaidens, which would fain speak for they knew the dead Man in his lifetime. Did ye not, children?"

And with one accord they answered her, "Aye, Mother dear!"

Then the assembly wept again, one among another, saying, "Is not this marvellous, here are others who were beholden unto him? Who was like unto this good Man in love? Who was like unto him in friendship? Therefor, say what ye will, for ye too were of his kind."

And Secrecy beckoned to the Seven and said, "Come children, but I pray you be modest in speech and decorous in. your behaviour."

And the first came forward and she said, "I knew him well, and who if not I? I am Sloth. We were wont to lie together in the gilded sunshine all the blessed livelong day and sleep—and dream—and sleep'! Ah! would that he were but alive again!" And she wept but yawned thrice in the weeping.

Then came the second and she peered cautiously and said, "Know ye, perchance, where he hath hidden his glistening coin and his bewildering treasure? Belike not. but I do! I am Covetousness, and together we buried his hoard by the light of an evil moon. Ye wist not that—nav!" And she rubbed her hands and chuckled aloud.

Then came the third and her cheeks were blown scarlet but her lips were white. "Out upon ye," she cried, "and wherefor do ye mourn? He was my kinsman and many a bout had we striven together. I could tell a tale, that could I, but no more, for I am Wrath and I bear no chiding whilst I live!"

And the fourth came and gazed neither to the right nor to the left but said, "I am Pride and I would that I could grieve for my dead friend but I dare not belittle my dignity. Farewell, Comrade!"

And there came the fifth who was attired in a robe of emerald and in her hand she carried a cup of jade. And she said, "I am subtle and slow of speech and for this am I best beloved of Secrecy. I am hight Envy and I brew the distillation of every man's poison. He who is departed I knew well for I whispered to him at midnight such things as the reddening daybreak would appal to hear. A good slumber, sweet Snake!" And she glided with a shiver from his side.

And sixth came and she was pursy and scant of breath. And she said, "Art thou indeed dead! I, who am Gluttony, was thy choicest companion, thy most dependable ministrant. Did we not feast together thou and I, until thy lips grew weary and I too, was fain to cry out my sufficiency. Woe is me that this should have befallen thee! Needs must I become lean for sorrow at the thought thereof. Alas! Alas!"

And there came the seventh whose eyes were dusk and hollow, yet lightened as with a living flame from within. And Secrecy whispered, "This is mine eldest, Lust, who grieveth as though her heart would break."

And Lust knelt by him and kissed him passionately with her red lips, crying, "Thou didst love me mightiest of all and wert most insatiate of mine enamoured embraces, yet am I last to declare my grief. Farewell! Farewell! I shall never forget thee, not even until the end of time!"

And when she had ceased certain ones of the assembly murmured and cried out, "Ye lie! ye are not his friends but of a league of enchantment. In the name of his soul's salvation begone, ere we do ye harm!"

Then Secrecy smiled hiddenly and she said, "I know well that ye dare not so long as my Seven encircle me. But come, children, we leave these folk to their task. Adieu, gentles!" And so they passed on, some singing and some weeping, all save Pride who smoothed her purple raiment and braided her long yellow hair.

And when these were gone they burled the dead man in silence and left him at peace under the stars.

The Dog
(*After the Russian*)

Basil Serebjakoff, a student in the first term at the Moscow University, attended a Christmas gathering at the home of one of his friends in Chariton Lane. The evening passed slowly and stupidly enough but at two o'clock in the morning after protracted adieus and endless promises to meet again, the party disbanded.

"Who goes with me?" asked Basil as they reached the street.

"I go down the Basmanaja," said one.

"And I go to the Red Gate," said another.

"We cross the River," cried a chorus.

"Well," grumbled Basil, "I can't follow you all, so good-night and good luck to you."

Their voices sounded strangely in the deserted lane. Again there was a general round of hearty handshaking and much to Basil's satisfaction the set parted. He strode on alone toward the Pure Ponds and turned to his right into the Boulevard. The walk was covered with snow, smooth and new-fallen. The trees shimmered with rime and the boughs and their branches appeared to be draped in the softest texture of cotton. Through all this miraculous whiteness the trunks loomed so nearly perpendicular that they seemed like ghostly pollards, transfigured into fantastic elements. Light-headed, but somewhat unsteady in gait, Basil felt particularly cheerful this night. He had helped a few more of the convivial ones partake of two bottles of cognac, but Basil would have been the last to impute his light-headedness and his wayward steps to drink. It was the beautiful Nate Zwantzeff, he repeated to himself. The girl had gazed upon him only once, but in that once, by all that was true and worthy, her eyes had declared themselves. Then he pondered—had it really meant something? He started to sing:

> "Like a free-born son of ether,
> I shall take to heaven's weather—"

but he gave it up in disgust. His voice was pitched in a wild falsetto and he actually felt ashamed of his attempt.

Then he started to declaim Andrejeff's welcome to the Belgians aloud: "There will be a day when the allies will enter into Berlin...." but this sounded equally absurd in the bewitched stillness of the Boulevard. He quickened his steps under the spur of imagination. His love for Nate and for the world seemed to increase momentarily, it became hot and glowing. After a while he felt that he must sit down. A few paces brought him to a bench in the shadow of a hedge. About him slept the enchanted city and its mystic peace and unity filled Basil with an unknown yearning.

"How good it is to live and love!" he thought. "How foolish and futile people are to seek their happiness in strife and turmoil. I, for instance, could find no greater blessedness than to sit here forever on this bench in the solitary Boulevard, and look immortally into the lovely eyes of Nate. That would be happiness!"

And yet Nate had chosen to remain over night with her friend instead of delegating him as her escort home. He would return to her again ... he lay back and enjoyed the luxury of the thought.

Suddenly he leaned forward and gazed to the opposite side. There was something silhouetted there in the open space ... could it be ... yes, it was a dog. And such a dog! it was lean and shrunken and shivered perceptibly. Its fur (the little that was left of it) hung in curls and tatters to the mere framework of bones. It was wet ... he could perceive by the glistening, and it swayed gently as if to balance itself against weakness.

Basil's heart became pitiful. He called to it, names of dogs that he had known in his far-off boyhood. It pricked up its wedges of ears, wagged its stump of a tail, and made one or two steps in his direction. Then, as if prepossessed with a suspicion of fear, it halted and stood limply.

"Come on, I'll not hurt you," coaxed Basil, "you mustn't be afraid." The intonation of his voice was low and caressing. Somewhat reassured the dog made one more attempt. Then it halted again. Basil held his hand cajolingly forward and bit by bit, step by step, it drew near until it could sniff at the outstretched fingers. Basil felt the warm breath on their tips.

"Poor little doggie!" he continued, "nothing to eat, no shelter, and with all the world against you. Come a little closer, please! How would you like to come home with me, eh?"

The dog looked at him intently and shivered. The stump rose and fell from side to side in a vain effort to show that appreciation was never lost, no matter how dismal the circumstances. Basil petted it with long, gradual strokes. It had ceased shivering.

"Well you shall go," exclaimed Basil. He arose and whistled to it. It followed him contentedly, flitting back and forth from the hedges. How it understood! Basil surveyed it profoundly, neither young nor old it typified to him the average derelict of humanity. He mused aloud.

"Well, my dear, one can't call you exactly handsome. True you possess the distinction of consisting of component parts. . . . I refer in point of breeding. That head, for instance, with nothing much of imagination, might be taken for a hound's. Note the long nose and the melancholy eyes. The ears, I regret to state, are unbalanced. Terrier blood, in 'em though, without a shadow of doubt. The tail. . . ." he drifted into a long burst of laughter. The dog turned its head and then pressed ahead.

They had now passed the lonely Strastnoj and Tverskoj quarters, then turning into the Bronnaja appeared near Basil's home. He stopped short. The dog sniffed the air; it scented prime cooking. There was a light in the house. The landlady, a spinster, was still entertaining her lover, who had come to the city on a visit. Basil could see them chatting in the parlor through the open blind. He was still youthful, but she— Basil swore at her mentally. True he owed her for lodging and had explained that payment was only a matter of days, perchance of hours. The remittance had been delayed, why he could not pretend to guess, but if she would only have patience . . . she had given him a sharp and short answer.

It would never do to take the dog into the house. Clearly, discovery of the animal would bring on a dreadful scene and Basil hated scenes and above all, excitement. There was the _____, however, with its carrotty walls and general air of refined _____. He remonstrated with himself for his sentimental mood.

"Sorry, my dear, but I can't do it," he said to the dog. "My intentions are of the best but the landlady's—" he laughed lustily—"are quite the reverse. After all, charity is a thing of the past—twenty—thirty years, back. You must find yourself other quarters. Good-night."

He ran up the stairs but at the first turning, paused. The dog had followed him. He became insanely angry and stamping his feet, bade him begone. He even picked up a piece of ice from the stairs and threw it at him. The dog howled and fled down the landing.

Mavra, the cook, who let Basil into the foul and ill-ventilated kitchen, had heard nothing, for she rubbed her eyes sleepily and extinguished the candle on a shelf. He entered his room and lit his small student's lamp. It was warm and comfortable after the night without.

"Blessed be God!" whispered the student, "I rid myself of him at last! What an incubus, I say!" His eyes fell on the two loaves of bread, a gammon of bacon, and a rasher of sausage in the pantry. He grew conscience-stricken. The dog had been wet, hungry, shivering and miserable... his sin against one of God's creatures was unpardonable. Would it ever be forgiven him?

He seized the gammon of bacon and went back into the kitchen, down the stairs to the yard, into the street... the dog was gone. He had struck him too and the dog had cried out for sheer pain. That was the worst of it. And he could never hope to right himself in his own soul again.

Ferris Thone

"Of all the people I have ever met," began Hesketh, "the one I regret most is Ferris Thone."

"Thone—Thone?" interposed someone from a cloud of cigarette smoke, "never heard of him. What was he—a financier or an artist?"

"Neither," replied Hesketh: "a poet."

We settled back to listen. Hesketh was usually interesting. This year in London, another in Zambesi, a third in Pisa, Cairo or Constantinople, existence seemed to have given him much of diversion, interspersed with hardship. And such people he had known! Lafrache, the Parisian, who had murdered seven of his guileless wives, only to be committed to the guillotine by the eighth; Hadden, an obscurity in his time, but since, the greatest painter in the world: Sarbine, editor of the vitriolic "Le Singe," long consigned to a madhouse among the incurables, near Marseilles. How many more there were! Now it was to be Ferris Thone, but who Ferris Thone was, not the least among us had an idea. We listened in silence.

"When I first knew Thone," he began with a strange smile, "he lived in Whitechapel. Mother, a Jewess; father, oddly enough, a landed proprietor from Warwick gone downhill. Drank much, gambled still more, and finished in the gutter. In his twelfth year Thone's mother deserted and disappeared. I've been told on pretty creditable information that she went back to her folk and her orthodox race. She wanted to forget the son, no less than the father, it seems. Racial pride and instinct are, after all, the strongest of the abiding traits in the Semite.

"For years Thone knocked about among the hulks. Then, I met him. Let me tell you that for all the admixture of races there was outwardly little of the Hebrew in Thone. Blue-eyed, hair the colour of gold or honey, and with the profile of a Greek, he seems to have taken after his Warwickshire father, who was as handsome a man as one could find. Emotionally, Thone was a perfect oriental. Sensitive to the point of tears, shy at one time, loquacious at others, pride and subtlety lurked visibly in the cameo-face. Yes, he drank. Brierson, author of his forthcoming biography, declaims him habitually addicted to haschish and opium, but I never discovered the pale-green pellets, although his eyes were somnolent and drowsy with what one might well have taken for the heavy and bitter dreams of tragic genius.

"In 1916 I found the boy. He wanted to enlist, he told me! They laughed and jeered at his delicate person and mannerly air, bidding him wait a few years. I was on Apperley's staff at the time and beheld him in a corner of the room wiping the tears from his eyes with his coat sleeve. Had him come to my room. Showed me his poetry . . . By all the fates, I knew him for a genius the moment I read the first line. It was a poem on something or other relating to the Greeks. The lines concerned flowers, vine-leaves and grapes—all that sort of thing; but it was poetry, nevertheless—amazing poetry, as Brierson takes every occasion to say. The boy was a genius, there could be no doubt about it.

"Well, I did get him into service; he begged and pleaded and so nearly wept for the opportunity, that I couldn't resist. He was sent to the vicinity of T——, on the Meuse, where he earned a lieutenancy in less time than it takes the average recruit to become proficient in ordinary infantry drill. Letters came regularly for a while, then ceased. I understood. That was Thone's way—not pure selfishness, you must understand, but the heedlessness of a young god to whom life and the radiance of the whole day blinded into a sort of dazzling fury. Then terror. Brierson quotes Svelton on the court-martial. Something dreadful had happened. The gist of the matter never came to me. He was drummed into a foul little goal of the countryside and after the armistice brought back under surveillance to England. His release transpired in a few months.

"My influence got him out but the authorities wouldn't divulge the charges. A friend of Thone's, Millay, was directly implicated in the affair. They became thicker than proverbial grease on a candlestick, after his liberation. I lived in dread. During this period, however, it seems that Thone did his master-work. "The Chimaera" belongs to his latest phase. Brierson and one or two others have found its splendors drugged with opiate and perverse poisons, but each luminously concedes that there is in the marvelous poetry, something—call it what you will—that no one else has succeeded in accomplishing before or since. Baudelaire, Poe and candescent fire of his passionate niche hollowed in a marble wall beneath the cypresses—and Thone has his—but lighted with the incandescent fire of his passionate visualization. 'Blue and divine is the burning heaven of his poetry,' writes Brierson, 'even the shadows glow and coruscate with colour and jewels. Toward the end there enters an element of pity. Thone understands that beyond his miraculously-depicted world lies the immensity of a vast outer darkness—call it suffering, call it humanity, call it what one will—only Thone has dared to give and interpret the cry of rebellion.'

"I saw him twice after his release. Once, Millay was there and not much could have been said on either side. Thone was obviously ill at ease. Millay recited glibly certain experiences in the prison at T——, over which Thone laughed nervously. I asked him about his work. There was little to be done, he answered with a trace of repressed emotion. Later—maybe, but at present he had to recover his poise of mind. Loved dining out among people and visiting the gay cabarets and music-halls. Millay had a Rolls-Royce in which they took excursions sometime to Stratford and Bristol, at another to the grave of Swinburne on the Isle of Wight within sight and hearing of the lovely waters of the sea. You will remember that all this period Thone was at work completing "The Chimaera," which Brierson tells us might have been written by a Greek on a headland of Lesbos or by some one from the Homeric age, so far as modernity was concerned.

"My last sight of Thone was in a bookshop on Charing Cross Road. He seemed shabby. His cap was frayed, tie tousled. The face was still the face of a young Olympian's. Broken with Millay, he had so he said, but thought a good deal of him as no doubt Millay did of Thone. Gave me his address. Besought me to call the following week. Had a bit of money but his hoard was considerably diminished. Did I see a painting entitled "The Symposium" in the queer old art gallery near the British

Museum? It was Greece come to life again. What the hell use was there living nowadays anyhow? Somewhere in Attica the archaeologists would sooner or later unearth the lost secret of the whole pagan civilization. He would go there himself—if only he had the money to do so. There were still vases of green bronze to be discovered with figures of gold dancing along the sides, enough to stock the richest collection in the world. He had dreamed of some forgotten mountain recess among the Hellenes where the gods were still alive and the sky as everlastingly azure as in the first, unfrequented dawn. He must go . . . must go, yes! Would I come to see him—surely? I promised again. It was growing dusk in the bookshop but there remained a halo of gold, an indescribable nimbus of light about the head of Ferris Thone. Poor, great, half-Hebrew! But I never saw him again. . . ."

"He died?" asked someone solicitously.

"Yes," replied Hesketh, flicking the ash from his cigarette, "died a few days later in a slum-lodging with his manuscripts scattered right and left about him, and a note on his desk begging that the ancient Hebrew rite of Kaddish be spoken over his body in case of death."

"Died a Jew!" exclaimed the same voice incredulously. "But Millay—what became of his friend Millay?"

"Millay killed him," answered Hesketh dispassionately. "He was hanged for it."

"How comes it that none of us ever heard of the incident, nor of Ferris Thone and his poetry?" persisted the voice.

"Simple enough. It never happened. Thone never existed, nor did his poetry. I merely created him for an hour's entertainment," replied Hesketh with a sad smile and a nod of departure.

An Impression

All day it had rained and in the evening a light came from the sunset and caught the heavens into a vast blue and orange flower with crosses and shafts of white light that turned the buildings of the city into a prism. In the country the roads lay brown, yellow, or ocherous, and little dabs of olive or purple splotched the pools and ditches that stared back to space without end. . . .

The faces of the two men who walked west were lighted with gold.

Behind them lay the east ominously darkened and to the spectator at the side of the road it would have seemed the end of a tragic world. But to the two men, intent on the pedestrian labor of a journey uphill, it was no such a thing. The east turned pale and duskier,—then black. There were bird-cries and snatches of bird-song. At the top of the hill the light flickered for an instant, then disappeared. With its departure the two men became a part of the great darkness—the darkness of the heavens, the darkness of the earth, and the rumor of mysterious darkened things in the souls of mankind.

A Hopeless Love

All day long the cripple Jehan stood before the Church of the Little Innocents and begged an alms. From early, clear-hued dawn, when that ancient verger, the god and gentle Michael Sauviat jingled the half-hundred keys that opened the different wonderfully-depicted doors of the most beautiful edifice in the most beautiful world, to shaken violet dusk when all things became ineffable with a subtlety beyond even mortal comprehension; when one by one the many vari-coloured doves settled with soft monotonous cries on the great statue of Our Lady who was compassionately carven above, and the day's business was ended, he stood there and besought a pittance. And some—the few—gave him a little, but many—the [most] part—gave him nothing at all.

First then, came the weazened, wrinkled usurer, Maitre Girard Gossoyn, who answered this day in response to Jehan's cry, "Thrive, an thou must, worm, but not by my purse," and spat venomously at the wisp of a weather-beaten cur who preceded him. This was the Girard Gossoyn, reputed of enormous wealth but sad to relate, infamously got, whereof many an uncourtly tale had been rumoured in the community of the Little Innocents, murder and piracy on the high seas in early youth being an accepted version of the unholy tattle. If so, the usurer had strangely and miraculously reformed. Barely did the verger turn his key in the well-oiled lock, when Gossoyn, whose face men were given to say bore a thousand wrinkles for ten thousand sins, ascended the thirty odd stairs for the morning's mass. This Gossoyn, a notary by profession in his later years, kept a vintner's shop directly across from the Little Innocents, and thither, be it said, Master François Villon the poet (of whom anon) and his roystering braggart crew were wont to fare of an evening's revel, while mine host stood by and muttered his Ave Marys in dire repentance over each new bit of indelicate spicery.

Then came the dignified Sieur de Maline, marvellously genial old gentleman but somewhat vinously inclined, who gave the cripple no alms but ever vouchsafed him a bright nod and who had once confessed that "the poor were best off without gold or the wherewithal to purchase the precedence of luxury." And to this, Jehan had responded with an inward sigh and a dubious shake of his bare head. "Quite true," he had reasoned with himself for an hour afterward, "but how is one to live? And if it be in each man's consciousness to preserve the crystal essence of the soul, how may one do otherwise?" Clearly where was something at fault in the Sieur's dissembling philosophy.

After this there followed the handsome and hearty Madeleine de Lardot with her wealthy Sicilian niece Rosina who was cross-eyed and hatchet-faced and whose teeth chattered so incessantly that the ill-disposed (God punish them for their waggery!) had been heard to declare that the devil played them a perpetual horn-pipe whereof the end was never to be until the poor girl had been laid clean and white in her shroud, but who was, all this notwithstanding, so charitably inclined that the beggar Jehan would have sworn her imperfections were as nothing compared with her saintliness. Surely the Most High, that burning divinity on a throne of beaten gold in a sea of everlasting azure, had anointed her one of His wandering seraphim which, folk still declare, pass over the whole pitiful earth in deeds of succor and newly-shed mercy, albeit greatly disguised. Such evidence was not to be gainsaid. Jehan spake his gratefulness with eyes moistened and trembling lips.

Then passed the fop Tabary and the mercer's bouncing wife Ursula, both shivering with their illicit affection; fat Margot, who had begotten the parish with three successive bastards in as many years, so that Master Villon had composed the now-famous distich which we remember but had best not quote. And at evening when Jehan had gathered his crutch under his one useless arm there came Master François Villon the pot-poet himself, with de Montigny and another hobbledehoy companion on either shoulder. Then, while his friends entered Gossoyn's hostelry did the said François furtively drop a shining silver coin in Jehan's unsuspecting pocket, the while singing,

> Quand Saturne me feit mon fardelet,
> Ces maulz y mist, ye le croy . . .

and departed in a gust of shaking laughter. Master Villon's purse, by reason of good or neatly executed card-playing, had been only lately replenished. True, there were odd ballades and sundry tearful elegies that might be composed for the express purpose of purveying the necessities of a night's revel or a day's feasting, but it was mainly on his exceeding dexterity with cards and dice that Master Villon hazarded his petty and (lest we paint the colours too roseate) grimy existence.

Now it chanced that the Maitre Girard Gossoyn being, in his dotage, enamored of an innocent maiden newly come from the provinces, Bourbonnais, to be more explicit, brought her one freezing winter's day into the Little Innocents for the purpose of there making her his lawful wife. Dom Nicolas, the pimple-faced, squat-headed Picardy monk, Vicar to Hell, say some—by reason of his great friendship for the notary, officiated. Jehan, crouching beneath the figure of Our Lady, now covered with new-fallen snow, heard the soft preludium within and his heart was filled in ardent joy thereof. Soon the wedding procession appeared and descending slowly and with much solemnity past the beggar's station wound its way across the street into Gossoyn's house. Master Villon chanted a resonant epithalamium of his own masterful making. Dom Nicolas, swinging a censer, led majestically. Relatives the usurer had none saving an elderly half-witted great-aunt who had served him for a score of years and who now smiled and nodded elvishly through the wrinkles of her five and eighty helpless years. Jehan crossed himself against enchantment, the old lady's reputation being none of the best.

The procession passed, but in the beggar's starved and lightless heart something akin to actual love had descended. The bride, a slim, flower-faced girl of barely twenty, had deigned to cast on him a look of such distress and utter pitifulness that the beggar had instantly and sacredly construed this as one of affection. It was true. Between these two supremely alien souls there was to be henceforth only such an interest which links natures sublimely correlated into the passion of mutual pity and intimate despair. The procession vanished into the house. There was a burst of song and a chorus of many voices. The beggar Jehan smiled.

At night the candles were lit and Jehan crept into the warmth of the crowded entry to watch the festivities. Here, the outcasts of the quarter were assembled and the beggar was greeted with a cry of, "Place for the Crookback! Way for the Aristocrat of Tatters! Ah, here we shall find good begging forsooth! What! would'st thou make faces at the bride, too? Jehan! Jehan!"—and many more like pleasantries. The smell of the wines and pasties mingled unpleasantly with the damp, penetrating odor exhaled from the rags of the uninvited. Jehan stared straight before him. Against his side there huddled Margot, who had crept in from the snow and cold without. The poor girl was quite drunken.

"Jehan, dear good friend," she whimpered, "methinks these gentlefolk are a deal better off than I am. O—O—O! How unfortunate! I shall never be a grand lady again. Ah, me—never, never again!" She sighed profoundly and then commenced a long, piercing wail. Jehan shifted his position and surveyed the party with interest. He knew that pity of any sort was lost on Margot.

Master Villon, by this time well in his cups, sat fingering a taper flagon of the usurer's best Rhenish, imitating in a somewhat shrill and uncertain voice the very sound and echo of a young damoiselle's wayward lute. This was greeted by the guests with huge sallies of laughter, the more so since Ramus, the burgomaster Leroune's youngest son, a fellow with an enormous faculty for extravagant, noisy humour, had risen unsteadily from his corner seat and after a frowzy fashion, embraced the discordant minstrel in such a manner as men are used to do with the women they madly love. Villon, no whit disconcerted, repulsed him mirthfully with a quatrain of Provençal poetry, quoted the devil knows wherefrom.

All this time Gossoyn gazed hard with his calf's eyes at his bride, who listened shyly and with slightly reddened cheeks to the occasional obscenity of the guests. After the truffles Dom Nicolas condescended to make a speech—and what a speech it was! Larded with erudite Latin, Greek, and (for all we know) Saracenic phrases; interspersed by such deft and intrepid allusions to the ancient heathen gods and goddesses perched on high Olympus, as must have struck many a heart with the precariousness of the couple's position—it was a mercy that the monk's sermon ever came to a fitting end. His auditors, however, applauded loudly and Margot, who had crept unnoted to Jehan's side again, sobbed out a loud "God help us" at the close, but would not cease her moaning and crying until the usurer's servants had forcibly carried her away.

By dawn the candles were guttered and the revelers asleep, one and all. Villon lay huddled a heap by the cold fireplace, his mouth twisted good-naturedly into the semblance of a smile. Dom Nicolas, with his head propped back against a high seat, snored as lustily a song as any devout psalm-singer in an orthodox congregation. Not a stir was there. Tabary twitched nervously and with ominous ill-comfort by an arch, dreaming perchance of his evil love for the mercer's Ursula. In the entry lay the outcasts and it was chill. The frost had made rarely beautiful flowers on the notary's mullioned windows but the yellow light gave promise of a fine winter's day. Jehan awoke and began very softly to repeat his prayers. At their close he opened the door stealthily and made his way into the street.

In the Spring the square patch of turret-haunted sky above Jehan's head became as blue as that adorable altar-piece of Paradiso, painted by the gracious Meynheer Jan Van Eyck of Bruges city, for the Little Innocents. In that picture, as is well known, one may observe how on either side of the golden region wherein are placed the then-happy Adam and his lovely spouse Eva, who legions of the heavenly host continually take flight into an azure heaven, and how this incessant play of radiance on their holy wings and ethereal vestitures have moved pious folk to say that God, who sitteth on top of the picture (as in heaven) for judgement, could an he but would, bid them ascend and descend as a proof of his divine experimental power and reciprocation. So, up and down, to the left and to the right, all the bright and blessed day long flew the swallows; for it was a season of love and it behooved these tiny creatures of God's own beneficence to bear the most of their slight, bittersweet existence. Once—ah, once!—a lark, strayed mayhap out of its demesne of green meadows and quiet waterways, arose sheer and precipitate from the street, but ere it has passed out of ken there fell such a song as made the tears to start into Jehan's eyes and blinded him inconsolably with a mist of weeping. Thereafter, he listened patiently for the same song, but the poor feathered thing, frightened apparently by the dust and din, much preferred its placid countryside to the spirited unrest of the Little Innocents. It had never ventured to return again.

One fine day the lords and ladies of the court went maying to the farther side of the Seine. The entire community turned out at their doors on this occasion. Lydie, the shrewish wife of the constable Regnault, who had once been ducked for beating her husband into a faint, left her day's washing and stood with arms akimbo and an ingratiating smile at the noble procession. Quill in hand, Gossoyn peered warily from his half-opened door, whilst Villon, sunning himself on a bench before the notary's house, smiled a bored smile, as though to say—"Do such matters interest you, O my neighbors? Welladay! May my soul perish utterly if I find therein aught but the veriest coxcombery!" And truly, it was an open secret that the King of France, than whom there was none greater in Christendom, had twice requested Master Villon to become his court-laureate, the which position held tithes and titles numberless, but that Villon had refused all this out of deference to the lowly circumstances of his friends and companions, and in such wise was to be commended for his humbleness as well as his genius.

As the procession, with a flutter of pennons, banners and insignia, paused before descending the steep and narrow declivity leading to the ancient Roman fortifications, Madam Gossoyn took her place at the open window. Jehan, who had waited for such an occasion many a day, eyed her raptly. Rumour had been only too true. The beautiful eyes, that grave and condescending mould of mouth and cheeks, as yet so graciously childlike, showed unmistakable visitations of sorrow. For an instant she gazed below, then quickly and tremulously her eyes met the beggar Jehan's.

"O my Love," whispered the beggar who understood, "O my Love, thou art mine! Mine, as lawfully as though I had taken thee in wedlock. We shall never know each other, thou and I—but take comfort. My heart is as a flame before an altar of thine own lighting!"

Day after day the failing Madame Gossoyn appeared at her window. On a single occasion (the only one, in fact) she had even ventured to accompany her elderly husband to his everlasting morning's mass. There descended a warm, gentle rain. The trees hung heavy and odorous with bloom. That great flock of doves which are constantly accustomed to seek their livelihood near the Little Innocents, fluttered and fell before Our Lady's figure as in a very miracle of hushed adoration. Gossoyn am-bled behind, arm in arm with the scrivener, one Aristides, a skulking, mongrel Greek. The usurer displayed quite a partiality for the fellow.

"A glorious creature, this wife of thine," remarked the scrivener covertly lifting his head.

"Aye," replied the usurer in a sudden burst of confidence, "but she fails quickly and wherefor I can give no reason, since—" his brow knitted darkly, "the woman hath every luxury I can find means to provide her with."

The Greek's face became a mask of old. "Gossoyn!" he whispered.

"Ha—," said the usurer interrupted from a profound revery.

"Would'st thou hear something to thine interest?" he ventured.

"So it be short and sweet," answered the usurer sourly, "what is it? God knows—" crossing himself devoutly—"I defy the devil and his lurid misrule."

"Thy wife will die." said the Greek in a tone of suppressed tragedy.

Now the usurer, for all his miserable, profitless existence, was endowed with his tittle of wit, so he asked grimly, "How now; and what is to become of the rest of us?"

"Ah," breathed the scrivener working the muscles of his lean face, "there it is! But to few of us hath it ever been given to perish for love! Oh, Love! Love! once it taketh one in toil, then

> Omnes humanos sanat medicina dolores:
> Solus amor morbi non amat artificem!

Which is to sain, no learned leech, no physician however skilled and versed in his profession, may cure the redubitable smart of Dame Venus. Some are mortified in their own pleasure but the most part survive aimless and similarly misshapen. Thy wife will die, Gossoyn!" repeated the scrivener heroically.

"Have a care!" thundered the usurer. His breath had begun to pant and wheeze in the fashion of old, decrepit men. He stopped short and gripped the scrivener fiercely by the shoulder.

"What old wife's flummery is this? Tell me quick! Tell me quick, or by God—"

"Soft, Gossoyn!" protested the scrivener, freeing himself. His voice was thin and pining. Now, it insinuated itself with well-chosen modulation. "I tell the truth and if the truth be ill-taken, methinks I err on the better side of heaven and virtue."

"Knowest thou then—" began the usurer.

"Not I, certes," replied the scrivener waving an airy, slender hand. "I do but conjecture."

"Then have done," said the usurer speciously. He reassured himself but nevertheless his heart was sick with an ominous fear. It might be Villon. But no, drabs and ill-starred queans did well enough for the poet when his muse fell into disfavor. Besides, the fortunate ones were certain of advertisement in rondel, chanson, or a perfect gem of a ballade. Nor by the slightest concession, Dom Nicolas. The priest had been in liquor since his last mass more than a month since. Not unlikely, the man of religion lay drunk in an out-cellar of Ribou's, where similarly inclined persons were to be regaled with a citation of select miracles and certain zestfully-told tales in one and the same munificent breath. The usurer covered his perturbation and gravely followed his young wife into the church.

One day she took to bed. Sabastien Gotet, a paunch-bellied little man with eye-brows like blown furze and a nose of unbelievable dimensions, was thereupon summoned to administer bodily comfort.

He quoted Plato, Zenoras and Aristotle, cited the differentiation of Galen, Celsus and Hippocrates on the efficacy of strengthening emulsions, and then with a conciliatory cough advised that the patient be forwith bled and given a prescription of his own making, hight Lithospermon. "The which," he added with a professional fervor not unmixed by dignity, "though incumbent of much discomfort in taking (being wry and acrid) hath never failed to heal and allayeth both the fret and fever in this particular ailment." So saying, he parted. The usurer had not spoken to him in twenty long years.

"Never!" cried he to Dom Nicolas, who stood at the bedside with a breviary, piously intoning his prayers. "Bleeding, forsooth! What!—a shadow? If we die, we die, God help us all! but I say that no ass of a physician shall hasten either of us to an early end!"

Nevertheless, Madame Gossoyn weakened with rapidity. On the third day she begged her husband to move her bed to the window. A fever of gradual unrest seemed to shake the dying young woman as she gazed in the direction of the Little Innocents. Particularly did it seem that her eyes were fastened to one spot.

"Vigilate et orate!" quoth the priest lifting his face paternally to heaven. "She craves the comfort of God's high and holy habitation, let us trust that it is not too late. Take heart, my friend, more omnibus communis, others have suffered the selfsame grief. Ah, me! how infinitely many!" Gossoyn turned moodily away.

By night the poor soul had become madly out of her head. Scraps of songs and stray ballads long since forgotten followed one after the other from her stricken lips. Insistently she besought Dom Nicolas to accept of an alms and after a moment's interval wept piteously over his imaginary deformity. The bewildered monk crossed himself hastily, being a devout believer in the devil's pertinacity at all times and occasions.

Suddenly she called an unintelligible name. Gossoyn bent over her but she seemed not to perceive him in spite of the light that shone full in her eyes. "Listen!" she said and then, "come close [for] I see thee not, for it begins to darken!"

"What is it, wife?" asked the usurer kneeling by the bed.

She stroked his face gently while her lips made a last attempt to fashion the syllables of words into speech. One would have likened her to an unhoused leaf swaying in the sudden impetuosity of an autumnal wind.

Then she said, "I have forgotten thy name; I have forgotten all else in the world—but I have loved the, kind one, since the beginning. Thou knewest that?" she asked.

"Aye," answered the usurer with lips a-tremble. The lie burnt his tongue, even his very soul, for it had begun to dawn upon him that her lover was nowise himself.

"Kiss me," she prompted softly and Gossoyn kissed her on the lips without another spoken word.

"So now leave me," she said when he had done, "but bid my husband give his money-bags to the poor and misfortuned. Haddest thou not need of them thyself? Yet sith I am tired, I must fain sleep." And so the usurer after closing her calm and glazed eyes left the room as one in a dream to make preparation for the disposal of the dead body, while the man of God and fell asleep over his prayers.

"And that," writes our unknown chronicler (from whom I derive this tale) in closing, "is the certain truth respecting the relation of Girard Gossoyn and his dead wife, but inasmuch as people disposed to deal foully with truth have privily whispered incredible tales into the ears of the insufficient and weak-minded, be it known (I speak with Heaven to witness) that these things were related to me by Dom Nicolas himself, when that worthy, then lean and shrunken with age, has passed his four score years and ten. And I mind well the chuckle with which the old priest was wont to tell how, on the next day following Madame Gossoyn's death, Margot with much lamentation gave birth to her fourth, a boy, but so nearly like his mother that the father remained secret and unapprehended; and that on the evening of the same day the body of Jehan, the beggar, was found washed in at low tide on those desolate reaches by the Seine, with one hand strangely folded across his heart, which was regarded as singularly out of accordance with nature."

The One Who Found Pity

I slew my friend in his garden at night and he cried out in his agony, "Alas! Have I not honoured thee before all men? Didst thou not partake of joy even as myself?"

And I said to him in mockery, "True, but I coveted thy riches and when I flattered thee most then did I most hate thee. Dost thou think I fear thee dead?"

"Thou shalt yet know it," he said softly.

"What meanest thou?" I asked as I drew him to me.

"Pity," he answered, but his eyes were already glazed and he fell back in death.

Then I dug a pit and buried the slain man therein. And I took unto me all that was his, even his house and his vineyards, his gold and his treasure. And I feasted to the full in my new possessions, save when darkness fell upon the face of the earth.

For each night the dead man stood at my side and when I had perceived him he said, "Hast thou much joy, O my friend?"

And I answered him, "Yes, I am surfeited." Then he said, "Thou shalt yet know my intent and therewith shall come peace unto thy soul!"

But I could not rest, so I sold his house and his vineyards and took away with me his gold and treasure. And I boarded a Phœnician galley to Tyre which was laden with ivory in exchange for vestments and purple dyes.

But it blew a wind and a storm arose at night and in the darkness the mariners called to their ancient gods, some to Ashtaroth and Baalim, some to Diana, and still others to Apis of the Egyptians, all of which were nailed on high against the masts.

And when they saw that I did not pray they marvelled and asked, "Why dost thou not pray to thy God? Is it because thou holdest ours in scorn before thine own?"

And I answered with laughter, "My God is as powerless as yours, yet of old they say he wrought wondrous things."

Then they grew wroth and would have cast me into the sea but they took counsel with one another and the foremost spake, "Abide, but thou shalt reckon with us when the tempest hath ceased. Peradventure, is this of thine own making."

But a blast of lightning clove the ship mid-ways in twain and the sea engulfed every living thing. And I clung to the prow on which was figured a siren and when it grew dawn I saw that there was still another who had done likewise, even the one who had threatened me in the night.

And he cried, "Either thou diest or I, so that I may avenge the souls of the dead!" And I answered him, "Be it thou, then," and held to him until the light of death shone in his eyes.

And at morn of the next day the sea cast me ashore where I lay on the sands as one deprived of speech. And when I opened my eyes there was an assembly that stood before me, and they were men of great dignity.

And they said to me, "Lord, we awaited thy coming."

And I asked in amazement, "How knew ye thereof?"

And one answered with an obeisance, "Three wise men who follow a certain star that is set in the pagan night. Our King being newly dead they counselled us to anoint thee in his place, yet further know we not, save that at sun-down they took their several burdens and rode away into the desert."

Then they placed me on a litter and bore me into their city. And when the inhabitants saw me they cried, "Hail to thee, all Hail! Thou shalt rule us with justice and pardon our enormities. Our last King did evil and we followed him blindly as sheep do their shepherd, but our eyes have since been opened and we would fain do what is wisest among ourselves."

And they clothed me in a robe of violet and led me to a throne which was hewn from one vast chrysolite and surmounted an eminence to the entire city. And they said to me, "Sit thou here, and whatsoever thy heart craveth, let it find fulfillment."

And I ruled over them for seven years but I did even as he who had been before me, for I crowned my head with roses and lay supine in lust and revelry. And they arose against me as one man and would have stoned me to death, but that I fled in the evening out of the gates of the city. And I entered the desert and sat down alone to brood over my perished hopes and my lost kingdom.

But a serpent came forth from the night and crawled up to me with glistening eyes. And it said to me, "Brother, I am forsaken of all things yet my heart is filled with love. Wherefore am I an outcast?"

And I answered without fear, "Thou didst evil in the time past."

And it murmured, saying, "But I repented me long ago. Beside, there was one who tempted me, one with golden hair."

And I asked, "Who tempted thee?"

And it answered with a moan, "Lilith!"

Then something stirred within me that I had not known before and I said, "I feel for thee." And the serpent murmured, "Ah, brother! thou hast pity," and it crept again into the darkness.

Then a hare limped up to me and it said, "Brother, I bleed to death. Bind up my wound so that I may at least not perish of thirst." And I tore mine own raiment and bound it thereto, to stanch the flow of blood. And I asked of it, "Was it one of mine own kind that did thee this hurt?"

And it answered, "As I lay with my young ones in a wheat-field the reapers came by at twilight and far and wide they cut down the shining breadth of wheat. And the sickles flashed and fell but when they rose again my young ones lay dead before mine eyes. Brother, wherefore did they slay them that nursed at my breasts?"

And I said, "I know not, but my heart is heavy for thee." And it cried, "Brother, thou hast pity" and went on its way.

Then a wolf came suddenly before me, crying, "Brother, I hunger. Give me to eat lest I perish."

And I said to him, "How can I give thee that which I lack myself?"

And he answered, "I would have slain thee but I dare not. Thou hast pity," and so saying he disappeared.

Then the dead man stood again before me and I beheld him after seven long years. And he said to me, "Hast thou forgotten me, O my friend?"

Then I bowed my hands in my head and wept. And he said to me, "Why dost thou weep?"

And I answered in abasement, "For pity."

And he said, "These are my tears, even as thy soul is mine."

And I said, "Do with it as thou wilt, for I did thee evil."

And he made reply, "Thou but slewest thy hate and thou hast found that which abideth with mankind until the demolition of eternity, that which is Pity. Arise and return to thy kin for they will make thee welcome. I leave thee forever."

And I went.

Christmas-Eve with Sherlock Holmes

All the way to Number 221-B Baker Street the heavens were filled with an impedimenta of what appeared to be cotton-wadding, but which was in reality, snow. It fell with a soft, sifting sound, occasionally punctuated by the wind, with a sibilance and murmuring that actually simulated the deliberate, low voices of human beings. The street-lamps glowed fuzzily through the white haze and the curbs of the streets were already heaped with high mounds and drifts of snow. I let myself into Number 221-B Baker Street with a key that Sherlock Holmes had given me many years ago. A lamp shone in his window, and under it was a wreath of red berries and holly. The apartment was dim with the one light and a fire burned cozily but not too conspicuously in the open fireplace. There was still a smell of Holmes's favorite tobacco-mixture, but my friend was not in evidence. An open book lay on the table, and I made so bold as to read the title. It was an excellent indication of the evening we were to spend together—"A Christmas Carol," by Charles Dickens. He arrived almost immediately, rubbing his hands and shaking the soft, glittering fleece of snow from his coat.

"You came directly from Limehouse," he said smiling and holding forth his hand. I shook it heartily and wished him a Merry Christmas, adding: "How did you know I came from Limehouse?" He gave me a short chuckle: "There's a small particle of the 'Aurifera Veritatis' on your sleeve, which I know is sold nowhere else but in the dusky, little herbal shop of Tung Fo in Limehouse." "You are right," I answered, "and it is to Tung Fo I went on a professional call. He is in a bad way with advanced consumption, and the joss-sticks are burning on either side of his bed." Sherlock Holmes filled his pipe, and applied a flickering match to it with the odd little gesture that I have seen repeated a thousand and one times. "Where is your wife?" he asked suddenly. I was filled with contrition: "With friends," I replied. "She begged me to come and share this Christmas-Eve with you." He nodded silently, then assented: "Unlike most women, she has understanding." He continued: "You can see for yourself that I was prepared to spend this Christmas-Eve alone with Charles Dickens. I was brought up on him. Was it not you, my dear Watson, who once sagely remarked that every human being had a bit of old Scrooge imbedded in him, and that you found an overwhelming similar quantity in no-less a person than your friend—myself?" I laughed: "A passing fancy!" "But it is good to know that you will spend this one night of all nights with me. These silent companions," he motioned to his row-on-row of books with the lamplight gleaming on their burnished bindings, "seem somewhat lonelier for all of my own brief conviviality this snowy evening. Shall we drink?" He poured us both a golden liquor from his half-filled crystal decanter whose cut facets shone like so many diamonds. "This is an amontillado of the Poe-period. Let us forget the messages of violence and vindictiveness that we have so often been forced to deliver. Surely, in spite of the scoundrelism, brutishness, rascality and evil credulity that relays certain victims into the by-paths of the unrighteous, there are ways of peace." I took his hand and shook it with feeling. "I have made up my mind," he said with great emphasis. "As to what?" I queried. "I shall leave Baker Street," he answered. I lifted both hands in amazement. "Nonsense—" I began, but he halted me. "There is a place in Sussex Downs. It is miles and miles removed from the nearest railroad, and all habitations are so far away that it is singularly perfect in its isolation. I shall raise bees," he added curtly. "You must come and visit me when the mood is on you. The cottage I have taken must by this time be buried deep in snow. I shall be at peace."

There was a sound of singing outside—fresh, young and clear soprano voices chanting a Christmas carol. "In the meantime," my friend continued, "there will be work for us to do on the morrow. You must come with me at the break of day." I was all alert with the cry of the hunt; I could hear the fury of the hounds once again. "You will remember that I was out when you first came in," he said, "and for a reason. I have been to the telegraph-office to wire our coming. On one of the wildest and stormiest portions of the coast of Cornwall—Trethven, to be explicit—they have discovered a body that bears every indication of being either a freak from a circus, or a monster. Rigor mortis had just set in. The fangs of this horrible creature, protruding from a salival mouth, were at least six inches in length. A strange, silver dagger with a blade sharpened to unbelievable slenderness, protruded from its breast. Runic letters spelled the word 'Otvos', on the widest portion of the blade. You and I, my dear fellow, will probably never again find an instance of such sheer moribund criminality, coupled with such frightful horror." His pipe had gone out and he lighted it again, puffing rhythmically. "We must have another drink," he said after a long silence. He refilled our glasses. "A toast to Christmas Eve, to London, yes, and to the whole world!" His voice became strong and his eyes sparkled. "You must return to your wife now, my dear Watson, and extend my wishes to her, too . . . for a Merry Christmas!" He took me to the door. It was snowing still heavier, if possible, and there were faint voices in the falling fog of snow—children were singing snatches of carols, cabbies stridently wishing their fares a Merry Christmas, and, as I descended the stoop, Holmes' landlady came panting and puffing up the four steps with a bright nod and a "Merry Christmas, Sir!"

Sherlock Holmes stood for a moment, with the lighted kerosene-lamp held aloft in his hand. His thin face shone with unaccustomed emotion as he called after me: "Remember, my dear Watson, that even if this holocaust of snow continues—bright and early tomorrow morning: 'THE ADVENTURE OF THE RUNIC DAGGER!'"

V. Nonfiction

Tips from the Hobo

Harry Boud's initial number of *The Quaker City Amateur* is very interesting. Keep it up, Harry, and follow in your brother's footsteps.

Whew! Great Scott! We were nearly roasted when *The Furnace* reached us, for "With the Fireman" is hot enough to drive away chills. We advise you to cool down to about thirty degrees below zero, Dillon, for your arguments are entirely too warm to suit "us northern folks." Your vocabulary seems to be limited to such words as "cad," "idiotic," etc. Get a good dictionary, Dillon, and find some decent words with which to express your *noble* opinions. A word to the wise, etc.

Mostly political news and squabbles in *The Night Owl* and *Juvenile Literati*. Why not give us something more interesting, for politics are quite monotonous.

The Criterion of Kansas City is a most meritable paper. "Criterion" by Melvin Thalman is most ably written. Why not drop the Negro Question, Miss Cohn. It has, like Socialism, been discussed so often that it is worn quite threadbare. Give the Negro Question a decent burial and be through with it forever, for we expect better things of you, Miss Cohn.

Foster does great honor to the office of Manuscript Manager by issuing such a good paper as *The Centurion*.

A very interesting paper is *The Book Worm*. It bores right through.

In the December *Marune* Miss Phelan gives the opinion that stories and poems should be excluded from the official organ. You are mistaken, Miss Phelan. We think there is nothing more enjoyable than a good story or a poem.

After a long absence the *Siren* again makes its appearance. The reviews by Miss Phelan and William Murphy are very interesting. *Le Diable* is "just lovely," although some articles are strong enough to drive a person hysterical. Can you give us a ticket to Hades, Dillon? We would like to meet His Satanic Majesty.

You can always depend upon "Hustle" to put some good things in *Good Things*. Mrs. Emory's story is, as are all her stories, very interesting.

Venus, Pandora and *Clara De Hirsche Journal* make a fine appearance. "The girls" must have "lots" of spare time.

By the Way

I first became interested in Amateur Journalism by seeing a statement in the *Golden Days* that Boud would send a bunch of papers to anyone interested in Amateur Journalism. On becoming a member of the U. A. P. A. I immediately started to write stories and poems with a vim. Had it not been for the efforts of Boud I am sure I would not have published a paper. But he wrote to me occasionally, sent me bundles of papers and cleared man)r of the difficulties that usually beset an amateur journalist. So that, I naturally have him to thank for starting me on in my career in Amateur Journalism.

As this is my first issue I beg to be excused if this number be somewhat crude, but the following issues will show that I can do "somethin'."

There are a certain few Uapaians who are terribly afflicted with a dreadful disease called "swelled head." I will not mention their names, but would like to know if any fellow member not afflicted with the disease could prescribe a cure for the sufferers.

Why do not publishers send their papers to members not publishing a sheet? It is a fact that sometimes during a whole month I did not receive a single paper. And yet some of the members grumble because a person gets inactive. Do you blame him? A new member naturally wants to hear all the news of the Association, and when he receives no papers he sizes up the Association as a hot-bed of selfishness. Can not this evil be remedied? It is "up" to the publishers to do it!

I shall mail this paper to every live amateur. No "dead-heads" on our list.

It is our intention to support John W. Boud for the presidency of the U. A. P. A . He is in every respect a loyal and earnest member and has only by hard work reached his present position. We advise every member, who has the interests of the Association at heart, to vote for Boud at the coming election. As to Cohen, we do not think he has done much to aspire to be president of the Association—in fact, summing it all up, he has done no work at all.

We also think that Dillon is in every respect suited for the office of Eastern Ms. Manager. He is at this time the most active of amateurs and works hard for the interests of the Association.

We shall *roast* anyone needing it, and expect you to do the same thing to us.

Cleveland Notes

By virtue of the inactivity of its members, the Cleveland Amateur Press Club has formally disbanded. When the organization was organized about three years ago with Brodie as its leading spirit, and Thrift, Zeigler, Harris, Kostir, and Fingulin, each sturdy in their united effort to attain the ideal of a literary club, it was universally conceded by the mother association, that the club was a strong factor to the making of the National. But "time drives flocks from field and fold;" after the convention the attendance dwindled down to two and three. Even one apathetic paper a month became an almost unknown occurrence; where heretofore each meeting brought a round half-dozen distributions. The worst and final blow was Tim's Resignation.

I am almost loth to write these words when I bethink myself of the long winter evenings spent down in Brodie's print shop. A knock at the screened basement window—an answered "yes, I'm coming"—and Brodie, candle in hand awaited us at the cellar stairs. I count those nights as the few really pleasurable times I have ever had—to treasure up in my heart for ever.

Richard Kevern is attending the Ohio State University. He intends to issue another miniature *Mite* in December.

William Feather served as "cub" reporter for the *Cleveland Press* during the last summer. As I understand it, he is attending Adelbert College of this city.

Zeigler has a splendid *Synthetique* in press. This will probably be his last offering to Amateur Journalism.

Ballads

Balladry, it has always seemed to me, is the one connecting and reverent link between the green and gold decadent era of the renaissance, and this, the modern commercial spirit of an age wherein one for very lack of the Midas' touch, suffers immeasurably the torture of an art for art's sake, creed.

"The more rude and wild the state of society," says Scott, "the more general and violent is the impulse received from poetry and music. The muse, whose effusions are the amusement of a very small part of a polished nation, records in the lays of inspiration the history the laws, the very religion, of savages. Where the pen and press are wanting, the flow of numbers impresses upon the memory of posterity the deeds and sentiments of their forefathers. . . . Hence, there has hardly been found to exist a nation so brutishly rude, as not to listen with enthusiasm to the song of their bards, recounting the exploits of their forefathers . . . or hymning the praises of their deities."

And this is aptly and conclusively true. For a perfect and punctitious chronicle of the dare-devil mastery and the innate glory of a departed time, these literally god-like records are priceless of the casual delver of the musty past. Of a necessity, time and the many itinerant commentators have so corrupted these ballads as to distort them out of all shape and sacred semblance. Scott, while his services wrought an inestimable good to the recovery and systemizing of the countless number of fragments extant, occasionally and alas, that too often, deliberately substituted his own tenuous falsities for the more archaic and, therefore better, transmutation of expression and exuberance. In all cases this vilification is easily apparent. The medieval ring strikes dead and sodden where even the least catch or phrase has been abstracted, and the lovely aptitude of grace and sweetness usually present in the original, sounds stilted and offensive with the sudden lapse of four centuries or more. A splendid example of these corrupted inanities, driftwood and ambergris interwoven alike, is Scott's famous version of the Binnorie burden. I quote in part:

> "The strings he framed of her yellow hair,
>   Binnorie, O Binnorie:
> Whose notes made sad the listening ear;
>   By the bonnie mill-dams of Binnorie."

The most inconvincible tyro will readily pronounce this an imposture. The transgression is almost unpardonable on Sir Walter's part. Having as he had, the best facility and favor for a Scottish border minstrelsy, and the versification should have been given to us clear and untrammeled, simplicity itself, yet without the very simplicity that makes strength and sweetness and purify.

Many of the ballads, however, have escaped maltreatment. With these one can best understand, allowing the few subservient changes, their sweet pregnancy and blossomy reach. Subjects that are esoteric Shaw might have treated with the utmost of leering duplicity, are here ventured upon frankly and fervidly; and it is this openheartedness, this same unperfunctory frankness, that undoubtedly held the rapt attention of the wayward country folk to the troveurs or minstrels. They sought no facetious problems pertaining to complex passions and dogmas of a spiritual habitation; an illicit love, and passing mistress or an unearthly wicked nobleman contained all the stress and tragedies needful to their little chanties. It is, too, in these ballads, that one comes across those occasional glimpses of strange terror-weird forebodings of an unknown fear, stifled by awful aching repression—a grimness to be met with in the later desultory Elizabethan dramatists—and our own, stern, iconoclastic Ibsen.

Of the later-day balladists, Swinburne is undeniably the best. His verses are like the swerve and rhythm of a summer sea, faultless in their omnipresent beauty and thought. He understands perfectly the art of ballad reiteration, and no where unless it be in the majestic might of Rossetti's "Troy Town and Eden Bower," may be found such gracious effect and understanding as are weft upon in the repetition and rendering of the alternative lines of each stanza.

Longfellow has done exceptionally well in his "The Wreck of the Hesperus"; also Whittier and Lowell in their redundant mass of folk lore. Yet even these, proper examples though they be, are merely the bastard after-glow of an unusually great and glorious sunset. In them, the elements provided for are weak and flabby—disproportionably so; and it is the personality and subject matter alone, that saves them from everlasting distrust and perdition.

NOTE—Preferably the best selections of the old ballads may be found in the "Golden Treasury Series." Mr. Allington, editor if this little volume, has contributed a remarkably dispassionate and succinct essay on their distinction, declaiming it his intention in presenting the volume for the matter of fact reader "to enjoy them simply as poems, unvexed with dull and trivial questions," hitherto largely a part of the old collections.

George Herbert

It is compatible and perfectly proper to assume that theological verse, allowing its bounds and subservience of expression, must by a necessity be confined strictly to the dull tenor of mediocrity. From the luminous fragility of Robert Wisdom's and George Wither's singing psalms, to the sniveling and whimpering morality of Horae Lyrica and The Christian Year, this with the single and positive exception of George Herbert, will apply. Following as the latter does, the extreme and indisputable brilliancy of the Elizabethan period; ushered and aided, as it were, "by the first poet of the world in some things"—John Donne, one is not loth to say, that for sheer simplicity of conception, and a "touch" of almost "Shakespearian felicity," this the most lovable of all divines, must take a place not higher and but little lower than that of Wordsworth. Herrick, "first in rank and station of English songwriters" though he be, has little that will rend the uneasy soul as the lives of Herbert:

> Until the years again restore
> Their dead and time shall be no more.

And while Donne, with his oft-quoted:

> A bracelet of bright hair about the bone,

has in a great measure this quality which drew for him the absolute praise of Ben Jonson, the measure of metaphysical science, he has saturated his elegies with, render them both inept and inadequate for serious and subsequent reading. George Herbert, however, has none of the good, old Doctor's inevitable obscurity and apish petulance. For this let us be thankful.

Charles Lamb

In all the wide and varying range of English literature it is difficult to find one on whom there has been accorded a greater and lovelier homage of benediction and adoration, than that of the average literary wrangler for the sweet and persuasive personality of Charles Lamb. A faith as pure and purely elusive as his unsurpassing love for little children, a depth and breadth of magnitude only equaled by Browne and Milton at their best—and shall we wonder that the acerbetic old Gebir stooped to kiss Lamb's exquisite, woven raiment with a very reverent humility?

Perhaps the only regrettable, (and to my way of thinking), peaceable transgression, second only to his unjust expression of some nationalities in the "Imperfect Sympathies," (a bit of balderdash which I take the opportunity to affirm we may well spare from the incomparable Essays as an outburst of erraticism fairly provokable on Elia's part), is Lamb's totally misconceived inappreciation of Scott and Shelley. It may be that Scott's unprecedented popularity had led Lamb to believe that anything appealable only to the novel-reading public at large, might hold little of ready interest to his, the rougher Elizabethan appetite. At any rate, it is hardly possible or probable that he had seen or read the "Cenci," which, without a doubt, his critical insight would have enabled him to pronounce the only tragedy since the "imperishable" Duchess of Malfi; comparable with "Othello."

Somewhere Mr. Swinburne has given us his opinion, and I quote from memory, that "no labour could be at once so delightful and so useless, so attractive and so vain, as the task of writing in praise of Lamb." It comes upon me suddenly, my first hap-hazard acquaintance with Charles Lamb. I had been browzing, as is my usual wont, in an old book-shop, when I unearthed a distinctly frayed but fragrant edition of Canon Ainger's admirably edited collection of Eliana. Somewhere years and years before, I had heard the Roast Pig essay quoted as one of the best and finest bits of prose in our round of literature. My find, need I say it, proved the treasure-trove I have held it in the succeeding years to come, and only the true and worthy lover of Charles ·Lamb knows what it is to make a life-long friendship with the countless Burtons, Taylors, and Kit Marlowes; to "linger long days by Swaynham brook," in the imperturbable gracious company of St. Izaac Walton, "sitting and singing" "whilst this shower falls so gently upon the teeming earth, and gives yet a sweeter smell to the lovely flowers that adorn these verdant meadows." O rare Charles Lamb!

Notes and Reviews

Plus mellis quam aloes habet.

Mr. Kevern and Huxley

A pitiable ignorance of the real Huxley and his prose style of writing marks and impairs an otherwise remarkably lucid note on that philosopher in the current number of "The Mite." Mr. Kevern, it seems, has long held a special grievance against a certain class of writers in our amateur papers, who persist (confessedly to cover their nakedness) in elaborating their rhetoric to the point of what Mr. Kevern succinctly terms "hifalutin." Has Mr. Kevern read Jeremy Taylor, Browne, Bunyan, and Pater? Can he trace the degeneration of the "splendid and terrible" arsenal of Dryden's prose down to that of our own parsimonious twilight of snivelling, drivelling manikins? And is he aware that our best prose is undergoing what Watts-Dunton has rationally defined as the Renaissance of Wonder; a period in which the bottomless barrier between prose and poetry is described as becoming less defined from the hackneyed strictures of that slough of affected classicism, the Georgian Era? We believe not. Dryasdust himself would arise from the sciential tomes of the dusty Bodleian in an avowed consternation, could he by any mischance read Mr. Kevern's extravagant estimation that "Huxley is to prose what Shakespere is to poetry." Evidently then, Mr. Kevern has never read Shakespere.

"Cartoons"

One finds it rather difficult to maintain the cool nonchalance of the reserved critic, in reviewing the December number of Mr. SinClair's "Cartoons." Typography and literary worth are so absolutely blended in the make-up of this booklet, that I am tempted to fling conventionality to the several winds, and indulge in an unwonted and irresponsible panegyric on all the manner of good things packed in this precious hamper of Yule-cheer.

I have always felt that about the best thing Mr. Thrift has done in the way of definite artistry, lay in that exquisite retrospection of the old Cleveland Club nights; and that, unless we except another, equally exquisite and marvelously Stevensonian in manner—"The Book of Silver Song"— nothing that Mr. Thrift has since done, and his sketches are all uniformly excellent, has quite convinced me that he is giving us his best work in A. J. I trust that I am violating no confidence when I say that Brodie himself declared to me on one occasion, that the "Cleveland Nights" sketch contained some of the finest writing he had ever read, amateurily or otherwise. As heretofore, the same unerring precision and the same insistent mellowness, heightened by an almost Rembrandt-esque shadowing, characterizes Mr. Thrift's "Fountain Town Sketches." Continued reading, however, makes one wish that Mr. Thrift would indulge in a bit of bluff Falstaffian bravado—show his "guts," as Mr. Woollen has it—if only for the sake of breaking the intolerable tension that gripes one so mercilessly and with such little forbearance.

"My Lady's Rose." by Arthur Goodenough, is pleasantly mediocre. The last verse naturally invites a comparison with that of Browning's "Evelyn Hope," but at no time does Mr. Goodenough rise to the supreme pathos and lyrical poignancy that Browning has attained in his immortal verses.

When Mr. SinClair first printed his "Day Dream" in the November, '06, number of "Cartoons," I wrote to him saying that I thought it the sweetest and purest idyll of child-life I had read since my first acquaintance with Blake, Lamb and Swinburne. I stand ready to repeat the assertion for the benefit of the few that may appreciate the love that surpasseth all things—the "blameless and stainless" love of little children. Since that time Mr. SinClair has progressed far into the intricacies of prose construction, and it was with unbounded pleasure that I perused his pathetic little Christmas sketch in the current "Cartoons." I can hold it no detraction or inference to Mr. SinClair's splendid literary capabilities in saying that at the present time he is strongly under the influence of Thrift, both in the subjective treatment of his idea, and the outgrowth of an extremely poetic prose which he uses in preference to the brand now so universally written. Riper scholarship will undoubtedly carry him farther into the way of originality of purpose and utterance, but I have no hesitation in saying that there are lines and paragraphs in his latest sketch which bear unmistakably the mark of the consummate master.

Harry E. Martin

I have before me two of Mr. Martin's tales—"After Many Years" and "The Face of the Flames," published respectively in the June "Dryad" and the July "Sprite." Mr. Martin has the considerable knack of telling an interesting tale. True, the language merges into triteness, undue sentimentality, and ornateness of purpose; but all this Mr. Martin can easily reprehend with a thorough mastery of such novelists, say as—Fielding, Dickens, Meredith, and Wilkie Collins; or if he prefers the short story writers—Poe, Du Maupassent [sic], Mary E. Wilkins, and Henry C. Bunner. The climax of the first, strikingly suggests what I believe to have been the greatest thing of its kind ever written amateurily—Mrs. Thrift's little passion-play, "The Outcome of the Matter." There is nothing quite so realistic, or for that matter, pathetically appealing to the average mind, than the breaking of the tense chord that binds both sense and soul to the body. Lear, great in his indomitable way, would never have conceived and attained the Aeschylean terribleness—

> "I will have such revenges on you both,
>   That all the world shall—I will do such things,—
>   What they are, yet I know not; but they shall be
>   The terrors of the earth—"

had his energy remained unexhausted and amiably content in the later years of his senility. Mr. Martin is to be congratulated on his worthy (if not wholly successful) attempt at portraiture of this kind.

Notes and Reviews

> On with thy fortunes then, what e're they be;
> If good I'le smile, if bad I'le weep for thee.
>   —HERRICK.

Orville J. Grisier

There is a certain frankness about Mr. Grisier's treatment of the rather perfunctory theme in the second of the "Rambler" sketches, that holds forth considerable promise of better things to come. Of course, the Romany Rye has been worked to tatters. Since the singular sunrise of Barrow's "L'Avengro" down to the more recent conception and publication of "Aylwin," there have been any number of the so-called "tales of the road"—all strictly and fluently modelled on their precursors—that have not found the attention of an audience of admirers wholly wanting. The idea, I believe, originating with Fielding and Smollet—or to trace it back directly. Cervantes and Le Sage—is a perfectly legitimate offspring of Dickens and (in a measure) Scott. I like the brawn and bearing in the terse phrasing of Mr. Grisier's sentences. In an attempt to overmatch the Thriftian tactics of rhythmic prose, our amateurs usually give vent to an exuberance, which in somebody's fortunate phrase, would take the breeks off a Highlander. Mr. Grisier persists in dragging the inevitable "woman in the case" without her inevitable inconstancy, into the slight story plot. Yet after all, we must bear in mind Luther's advice—I believe it runs

"Wer nicht liebt Wein, Weib, und Gesang.
Der bleibt ein Narr sein Leben lang—"

Or something of the sort. I am scarcely old—or cynical—enough, to commit myself entirely to his peculiar point of view.

THE QUAKER

One of the best things in "The Quaker" is Mr. Oliphant's appreciation of that rare personality, Harry Marlow. "He is one of the most interesting persons I have ever known," says Mr. Oliphant, "... a sort of continual surprise, misunderstood by many, but a friend to all. The world would be better if there were more like him in it." All which I heartily affirm is correct. Mr. Oliphant writes an easy, luminous prose, but there is hardly enough of it to enable my passing any judgement on its characteristic worth or construction.

W. R. SCHŒNBERGER

In one of Keats' letters to his brother George, then residing in America and whither the poet had resolved to immigrate, he remarks, probably at his brother's inference, on the dishonesty of Audubon, the early ornithologist. I have not the volume by me, nor have I since verified what I think would make extremely interesting research; yet something of undoubted and unusual significance must have passed between them in the course of what was inferentially a close and ultimately unsatisfactory acquaintance. In his sketch of Audubon, Mr. Schœnberger has given us one of the must unaffected bits of prose writing I have ever seen this long time. I await more of his work with interest.

SAM'L BEGLAND

Among the dozen poems published by Mr. Begland in his initial "Thistle," there is one in which occur two lines worthy of Burns at his inexpressibly best. On the strength of these

> "Bit wi' the tales I wasna frichted,
> Ye ken I wis at mither's knee—"

I urge Mr. Begland to flee the pseudo-Byronism of much of his verse, as he would the very devil. Such a poem as "An Acrostic" on a baby approaches very nearly to good, substantial work: but surely Mr. Begland has mistaken the meaning of the last word in the closing lines

> "Earth's rare beauties are but vapors,
> Rivalling all dost thou EN MASSE!"

This is inconceivable nonsense. For a baby (however cumbersome and weighty) to match and possibly outrival this earth in avoirdupois were manifestly an impossibility—yet this is what the word literally implies. Erudition, unless it be of the unassuming sort, has no place in poetry, except (and I might cite Milton and Browning) in the hands of a master, which Mr. Begland is as yet unfortunately not. With his delicate delineation of what I take to be the Gnadenhutten type of beauty—

> "Hair of night
> With eyes as soft as ocean's foam.
> And smile that only angels own—"

I can very heartily sympathize and attest to.

George Meredith

I presume that of all the greater Victorian poets, probably the least known, and surely the least appreciated, is George Meredith. That the author of "Richard Feveral" must eventually be conceded to a place beside Browning is an apparency which any one with any capability in summing up the poetry of the last century must consciously and seriously affirm and uphold. It has been accorded us by a certain luminous faction whose immediate claim for a proper portion of immortality lies in their firm adherence to Wordsworth as an apostle of nature, that Meredith, out of an extreme turgidness and an inability to proclaim his mission in the true and truly simple Wordsworthian style, cannot in all conscience be called a great poet. Notwithstanding the profound respect I hold for many of the latter's staunch supporters, and in particular Mr. William Watson, whose "England, My Mother" must number among the greatest of its kind ever written for any conservative country, it is my steadfast opinion that time alone will show how completely under a misapprehension he and the many beneath him are laboring. In my humble estimation I should not hesitate to pronounce "Modern Love" the finest sonnet-sequence we have had since the days of the star-studded "Amorette" and the immortal "W. H." sonnets. Absolutely no greater single line has been written than the

"Shrieking Bachantes with their souls of wine."

Of "Love in the Valley" one can only say, that across its nascent golden pages runs the scent of innumerable meadow flowers, "and for a moment, by the sweet sophistry of association, we stand again among them where they grew." The Woods of Westermain" is comparable only with Shelley's most exquisite lines among the Euganean Hills, and even in this instance I should say that Shelley's noble verses suffer in a distinct comparison with the former. When one comes across lines as haunting, as highly imaginative and as perfect as the opening importunation:

"Enter these enchanted woods,
   You who dare.
Nothing harms beneath the leaves
More than waves a swimmer cleaves.
Toss your heart up with the lark,
Foot at peace with mouse and worm,
   Fare you fair.
Only at a dread of dark
Quaver, and they quit their forms:
Thousand eyeballs under hoods
   Have you by the hair.
Enter these enchanted woods,
   You who dare;"

even Dante's flaming hell-fire signal shrinks and shrivels before its stolid immensity into the oblivious dust of many centuries.

Amateur Poetry

Allowing Mrs. Zeigler's singular inactivity, there is only one among our younger writers upon whom the crown for serious and unquestionable poetry, should in the course of events, augustly and right-reverently descend—I refer to our celestial plagiarist, Mr. Richard Braunstein. A lovelier sonnet than the one which procured him the laureate title, I have never read. Mrs. Campbell is doing splendid work. Her "Recompense," which I believe appeared in the December, 1906, "Cartoons," equaled, and in a measure surpassed, Mrs. Dithridge's laureate poem, "Lethe."

I remember a conversation in which it was unanimously agreed upon, that a great part of our best amateur poetry, had it but been signed by such illustrious names as Tennyson, Browning, Rossetti, or to instance a lesser and infinitely inferior person, whose real vocation lies in the stoker's hole of a smutty lake trailer—Rudyard Kipling—the world would scarcely have found terms fit enough with which to welcome it into the limelight of publicity. But being an untitled and unprofessional instance, and lacking in the first and essential requisites that go to the making of a pecuniary success, the reedy and rotten wharves of Lethe easily acquire and eventually consume these pearls of purest price in their own festering depths and fastnesses.

Such a gem as Charlie Heywood's "Mariana" has scant excuse for oblivion. There are lines in it far and away better than the poem of the same name by Tennyson. We are wont to vaunt Swinburne and Rossetti as masters of supreme spiritual significance, but where, may I ask (unless it be in the former's "Thalassius") have either of them approached the singular and characteristic biographical beauty of Mr. Edkins's commemorative lines to his friend Woollen? By this I do not mean to infer or imply that our entire output of amateur poetry is creditable, or even noteworthy. Much, I fear, is unblushingly provided for as a space-filler; and about nine-tenths of it has been written without the slightest regard as to what that miscalled and much abused word "inspiration" signifies. "Poetry," says Poe, "is a response to a natural and irresistible demand." "That most exquisite critic," Swinburne calls Poe. I feel that I am under obligation to Mr. SinClair for so kindly and considerately calling my attention to certain qualities in Poe, that I had allowed myself to treat of in a momentary mood of irritability with a most ungenerous depreciation. Phidias or Praxiteles—what little remains of them—have never designed anything as classically perfect as that ivory intaglio, "To Helen." There is nothing that so nearly equals the grave Hellenic consistency of Keats' "Ode on a Grecian Urn," as do these three "faultlessly faulty" stanzas of the poem which Mr. Andrew Lang has placed at the very beginning of his edition of Poe's poetry. Ranked as a critic, I should place Poe beside Lowell; who, if we accord him not the position of second or even third-rate poet, we must unquestionably confer the post of a highly meritable and sympathetic writer on the literature of the seventeenth century. As Mr. SinClair has generously pointed out to me, the perceptible fault and recurrence of Poe's critical sketches and papers, is the ridiculous pretensions he has taken in reviewing a lot of tenth or twentieth-rate "ranting authors and plagiarists." On some, his laborious reviews are unusually severe and structural, and one is apt to weary of the interminable charges of chicanery, theft and plagiarism, which he passes off with a sort of spiteful satisfaction on the head of the luckless Longfellow. Had he confined himself to his poetry, our literature might have been infinitely the richer in what now appears only as glittering ore and elaborate star-dust—yet assuredly of the woof and texture that such titanic fragments as "Hyperion" are made of.

Properly speaking, however, the writing of the poem is wholly reminiscent of the inspiration itself. I venture to affirm that the lines—

> "Her silken robe and inner vest,
> Dropt to her feet, and full in view,
> Behold! Her bosom and half her side—
> A sight to dream of, not to tell!
> O shield her! shield sweet Christabel!—

were composed by Coleridge under the very fortifying influences of a tumbler of Madeira and a comfortable meerschaum pipe brimmed to the bowl with tobacco.

Critic's Letter

Cleveland, Ohio, October 1, 1908.

Gentlemen:

Prose writing has so nearly always been the most laborious of tasks to me, that while I reverence the honor of Mr. Oliphant's request for a lengthy report on my "official" duties of at least 500 words, I must, in light of my double duty for the accompanying *Notes and Reviews*, beg to be excused. With Mr. Harry E. Martin at the head of our association, matters should progress speedily and with record.

Faithfully yours,
SAMUEL E. LOVEMAN.
7206 Harvard Ave., S.E.

Notes and Review

"I had rather than forty shillings I had my Book of Songs and Sonnets here."
—Master Abraham Slender.

May "Cartoons."

A word (much as I should like to make it two) anent the simple beauty of Mrs. Campbell's bright little lyric in this number. For sheer exquisiteness of sense and haunting pathos, the third verse must take its place among the precious classics of amateur literature.

Timon of Athens

Timon, is a temporal Lear. Spiritually on an infinitely lower plane than the latter, and provocative; of desires that might have admissibly have intercepted the progress of a greater and gentler soul, there is still (and assuredly with no little insistence) the probable and crucial instinct in the network of his nature which tends to move heaven and earth in propagandizing the existing state of society. I know nothing to equal Timon's prayer to the indivisible and benignant Mother of pity and pleasance. Here was one that drew and desired life with no less a fervor than Wordsworth, from her all-material, shining breast. Hear him—

"Common mother thou,
Whose womb immeasurable, and infinite breast,

> Teems and feels all; whose self-same mettle,
> Whereof thy proud child, arrogant man, is puff'd,
> Engenders the black toad and adder blue,
> The gilded newt and eyeless venom'd worm,
> With all the abhorred births below crisp Heaven,
> Whereon Hyperion's quickening fire doeth shine;
> Shield him, who all thy human sons do hate,
> From forth thy plenteous bosom, one poor root!

Scenes and parts of this play bear a marked hand other than that of Shakespeare; yet altogether in a less and subsidiary proportion than in the *"Two Noble Kinsman."*

ROMEO AND JULIET

Here, through the intermittent spaces of dusk and deepening twilight, the Libyan nightingale sings with a rapture that might have reclaimed fabled Tempte or towering Troy from "the Tracian ships and the foreign faces, the tongueless vigil, and all the pain." In this, the most perfect, passionate, and pathetic, of Shakespeare's poems or plays, the soft sweet spirit of the everlasting immortality of youth, fires and pervades the simplest speech of the least or subordinate character with a painless passion, entirely unapparent though in the later *"Hamlet," "Lear,"* and *"Othello"*; and not resuscitated again until the closing sunset and signal-light for departure in that perfect trinity of wife and all womanhood, Miranda, Perdita, and Imogene.

THOMAS CHATTERTON

Chatterton, it has always seemed to me, is the one poet upon whom for reasons conspicuously unknown, no sufficient justice has been done in the way of determining the indubitable greatness of his poetry. Keats, in whom the critical acumen matured at such an early date as the publication of his first poems, unfailingly pronounced him in an inscription that shines and singles itself out by mere force of gracious gratitude, as "the most English of poets except Shakespeare"; and Scott, Wordsworth, and Shelly, in an age when the Scotch quarterly reviews twaddle their thumbs at their noses in pure despite and derision at all decency and self-righteousness, staunchly supported "marvelous boy" with an adherence truly worthy of their nobleness and ultimate kinship. Time and time again has the remedial revision and modernization of the poems been proposed, propounded, and herein, I believe, lies the direct difficulty of the matter. I mind me perfectly the mark of irrepressible impudence (myself not the least) with which the study of Chaucer was greeted in the earlier half of my Sophomore year; and (needless to say) I have since seen fit to change and counterchange my distaste to something little short of absolute adoration. The specimen of roundelay in the tragical interlude of Ælla is probably finer than the finest Elizabethan ballad of Lovelace or Suckling and Ælla itself, shines with a radiance and rings with a sonorousness not unlike the first fruits of Blake, and Swinburne. Mr. Watts-Dunton, as is well known, has singled out the *"Ballad of Charite"* for special and significant praise. Truly, here is something "not to be read without a renewed sense of tears in mortal things"; and at a time when—to quote Wm. Watson—

"Song from celestial heights had wandered down,
Put off her robe of sunlight, dew and flame,
And downed a modish dress to charm the town—"

To proffer a poem of thanksgiving and prayer that such things be possible on earth.

Measure for Measure
Something not unlike the brooding, batlike pessimism of Ibsen, shadows with silent, inscrutable wings the fearful foundations of this play. Only Isabella, a snatch of spiritual sunlight caught and weft upon in the witchery of a single moment, shines through the terminable shifts of its tapestry, and by sheer presence of performance and power touches and tests to the point of finer issues, the rottenness of the principle characters.

Twelfth-Night
Mr. Swinburne's assumption that this excellent comedy owes its ripe and heady humour to the most revertible railing of Rabelais is not at all improbable. What a spirit of mere mischief and wantonness is Maria! Malvolio, malcontent and mercenary, is a very Tartuffe in the distraction of quaint and querulous devices. Here is "the Alsatia of hunted casuistry."

KING LEAR

From the opening speech of Kent where the storm gathers sound and sovereignty, to the tempestuous night and insufferable anguish of the closing scene, the characters, Lear not the least of all, speak with "a snatch of Tartarus and the souls in bale." There will never be a second Cordelia, I fear. All the imaginable loveliness of what is most lovely and lovable in life and death, finds, as it were, an outlet or occasion in her sole speech and action. The Fool might have been a man of ripe wisdom, but alas! Shakespeare called him a fool, and as such then, let him make immortal the pages of Lear.

> We press too close in church and mart
> To keep a dream or grace apart.
> —Elizabeth Barret Browning

MACBETH

Here, more so than in any other of Shakespere's plays, we have the naked, headlong, and inaccessible passions of the soul stript to the very "sulphurous pit." Over and across the withering night and the blasted heath, starless save for an occasional cessation of the tempest, Lady Macbeth, ancient beyond immutable chaos, frowns for a space—and then everlasting night "past and to come" closes over all. Shelley alone, in the incomparable and inexpressibly tragic scene of the slaying of Cenci, approaches nigh perfectly the murder of Duncan. "A trouble not of clouds or weeping rain" softens and sheds the unimaginable horror of the sleep-walking scene, by which (and only by which) actualities and infinities are tempered to a tension that predetermines nightmare or imminent insanity. Here again (Act IV, Scene II,) it may be conclusively proven that the great, and only the great, are capable of conscientiously reporting or representing the actual lisp or fragrance of childhood and babyhood at its best.

THE QUAKER

Through the courtesy of Mr. Oliphant its editor, I am in receipt of an advanced copy of the September *Quaker*. Mr. Greenfield contributes a satirical essay on the qualification and advantages of the gentler sex:—"a future now beyond the fowler's nets"—and under the caption of "As the Spirit Moves," Mr. Oliphant discourses on amateurs and amateur affairs.

THE LUCKY DOG

So much has been said and written in lieu of Mr. Thrift's method of prosodizing prose, that I am loth to reawaken a controversy as profitless as it is wearying, as non-essential and as bootless as a succinct and satisfactory appreciation of Mr. Thrift's better and brighter efforts is essential. There is, to my knowledge, no set or single rule which governs the gainsaying of what shall be this or that in the permanent parts of prosody or prose. The ear, and the ear alone, must stand the factor and sponsor of what may be insisted upon and interpreted as speech or silence in the irremedial efforts of the pen. Ruskin (and I have never been in a position to assail or to appreciate him) interspersed his choicest and most elaborate description of sight and scenery with a species of so-called blank verse. I have in my possession the reprint of an early prose romance—*"Guy of Warwick"*—originally published as far back as 1570 and entirely written in blank verse that was printed like prose. "Prose has its music," says Mr. Morley in his introduction, "but is always bad when it so runs into successive lines of metre that the artifice is obvious. Such artifice of manner weakens faith in the sincerity of what is said." More need scarcely be affirmed.

JACOB ADLER

Mr. Adler, I believe, is the greatest tragedian of his time. I have seen him in *"The Imbecile,"* a version of Enoch Arden, and *The Merchant of Venice,"* and successively, I make bold to say his art and responsibility have impressed and inspired me in a measure beyond that of any of his English contemporaries. The slinking and shameful insanity of the first, the intolerable pain and pathos of the second, and finally the crowning and unquestionable proof of greatness and genius in the third, leaves little doubt in the mind of the impressible playgoer.

IN THE VEIN OF ELIA

S. has a magnificent deckle-edged edition of Charles Lamb, but mine, unlike these apples Hesperidean, have had their golden fruits plucked long ago. In short, I purchased them at a dusty old bookshop on our

Cheapside, where S. tells me he jewed the urbane proprietor down a goodly number of ducats on a passable three-volume edition of Keats—to the latter's voluble protestation that the amount paid could not cover the cost of their elegant blue binding. I have my doubts!—but of course S. will never know that even at the aforesaid reduction, a little less-diffident argument on his part might have resulted in a considerable advantage to his pecuniary resources.

Grouping ones books requires as much gracious art as does the execution of a Leonardo—say the Mona Lisa with all her benignant loveliness. I should never dare to place my Swinburne beside the oracular majesty of *"Sartor Resartus."* Their very antithesis might produce a conflagration, by comparison of which, the burning of Ilion—topmost towers and all—would speedily sink into minor significance.

I have no strong leaning toward the erotic in literature, but I bear a world of pity for these few unfortunates whom the elect have revised at their worst and misunderstood at their best. With S. whose tastes (I imagine) are strongly and sturdily conservative, I can even appreciate and determine the soul of such a rake as Dowson. True, I have my little petty prejudices, yet in the main I bare my head as reverently before the obscenities of the Elizabethans as I should in some sacred synagogue, with the old cantors droning out an elaborate evening prayer.

> This is the place where poets pause to dream—
> Where thrush and nightingale are never mute.

Had I but one wish left me, and that with a certainty of fulfillment, I should pray that my love for all that is beautiful might never forsake me—even unto the brooding sleep of death.

It has been my misfortune never to possess a folio, and in these days five pounds is the least that will purchase one. I have seen these stiff saints behind lock and key, and always my heart has bounded to them. Some day perhaps I shall be fortunate enough to acquire one (I fluctuate, gentle reader, between Sibbe's *"Returning Backslider"* and—what think you?—the *"De Piscibus"* of the elder Aldrovandus!); but until then I must abide the commands of an extenuated purse, and a prospect by no means so inviting as to afford me "the bounteous golden pomps that do beget" the latent serviceability of a Fortunatus.

The Cleveland Amateur Press Club Comes to Life

At a second informal meeting of the old Cleveland Amateur Press Club, held at the home of John S. Ziegler, plans were laid for a re-organization of the club. The meeting was well attended and enthusiasm ran high. The association will remember the good work done by the old C. A. P. C. and will welcome this announcement of a return to former activities.

Another meeting will be held the eighteenth of November at the home of Tim Thrift, where the club will be formally organized and a year of activity planned. Many of the old members have signified their intention of once more becoming active and resuming publication of the many handsome papers that made the old club in its day the leader in the association.

It is rumored that Cleveland will be in the field for convention honors in 1910, and those who remember the good convention held there some three years ago will doubtless welcome this bit of news with interest.

Watch Cleveland will be a good slogan from now on. There seems to be something doing there, if reports are true. It is even said that Brodie, the great and only, will get out another *Random Amateur*.

Samuel E. Loveman, *Secretary*

Cleveland Club Notes

At the first formal meeting of the re-organized Cleveland Amateur Press Club, held at the home of Mr. and Mrs. T. B. Thrift, November 18, 1908, the following officers were elected. T. B. Thrift, President; John Ziegler, Vice-President; S. E. Loveman, Secretary; W. J. Brodie, Treasurer, and Margaret L. Thrift, Sargeant *in* Arms. The members present were Mrs. T. B. Thrift, Margaret L. Thrift, Miss S. Marie Nye, W. J. Brodie, T. B. Thrift, A. V. Fingulin, C. B. Harris, R. R. Kevern and S. E. Loveman. Promises of a *Mite* from Kevern, and an *Ambassador* from Harris, a *Waste-basket* from Fingulin, and a *Robin Goodfellow* from Loveman, were received with responsive enthusiasm. Mr. Thrift, it is understood, has a *Lucky Dog* well on the way. Brodie may be induced to publish a series of *Random Amateurs*.

Mr. Sterling and Minor Poets

The New York Times Review of Books:

It seems a singular anomaly that a poet of Mr. George Sterling's rank and responsibility should be referred to as a minor poet, and still more so that Mr. William Watson should be mentioned in the same connection. Mr. Sterling is not only a great poet, but inconceivably the greatest living, in either England or America. The sense of his art as a divine mission—

> "Remiss the ministry they bear
> Who serve her with divided heart;
> She stands reluctant to impart
> Her strength to purpose, end, or share—"

—stamps the high seriousness of one whom Shelley, Poe and even Keats would have been the first to welcome. Let us honor the living as well as the dead.

SAMUEL LOVEMAN.

Cleveland, Ohio, May 20.

A Keats Discovery

(*To the Editor of* THE DIAL.)

The acquisition of a bundle of unpublished letters written by John Clare, the Northamptonshire peasant-poet, to his publishers, Taylor and Hessey, who, it will be remembered, acted in the same capacity for Keats, brings to light the most extraordinary association-interest between two contemporary poets, one great and both unfortunate, that has been recorded in recent years. For a supreme instant Fate seems to have brought her two nearest of kin together.

In March of 1820, Clare came to London. His poems had already been printed with a preface by his publisher. "There was no limit to the applause bestowed upon him," says his biographer, Frederic Martin. "Rossini sets his verses to music; Madame Vestris recited them before crowded audiences; William Gifford sang his praises in the 'Quarterly Review'; and all the critical journals, reviews, and magazines of the day were unanimous in their admiration of poetical genius coming before them in the humble garb of a farm labourer." It was also the year of "Lamia" and of Keats's departure for Italy.

But a few months later Keats lay dead in Rome and Clare's popularity had so far subsided that he wrote to James Montgomery, "My New Poems do not sell, Taylor tells me, and so I must either do better or do nothing. I expect the rage for novels being predominant is as much the cause as anything, and I hope a better time, if not a better taste, is to follow thereafter—but I dare not question that." Apparently, the rage for fiction continued long in the ascendant, for in 1837 Clare was led half starved and wholly insane to the county madhouse at Northampton, where there commenced an oblivion for the poet that lasted to his death in 1864. It is recorded that he "wrote occasionally to his son Charles, but appears never to have been visited by either relatives or friends. The neglect of his wife and children is inexplicable." And yet it was during this period that he contributed his finest efforts to literature.

Among these documents is a single folio sheet torn from the context of an entire letter, bearing on one side the address, dated June 5, 1820, with Clare's inscription, "Cut round the Seal, Clare," and on the reverse a sprawling postscript commenting pathetically on the vicissitudes of his success with a noble patron—"I forget to mention that I yesterday wrote a very strong letter to Sir Thos. Plumer. I am in hopes to receive from him Three pounds, not more. I have had some failures but this must necessarily be look'd for...." Below this, in Keats's characteristic and beautiful handwriting, are lines 293 and 294 from "Lamia,"

> From Lycius answer'd, as heart-struck and lost
> He sank supine beside the aching ghost.

which read in the original manuscript (H. Buxton Forman's edition)—

> From Lycius answer'd, as he sunk supine
> Upon the couch where Lamia's beauties pine.

It has been conjectured that Keats, visiting his publishers at their place of business, wrote the emendation for the original passage upon the nearest piece of paper that presented itself, and that this happened to be (strangely enough) a letter from Clare, then in London on a visit. "Poor Keats!" writes Clare in one of these letters concerning the preface to his "Village Minstrel," of 1821. "I mention his name with reverence and regret. As to letting his name stand, do as you please, but it strikes me that 'except one' would be more appropriate—not so personal and less fear of being misjudg'd partially as some would call it ... you know from what quarter I mean." By which it may be concluded that even Clare knew the pitfalls and pusillanimity of the critical eighteen-twenties.

SAMUEL LOVEMAN.

Cleveland, O., July 8, 1917.

COMMENT

"I do not claim," says Baudelaire, "That Joy cannot be associated with Beauty, but I do say that Joy is one of its most vulgar ornaments, while Melancholy is, as it were, its illustrious companion, to such a degree that I can scarcely conceive (is my brain an enchanted mirror?) a type of beauty in which is no misfortune."

The following prose-poem "parable" from Heine, seems to be peculiarly applicable to modern poets and poetry:

"The old Harp lies sunk in the deep grass. The Harper is dead. The talented Apes descend from their neighboring trees and juggle with it— the Owl sits moodily hooting—the Nightingale sings her love to the Rose; as soon as it darkens, overpowered by love, she presses her breast against the thorns of the rose and bleeds..........The Moon rises—the night-wind wails incessantly against the sides of the Harp—the Apes, believing it to be the dead Harper, scatter in dismay."

We hope, in our next number, to present our readers with an appreciation and appraisal of the poetry and drawings of Clark Ashton Smith, the young Californian. Mr. Smith is the author of two great and profound volumes of poetry: "The Star-treader and Other Poems," 1912; "Odes and Sonnets," privately printed, 1918. His drawings are unpublished.

COMMENT

It is with regret that we postpone our original intention of dedicating this number to the work of Clark Ashton Smith, until the next issue. This will contain reproductions of two or three of the imaginative drawings, notably the magnificent "Fear." Preparations for an exhibit of Mr. Smith's pictures are now being made in San Francisco.

As we write, George Sterling's "Lilith" comes to us, and reading its amazing beauty and visual philosophy the distinction is revealed, that not only is it great American—but equally great world—poetry. The cry of Lear in the tremendous night:

> "Poor naked wretches, wheresoe'er you are,
> That bide the pelting of this pitiless storm;

The moan of the plucked tree to Dante in the enchanted wood:

> "Perche me acerpi?
> Non nai tu spirto di pietate alcuno?"

or the monumental speech of Tancred in "Lilith":

> "I have been blind indeed,
> But my humanity I put not by,
> Nor turn from the great Army which betrayed
> By many captains and by many years,
> Goes up against the darkness—"

is there any difference? None their humanity is one and the same.

> "Who is there lives for beauty? Still am I
> The torch, but where's the moth that still dares die?"

So questions Arthur Symons in his poem, "Modern Beauty." And the Sphinx, in an unpublished play by an unknown, speaks somewhat reminiscently: "Many men have sought Beauty. Euryanax, the lovely son of Iacchus, set sail from Zacinthus in a bronze galley with his comrades, one blue dawn. Ah, whither goest though faring? cried the bearded Ionians. Abide with us, O Youth, and we shall make thee king of all this ancient realm. Yet he heeded them not and their cries were futile and unavailing. And after many days they came with their torches at dusk to a moon-white isle in the Asian sea of Syme, whereon my beautiful, pallid mother abode in a palace of green alabaster with her lordly minions of civil. He sought Beauty........ (She laughs softly.) He sought Beauty........ (Her mirth becomes louder and her face grows monstrous.) He sought Beauty........ (She screams.) He found ashen corruption hideous putrefaction, charnel Death!"

Bureau of Critics

It is the intention of the Bureau of Critics to make a departure, whenever possible, from the review of an entire sheet, substituting in its stead, individual effort. This month, we present the poets—"current in any realm," good, bad, indifferent—in all the papers that have come to us in the past four months. We begin with Miss Edna Hyde.

"Armistice," by Edna Hyde in the November, 1919 "Inspiration." To the writer, at least, there is no question as to Miss Hyde's being the greatest writer of poetry in Amateur Journalism, and the little poem of eighteen lines, "Armistice," goes far to prove it. Surely no one else combines with an exquisite emotional appeal the sense of such perfect artistry as is contained in some of her brief and recently lyrics. Instead of the customary patriotic obituary "done into rhyme," one finds the following final stanza, lines in which the flash of poignant heartache and grief dying into unforgetting silence, read like a tributary poem from the Greek Anthology:

> "The twilight thrills with memory—
>   Lost comrades come and sit
> About the friendly hearth where we
>   Are joined to talk a bit—
> *But still in silent fields afar*
> *The little wooden crosses are."*

(The italics are ours, but the poem does not need them.)

"The Web," "Before Sleep" and "Tears," by Elsa Gidlow in the September "The American Amateur," Miss Gidlow seems to be on terms of easy familiarity with her Creator. In "Tears," for instance:

> "I think this man could look into God's eyes;
>   He is not ashamed when he cries."

Others have felt the same mood—Blake or Arthur Symons, men of genius, and Garth Wilkinson, the Swedenborgian, in a volume entitled "Improvisations," a book remembered, if at all, for the frequent references by James Thomson of "The City of Dreadful Night." And in any of the three, the vision or touch of hallucination visibly phrased or worded trembles into the loveliest of poetry. A poet, Miss Gidlow is, but this quality she does not possess. Yet the closing lines of "Before Sleep' are beautiful enough and seem to have been written in all sincerity:

> "There are trembling hands on my eyelids,
> A dim foreknowledge of tears,
> And dreams patterning ultimate slumber.
> There is an Autumn sadness upon me;
> There is a falling of leaves in my soul."

Miss Gidlow would be as fine and certain a poet as Miss Hyde if she could forget herself.

"My Moon," by Frances Alexander, in the September "The Blotter." Miss Alexander's name is new to us, but the reading of this magnificent sonnet leads us to believe that the writer is no novice in poetry. We must quote it in full. It deserves professional notice.

> When I, a child, first saw the stars I wept,
>   In dread I thought some giant's ruthless hand
> Upon my sailing moon with greed had crept,
>   And crushed its gleaming shell to twinkling sand;
> And having thus my shining toy laid waste,
>   Casting its powdered gold across the sky,
> Had silent gone, as he had come in haste,
>   Nor cared that I should gaze with grief and cry.
>
> Since then has often disappeared my moon,
>   And I have wept because but stars remained;
> Slow learner that 'tis only tinsel strewn,
>   And all its passing loveliness but feigned.
> Slow learner that a moon's cold shattered jar
>   Could not be mother to a burning star."

Anything by Arthur Goodenough. We confess that since our earliest days in Amateur Journalism, no poem by Mr. Goodenough in any of the multitude of his contributory papers has passed unread. Something—shall we call it tritely, the "Wordsworthian quietude"—or is it an artist's hieratic simplicity and an invocation to whatever is wisest in an unsordid wisdom, make for this quality. Think of dozens and tens of Mr. Goodenough's specimens from his Muse! Yet there are, we dare say, not one which the average lover of poetry would find unreadable. Mr. Goodenough is an artist and a poet. Who that reads "A Song of Dusk" in the "The Tryout" for June can doubt it?

> "The dusk, the dew and the daisies,
>   The scent of hay new-mown,
> The cricket's cry and the fading sky
>   With shadows overgrown.
>
> The dusk, the dew and the daisies,
>   The call of the cows that wait
> By the farm-yard bars and the light of stars
>   Calm and serene as fate.
>
> The dusk, the dew and the daisies,
>   And two in a twilight roam,
> Who are speaking less than with their lips than eyes
>   And blessing the scented gloam.
>
> The dusk, the dew and the daisies,
>   And Nature's soul in prayer,
> Moving the leaves of the patient trees
>   And stirring the evening air!"

"The Soul's Autumn Time" and "Paradise Regained" by Dorrie M. Moiteret in the September "The American Amateur." The latter of these two poems is especially fine. The author is a poet in every line, every word, every phrase. Reading and re-reading it reminds one of that grave and beautiful passage in Charlotte Brontë's "Shirley"—the fictional description of her sister Emily throned as a Titan woman in a paradise of azure, also with the light of elegiac maternity.

> "Then she was glad again, and young and gay
> With her new love; for, gazing in his eyes,
> She saw reflected lights of glory shine,
> And found in Motherhood her Paradise."

"Like Burnish'd Stars," by Eugene B. Kuntz in the June "The Tryout," Mr. Kuntz is typical of the many. No new thing to say and if there were, no new or distinguishing way of saying it. "Quiv'ring beams," "gladsome dreams," "burning fires," "enrapt desires," are hardly poetry. Forty and fifty years ago the poetry columns of the county newspapers retailed the same descriptions and, no doubt, were read by the since-extinguished, languishing ladies with violet eyes and pale faces, in deliberate rapture. But the thing is done forever. Mr. Kuntz should read the moderns—Ernest Dowson, Francis Thompson, Lionel Johnson, Keats, Shelley—yes, even Algernon Charles Swinburne. There is no poetry save the poetry of ecstacy—and great or minor, this quality all poetry must have. All the costive and moribund emotion insincerely interpreted that a writer proffers his reader, will not save him. Somehow, somewhere—an inmost flame, and light of signification, passion and the wording of imagination evenly matched—the poetry must come of its own accord and come freely.

Something in the way of relief are the *Vers Libre* poems of Roswell George Mills. Mr. Mills knows his medium perfectly. In the two poems in the September "The American Amateur," "Stadium Concert Nocturne" and "Soldiers' Monument Argentee," a light, slim yet absolute, is focused on certain phases of city life. The effect is brilliant. Floaters, roustabouts, the flash gentry of both sexes are suddenly stained as with an infinitesimal radiance. Almost one feels the pity of it—for the motley victims of a materialistic civilization. And Mr. Mills also seems to feel this with a curious sense of participation—or is it satisfaction? Within his limits, Roswell George Mills is an artist.

As to the prosodical efforts of Mr. Howard P. Lovecraft there are many and varied opinions—personality allowing even for the magnificent Poesque horror of "Nightmare Lake" in a recent number of Mr. Cook's "The Vagrant" the writer does not take them seriously. The curse of the eighteenth century classicism hangs like a thundercloud over all of them. And Mr. Lovecraft knows this, most assuredly, for do not all men of genius realize and in a measure survey with a disembodied interest their limitations? But the stories of sorcery and bedevilment of which Mr. Lovecraft has contributed at least a half-dozen recently to the amateur press—that is another matter. Mr. Lovecraft is the greatest master of short-story craftsmanship and artistry who has ever written for Amateur Journalism. This wish-wash of the last forty years falls like a faded tapestry before it. Mr. Cook is right. "He is at this day the only amateur story-writer worthy of more than a polite passing notice."

Official Criticism: Bureau of Critics

During a brief participation on the Bureau of Critics last year, the present writer in an all-too slight appreciation of Mr. Howard P. Lovecraft's work, declared it his intention to return to the subject at a later date. That time seems to have come. The few scoffs and jibes at Mr. Lovecraft's attempt to rehabilitate Georgian poetry seems to have been silenced by the speedy transition to a succession of tales of diablerie, productions so distinct in their atmosphere and individuality that there should be no question as to their value not only to amateurs, but through whatever channel they fare in professional literature. Stories of terror have been, since the days of Poe down to Ambrose Bierce and Thomas Burke, purely the medium or the exploitation of a little whip, or, so to speak, the touch of salt on the open wound at the close of the tale. Mr. Lovecraft applies no such an irritant. In the "Facts concerning the Late Arthur Jermyn," published in the March and June numbers of Mr. Horace Lawson's *The Wolverine*, we have what may well be called a singularly perfect specimen of his method of handling the subtle but hair-raising material. "Life," begins the writer, "is a hideous thing, and from the background behind what we know of it peer demonical hints of truth which make it sometimes a thousand-fold more hideous." And here in the first sentence at the very beginning of his magnificent but malign inspiration, Mr. Lovecraft conjures up an unholy atmosphere; the wind of "unguessed horrors" slowly revolves until with something akin to the Shakespearian activity of Macbeth, his characters, pure fiction no longer, but creatures satanically endowed to obey the minutest impulse of the gods of haschish, opium and mandragora, sustain and complete their doom to the darkening and inevitable end. One finds no theatricality, Mr. Lovecraft understands well enough the danger of that. Nightmare, turbulent and all-embracing there is, and not unlike those dreams that betake themselves to mortals when the "good things of day begin to droop and drowse," their simplicity is their genius, and the utter absence of complexity testifies to the abiding worth.

The statement of John Milton Heins in the July *The American Amateur*, that his "order to my mother to write on the social side of the Convention, has brought me, I believe, a very splendid article," reads well for the incitement of Mr. Heins. Mrs. Helen C. Heins writes a pointed and particularly readable prose, not altogether conversational nor entirely literary, but with enough of both to warrant the praise of her son. Readers of *The American Amateur* will be interested to read of "Houtain's magnetic tongue," Cole's "stately effective toast," Mr. Dowdell's "aggressiveness," and last but not least, Mr. Lovecraft, "without a smile on his face ...... who, wherever he was, seemed a book a-talking." More power to Mrs. Heins who writes so interestingly.

And here, in the September *The Tryout*, we have our dear, old friend, Arthur Goodenough again. He writes of "September" and as with everything that Mr. Goodenough says, it is not the matter but the heartfelt and unsubjective emotion crystallized in a personality of unobtrusive but entirely poetic vision. Let me quote a verse—the first one:

> "When the Bronze bacchante, Autumn,
>   On the woods her splendor spills;
> When the foam-flung Aphrodite
>   Vapours hover on the hills—
>
> When the Summer has departed
>   And the bright blue days are brief,
> Then the season is September
>   And the red is on the leaf."

The finest tribute to the memory of any deceased amateur it has ever been our privilege to read is the beautiful *In Memoriam* to Mrs. Jennie E. T. Dowe, edited by Michael White and published by W. Paul Cook, of Athol, Mass. To one who remembered Mrs. Dowe only through a chance meeting at a convention, the testimony and tribute for those who knew her intimately, comes with something of regret—regret for the lost opportunity of knowing a woman of genuine inspiration and high ideals. One would have liked to ask her the immortal question of Peter Pan to his audience, whether she "believed in Fairies," and if so, whether she preferred the lovely, daintily-colored Celtic ones in an Ireland of a century ago. Her daughter, Mrs. Edith Minter, contributes a charming tribute "My mother—as She Seemed to Me." "My mother's taste for fiction," she writes, "was eclectic. She particularly liked stories of strong plot, mystery stories, and stories of eccentric characters in unique settings. Wilkie Collins was an intense favorite, she read and re-read 'The Woman in White,' 'No Name,' and 'Moonstone.' When 'She' dawned it was an episode in our world, and Hugh Conway's 'Called Back' was doubly interesting to my mother because she herself had for years considered a story of similar loss of memory."

William (no longer Bill) Dowdell's *The Bear Cat* for September appears with a startling slate-cover done to life, and with a leading article from his journalistic pen entitled "Bosses and Boston." Mr. Dowdell, it is needless to say, is particularly in his element in recounting political strategy and the whereof and witherabout of presidential campaigns in the Association. Mrs. Dowdell writes two entertaining notes. Miss Edna Hyde contributes a quatrain entitled "Anniversary." One has only to remember certain fine laureate poems by Miss Hyde in the past and shudder. Nevertheless, Miss Hyde is always the poet.

A glance at a few numbers of *The American Amateur* or *The Tryout*, sums up fairly well the situation so far as poetry is concerned. There seems to be no serious attempt to write much beside the customary squibs and prettily ineffectual "Stanzas to Nature." Mr. James Morton does indeed write a poem of seven verses to Edwin Markham, but the result is negative. Elgie Joseph Andrione tells about a little sapling, Mary H. Lehr-Guthrey about love, Margaret A. Richard writes of absence—but passion, "the all-in-all of poetry," as declared by Charles Lamb, one shall not find. John Osman Baldwin deserves to be better known. Mr. Baldwin writes of nature and loves her as only a poet can, in his obliteration of worldly essentials. What he says has been said before, and will be repeated again, no doubt, but for the moment he impresses us with a sincerity that need never be questioned:

> "I love to dwell where paths go winding,
>   In and out by columns old:
> Where tendrilled vines go slowly finding
>   Their upward way to blue and gold."

Mr. Baldwin belongs to the tribe of John Clare.

November 1921

Modern Poetry (An Exorcism)

We are told with something approaching portentous significance, that the new era in Poetry has dawned, and from the remotest gutterhole and sewer-trap in Greenwich Village, to the heroic skyline on Michigan Boulevard, vers-libre squalls and moans with the gusto of something newly-created, resolved to announce itself at the very outset as the one thing worth while and permanent in literature. Magazines with strange names, geometric illustrations and Euclidean contributors, spring up overnight with as determined a plea for existence as do enchanted mushrooms by moonlight. Emotion and beauty, the pity and the tragedy, the loneliness and oppression of life and humanity—are all to no purpose or concern in a movement that seems to have discovered itself originally within the chaste and holy precincts of a Parisian latrine, taken third-class passage on a freighter laden with hogs across the Atlantic, and brought its corporal and personal characteristics to the vicinities of Hester Street or Coney Island with a pomp and dignity not unbefitting mightier artistic influences. A cube, a straight line, or a circle, asseverate these plastically-minded folk, are as capable of performing or perpetuating a direct emotion, as any of the tremendous passages in *King Lear*. Life, in a word, consists of three or four dimensions solely. . . .

And so, the movement wags as it will and increases with vehement and widening rapidity. The few who steadfastly remain aloof, find themselves as steadfastly ostracised or outmoded. Already is Walt Whitman a legend of a colossus, but the flowers at his feet of clay are those planted by other than his fervent disciples. Ezra Pound gathers the clouds upon his aureoled head even as the earliest of the Nietzscheans, Moses on Mount Sinai. T. S. Eliot acclaims with the precision of a bronze gong his discovery of literary genius among the Elizabethans. The Sandburgs and the Kreymborgs shriek and display their meticulous wares in chromatic stalls on the market. Mr. Frost, not inconsistent with his desire for the peace that is not of this world, turns freezingly a brilliant eye on the aridity of New England plowshares. . . . In the meantime, the endless, metallic lines fizz and splutter, minus all capitalization and punctuation, in their endless periodicals; fragments of glass and the clear sheen of silks are assembled by Miss Lowell and sharded into lines with a consummation of dexterity that would have set the Chinese heart of old Po-Chui afire with envy . . . and the end is not yet. . . .

Brethren, let us pray!

Ernest Nelson: In Memoriam

Artist of a few lovely drawings, poet of a few divine fragments, musician to whom the actual creation of music was denied . . . . one of the two who remain gives you the soul-shaking cry of still another . . . . a young Roman poet, two-thousand years ago among the Italian Lakes with the violets in the springtime . . . . AVE IN PERPETUUM, FRATER, AVE ATQUE VALE!

COMMENT

This issue of "The Saturnian" is inscribed in fealty, as in friendship to the three following: W. Paul Cook, Sonia H. Greene, and Howard P. Lovecraft.

The music of Bach is the fruition of ecstasy, but it is also the emotion of the perfect intellect. These gigues and gavottes, these concertos with their leaping and crying largos in which the soul bewails its inhibition to a greater freedom than this life affords it ... their dedication is deliberate and wholly to the artist. In Beethoven we find for all time the barrier broken. So brief yet so beautiful has been the earlier demarcation, that with a single profound gesture the giant, exultant in his liberation of symphonic melody, gives the cry of Dionysus and the marvelous Greek gods return once again into a world and an alien civilization so long estranged from them. At least once, was Beethoven the creator of such a world. Note by note, bar by bar, harmony by harmony, it springs blindingly yet intelligibly in its poignancy and innocence, from chaos into light. Men awaken with the sun and gaze at the lucency of a new dawn; fields are ploughed; kine are fed; wine is drunken newly-pressed and reddening from the grape; evening brings the evening-star and a moon lowly and comforting in the heavens; at last, sleep. Beethoven prays over the world. Then suddenly evil and oppression enter as of old. The weeping is not of sorrow but of lost faith and broken reticencies. Tyranny has become omnipotent and conscious of its aim and fulfillment the music grows ominous. Beethoven understands; what he has created he must destroy; that which gives life, dare even take life, compassionate in its destruction. Yet imprisoned and intellectually bound, the disembodied soul, a miracle in itself even as the voice of his music, dare not lose hope. To destroy? ... yes .... to destroy evil.....

> "To suffer woes which hope thinks infinite;
> To forgive wrongs darker than death or night;
> To defy Power, which seems omnipotent;
> To love and bear; to hope till Hope creates
> From its own wreck the thing it contemplates;
> Neither to change, nor falter, nor repent!"

The Ninth Symphony tells the tale.

A Note [to *Twenty-one Letters of Ambrose Bierce*]

Nine years mark the disappearance of Ambrose Bierce and yet a biography or critical essay in appreciation of the poet, satirist, adventurer, journalist and supreme story-teller, still remains to be written. In the meantime, Herman Melville, touted with Poe and Whitman as one of the three distinct landmarks in American literature, seems to have achieved hectic permanence. The past half-dozen years have seen the decline and fall of O. Henry. Edgar Saltus, a man of genius with the limitation of his environment and a public that has seen fit to sniff over "Imperial Purple" and utterly ignore "The Imperial Orgy," is dead for a year and the brothers of the rare book alone attest to his limited but safe security. Of Messrs. Hergesheimer and Cabell let us say little—very little. Pater and Stevenson, with a combination and admixture of Yankee perspicacy, never yet conspired to make two helpless and hopeless souls, men of genius. One chapter in "Jurgen," alone saves the book from altogether chaos. The sleekest of the contes brandished by Mr. Hergesheimer in his much lauded collection, "The Happy End," founders undefensibly before the least in Ambrose Bierce. Of pure pity and terror Mr. Hergesheimer knows nothing.

In Bierce, the evocation of horror becomes for the first time, not so much the prescription or perversion of Poe and Maupassant, but an atmosphere definite and uncannily precise. Words, so simple that one would be prone to ascribe them to the limitations of a literary hack, take on an unholy horror, a new and unguessed transformation. In Poe one finds it a *tour de force*, in Maupassant a nervous engagement of the flagellated climax. To Bierce, simply and sincerely, diabolism held in its tormented depth, a legitimate and reliant means to the end. Yet a tacit confirmation with nature is in every instance insisted upon.

In "The Death of Halpin Frayser," flowers, verdure and the boughs and leaves of trees are magnificently placed as an opposing foil to unnatural malignity. Not the accustomed golden world, but a world pervaded with the mystery of blue and the breathless recalcitrance of dreams, is Bierce's. Yet curiously, inhumanity is not altogether absent. Think of the episode of the deaf and dumb derelict at Chickamauga and the altogether lovable little Jo—Dickens done to life but with how much more consummate artistry.

The following letters written by Bierce to the writer, make a plea for just such literature as can be gathered into the final and authoritative book on the subject. And written eventually, it must be. Mr. Starrett's brief and notable but wholly ineffective brochure on Bierce, is valuable for the inclusion of the three last letters dispatched by him to his friend in California.

The present collection, slight but unbroken, ends only by Bierce's mysterious departure into what one would consolingly believe may have been the secret but not necessarily tragic finality of South America. "Lies—'s all lies," cried Trelawney concerning the legends, vile and splendid, that even in his lifetime were dinned and perpetuated into his ears. Ambrose Bierce, but for the lonely and immortal austerity that veils him in all eternity from view, may well have uttered the same. And whether one could have wished it thus or otherwise—"the rest is silence."

September 12, 1922.

Preface [to Oelenschlaeger's *Hakon Yarl,* translated by George Borrow]

The "Veiled Period" of Borrow, beginning in 1826, ends seven years later, in 1833. "A large portion of these voyagings in the veiled period," we are assured by Dr. Knapp, "and even after it, were purely apocryphal and imaginary." Information exists, and in no uncertain measure, that much of the wandering ascribed to Borrow, was purely cerebral. A vagabond journey to the south of France was probably undertaken. As to something of like nature in Spain or Italy, proof positive is nebulous or altogether lacking.

Huge reams were consumed by the industrious Maestro from 1826 to at least 1830. The British Museum was ploughed as a fertile field that all succeeding students have since found it. In this instance, the industrious Dr. Bowring, from whom Borrow was later to alienate himself, wisely made the suggestion—"You have claims, strong ones, and I should rejoice to see you *niched* in the British Museum." This was in 1830.

Much of the translation done then by Borrow was from the Danish, and most of it from the great nationalist poet, Oelenschlaeger. The "Romantic Ballads" show with little necessity for discursiveness Borrow's faults and amenities as a literary translator. "Svend Vonved," for instance, with its fine, wild and poetical rhythms, is done with incredible eagerness and rapidity. "Vidrik Verlandson" has gleams and not a few hints of the Scot border-song. "The old Danish poets were, for the most part," says Borrow, "extremely rude in their versification. Their stanzas of four or two lines have not the full rhyme of vowel or consonant, but merely what the Spaniards call the 'assonante,' or vowel rhyme, and attention seldom seems to have been paid to the number of *feet* on which the lines moved along. but, however defective their poetry may be in point of harmony of numbers, it describes, in vivid and barbaric language, scenes of barbaric grandeur, which in these days are never witnessed; and, which, though the modern muse may imagine, she generally fails in attempting to portray, from the violent desire to be smooth and tuneful, forgetting that smoothness and tunefulness are nearly synonymous with tameness and unmeaningness."

The "Scene" from the "Hakon Yarl" of Oelenschlaeger, here printed for the first time from Borrow's beautiful seven-page manuscript, is believed to be the only specimen of play-writing or play-translating ever attempted by the author of "Lavengro." The paper is water-marked "1827." This translation is signalised by a nervous and delicate precision in the instrumental handling of his blank-verse and a care for phrasing unusual with Borrow—if much of his pedestrian, published verse be given consideration. It seems to have been a task of labour and loyalty. Lines and entire passages were later excised or wholly rewritten in handwriting that dates many years afterward. In each instance, the emendation made was for the best.

One passage alone would bear Borrow's stamp as an artist. The altercation between Hakon and Yarl, something certainly reminiscent of the shining Elizabethans, stamps itself in a handful of jewelled lines as true and as noble as anything in Marlowe or Chapman:

HAKON
(Proud and calm.)

The last I choose, I choose the last, O Olaf!
Thou callest me a nidding and a thrall,
Which lureth high a smile upon my lips.

> One may perceive, thou art a stripling, Olaf!
> Thy insolence and wordiness thy age
> Itself announces. Please to look me, Olaf,
> Didst ever in a thrall find such a glance?
> And dost thou find that cowardliness and guile
> Have folded narrowly this forehead wrinkled?
> I caused thee to be envied? Yes, naturally
> I knew that thou requiredest but a beck
> To straightway pounce upon the heart; that in
> Thy soul thou valuedst thy affinity
> To an extinguished race of Kings, much more
> Than all the wonder'd deeds of Hakon Yarl.

Truly, a tidy bit, as Sir Clement Shorter, whose experience with Borrow's posthumous manuscripts has been so extensive, informs us. And for once—we agree with him.

September 24, 1922.

Bureau of Critics

Mr. Dudley Carroll's "An Inhibition" in the November–January *National Amateur*, is a fine example of modern short-story telling. Mr. Carroll confines himself with imaginative precision to the simplest of effects, yet his simplicity is vivid and revealing. "An Inhibition" is the story of Father Angelo, a young monk who assists the Abbot of his monastery "in administrative matters." Clearly and with convincing "actuality"—as Mr. Carroll phrases it—there comes to him one day "a turbulence that he could not repress, however much he knew or felt it was sinful, and his endeavor to mortify himself was futile." The tragedy is culminative and certain. A girl, discovered by Angelo in the hills above the monastery, inspires a fiery outlet to the enormity of the Father's passionate demonstration of full bloodedness. It is the thing that Sappho called at once "sweet and bitter"—and in an attempt to verify the object of his desire Angelo loses his balance and topples headlong from the steep cliff.

"They found his body cut and bruised, his left hand lay on his heart, and in his right hand was a small piece of twig; his face showed a peculiar contentment, his sunken eyes and the heavy lines that ran down his face beside his mouth seemed deeper; but they, somehow, put an indescribable beauty in his face."

Mr. Carroll knows his medium, and the writer will attest that at least one other story, still unpublished, certifies to his growing mastery of the short story. What is needed, is an added refinement.

A Convention Address

Fellow members:

You have heard—or will hear—this evening, what Amateur Journalism has meant to many people. To some it gives one thing, to some another. To many it means the first door that opens wide to them the gate of life, whether it be to emancipate themselves by the power of expression or by sturdy leadership. But if it gives anything, as it assuredly has in its nearly fifty years of service, Amateur Journalism has served its purpose, an existence that seems nearly miraculous when one remembers how many organizations similarly intended have foundered or drifted so far into chaos that even the memory of them is forgotten. And Amateur Journalism still thrives, still connives with Fate into perpetuating its species, its distinctive sort—namely the few, the very few, social beings, who, without a single possibility of pecuniary advancement or advertisement, are willing to give their everything for a cause that holds within its limits, nothing but a profound love of letters.

I remember my entry into Amateur Journalism as though nothing else had intervened in all those years. I remember the papers that flooded my mails. I remember the shiver of delight with which I beheld my first contribution, a poem, and I remember my first convention, when, for the sheer ecstasy of anticipation, I could not sleep for two weeks ahead, awaiting the glorious event. I remember Brodie's boyishness, Thrift's idealism, (cabinet making had not then called him) Ziegler, the then-philosopher, Fingulin, impulsive and warm-hearted, Kevern, and Feather and Kostir—and these things that I remember, I assure myself can never be forgotten, for they have entered into the making of whatever has been worth while in my life, whatever has been vital, sincere, artistic and strengthening, in an otherwise not very successful literary career. For Amateur Journalism gave to me at that crucial period, what it has given to so many others, what we hope it will continue to give to so many an impulse and a defined incentive for keeping a flame in the torch, a light to go by, in an age almost hopelessly money-mad or material.

Amateur Journalism has its perils, its pitfalls and its darker side—do not forget that! You have in this world in miniature, as in actual life, the danger of personality—of personalities so engrossed in their own bitter and mediocre ends, their narrow and vehement outlook on the actual purposes, the definite needs of the Association—that no limit can be placed on their selfish ambitions. These people are to be feared as well as hated. Their object has been, not only in this smaller, but in the vaster and greater world to wreck the things, beautiful and learned and wise that men have most set their hearts upon and best divined for the use of their fellow humans. Drive them out! Destroy them utterly! Their presence in our Utopian Association is cancerous and a fulmination for the destruction of our own, good aims and our continued activities. When you receive their papers, annihilate them. When you hear their gossip, when their little, petty, tell-tale, infernal scandal comes to you on a breath of the wind, close your ears to it, as you would to a thing anathema—for their intent is as the serpent's who has been in pretty fair evidence since the early days of Paradise. We have no place for these folk. One and all we must band together to obliterate them utterly in the years to come. Argument, criticism—destructive and also constructive—Yes! But spite, insincerity and malignity that masks itself in the guise of good intentions—No! Fellow Members. The National Amateur Press Association!

Cleveland, Ohio
July 4th, 1923

A Foreword
With Don Bregenzer

In justice to the reader of this symposium the Editors desire to state that the occasion for the publication of these papers arises from a feeling on the part of members of The Colophon Club that comparatively little has been done in appreciation of the life-long sacrifice and assiduity of James Branch Cabell to creative literature.

Instances of the neglect of literary artists are not uncommon—

especially in America. Herman Melville, saddened by the attitude of his contemporaries that almost openly proclaimed him a pariah, drew his mantle about him in his later years, and died embittered-convinced that posterity held little for him beyond the, mere linking of his name with that of the transcendental, Hawthorne. To Ambrose Bierce, now an acknowledged master of the short story, recognition came slowly. In the non-acceptance of Edgar Saltus lies the epitomized tragedy of an entirely unrecognized man of genius.

With Mr. Cabell we have come perilously close to a repetition of the old story. It is in an effort to forestall any recurrence of such a public misfortune that this collection of papers, with Mr. Cabell's own unselfish contribution, is offered as a permanent tribute.

Thanks and obligations are due to the friends and contributors that have made possible such a measure of appreciation. Gratitude is expressed for the voluntary assistance given by Mr. H. L. Mencken, Mr. Christopher Motley, Mr. Ben Ray Redman, Mr. Ernest Boyd and Mr. Burton Rascoe as evidenced by their various contributions; thanks, again, to Robert M. McBride & Company in general, and Mr. Guy Holt in particular, for permission to reprint certain excerpts from Mr. Cabell's published work, and to the editors of *The Reviewer* for the use of Mr. Redman's essay, *Bülg the Forgotten*, first published in that magazine.

Enduring gratitude is tendered to Mr. Cabell, without whose friendly support and generous co-operation this publication would not have been possible. Mr. Cabell, be it said, requested that his contribution appear as the last item in these pages, upon the ground of some natural unwillingness to seem to lead and marshal a procession which brought tribute to him. We have, none the less, esteemed it preferable to place this peculiarly revelatory paper first.

THE EDITORS

Cleveland,
January 13, 1924.

The Book of Life

Jurgen gives us in its semi-satiric, romantic amplitude the fecundity of the life-forces and of the procreative urge that is the very self and savour of life. Metaphorically it deals with the little half-pathetic fallacies that make illusion of existence, but in symbol it looms largely as a part of that literature veiled as yet to Western eyes, but entirely naked in its open candour to the Orient. Whether it be the darkened cone that Herodian tells us the young priest Elegabal danced before in a courtyard of a temple in Syria, or the lance that Jurgen breaks with Anaitis in his search for the adytum, the symbol remains the same.

Ever, the enormous shuttle creaks, and the diverse fabric woven is the same that Nature has enforced on her wayward and graceless puppets since there first appeared on the scene the perilous apparition of Time. *Jurgen* is clairvoyant with the subtlety and knowledge of these things. Mr. Cabell stands in the wings with a half-tragic smile and a not altogether dishumanizing attitude toward the delicate unreality of his world. But whether his creatures love with vehemence or sin with the audacity that their author could only have given them in a fierce dissatisfaction over the traditions that obstruct all freedom, one must admit the verity of his heart. That verity is non-existent in much contemporary writing.

Jurgen is equally the manuscript of the Book of Youth and of Age. No other literature, certainly not that of the French represented by M. Anatole France (with whom Mr. Cabell has been most frequently compared) can produce its like. You will find quite obviously, as in M. Anatole France, an irony at once delicate and sensual that connotes very possibly the same flow from the identical racial spring in the same lofty region—but something has half-bewitched and enfranchised the American writer into a world at once alien and fantastic, yet still eternally fanciful and terribly symbolic of its own secret beauty. The Frenchman has the sophistication of centuries and a weight of lore and wisdom beside which Mr. Cabell may actually seem a neophyte, but of the sentiment that profoundly touches the hem of tragedy in *Jurgen*, you will discover in the former little, if anything at all.

And Mr. Cabell brings to the force and genius that make this book his masterpiece, an unparalleled elasticity of style, at times elliptical, at others veiled, and again, brilliant with its distinct empirical flame.

Jurgen is illusion, stripped chapter by chapter and page by page, until in "The Vision of Helen" with its blinding peroration to Beauty, or in the final chapter with Madame Dorothy on the dusked, moonlit terrace, a lyric materialism brings the book to a close. One finds pathos, comedy and the hugely exalted tragedy of sentiment. That is *Jurgen*. That is also, Life.

A Preface [to *The Fear*]

The literature of insanity is a long and interesting one. It includes, aside from the giants, such names as Emily Brontë, with her Heathcliff in "Wuthering Heights," the author of "The House with the Green Shutters," and the fine, fourth-dimensional delusion of Edgar Saltus's Tristram Varrick. But in the highest and mightiest depiction of madness—the Lear of Shakespeare, the Furies of the Sophoclean Orestes—the soul becomes so sensitized and occult that not a vestige of materialism remains to dross the physical or outer existence.

Mr. Spira's "The Fear" is unusual. There are parts, especially in the steady ascent to a climax, that contain the authentic, spiritual shudder which only the soul can give as it engulfs itself in abysses that the tragedy of life may have plunged it into. The Mother's emotion is genuine and heart-rending, her unfortunate son is pitiful and tragic. A phase of Vladimir's madness is the enormous cunning of his cruelty. This reads sincerely and is startling in its candid and open realism.

Edna Hyde: A Preface

Women who have written successful poetry are numerous enough in literature. From Sappho down to Millay the purple line has had its undeviating individuality, and if certain aspects betray the feminine lack of definiteness, it is equally certain that no masculine poet has ever displayed such a marvel of tender and epitomized lyricism as one finds concentrated in the poetry of Emily Brontë, Nora May French, Edna St. Vincent Millay, or the author of the present volume. Edna Hyde belongs to this group. She belongs to it by reason of the same definite and balanced emotionalism combined with a cameo-apprehensiveness for form, felicity and beauty, that gives to each of her lyrics—even the slightest and weakest—a touch of genius. Poetry, whether you clothe it precisely in formalism or denude it into sheerest free verse, remains essentially poetry. The muses, those mythical yet certainly real attributes, have well assured themselves of this. Edna Hyde's poetry is the poetry of spring-time youth and the half-articulate ecstasy that will always be a portion of those that are, or choose to remain, eternally young.

If her poetry deals with the pathos and accumulated tragedy of modern existence rather than with the joy of the moment, remember, that while the mills of the gods grind slowly and in complete proverbial accordance, the process still remains an interminably heart-rending one. A new great poem, not unlike Mrs. Browning's "Songs of the Children," could be written as the demonstration of an age that numbs and tortures its applicant-artists in factories, in steel-mills, and in the oblivion of rear-offices.

In the meantime we have Edna Hyde.

A new poet, O my friends!

Foreword [to *Poppies and Mandragora*]

We have here a collection of sonnets written by Edgar Saltus, several antedating his earliest published work, with a few written within a decade of his death. These sonnets, painstakingly copied from an old notebook, yellow and brittle with age, are now printed for the first time, with the exception of a few included in "Love and Lore," a volume of poems and essays published by Mr. Saltus in the Nineties.

Mrs. Saltus is authority for the amazing information vouchsafed us, that Frank Saltus "was the underlying inspiration of Edgar Saltus's poetical efforts. His admiration for his brother's ability was such that the one desire of his youth was to write verse of which his brother could be proud. Toward his brother Edgar Saltus had a decided inferiority complex,—Frank Saltus's unique genius stimulating him not only to write in verse but to re-polish in prose."

The verse called "Myself," with which the volume opens, was written in fun and not intended for publication. To make the collection inclusive, however, and give a glimpse into the playful side of Mr. Saltus's nature, it was decided to put it in as it appears in the old note-book.

In the unique dedication, written in 1882, when Edgar Saltus was the supposed agnostic, one sees the real man, who had even then the subconscious beliefs, which coming to the surface at a later period, coloured his life to the end.

Following the compilation of her husband's sonnets, Mrs. Saltus was asked by her publisher to include a selection of her own poetry,—not only to show Mr. Saltus's influence, but because her intimate and tender association with his life for twenty years made her work in a sense a part of his. This she has done. Many of her poems written during girlhood and several in the period of her life with Edgar Saltus, represent the soul of a woman who has grasped with more than ordinary insight the futility of all creeds beside that one over which Buddha sits brooding in bronze immobility—perpetual warder of the gates that to some flicker perilously before the vast reaches of chaos—to others into new and radiant life.

In at least three of her poems: "London in Fog," "Hesitation," and "Karma," we have the sheer liquescence that is to be found in our best English poetry. "Karma" touches without trepidity, the vehemence and daring of Emily Brontë's "Old Stoic."

And so, the reader is finally and definitively permitted to receive the bulk of Edgar Saltus's poetry into one volume. The result is one of decided and valuable interest to the students of Saltusian prose. Much of the inebriation that tends to make his work heady with life and light, succumbs here into the crystallization of fragile and exquisite, but unimpassioned, poetry. The sonnets written in Venice are faintly coloured by the splendour of the Italian scene. Another, "The Feast," prosaically and emotionally perfect, takes its place with the greatest sonnets in the English language. Yet the writer of "The Imperial Orgy," still stands by reason of his prose and not his poetry, as a great writer and probably the greatest stylist in modern American Letters.

New York City

Preface [to *The Man from Genoa*]

Homer was the first and greatest of romantic poets. Helen with her filleted golden hair and cupped breasts, on whom the shadow of no elder civilization had ever fallen, has her moments of deific depth, but it is a depth evolved from the supremely romantic mind, not the outwelling of supremely tragic poetry. Strife there may be in all of this, but tragedy is to follow later if it is to follow at all. In the meantime one may well be content with the ancient, beautiful things—gold, raiment and gems, perfumes ascending sheer from braziers into a blue world, with men and women glamorously conceived as a foil for the unworthiness of actual life.

Frank Belknap Long, then, is our new poet—writing poems that might have been penned by the greatest of the lesser Elizabethans, with at least one, "The Marriage of Sir John de Mandeville," worthy of Christopher Marlowe. To Long the hideousness of life as it may be found in the modern city ceases to exist, but in his refusal of realism as his contemporaries see it there lies a shining road to finer things, and to the momentum of pity that spins into permanence all tragic and major poetry.

Hubert Crackanthorpe: A Realist of the Nineties

In an age that leads itself with inquisitorial sapience to open courts of criticism the name of Hubert Crackanthorpe remains singularly unknown. A fine and searching essay by Arthur Symons, a note by Richard Le Gallienne, seven citations in Holbrook Jackson's *fin de siècle* encyclopedia, as many pages in Bernard Muddiman's "The Men of the Nineties," J. M. Kennedy's "English Literature: 1880–1896" and the tale is soon told. Vincent Starrett, it is true, makes an interesting attempt to bridge the vast gap toward the recognition of Crackanthorpe in his "Buried Cæsars," but there the honors are evenly divided with Richard Middleton (a strange and unfortunate choice for a bedfellow) with no great critical appraisal of either.

To many Crackanthorpe occurs as a sort of modified "Enoch Soames," with all the tragedy and none of the exhilarating farce of Max's famous verbal caricature. Born May 12, 1870, his body was found in October of 1896, a suicide in the Seine, after six weeks of mysterious disappearance. Contemporary newspaper obituaries mention his "morbid lucubrations," while a notice in *The Critic* for January, 1897, refers to his "literary work of a strange sort," followed by the inevitable "Who's Who" assortment of instructive facts. Lionel Johnson alone, in a note in the "Academy" for March 20, 1897, quotes Rossetti in defence against the assertion that his "work makes a goblin of the sun," and with words that veil his own personal tragedy writes: "The terrible pages are full of an aching poignancy. The straightforward sentences hide an inner appeal. The telling of misery becomes a thing of dreadful beauty and its intensity goes nearer to the heart of the whole dark matter than many a moving sermon. The artist's abstemiousness in Mr. Crackanthorpe, the refinement of his reticence, never chilled his reader. 'The pity of it! The pity of it!' That was the unspoken yet audible burden of his art."

Crackanthorpe was the author of four books in a literary productiveness that extended for less than five years, yet in that brief boundary of a life of sheer tragedy began (as we now know it) the genuine realist movement in modern fiction. "Wreckage," the first book, published in 1893, marks a monument to realism of the modern period. Hardy's "Jude the Obscure" was to come in 1895. George Moore, it may be, had gone a step further in "The Mummer's Wife" than any one since Trollope, Hardy, Gissing, or Henry James in depicting the sorrows and bypaths of pessimistic impressionism. But if the hand was the hand of Moore, the voice was assuredly the voice of Zola. The sodden sodality of the provincial theatre, the tart yet nebulous taint of viciousness made manifest in the commonplace heroine, are all identities boldly abstracted from the men and women in the series Rougon Macquart. In Zola, at least, we touch life and soil our fingers in boldly touching it. "The Mummer's Wife" mirrors the real thing only as one would find it in a spectroscope. The emotional actress, so pathetic in her drab negation of the joy that could actually have been hers, suffers and dies in true story-fashion. The whole book is a coroner's inquest. The process of dying has been a business—no more.

With Crackanthorpe's "Wreckage" we come to something definitely new. Here are seven stories told in the English idiom, with excellent touches of art. We read in the prefatory quotation: "*Que le roman ait cette religion que le siècle passé appelait de ce large et vaste nom: 'Humanité';—il lui suffit de cette conscience; son droit est là.*" Humanity—that was what Crackanthorpe never forgot. It makes each of the stories in his book the shelter and vindication of pity, with a something underlying, an intelligent tragic sense that De Maupassant, for all his vivid, illusory world, never quite persuaded himself into conveying or projecting.

"Profiles," the first, is much the longest of the set. It is not, as Mr. Muddiman infers, entirely unsuccessful. Lilly, the heroine, finely manipulated in the transition from her innocent girlishness to the horror of prostitution, burns violently if with some crudity. The story of the girl whose temperament takes her from average domesticity to a ghastly life in the streets has a force that still drives home. "What had become of her, no one knew and no one cared," says Crackanthorpe simply at the end. The second, "A Conflict of Egoisms," really an annihilation of two discordant individualities by marriage, ends first in the spiritual then physical suicide of the hero as an idolatrous offering to his sickeningly sentimental wife. One may find passages that are obviously autobiographical. "As time went on the thought of death began to haunt him till it became a constant obsession," we read of the hero who is a novelist. "In the daytime, fascinated by it, he would lay down his pen and sit brooding on it; at night, he would lie tossing feverishly from side to side, with the blackness that was awaiting ever before him. And with the sickly light of the early morning, there met him the early relief of having dragged on one day nearer the end."

"The Struggle for Life" and "Dissolving View," the first merely ordinary but the second magnificent in its concentrated pathos, are followed by "A Dead Woman," the story of a volcanic upheaval among the ordinary types of an English countryside. This is Crackanthorpe's masterpiece. The austere and heroic suffering of a reticent peasant who by chance discovers the betrayer of his dead wife in the person of a lifelong friend, a neighboring inn-keeper, is the very essence of tragedy. Rushout, the husband, lifts her photograph from the wall. "He watched the whole scene as it was played before him; she, giving herself with all the gestures and caresses with which he was familiar, till its vividness became almost unbearable. He lifted up the photograph once more. But underneath the faint smile lurked a wealth of smothered corruption; on the half-parted lips he detected the imprint of Jonathan's kisses."

"When Greek Meets Greek," the tale of a faithless wife of a card-sharp at Nice, is melodrama, quick and poignant, but with a method and consideration for the sordid malefaction of the principals that sears in the telling. Duncan Ralston, the lover, is passive but vehement. The woman Pearl is best described in the flickering light "which played about her face" as fragile and "little more than a child." Simon, her gambler-husband, the peak of the triangle, plays more than an average game of cards. His is a compelling soul, hard and reckless in effrontery, but with something of unusual largess for the possessor of so despicable a vocation. "Embers," the last story, directs two intensely parallel temperaments that pause, give each their sign of divergent recognition, but in the tragic depository of the writer's brain never meet.

Crackanthorpe's second book, "Sentimental Studies," with the subtitle of an additional "Set of Village Tales," was published in 1895. The "Village Tales," which take up only a small portion of the volume, may be briefly dismissed. They contribute, with a gesture of plot and dé-

nouement, some slight elaboration to the "Vignettes" of a year later. Unlike the Anglo-Saxon studies in "Wreckage" and totally dissimilar from the "Sentimental Studies," these miseries of the poverty-stricken peasantry in the hazy, French villages, with their long roads and slim poplars, their peaked roofs and "noisy battering rains," are inextricably woven to make distinct the overwhelming misfortunes of the inhabitants. "The White Maize," not more than the hint of a sketch, contains probably the best descriptive writing in the book:

> "For eight days and eight nights the ceaseless hiss of rain. During the daytime, neither sky nor sun, nor breath of wind—only the gray veil of mist enshrouding all things. The nights were dark as pitch, and full of the hiss of rain; and from sunset to sunrise the frogs chanted their long, dismal mass.
>
> "On the eighth day of the rain, about six o'clock, in the afternoon, I went out. A sickly glimmer of muddy light flickered from the west; a breeze was shaking drops from the trees; the road was powdered with acacia-bloom, lying thick like sodden snow; great pools of yellow water were in possession of the lanes; and new-born streams, bubbling of their own importance, trickled sleek and swollen, across the fields and under the hedges."

In "Sentimental Studies," consisting of three long and two short stories, we find a real advance over the earlier volume. For the first time, if we except "A Dead Woman," literature begins to creep in. Never altogether absent, the influence of Henry James is made more suggestive and conspicuous in the motivation or mental activities of the characters concerned. They suffer, not so much for the things they do as for the things that of their own diffidence they leave undone. One and all, analysis would find them potential victims of what Crackanthorpe discerningly terms their "trepidating curiosity," a delicate but aloof spiritual sluggishness that continually fringes the line of complete decision—yet never quite comes up to it.

"A Commonplace Chapter," really a novelette in two parts, opens the volume. Here we have Crackanthorpe with his favorite *motif*, the man of genius, in this instance a successful poet, beloved by a beautiful and impulsive young woman. This type of Crackanthorpe's femininity possesses the power, when occasion calls for it, to leap into instant maturity; adolescence being only temporary and a foil to match the complete sophistication of the male. Hillier Hasleton, the poet, dreams of marriage, "an ideal marriage—a simultaneous satisfaction of intellectual, emotional and physical desires." Yet over this marriage, following an association of professed respectability in which the heroine, Ella, remembers "nothing but his goodness and the abandonment of the intoxication of his love"—arises the shadow of another, a certain Mrs. Hendrick, beneath whose smile and gentle voice there lurks "an air of bitterness restrained and refined." Hillier is drawn body and soul into her toils. So completely does he justify himself in his intrigue, that he finds himself unable to live without her. Swann, a cousin of Hillier's, enters into the story, and between the alienated wife and this high-spirited relative an attraction is formed that grows insensibly into love. "Swann had become necessary to her, almost the pivot, as it were, of her life; to muse concerning the nature of his feeling towards her, to probe its sentimental aspects, to accept his friendship otherwise than with conscious ease, that was not her way." Aware of Hillier's unfaithfulness, Swann approaches him and in a burst of pleading exacts a promise that the poet, who is traditionally weak, will explain the entire matter to his wife. This he does, but not before Swann has secretly bidden her farewell. We are led to believe that ever after this man who had so spurned and cheapened her love would be hers devotedly and alone; we are certain, however, that this woman could never love her husband again. He kisses her as he pleads:

"'I have been punished, Nellie,' he began in a broken whisper. 'Good God! it is hard to bear ...... Help me Nellie ...... help me to bear it!'

"She unclasped his fingers, and started to stroke them; a little mechanically, as if it were her duty to ease him of his pain. ...."

"Battledore and Shuttlecock," the second long story, with its gentle yet bitter cynicism treats of the eternal *cocotte*, the refined woman to whom fidelity or infidelity are merely experiences in a life of absorbing futility. Of all Crackanthorpe's heroines, "Midge" (Nita) Bashford is by far the loveliest. Ronald Thornycroft meets here in a theatre and beside her "he felt himself clumsy and clownish." He notes her "large-brimmed black velvet hat; the soft duskiness of her skin, which a feather boa caressed; her white, tight-fitting gloves, and the golden bangles on her wrists."

They spend days together, idly and pleasantly chatting in her rooms, walking the streets of the city that ceases to be only a conventional assembly of dreary thoroughfares; the man, on his part, never entirely unconscious of the complete elusiveness, the delightful uncertainty of this mercurial being at his side. She disappears, and her return a few days later elicits the astounding information that only recently had she been separated from her husband, an actor. He had beaten her, she tells him. Her trip to Brighton was with another man, she confesses with a tinge of cruelty: "I suppose I can go where I like, can't I? I needn't ask your leave first. Since you're dead keen on knowing—well, I went because I was hard up.—There!" But she deserts him for good, leaving a note in which he is admonished, "never, never to find out where I've gone, and never to come down after me." He meets her, all unknowingly, twelve years later in a stable-yard at Huntington. "Her husband kept the yard, and she was the mother of three chubby-cheeked girls.... She knew him at once, but because of her husband refrained from betraying it. And he just glanced carelessly at her and never recognized her."

The revival of a love, bygone and forgotten, forms the substance of "In Cumberland." It fails to keep close in rendering convincingly the sense of appeal in Alec Burkett, who, taken ill in a tiny, unkempt mountain village, "a choppy pool of black slate roofs, wanly a-glimmer in the wet," meets once again with a former sweetheart, and in the course of events (she had meanwhile married), being passionately urged by Burkett to elope with him, she brings the affair to an untimely end. The close of the story bites like etcher's acid. "He strode away across the lawn, and as she watched his retreating figure, she felt for him a shallow compassion, not unmingled with contempt."

"Modern Melodrama" and "Yew-trees and Peacocks" are two short stories that close the "Sentimental Studies." In the latter we find great verbal beauty and retrospection. "Modern Melodrama" reverts to the naked style of journalism so succinctly used in narrating the stories in "Wreckage." The two characters, who have been coarsened in a world that makes life adventitious only to those steeled and hardened by it, talk of hell-fire and "wince under the fierce feeling of revolt"—but for all that their flame and fury scarcely suffice to make them live. The mood of a languorous afternoon, with the foliage turned ever so faintly by Autumn, is in "Yew-trees and Peacocks." The heroine is delicate and mobile, her lover perhaps a little too vague and courtly. An atmosphere of saddened and mellow placidity colors this tale, which makes the common contention that Crackanthorpe was concerned solely with the trough and gutter of existence a fallacy.

A motto prefixed to "Vignettes" (1896) reads: "The pursuit of experience is the refuge of the unimaginative." In this slender volume of only sixty-three pages will be found some of the most stimulating and exuberant prose of the Nineties. "In a work like this Crackanthorpe was perfect," writes J. M. Kennedy. "And if there are beautiful subjects to choose from, there is no special reason why an artist of Crackanthorpe's qualifications should deliberately choose ugly ones. Even when writing about Naples he does not forget to remind us of the garbage in the Strada del Porto and the squalidness of the Strata del Chiaia." None the less it is this very insistence on Crackanthorpe's part to accentuate the occasional misshapen hideousness of the human scene that converts with touches of verisimilitude his perfect but ordinary prose, into broad and astonishing writing. Beauty alone he could never altogether disassociate from the element of humanity. "I dreamed of this great, dreamy London of ours," he writes on returning to England, "of her myriad fleeting moods; of the charm of her portentous provinciality; and I awoke all a-glad and hungering for life." Movement and the joy of movement there are in even the least of these notes, with the never-failing, ever shifting, emotional agony that makes them distinct and discoverable as a part of life.

The "Last Studies," a collection of three long stories, was posthumously published in 1897 with a memorial sonnet by Stopford Brooke and an appreciation by Henry James. "The troubled individual note" of Crackanthorpe, we are told, is a difficult thing to interpret. Of stories of this type, we further read, "it may be an effort preferably pictorial, a portrait of conditions, an attempt to summarize and compress for purposes of presentation, to 'render' even, if possible, for purposes of expression."

The first, "Anthony Garstin's Courtship," is written in complete subjection to a tragic mood. It shows the subtle but resistless antagonism of a dominant, masculine woman who pits herself in all hardihood and contention against a light and flighty creature, the choice of her son. She declares: "T' hoose be mine, t' Lord be praised.... an' as long as he spares me, Tony, I'll not see Rosa Blencarn set foot inside it." The same sort of solidity makes Anthony at odds with her. This story is faintly reminiscent of "The Return of the Native"; Mrs. Garstin, "stalwart almost despite her years," derives in strength of purpose, not wickedness, from Heathcliff in "Wuthering Heights." She would have dominated any person, anywhere.

"Trevor Perkins," second of the three, stresses the element of sex. Trevor, who loves a waitress in a bunshop, is typical of his kind. Here again we see how easily and with what deliberation Crackanthorpe can conjure up and clarify a situation at hand.

The last story, "The Turn of the Wheel," is weak and fine-spun in spite of its inordinate length. It gives us nothing new, but the description of London society is good. The rebellious daughter who worships her father but despises her deserted mother reveals with perhaps too much fidelity the complexities that force themselves into Crackanthorpe's characters. Yet their lives are lines, pure and severe, like Crackanthorpe's own, that run with no deviation straight to an end.

The re-discovery of Herman Melville, of Ambrose Bierce and (thanks to Thomas Beer) of Stephen Crane, leads one to hope that not so far in the future will come the recognition of one who wrote not only with consummate courage but who—more than any one else of his time or period—showed unmistakable signs of a superlative talent. "He was one of those who fight well, who fight unselfishly, the knights errant of the idea," says Arthur Symons.

Marcel Proust
"Le Temps Retrouvé"

Up to the period of 1913 it may be stated, with fairly explicit definiteness, that the affirmation of a single slice of modern civilization, as expressed in the brain of a single creative talent, was invested in Balzac. Zola can be at once dismissed, since the manufacturer of the family Rougon, synthetically in common with much that was done by the late Arnold Bennett, lacked even the ordinary requisites that should have entered into the making of a work of genius. 1913, then, saw the publication of the first new and great novel that was to enter into the completely conscious, modern order of things—"Du Côté de Chez Swann" ("Swann's Way")—to be followed by the posthumous publication, after an interval of five years, of "A l'Ombre des Jeunes Filles en Fleurs" ("Within a Budding Grove") and ending with "Le Temps Retrouvé" ("Time Regained"), completing the entire novel that we now know as "A La Recherche du Temps Perdu" ("Remembrance of Things Past").

To the translator of Proust's first seven volumes, C. K. Scott Moncrieff, the reader of the English version was one of the incalculably finest and greatest translations of any work rendered into English since the "Rabelais" of Sir Thomas Urquhart and "The Arabian Nights Entertainment," by Sir Richard Burton. In that curious world, half of shadow and half of fulfillment, must ever remain the inexplicable irony of the English translator's death before the final volume could have been translated. To Stephen Hudson, one of Proust's most intimate friends and confiding spirits, was delegated the task of completion, and we now have this volume (London: Chatto and Windus; New York: Albert and Charles Boni) in a translation that approximates, if not the lyrical or poetic suavity, at least with engrossing verbal literalism, the symphonic direction of the original.

By no mere chance does Proust in this last volume gather together the threads of his hitherto widely strung plot and the divergence of his practically inchoate chain of loosely manipulated people, into the one gigantic upheaval that decided the fate of the Guermantes world in 1914. Here they return to us, much as we should have expected them to—M. de Charlus, Jupien, M. and Madame Verdurin, Morel, Robert Saint-Loup, Albertine, Odette, Gilberte, Block and the Duke and Duchesse de Guermantes. Nothing less terrifying remains to the reader than Proust's conventional insistence, in every instance, that the spectator, who has followed with expectation and possibly with inconvenience, this concentrated world as depicted to its outer and nethermost limits—be tendered the final justification of each character and every situation uncleared, up to the beginning of the last installment of his novel.

For M. de Charlus, demoralized and decayed to a degree scarcely credible at the outset, is delegated the role of master of ceremonies—in a performance that reminds one, oddly enough, of one of the York Miracle Plays depicting the literary torments of a territorial hell. The maddening savor of bitterness and apprehension in this novel reaches its apogee perhaps in the bewildering and stupendous scenes of sadism enacted in Jupien's perverted brothel. Here then, for the first time since Lear, is portrayed the inescapable drama and tragedy of the material soul. Not even Proust's insistence in an off-handed passage, on "an ineffable vision on the threshold of sleep," disperses the stupefaction experienced by the reader in the disclosures presented. In M. de Charlus alone is endowed the capacity to be "solid, immense and resistant," and if one were permitted to delve even deeper, to Saint-Loup solely is delivered the capacity for the one precise attribute of pathos and actuating human sympathy (always excepting Swann and Albertine, figures in silver or platinum) in the entire range of this enormous novel.

"Hell is myself and where I am is Hell," cries a figure in an Elizabethan drama. That, one may conjecture, must have been Proust's idea.

Literature and Dry-Rot

A Review of Mr. Lewisohn's "Expression in America"

When a final summarization of American Literature is written, Mr. Ludwig Lewisohn's present "Expression in America" (Harper & Bros.), will prove to be little beyond an inexpert and synthetic documentation of the case. For Mr. Lewisohn's book declares nothing of the tragedy of failure that has had its appalling tenure in American Letters. The youngster who was once taken by his father to hear a symphony, and who cried out shrilly and vociferously that he liked the noise of the big drums best, would find an instant fellowship in those readers of Mr. Lewisohn's cyclical work who believe that the fraudulent, old household gods—Longfellow, Whittier, Lowell and Holmes, together with Emerson, Thoreau, Howells and Mark Twain, still loom largely and ominously on the horizon of American Literature—while Herman Melville is relegated and pinned to annihilation by Mr. Lewisohn, in such an astonishing and disturbing statement as the following: "Melville is not even a minor master. His works constitute rather one of the important curiosities of literature. He will be chiefly remembered as the inventor of a somber legend concerning the evil that is under the sun. But to embody this legend in a permanently valid form he had only half the creative power and none of the creative discipline or serenity." Of Mark Twain we are asked to believe that he "is related to Homer himself who, also, raised into the immortal realm of the imagination the life and conflicts of obscure villages among otherwise forgotten Ionians of the isles and the Asian shore. A poor relation, a late descendant, but of the authentic lineage and blood." This is either the snare of an artistic delusion or a deliberate untruth. An intelligence such as Mr. Lewisohn's, which rates Herman Melville as less than a minor and in nearly the same breath apotheosizes Mark Twain to an Homeric stature, would scarcely be trusted as a safe guide over the teetering tight-rope that spans the empty abyss of American Letters.

Concerning Edgar Lee Masters, Mr. Lewisohn vouchsafes to us that he "has that serenity of mind and character that makes for style," but that "Hemingway's manner became style, and fragmentariness became structure, and his bluntness won resonance and overtone, because he was inspired by the affirmation and not the denial of passion." Of such a roaring and swashing tenth-rater as William Faulkner: "He has preserved one active emotion, a very fruitful emotion for the naturalist: a fierce hatred for all that has given him pain." Edwin Markham's "The Man with the Hoe," is given a sinecure as "his contribution to the civilization of his country." Of Theodore Dreiser, the American Moses whose prolonged ascent still continues up Mount Nebo, we are told that "his power and truth are so great that they will long irradiate their muddy integuments"; while Henry Adams "is a symbol of American tradition hurling itself into the flame of the altar to be consumed so that another tradition and another life might come to be born." Still farther, we read of the "acrid vision" of Mr. Ring Lardner, and of Eugene O'Neill's "place in the flowering period of national expression."

Mr. Lewisohn's book clearly presents the fallacy of attempting or at least relegating to the brain of a single consciousness, the task of indexing, classifying, elucidating and aestheticising a civilization of writers. To the historian of races and to the chronicler of art is given either the juggling of spacial and remote dynasties or the colour of words, in describing something of a visual beauty. To the historian of such a work as Mr. Lewisohn has attempted in the architectonic terms of his present book, the result can only be achieved by an articulate and strict definition of the matter in question. To Mr. Lewisohn this comes rarely in the course of his running and rapid-fire criticism. "For what is here attempted," he writes in his "preface," "is a portrait of the American spirit seen and delineated, as the human spirit itself as best seen, in and through its mood of articulateness, of creative expression. To this end selection under the appropriate guiding principle was inevitable. It was equally inevitable that I use the organon or method of knowledge associated with the venerated name of Sigmund Freud." It is his "use of the psychological method," however that flings Mr. Lewisohn headlong into the proverbial pit that was a long time ago dug by all bad critics for their entirely good but immoderate selves.

The Theatrical Season

From Chicago, comes the disquieting news that Mr. O'Neil's "Mourning Becomes Electra," as acted by the Theatre Guild's Touring Company, has not been taken to so kindly by its audiences, nor was the ballyhooing that accompanied the uniqueness of its original production, here in New York, commented on with as much patience as is ordinarily the case. This was to have been expected. The procedure of Mr. O'Neil and the American Drama, always a matter of suspicion, and inevitably a question of doubt circumspectly delivered, would seem to have been sufficiently settled when his preceding play, "Dynamo," found itself the center of a disturbed appraisal that has rarely been bestowed upon a playwright of Mr. O'Neil's accredited standing. Technically perfect, it was discovered that its writer, in spite of Mr. Nathan and a few of the others—"cum laude"—had, so far as the rating of an intelligence was concerned, the aesthetics of an adolescent. Here were, as are generally associated with a period that delivers itself deliquescently from the Bible to be absorbed by the flagrant heresies of Darwin, Tom Paine and Ingersoll—huge gobs of controversial and agnostic matter, ordinarily assimilated and forgotten after the departure of adolescence. Nothing daunted, "Dynamo," as with all of Mr. O'Neil's other productions, excepting his casual and ill-fated "The Fountain," was subjected to the cold and merciless analysis of print.

With the appearance of "Mourning Becomes Electra," the controversy was revived. A feat the play has unquestionably proved to be—huge in its dimensional phases, seemingly more deft and recondite than anything since "Strange Interlude," and in its emotional aspects and dramatic cliches, certain or "sure-fire," as the average theatre-goer would be led to say. That the play is "fine theatre" no one would care to question, and that even its press-agented stunt of taxing the patience of its auditors by the production of three plays in one, without a hiatus, does not deter its success—leads us to the extraordinary good business sense of

Mr. O'Neil. That the reading of the play itself reduces us to the certain feeling of its failure as literature, is another matter. For one and all, they "date"—"Anna Christie," "The Hairy Ape," "Desire Under the Elms," "The Great God Brown," and what-not-else. And the literary element—that absolute preservative of all artistic and timeless work—is alarmingly absent. For a positive decree, Mr. O'Neil must abide the verdict of the next quarter of a century, but if past history in such adventitious instances prove prophetic, it may be even less. The production of "Mourning Becomes Electra" is made more than remarkable in its classical New England setting by the beautiful acting of Alice Brady and the magnificent realism of Madame Nazimova. One scene alone, that between the mother and daughter, with its metallic percussion of malice and its inviolable delivery of rhetorical poison, make it a scene to be remembered so long as memory serves that purpose. Sheer and high arises the consummate wall of artistry, erected in denunciation, by the shafts of the Russian actress's icy yet fiery vituperation. We remember no acting comparable to what Coleridge calls the "overmastering sense of reality" projected in the drama at this point. Over and above the ellipsis and verbal provocation of the lines ensues something so real and poignant that the situation is scarcely to be endured. Emphasizing much that is otherwise trivial and tame in contemporary miming, one must, perforce, retain one's hope and respect for the future of the American Theatre.

Hamlet

The past season's "Hamlet," a production designed and directed by Norman Bel Geddes, with the lead played by a young Canadian actor, Raymond Massey, fell foul of most New York professional criticism, yet it would seem not entirely with justifiable cause. To the present writer it would occur that the mere ordinary reading of the lines by Mr. Massey, the excellent portraiture of the Queen Mother by Mary Servoss, and the exquisite and universally-acclaimed Ophelia of Celia Johnson, should have given it longer shrift or at least some term of mild extenuation. Mr. Bel Geddes's marvellous lighting seemed almost superhumanly brilliant and beautiful. The cast in enacting the story, however, wandered on and off the stage in effect, much as one might imagine an excursion of the entire population of New York on its annual moving day in fall.

The Barretts of Wimpole Street

A great portion of what has been written or delivered of the practically perfect performance of Miss Katherine Cornell in her production of "The Barretts of Wimpole Street," attests to the lifelike and sympathetic creation of the two literary characters whose adventures conspire to make one of the most perfect dramas ever enacted in real life. Here, Miss Cornell's monotonous emotionalism serves its purpose to a degree that no play has ever delivered her to. We are told that the motif of incest, so strongly accentuated in the American version was barely made perceptible in the English presentation. One could have wished it otherwise in the performance by Miss Cornell, but curious readers or spectators of the play will hardly need to be told that the plot and planning of the entire unfolding of the drama, even to its odd or deliberate bearings in the machinations of the 1845 elopement by the Brownings, may be found nearly verbatim in an actual letter by the heroine, written to a friend in England.

[Untitled]

365 Ghost Stories. The Collected Ghost Stories of M. R. James. Sq. 8vo. N.Y. and London, 1931. $2.50

Nearly 650 pages of enchanted and haunting fiction by the one man living, who can—with a single exception—retrace the footsteps of loneliness on the wizard beach once trodden by Edgar Allan Poe, Ambrose Bierce, and Mary E. Wilkins-Freeman. THAT SINGLE EXCEPTION IS HOWARD PHILLIPS LOVECRAFT, OF 66 COLLEGE STREET, PROVIDENCE, RHODE ISLAND—THE GREATEST MASTER OF WEIRD STORY-TELLING SINCE POE.

A Letter on Hart Crane

EDITOR'S NOTE:—*In response to a request by the Editor of the* LIT *Mr. Samuel Loveman of New York has been kind enough to contribute a few recollections of Hart Crane.*

Mr. Loveman was the poet's closest friend during his years of creative activity. The letter quoted in the last paragraph was the poet's last communication before his death.

You ask me to perform the most difficult task in the world—to write about a human being whom one has loved, not because of his career as an artist nor for what the world has qualified as his genius, but because of some innately loyal feature that predominated in his makeup, in a personality drenched with sensitiveness and imbued with sincerity.

I first met Hart Crane in the spring of 1919 in Cleveland, Ohio. He was full of keen communication, a boy out of school at work for an insensitive father. Thus it was that I first learned of the existence of the left wing in modern literature—of Tristan Tzara, Jean Cocteau, Guillaume Apollinaire, James Joyce, *The Little Review*, Gorham Munson and T. S. Eliot. I was shown his sheaf of correspondence with the Intelligentsia, not the least being an unpleasant letter from Ezra Pound, the contents of which I forbear to describe. He was filled with his life in New York—of Amy Lowell, Jane Heap, Margaret Anderson, Djuna Barnes—and there clings to me his unforgettable anecdote of Amy Lowell's bi-yearly visit to the office of the Editors of *The Little Review,* flinging her huge ton of a bearskin coat at the foot of the high flight of stairs before her ascent, and hallooing and panting all the way up. An account by Mr. Charles Brooks in one of his early books of essays, published, if I recollect rightly, under the title of *A Modern Poet,* gives a fair photographic picture of him as he must have appeared to others in those days. Hart read it in huge glee, but not without a touch of lingering, ironic malice. His desire to return to New York was strong and made him restless; he began to entertain his friends and later to drink wine alone in the solitude of his third-story room. Our circle of people in Cleveland grew and then dissolved, as groups naturally do in a town of any considerable size. One of his closest friendships was with William Sommer of Macedonia, Ohio, an artist whose dimensions America must still find its way some day to recognize.

My residence in New York followed Hart's by only a few weeks. I arrived here, as one would say, "on my uppers," and was installed by him in the room at 110 Columbia Heights which he was later to occupy and in which he was to write *The Bridge,* a room from which Colonel Roebling, sick and paralyzed, had watched and awaited the construction of Brooklyn Bridge. From it, Ivan Opfer's father had only recently been taken to his death-bed in a hospital; but it bore no relation to all of this, except for the scene that enchanted and fascinated its occupants by day and night—the marvelous harbor view, with an incrustation of the glittering and flashing New York skyline; the boats and tugs and liners that constituted an incessant and variable pageant at any hour of the day. The room was long and narrow and whitewashed, with a cot against the wall. At dusk, with the lights out, the bare walls turned blue, while always before one was the scene that Joseph Pennell, who lived across the way at the Hotel Margaret and whom one could meet taking his morning's saunter, had declared to be without a peer in the whole world. I moved a short way down the street, but was never long separated from Hart. "You must always live on the Heights," he had earnestly advised. "Wherever I go and whatever I do, I'll always return here and it will be some comfort to know that you live nearby."

Life was beginning to become more complicated for him. Acquaintances increased, mostly of the drinking and carousing sort. *White Buildings* was published, but in spite of a second edition, fell like lead. *The Bridge* was projected and writing began. With it, came the process that linked his writing with drinking, i.e., the acceleration of the impetus to create that could only come with drink and music, until the process, or, if you choose to call it the combination—became inseparable.

Hart had gone abroad convinced that America was no place for the artist. He discoursed and objurgated vehemently at the suppression of the individual in the land of the free, and of the complete deliverance that awaited him with the rest of the expatriates in Paris. England came first—a stay with Robert Graves and Laura Riding, who had a houseboat on the tranquil Thames. After a brief stay in Paris, he made his way along the Cote d'Azur, with a visit to Roy Campbell in Southern France, which, I believe, ended disastrously. But the high point was Paris. Here he became involved, or rather enmeshed, in the coils of the French law, and was thrown into jail because of a brawl with gendarmes and sailors. Hart's shuddering description of the bestiality of a French jail and the brutality of the Parisian judge were unforgettable. His verbal narratives (I recall his amazing account of the West Indies hurricane) were Homeric in their episodic completeness and freedom from verbose locution. He was released after a few days, on the concerted plea and recommendations of several French intellectuals and artists, among whom were Chirico and Jean Cocteau.

His return to New York was signalised with as fantastic an outlay of clothes as I have ever seen—shirts from Provence, blazers from Marseilles, a raglan from London, and a beret from Paris. But it was a new Hart Crane, American to his finger-tips, a devotee of Walt Whitman and Emily Dickinson with Isadora Duncan as a side-issue, that arrived. *The Bridge* was slowly, and with an accretion of torment incredible to all but those that know the process of Hart's composition, worked into something that might approach but could never reach a complete unification. Dependence on the element of spiritous liquors was unbroken. To me, he had confessed his complete inability to break himself of the habit. Something seemed to have burned itself out within the boundaries of his creative consciousness, after the actual publication of *The Bridge*. There were flares and flings of the oldtime Dionysiac light and gusto that those who knew Hart will always and considerably associate with him. His return to Mexico the second time, after the death of his father, was as one who goes to his doom. I know little of that last phase.

Here is the postscript that accompanied "The Broken Tower," mailed to me a few days before his death, Easter, 1932. I copy it in a blind mist:

"What a jolly long letter from you, Sam! I can't get time to answer immediately, but here's a poem—about the first in 2 years. Tell me if you like it or not. Happiness continues, with also all the gay incidentals of a Mexican Easter—exploding Judases, rockets, flowers, pappas (excuse me, that's the spelling for Mexican potatoes!) mammas, delicious and infinitesimal children wearing masks and firemen's helmets, flowers galore and a sky that carries you ever upward! More anon and soon! Love always, Hart!" Hail and Farewell to you, Hart Crane!

Collecting Curious Books

We assure you that the title isn't at all what you may be led to believe. By the collecting of curious books—curious in the actual sense of the word—we mean books on odd subjects, out-of-the-way poetry, low- or high-cast novels written in such a state of actual unsophistication that the years have made them subjects for hilarious laughter rather than that of the deep and thorough profundity inculcated or intended by their author. Literature of this sort arose early. Elizabethan England, with its wholesale slaughter of pamphlets of prose and poetry, began the steady and varying stream that was to trickle with such persistence through to the 18th century, when the renaissance started anew. We have now no parallel in the number of books and pamphlets, all curious, that smothered, or (as Rabelais would have phrased it) "larded" the open literary market.

Shining examples of the 18th century English curiosa may be stipulated by such works as Amory's "John Buncle" (beloved by Lamb), Paltock's "Adventures of Peter Wilkins and the Flying Women," Ned Ward's "The London Spy"—while from the printed shambles of the shameless Edmund Curll, Pope's vociferous adversary, came a verbal inundation that flooded the sinks and sewers of London's Grub Street, and finally precipitated their publisher into the stocks for a timely, penitential whipping.

American has been consistently a home and harboring of the curious book. Beginning with 1820, the literature of roguery and confession flourished at its height like the proverbial green bay tree. Every unprotected female who had ever been the victim of deliberate seduction, flew to her reputation's rescue in the solidarity of print. From the criminal end came wholesale, early reports of trials for murder—veritable fests of rapine and revenge in a civilization that was to all other intents decent and violently sweet-smelling. Dainty, leather-bound tomes entitled "Gift Books" and "Tokens," with borders of illuminated amaranths centered by young women provided with extensive posteriors, who leaned against gilt funerary urns—made life just the vale of tears or hell on earth that it has always been suspected to be. The virgin of fifty sat herself down to read with all the abject, outer humility of one for whom hope had departed, "The Weeping Willow," a miniature volume of poetry published by Lydia H. Sigourney at Hartford, Connecticut, in 1847. A female of the same unblemished status but duly more kittenish, would have perused "The Floral Gift from Nature and the Heart," by Miss Mary Chauncey, a darling bijou printed in Worcester, Massachusetts, 1846. Its frontispiece depicts a red, red rose, with thorns, buds and emerald foliage—a rose that must have risen and fallen on the alabaster bosom of many a meek maiden of the Poe period. From Philadelphia, in the 1848, stems a tiny volume bound in full sheep, entitled "The American Joe Miller." Among its titles that must have set them hee-hawing, may be noted the following: Colonel Crockett's Quandary; Vocals in Rhode Island; Negro Jockeys; Dialogue in a New Jersey Tavern; a Kentuckian among Ladies; Maryland Wit; Scene in Nashville; A Kentucky Steamboat, etc., etc. In it, masculine virility may have sought refuge by combatting, in a sort of savage and belligerent rough-neckery, the influence that threatened to smother its valor in sentiment spread thick with drivel and honey. The seventies and eighties beheld a still more advanced phase—the utterly elegant and divinely trivial. Presses groaned, moaned and protested, but nevertheless tossed them off—books on etiquette, dancing, courtship, fortune-telling, sex, Mormonism, New York low-life, Henry Ward Beecher, Tennessee Claflin, Lola Montez, Adah Isaacs Mencken, *ad nauseam* and *in perpetuum*—without rest, without hope, without even a future. And then—miracle of miracles!—

Along came Nietzsche!

A Conversation with Ambrose Bierce

Now that dear George Sterling is dead and books about Ambrose Bierce already number a proverbial baker's dozen, posterity assumes proportions that make the latter a permanent literary legend. I visited Ambrose Bierce in the summer of 1913, only a few weeks before his disappearance from Washington, D. C. "Massive" and "leonine" were the two adjectives that best describe him, in perfecting a portrait that he has clearly remained before me to this day. Beneath an exterior of fierce irony, there was something definitely soft and alarmingly gentle. He was kindly, he was condescending, he was surprisingly human. He appeared not a day over sixty, although printed records had placed him at seventy-four. "Come in and have some beer," he promptly accosted me with, at the elevator on the floor of his apartment. I declared my instant aversion to beer, but the temptation to include "skittles" also, was overwhelming. "Come in anyway," was his smiling response, and so I entered. "You look like a poet," he remarked. "Can't be very old, either," he continued, after introducing me to the guests—his publisher, his friend and secretary, Carrie Christianson," [sic] and a Miss White. I nodded with due modesty. Conversation sprang into being like an incorrigible firefly dance of the far-flung atoms. So far as Bierce was concerned, it ran the gamut from an egoistic forcefulness usually associated with the omniscient period of Johnson or Pope, to an Ariel-like manipulation of subjects that must always characterize the born conversationalist.

The actual topic was, of course, George Sterling. Bierce fired his first salvo. "George is very ugly," he began, "something like Dante—they call him Dante, Ha! Ha! .... Sterling, unlike so many other poets, has never known a time when his published work was other than mature. Curious, isn't it, that a poet who has failed to reach the highest peak, is, in the eyes of his public the most despicable of human creatures. It is hard to understand. Men like Lord Tennyson are lauded to high Olympus, while the minor poet is relegated to the degradation of an insect. The truth is, that great poets are rarely, if ever, understood by their wives. Look at Heine, married to a woman so stupid she couldn't conceive what the world meant by calling her dead husband a man of genius. The average man is a fool—and so is the average woman, too, for that matter.

Talk veered to Shaw. "An imposter!" vociferated Bierce bringing down his fist, "all that is good in him I have written myself. It is difficult to say who is really the great light at present. Hardy is a decidedly vague name. Kipling, I believe to be the greatest living influence. I don't exactly see a necessity for the silly laureateship, but a man like Tennyson gave it an upward boost that will never be quite forgotten. The rest were batterheads!" Whitman and Masefield being next discussed, he declared tacitly and with finality: "Whitman was no poet. In Masefield I can see no good whatever. A correspondent has written me," he added, "that Sterling by way of comparison with Masefield, has signed himself in a letter as 'The Worm.' Imagine," he chuckled uproariously, "a great poet such as Sterling indubitably is, ever doing a thing as incredible as that!"

"Does this 'Collected Edition' mean that your work is completed?" was asked in parting. "Yes," he replied. "I have a half-humorous idea that the proceeds will support me—if not in luxury—at least in comfort, for the remainder of my life. But such things are for futurity. Journalism has been my work for the past thirty years. Of course, I had the cream and could pick exactly what I wanted."

A Holiday Post-Card

Offhand, we should say that by far the worst place to be in, during the year's holidays, must be a large city. Retrospection brings an endless chain of winding country byways, indefinably buried in snow; roadside trees and hedges, heavy with clinging rime; field and pasturage, covered with a spaceless carpet so white and unsullied that beside it, certain lines in Whittier's classic "Snow-bound," are endowed with permeating warmth or undeviating heat. Heaven conspires with the season in a perfect color-scheme, an endless mockery of blue. Not the blue as we know it on the fringe of a garment by Titian, a sonnet of Keats, or in the flashing and glittering skies above the Mediterranean—but a flawless resurrection of something that burns as well as freezes—an ode that might well have been written to a piece of Attic sculpture set in a temperature of minus zero.

Yet in our parasitic moments we prefer the city. Here you have us—seven or eight million souls tossed on one gigantic location, each as certain of its indomitable identify as the tiniest contributory figure in the cosmic calculation of a thundering theorem by Dr. Einstein. Here, is the one place in the world to forget everything—or to remember nothing. Charles Lamb loved it; George Gissing wrote about it; Walt Whitman prophesied for it. In the face of creation as Nature presents herself to us, men must ever remain the remote but invincibly sturdy and nihilistic figures represented as dancing motes by Thomas Hardy in his "Dynasts." Dwellers and inmates of a huge city, the spirit of their stalwart bravado persists, even as a sense of their just irony remains.

Love the city we do, much as those who have gone before us—lights, types, throngs, theatres, buildings, music, bookshops—bitter, sordid, witty, brilliant and gay at all times, but especially so at Christmas and the close of the old year. In it, are compounded to an infinitesimal fraction of correctness, the mysterious components of that profound chemical prescription commonly known as the "Joy of Life."

The Coast of Bohemia

The backwoods of literature are filled with books about the never-never lands—elusive marginalia on the desire of human beings to escape the dead-rot of civilization, the boundaries that provide for the jumping-off place in many a man's materialistic life. To it, some of the majors have largely contributed—notably De Foe, for whom the unreal was as actual as a bubble of dew solidified in crystal, and in our own day, W. H. Hudson.

It is rather for the minors of this particular aspect of literature that we choose to make our plea—a field that is seemingly as limitless in number as are its outrageously obsolete or forgotten specimens. Who, for instance, has ever heard of "Revi-Lona" by Frank Cowan of Greensburg, Pa? Originally sold for as low as five cents a copy, prices eventually gained an ascendancy to five dollars. We haven't seen a copy in three years, but this is one of the best of its sort. The hero is described as a brave man, with all of the vices and a few of the virtues of his sex, who becomes sick to death of the routine of everyday life. He embarks on an oldtime whaler which sets sail for the South Seas, where a shipwreck (and what a shipwreck it is!) casts him on an unknown island inhabited only by Amazonian women. We defy even De Foe to produce anything so similarly brilliant and unconsciously witty as the hero's espousal with nine or ten Amazonian woman, each on a successive nuptial night. Beautifully written and horribly printed, here is one book that cries for a modern edition. It deserves clear type, good paper and a sympathetic editor.

Better known, but more fastidious in its conscious, fantastic phases, and more deliberate in its conformable appeal to the reader's element of realism will be found John Uri Lloyd's "Etidorpha." This is a far-better book than anything ever written by Mr. H. G. Wells in his much-touted, earlier, pseudo-scientific vein. A breathless but tragic pathos hangs over the mysterious narrator: "I admit anything, everything. I do not know that I am here or that you are there. I do not know that I have ever been ... perhaps vacuity alone is tangible."

The 18th century gave us two novels that were to win the immortal laudation of Lamb and Coleridge—Paltock's "Peter Wilkins and the Flying Women" and "The Live and Adventures of John Buncle" by Thomas Amory. The first contains some of the most sheerly beautiful, imaginative writing of any period since "The Tempest" of Shakespeare. The curious wedding night of "Peter" and "Youwarkee" has been praised by no less a person than Hazlitt, for its rich, romantic flavor. It deserves that, and more. Meredith's "Richard Feverel" alone holds up beside it, for oddly-heightened ecstasy. In "John Buncle," the realistic type of the fantastic novel reaches its apogee. Mistakenly, this book has been compared to Rabelais, but George Borrow would be far more to the point. Such romping bluster, self-sufficiency and virile bravado, belong—not to the 18th—but to the 20th century. Somewhat with more dignity, but certainly with no less exaggeration, an 18th century novelist lands cheek-by-jowl with the virulent virtuosity of Mr. James Joyce.

A Whittier Discovery

In the days when our American literary torch flared with specious glitter, Poe's attack on Longfellow, accusing him in no mild or moderate terms of plagiarism and piratical theft, was designated as the last word in sensational word-baiting. True enough, the illustrious victim, from whom Poe had previously solicited and received a loan of money, remonstrated only in a private letter against the unjustifiable rudeness of his opponent's charge. Open or anonymous, defence of Longfellow became numerous and warmly partisan. But the born dreamer and gentleman-poet, seated like one of his own legends in the book-lined study at Cambridge, kept his own counsel and (in justice to his memory) his entirely equable temper. Only then, had Poe's foaming anger slowly subsided.

The literature of verbal analogy and plagiarism knows no greater and more delicately-refined work than "The Road to Xanadu," where a mind so beautifully unbalanced and nebulously-colored as that of Coleridge, is finally tracked from traces that are blindly intermingled and waste, into a single, clairvoyant source of inspiration. Mr. Lowes proves to such of us who need proof, that the brain, like the "loop'd and window'd raggedness" of Lear, is open to the persuasive habitation of all elements, even as its vigilances are accessible to every phase of emotional truth.

We have before us a copy of a bygone London annual edited by Allan Cunningham—"The Anniversary," for 1829. In its table of contents may be found a surprising number of first-hand contributions by George Darley, John Clare, James Hogg, J. G. Lockhart, Miss Mitford, Caroline Bowles and Robert Southey. Many of the additional contributions are unsigned or merely initialed and it is one of the latter that excites our instant attention. This is a poem of sixty lines in the metre of Whittier's "The Barefoot Boy," entitled "The Blackberry Boy," identified, at the end, with the initial "C," and accompanied by an illustrative plate. So startling is the similarity between this poem printed in 1829, and Whittier's famous lines, published many years later, that one is moved to believe Whittier's actual reading of this poem and its eventual use for his composition.

Incredible as it may seem, practically every mood and color of phrasing in the American poet's one hundred odd lines, find their equivalent in this earlier poem. Here is an instance:

> "For gladness as the bees which sup
>   On honey when the sun is up,
>   Was I; and pure as rose in June,
>   Or star which rises next the moon,
>   And restless as the running stream,
>   And joyous as the morning beam,
>   And light of heart and bright of face
>   I started on life's oft-run race."

And in the allusions to nature:

> "Ah! Different when, sweet Child, like thee,
>   I hunted wild the murmuring bee;
>   Or loitering o'er my school-boy task.
>   In sunshine stretched me out to bask;
>   Chased speckled trout from stone to bank,
>   Made whistles, swords of rushes rank;
>   To trees and streams as brethren spake,
>   And dyed my lips with berries black;
>   **The wild fruit, in the wildest tree,**
>   **Might 'scape from birds, but not from me."**

Had Whittier read this poem, and if so, did it seep into his consciousness? Or again, is it simply another instance of those curious but undefinable transmigrations that occur in literature as well as in life? One hesitates to hazard an answer. Yet those haunting, wizard lines:

> "The wild fruit, in the wildest tree,
>   Might 'scape from birds, but not from me—"

Whose poetry could it be, but that of Samuel Taylor Coleridge!

Books in Summer

"Dear Mr. Cataloguer, now that you have blurbed and extolled and emphasized some ten thousand books during the past season in your eminently readable DAUBER AND PINE Catalogues of General Literature, just what volumes are YOU going to take with you on your vacation? The writer is curious. (Initialled) C.D."

Well, C.D., we don't in the least mind telling you—we have decided on four books. Not that we propose to read each of them all the way through—heavens and earth, no! Two, we have read several times from cover to cover; one, we swear by Allah, has remained unread even by a single human being for a period of at least two hundred years. Truly, we shall consider ourselves

> "To be the first that ever burst
> Into that silent Sea!"

So, here they are: The "Collected Letters" of Jane Austen, in the handsome two-volume Oxford Edition, shimmering bits of quiet staccato that connect the flower-strewn abysses between her so-few novels, much as the jeweled Lapland day does its long and lonely Arctic night. Second, "South Wind," by Norman Douglas (Evoe! Evoe!). We should think ourself ill-adjusted, indeed, if an occasional reading did not bring us back again to the most wonderful book ever written by a discontented human being. Meet us, if you like, in the Count's sunny, archaeological garden, forgetting for once that, you or credulous American multi-millionaires—remembering only, that behind the charming fable lies its exquisite Italian scene, an wonderful island, blue and wave-encircled and hyaline, with most enchanting group of people ever assembled for the purpose of making literature.

Third: The "Collected Poems" of Hart Crane. Cognizant of the legend that has already formed itself around his brief, unruly existence, we propose to read his poetry once again to prove to ourselves that he was really the great American poet so many of his fervent admirers claim him to be. That his life and poetry are inseparable, we have not the slightest doubt. Poe himself, and Marlow certainly, never crammed into their headlong courses so much of what we call the "tragic element"; nor did Villon and Lord Rochester, Rimbaud and Verlaine, drink the dregs from as riotously bitter and deadly a potent cup.

Last, but not least—"The General Historie of the Turkes," by Richard Knolles, anno 1603. Honestly, we are resolved to read this book and to read it through, for all its portentous folio size—even if we perish by so doing. What were the unspeakable imprecations of the rival Commanders of the Faithful, as they uttered gigantic maledictions in their daily prayers, each one vociferously blaspheming the other? Who said to

Fatima, daughter of the divine Mohamet: "Thy father was better than I, but thou are better than my daughters"? Why did Abu Bekr, A.D. 632, dye his beard a flaming red, ere he entered the great Mosque at Medina?

We haven't the slightest idea; ours be the duty to find out. Be sure, however, that with the exception of the above noted, we propose for the period of our vacation (two weeks, my hearties!) to forget not only the gentle art of cataloguing but the very existence of books themselves. And yet ... and yet ... those unread nineteen volumes of the Paget Toynbee Edition of Horace Walpole's Letters; Doughty's "Arabia Deserta," complete in two marvelous tomes; the Wheatley Edition of the "Diary" of John Evelyn, four volumes of sheer delight! Have we made a vow and do we contradict ourself by breaking it? Very well then—we contradict ourself!

A Sea-Coal Fire

Few of us possess the "sea-coal fire" that Shakespeare conjures up in that miracle of historical plays, "Henry the Fourth": "Thou didst swear to me upon a parcel-gilt goblet, sitting in my Dolphin-chamber, at the round table, by a sea-coal fire...." but if one actually had a "sea-coal fire" in the aforesaid chamber, with the possibilities of a "parcel-gilt goblet," would *you* dream your dream as we would ours? We have a vision of all the people we have loved in literature, much-memoried and beloved, coming to life again from between the covers of books. If you were asked to make your choice, could you do so? Out of the orange and blue light of the flame, we bring to you our own—some in fact and some in fiction, but all so real that their actuality requires only a matter of belief:

John Keats, peering through the casement of Leigh Hunt's cottage in the Vale of Health, Hampstead, waiting for Fanny Brawne to pass by; Shelly in Elinor Wylie's "The Orphan Angel," flickering through the forests of Kentucky, a radiant wraith with eyes still misted by the far-off waters of the Gulf of Spezzia; Isadore Duncan in her pathetic, final phase—"Adieu, mea amis—Je vais a gloire!"—embarking to death in the snare of her Chinese scarf; Shestov's account of his visit to Tolstoy: "He is like a god, not an Olympian, but the kind of Russian god who sits on a maple throne under a golden lime tree; not very majestic, but perhaps much more cunning"; Emily Dickinson's last words to the living: "Little

Cousins, called back"; Sarah Orne Jewett's "The Queen's Twin," a gentle, harmless and half-hallucinated, old lady, who believed herself divinely affiliated with—no less a person than Victoria, Queen of England; the hero of Thomas Hardy's "The Well-Beloved," ingeniously eager and everlastingly pursuing the intolerable image of love dawn three generations of elusive femininity; Shakespeare's "Hermione," the pattern of everything gracious and beautiful and wise, in the heartache covered by her ivory serenity, pleading her own just and inviolable cause:

"No life,
I prize it not a straw";

Compton Mackenzie's marvelous portrait of "Rory," in his odd but entirely creditable novel of Capri, "Extraordinary Women"; Meredith's "Sandra Belloni," singing her nightingale-song in an English forest, when a sleepy fire of early moonlight hung through the dusky fir branches"; "The Private Papers of Henry Rycroft," a spiritual autobiography in golden tints and perfumed prose, completely at variance with Gissing's personal, sordid life; Gibbon, drinking his brandy and water from a teapot exactly three-quarters of an hour before his death; Lear's rending cry of momentary recognition to Kent, in the greatest tragedy every written; the parting utterance of Medea: "Be happy," in William Morris's "Life and Death of Jason"; Southey to Carlyle: "I have told Hartley Coleridge, that he ought to take up a strong cudgel, and give De Quincy, publicly in the streets there, a sound beating"; Hart Crane reading his poetry to a stoker and a sailor from the Battleship "Wyoming,' in his basement apartment at 190 Columbia Heights, Brooklyn; Beddoes setting fire to Covent Garden with a five pound note; Swinburne, carted off by Theodore Watts-Dunton to the Pines, Putney, to be cured of drink; the love-letters of Mrs. Gilchrist to Walt Whitman and the love-letters of Whitman to his Washington street-car conductor, Peter Doyle; Peer Gynt's last ride with his old mother across the pine-haunted forest to the lighted Castle of Soria-Moria, east of the sun and west of the moon; the funeral of Francis Thompson—the lowering of the coffin covered with violets from George Meredith, Edmund Gosse and Sidney Colvin vehemently discussing Stevenson's prose style at one end, Mrs. Meynell at the other, copiously weeping into her pocket handkerchief but sufficiently aware of the drift of the conversation to lift her head with flashing eyes and cry out: "Stevenson had no style"—then to proceed weeping again

Try it before your own "sea-coal fire!"

New York Dynamics

When, in 1913, the writer visited Ambrose Bierce for the last few weeks preceding his mysterious disappearance, he was greeted sardonically with something that ran as follows: "Watch yourself in New York. Manhattan is hashish, opium, cocaine. No drug, as a matter of fact, is so deleterious as the poison that awaits you there. You are met at the Pennsylvania Station by the colored porters themselves dancing away with your luggage to the tune of their ingratiating but obscene rhythms. They build their monolithic skyscrapers to it. Walk through the downtown streets—the Wall Street section specifically—and see if the very buildings don't desert their foundations and dance toppling down the street following you to East River and into the bay. New York is something apart from anything else in America. Its dissonance spells chaos to the marvelously attuned metrics of the sensitive ear. It ruined George Sterling during his prolonged stay there, so far as his genius or career for writing great poetry are concerned. But what I want to warn you against is the rhythm, the insistent, negroid rhythm and movement of this uncanny and diabolically unholy, cacophonous city. A passage in Plutarch's life of Mark Anthony illustrate just what I mean. 'In *Euphesus,*' he writes, 'women attired as they go in feasts and sacrifice of Bacchus came out to meet him with solemnities and ceremonies, with men and children disguised like fauns and satyrs. Moreover, the city was full of ivy, and darts wreathed about with ivy, psalterions, flutes and hautboys. In their songs they called him Bacchus, father of mirth, courteous and gentle. So he was to some, but to the most part of men, cruel and extreme.' Now substitute for Bacchus in a leopard skin, the great god Mumbo Jumbo of the African jungle, primitive, uncouth, a gigantic and gestative, phallic deity, and there you have the pervading monster that now rules New York."

When, not so many years later, the advent of George Antheil returning to this country, heralded by Ezra Pound, was to be made an actuality by his single concert at Carnegie Hall, excitement rose to a very high pitch. That this was warranted is attested by the fact that never, in all the years of professional music here, have such scenes been witnessed as auditors were to witness that night. Antheil's *Ballet Mécanique* was the *"piece de résistance."* Described by those who had previously heard it in Paris as purely modern American music, it resolved itself in a gigantic unmelodic rhythm that was thumped out on their elbows by a number of relentlessly-determined pianists on their several pianos, while a specially-contrived machine at which Mr. Antheil himself officiated, overtopped by a screaming and vociferous siren, took heaven and its silver music by storm with much more fury than ever did the vocal portion in the final movement of Beethoven's 9th Symphony. Purely American music had come, was the cry. But had it ever been absent?—was succinctly queried by others.

For here, in something composed of about ninety-five per-cent cacophony and five per-cent music, was the long-lost answer to the modernist's midsummer night's dream. Here, too, were to be found those casually disregarded yet curiously related components of rhythms that the penetrating observer could find in a million and one active city minutiae ... rumble of subways, pounding of airblasts, deafening of rivets, clanging of bells, clashing of sounds, cries of hawkers, press of people and faces ... always faces; a distinct cosmography in which one city that, city being New York, seems to have been accorded so much, that every other place seems less richly endowed, less potently profitable.

Something beside the noise of Mr. Antheil's concert that evening, his auditors were assuredly given. Those in the audience who remained unbefuddled by the throwing of missiles at performers and this boisterous cries of opprobrium or dissent, were vouchsafed a glimmer of what the composer had contrived to project during the course of his astonishing program. Gone forever, were the days of the old-fashioned technique that had accustomed us to the stereotyped but endlessly pleasing patterns of symphony, sonata, concerto and *air de ballet.* In its place was a concept seemingly as formless yet as clearly sanative as the phenomena of formlessness and sanativeness that we have come to associate with Gertrude Stein's highly-proscribed prose. It has its derivation for the whole world of contemporary art, by this time clearly defined and precisely stated—the art of Cezanne, Picasso, Modigliani, Gaudier-Brzeska, Henri Rousseau and Matisse. Like these it was informed with the same power that made for antagonism to precipitate artistic hatred. In it, were already placed those properties that we now associate with Mr. Wilenski's recent definition of sculptural imagination—"The Power to organize formal energy in symbols for the universal analogy of form."

Forth from La Mancha

Legend has it that in late years and a long time after his master's passing, grown rubicund with ease and comfort, Sancho Panza resolved to revisit the scenes of his former vicissitudes, as described in that admirable work, "Don Quixote," by the worthy Miguel de Cervantes. It was spring and the air had a foretaste to it like the best wine of Amontillado. True enough, Sancho who knew only the rough but serviceable vintage of his own village, could not have declared the difference. But that all heaven was blue he must have been cognizant of by its resemblance to some azure altar cloth in the cathedral, and that the wayside was scented he knew well—because there is no odor so sweet and penetrating as the perfume of the burgeoning hedges of La Mancha in the heart of spring.

Descending the steep declivity that led down to the green and well-watered valley shining pleasantly below, Sancho prodded the sides of his sleek and lazy-paced mule. "Whither, Sancho," screamed a young girl with arms akimbo from an open doorway, "and why caparisoned with shield and armor?" "Hold thy mouth, lass!" admonished Sancho with a scornful wave of his free hand. "However, if secrecy be thine, let me unfold it unto thee. First, I go once more to wage puissant war (as did my master of blessed memory) with those immortal giants, miscalled by some 'wind-mills;' second, to witness yet again that comely semblance of unparalleled divinity, my master's beauteous Dulcinea; third, to rule justly and wisely among the noble islanders of Barataria, as I did during the days of my omnipotent, fiery youth." "Nit-wit! Nit-wit!" screamed the young woman after him. "Silence, witch!" thundered Sancho, not greatly perturbed, and rode leisurely down to where sunshine and legend swallowed him up in the aureate mist of over four centuries ago.

Incredibly enough, in the core of this legend lies fair proof that insecurity exists not alone for us as human beings in life—but for the fortunes of our imaginary characters in literature. Did you think (as we thought) that Sancho went back for good to his old home, embowered between food and drink, among the burning oleanders of his sleepy hamlet? Not our hero! Beholden to no one, but master of the one memory that had sped him in earlier years to fare with the maddest idealist who ever sought the high road in search of the most fantastic adventure ever conceived by a human brain, there flickered within his indomitable and incorrigible soul the essence of something that roamed and roared and blazed. Once again, the winding and sloping road to Segovia beckoned him. Not wind and rain, not hail and sleet not burning sun or freezing snow, could keep him from his appointed quest—

FORTH FROM LA MANCHA!

Boswell Redivivus

There is a conversation that a lover of Dr. Johnson will not find perpetuated in his beloved Boswell, nor is it duly but drearily recorded in the sacrosanct if somewhat irrelevant pages of Sir John Hawkins, in the winsome wit of pretty Mrs. Thrale, or in those countless indefatigable chroniclers of colored minutiae and small beer that follow precisely in the wake of a man of genius. Briefly, it follows; how brief—the reader will at once perceive.

Scene: The Mitre. Present: Dr. Johnson and Boswell.

Boswell. Garrick has confided to Tom Davies, to Reynolds, and to half the town beside, that his last production, writ by himself, is the greatest drama since Shakespeare. Tell me sir, why does Garrick exaggerate?

Johnson. Garrick is a dolt, an imbecile, a pseudonomycule, a— a— a mime!

Boswell. Yet he asseverates his complete and ardent friendship for you, Sir.

Johnson. He forfeits it three hundred and sixty-five days a year! Had I a son, Sir, he should read nothing modern, see nothing modern, partake of nothing modern—but live for the first twenty-five years of his life impanelled in a library.

Boswell. Impossible! But why, Sir, in a library? Would you not at least permit him to confront the world? Then, too, it should be most desirous and certainly most natural that he meet and mingle in the society of the fair sex.

Johnson. No, Sir! There is no such safety in all the world as in books—I mean in old books. I remember my father's own bookshop and during my period of apprenticeship there, was acquainted with every nook and corner, with every separate quarto and folio in the place. Sir, I read more in Litchfield than I have had occasion to read ever since. My candle guttered nightly in the pleasant and profitable pursuit of knowledge. Saint Augustine and Epictetus taught me much of the material ways of life. I partook of the Apostolic Fathers and read the Roman Poets with great, familiar gusto. I learned to make love from the passion in their lines, as indeed most of us should do.

Boswell. The Roman Poets were vicious, immoral and profane. Your love, must have been of the highest order, Sir!

Johnson. Only a fool would think so. No, Sir—love is love, and differs not a whit with anyone, anywhere. The function of the human animal operates instinctively alike, in each of us. I have never set myself up to be a saint, nor could I be picked out in a crowd for a villain. But it is of books we were talking, not women, Sir!

Boswell. Dear Sir, you endow me with a new impetus. I warrant you that I shall lay siege to my library with renewed assurance when I return again to Auchinleck.

Johnson. Do so, Sir. There is no life beyond the four corners of the room that contains your chiefest possessions, your books. Had I my wife, I would hold her subservient even to these. One should be constantly reminded of that fabulous spot in no wise attributed to orthodoxy, but set in the Elysian Isles of the South Seas, where the rains beat and hail fell, save in one sanctified circle of sunlight. These are your books, your good books, Sir. Keep them innermost and close to you; nor shall you regret it.

Johnson's Servant. Master, it snows heavily; the streets are already drifted deep; I have brought a lanthorn along with me.

Johnson. Bless us, Francis, so you have. Sir, it has been my unbounded pleasure to have dined with you here, this evening. Tender my worthy respects and my most felicitous regards to the dear lady, your wife, when you return again to Auchinleck. She shall yet learn to love me! (*He chuckles and repeats as though to himself.*) Little rogue, she shall yet learn to love me! (*Exeunt.*)

A Feast of Charles Lamb

Now, that his collected letters have been finally published in the handsome three-volume edition so admirably edited by E. V. Lucas, lovers of Elia will have before them a full feast—flavorous as well as informative—of the delicate mechanism that functioned in the most charming personality ever created, to manifest itself by a series of unsurpassed essays.

Here, for once, are the original letters, printed as Lamb actually penned them—unhampered by expurgation and heightened by the candor of a soul who could be as forthright as the greatest in literature. Here, are the letters we have known so long, the early letters to Coleridge advising him of the cataclysm in his family, that mighty horror, when—he writes—"my poor dear dearest sister has been the death of her own mother. I was at hand only time enough to snatch the knife out of her grasp. She is at present in a madhouse ... God has preserved to me my senses—I eat and drink and sleep."

Here, too, are all the wonderful letters to Manning, the Lloyds and to Bernard Barton, long consigned to other editions or the oblivion of separate volumes, and at last placed into the miraculous progression of their proper sequence. Dare we forget the heart-rending letter that Lamb wrote to Fanny Kelly, beseeching her to relinquish the theatre and become his wife?—"Can you quit these shadows of existence, and come and be a reality to us?" We know now that her refusal was due to the maenadic insanity of Mary Lamb.

Present also, in an initial reading to us, is Lamb's unabashed but tragic confession of drunkenness at a party the evening before, given by his physician, Dr. J. Vale Asbury: "It is an observation of a wise man 'that moderation is best in all things.' I cannot agree with him 'in liquor' ... I protest I thought myself in a palanquin, and never felt myself so grandly carried ... My sister has begged me to write an apology to Mrs. A. and you for disgracing your party; now it does seem to me, that I rather honoured your party, for every one that was not drunk (and one or two of the ladies, I am sure, were not) must have been set off greatly in contrast to me. I was the scapegoat."

Reader, are you sick to death of the angularities and contumely, that have gone to the making of modern literature? Have you wearied (as we have) of the deliberate distortion that has conceived life as a succession of machines—monsters without joy made by man to parody the image of huge madness in the firelight of his dancing brain? Would you (as of old) care to cast your lot again with human beings?

Then read the letters of Charles Lamb. Track him through the haunted streets of London—"Noise of coaches, drowsy cry of mechanic watchmen in the night ... inns of the court, with their learned air, and halls and butteries, just like Cambridge colleges; old bookstalls, Jeremy Taylors, Burtons on Melancholy, and Religio Medicis on every stall." The quiet, shy, stammering, informal Charles Lamb, unrecognized royalty in his own right, dressed in threadbare, rusty brown, thin hair flying in the jolly Edmonton breeze, following the path lined with flowers and sedge along the old canal; Lamb at the Leigh Hunts; at the bedside of the dying Hazlitt; at whist with the gay Badams in the flying dusk of a stormy Saturday evening; at the immortal supper given by Haydon—his hilarious, tipsy incident with the dumb Comptroller—while present, in the guise of a divine chorus, were Keats, Wordsworth, Ritchie and Monkhouse ...

Would you ... would you? There is no better company in the world!

We Break the Silence

There are books that one reads not only from a sense of duty to the outside world, but as an act of voluntary obligation toward one's self. Reading them, one is constrained to declare, after the last word of the final chapter has been arduously reached: "I shall never read this book again. Such books (to us, at least), are Carlyle's "French Revolution"; Browning's "Ring and the Book"; Evelyn's "Diary"; De Gourmont "On Love"; Thackeray's "Vanity Fair"; Fielding's "Tom Jones"; any book by G. K. Chesterton; Spengler's "Decline of the West"; much of the later Ruskin. The list could reach into infinity. We shall never read them again for various reasons, but probably because of the books that we really love, whose insistence that we return to them again is like the knocking of the porter at the gate, in "Macbeth." Their urgency to reenter again into our consciousness, is too great to be withstood.

What then, you ask, are those books with undefinable and perhaps unusual charm, that cry for a re-reading? Each of us, a human personality within a world of its own, demands the privilege of making a personal selection. There are some books such as Jane Austen's "Emma" and "Pride and Prejudice," where the mere dilemma of parting with the characters at the end of a twentieth reading, works such havoc as could never be understood by a layman—and leads one to wonder what the anguish would be if one were cognizant of separating from them forever. Pepys's "Diary," the "'Letters" of Lamb and Keats and Shelley, Plato's "Dialogues," Casanova's "Memoirs," Thayer's "Life of Beethoven," Van Gogh's "Letters to His Brother," Shakespeare's "Sonnets" . . . here again, all are cut from the same pattern and the roll is endless.

There are books where the sheer torment of acquisition is more than compensated by the lofty declaration of their tragic heights—Shakespeare's "King Lear," Emily Brontë's "Wuthering Heights," Douglas's "House with the Green Shutters," "The Trojan Women" of Euripides. We read them because of the double purgation by suffering, where the soul, peering into the pool of its own consciousness, views beneath the spectral placidity, this incomparable tempest of life.

Each of us chooses the books that become meat and drink and even existence unto ourselves. Have you read "South Wind," and has its lighthearted, but not exactly brittle gayety, fashioned for you the image of an insouciant planet heaving off into the vast empyrean? Or Beardsley's annihilating last prose fragment, "Venus and Tannhauser"—so gigantic a bit of ironic or defeatist writing that the end could only have been the death of either Beardsley or his unsacrosanct opus? Do you know of a book by Edward Hutton, entitled "A Glimpse of Greece"; an account of a tour made by the latter in conjunction with Mr. Norman Douglas? Nothing in the literature of delight can equal the registration by the author, of his Hellenic conversations with Mr. Douglas. Embarking on the second reading of Proust's "Remembrance of Things Past," we become keenly and sensitively aware of our poignant reaction to the first reading, in relation to the growing realism and suffering of the hero—or rather, of Proust himself. The fifth or possibly sixth reading of the huge scene of justice in "Don Quixote," where Sancho Panza sits in the parody of a tribunal—unfolds again for us a scene of pure comedy lifted to a peak of poetry as direct and deliberate as the fall of Lucifer in "Paradise Lost"—a trackless but swift excursion of genius into a realm flooded with light and understanding.

Some day, we promise you, that we shall again form our own library—plays, essays, biographies, novels, and even oddities of literature—the right books, the inevitable volumes, so secure and unshaken in their perfection that not even so-and-so's latest list of the best one-hundred titles, will ever budge them from their massive, oaken shelves.

On such a day and in such a place, we shall invite you to enter.

Literature and Life

Life parallels literature, but unless you are guided or determined, you will know no more of it than the last of this year's snows are aware of the trembling of their white world into green, or the change and transmutation of sunlight into shadow. Yet we are confirmed in believing that there are moments in life as expressed by the power and perfection of literature, that may be ours only through the symbiosis of the written word. Then it is that the media of the dream becomes vividly real. All else that you invoke into the immutable processes of the imagination, is otherwise futile. But come—we offer a solution to a world well-lost. These then, are the great moments, for any one of which we would have vouchsafed a portion of our lifetime to have witnessed:

Shakespeare, in the apartment of his notary . . . "I give unto my wife my second-best bed with the furniture" (and to some light of love his very soul); an early awakening of Pepys by his jealous French wife, who threatens him in no uncertain terms, with a heated poker in her hand; Wilde, on his way to a two years' sentence in Reading Gaol, hissed and hooted and outraged by a mob in the rain; the burial of William Blake in Potters' Field; the separation of Duse from D'Annunzio—her broken utterance: "Ashes—ashes—before my eyes, on my lips, in my empty hands"; Emerson, his mind completely effaced, staring mistily into the coffin at Longfellow, then confiding to William Dean Howells: "His was a beautiful soul but I forget his name"; Poe, dying in a drunken stupor on the streets of Baltimore; Shelley, by the sea at Viareggio and the vision of the golden Allegra, Byron's little daughter, arising from the waves and clapping and beckoning to him with her childish hands; the deaf Beethoven leading his gigantic Ninth Symphony; Chatterton, in a cheap London lodging, swallowing his vial of arsenic; Mary Lamb, old and demented, in gusts of tears and laughter at her brother's funeral;

Beddoes setting fire to Covent Garden with a five-pound note; the poisoner Wainewright, a crony of Lamb's, recognized as a convict, in Australia.... "They think me a desperado. Me! the companion of poets, philosophers, artists and musicians, a desperado"; Cowper, raving, quieted by the portrait of his mother; Garrick as Richard the Third and Mrs. Siddons as Lady Macbeth; Therese, lost to the sight of Casanova for twenty migratory years, but nursing him unrecognized and lovingly through an illness in the poverty of his old age; the great Balzac dying in one room and Madame Hanska, his Polish wife, emerging after an assignation with her lover, from another; Thomas Hardy, alone at midnight under the stars, on Egdon Heath; Horace Walpole, in his castle of stucco, pinchbeck and glass, making love to charming Kitty Clive; Swinburne, evading the wary Watts-Dunton to steal past his open door for his bottle of ale at the "Pub" across Putney Common; Dr. Johnson, in an ante-room of the Earl of Chesterfield.... "Seven years, my Lord, have now passed, since I waited in your outward rooms, or was repulsed from your door"; the summary and weeping departure of Keats from the household of Leigh Hunt, due to the inadvertent opening of a love-letter from Fanny Brawne, by one of Hunt's children; Beardsley, in his death-agony, beseeching his friends to destroy his obscene drawings.

Whether it be Lear who cries out to you: "All's cheerless, dark and deadly," or Hazlitt confessing, with the light extinguished from his once-ardent eyes: "I have had a happy life"—the business of living revolves itself into an escape, and mainly into literature. Look out through your window, for Autumn is come again. If you be so fortunate, you shall see day by day the miracle of the foliage, dyed as no tropic moth has ever been—falling, falling steadfastly across the thin, blue horizon of the farthest hills. Turn to your books then, for between their covers is release.

Back to La Mancha

When Don Quixote, sometime Knight and eternally resident of the tiny, rain-beaten village of La Mancha, after a thousand and one extraordinary adventures which the world still thrills and resounds to, returned home, he announced in no uncertain terms his intention of henceforth leading a shepherd's life. His niece, Antonia, implored him to desist. "Bless us, Uncle," she exclaimed, "what new maggot is gone into your head! We thought you were come to stay here at home and live like a sober and honest gentleman." "Hold your tongue," was the good Knight's answer, "only help me to get into bed for I find myself somewhat out of order."

We know that he was old, half-mad and tired. We infer that he drew his coverlet of soft, Asturian fleece about him with trembling hands, wept some, prayed more, then quietly passed out of the scene. Secretly, we doubt it. He was too good and glorified a bookhunter to dispense with so fine a sport at that stage of the game, even after the Curate's irate conflagration of his own fantastic and somewhat notorious library. They would have cajoled him, beckoned him on ... the dust and must of all the accumulated bookstalls in his neighboring countryside; the resonant hawkers of romantic, dramatic and chivalric ballads on the broad, marble stoops of its delicate, skyblown cathedrals; the stained wine-sellers, dispensing from yellow and scarlet skins, a rich fermentation of the choicest and fieriest vintage in hazy La Mancha; sunlight like fire, glowing heat, awnings of orange and rose, pervasive blue fogs ... everywhere life and everywhere color, coupled with this one, consuming passion for books, which alone could have contributed to keep his undaunted and indomitable old soul alive.

To concern oneself with life so deeply that everything else is swept aside, to place a species of cosmic italicizing on the restlessness of the throng, the endless attraction and repulsion of personalities, the finite and kaleidoscopic variation in the vast or sinister scheme of the Human Comedy—then to come back and find that after all, the best and most immortal part of it lay close enough between the covers of our books— this we hold to be (as did possibly Don Quixote) the inevitable solution. No other objective is so certain; nothing else can equal the thrill of its illimitable expectancy. Even so, did William Blake retire to his shabby but shining room, high above the gray tracery of the Thames; Robert Southey to his marvellous mountain-study at Keswick; Charles Lamb to his pleasant, book-thronged cottage in green and leafy Edmonton.

For one's indissoluble refuge, after the foundering-wreckage of all that is too substantially concrete or too illusively unreal, is a return to this earliest and only love, the timeless and unchanging world of Books—

Or to La Mancha.

Under the Mistletoe

Where we come from, it begins to snow a week before Christmas. Ever so imperceptibly signalised by the pattern of a few idle flakes across the window, it becomes by nightfall, a spaceless and giant gale that flickers and howls and slashes the darkness into a monument of tenantless fury. By the close of day, all cognizance that one has ever had of the familiar traces of streets, paths, trees, hills, fences, fields and roads—anything and everything contributory to the actuality of life around us is lost, while softly persistently and unevasively the obliteration proceeds.

Be comforted—there are still books. Not Whittier's "Snow Bound:"

> "*A night made hoary with the swarm*
> *And whirl-dance of the blinding storm;*"

not the Pearys and Shackletons; works on the infinite and almighty Gothic cathedrals of the gray North; the New England poets, as strictly and sternly disciplined as the arid earth that yields them their slender, poetic foison—ah, no! not these. But books on Italy, Greece, Provence, the Mediterranean, the Carribs, the South Seas—a jewelled civilization of light, heat, radiance perfume and green vegetation, where

> "*For hours and hours,*
> *On the still deep,*
> *Comes the odor of flowers*
> *Comes the color of sleep.*"

And nothing else. It is there that one would mostly care to turn to.

Certain books fill this desire, and certainly this need—such as the "South Wind" of Norman Douglas. Read it in the dusk of an inclement day and you shall see (such is its magic) the white foam of the bluest seas wavering in shell-like coruscations around the enchanted coast of Nepenthe (we had nearly written Capri), and if the reader will promise to be ever so moderately discreet, he may even glimpse the fascinating but mysterious Mr. Keith, "vanishing for a day and returning with some rare orchid from the hills, a piece of Greek statuary, a new gardener, or something." There are others—D. H. Lawrence's "Sea and Sardinia," the gorgeous travel-essays of John Addington Symonds, Goethe's "William Meister" ("Kennst du das Land wo die Zitronen blueh'n?"); Herman

Melville's happiest South Sea books; the delightful, derelict essays of Vernon Lee; Simeon Solomon's "Vision of Love Revealed in Sleep"; Arthur Symons's ineluctible "Cities of Italy;" the Poems of Sappho; the entire Greek Anthology—beautiful books, all of them. So many have clustered in our brain, that we forget the flying wilderness of snow outside.

In Macedonia, Ohio, Bill Sommer takes his yellow lantern and stumbles in a drift knee-deep, from the studio to his house; the valley of the Brandywine is white, white with a screen of perpetually falling snow; his waterfall, heard like a murmur by day and by night in the early Spring, is long since silent. Greetings, Bill! In the city of Cleveland, our old friend Richard Laukhuff closes his shop an hour earlier, to go home. Number 40, Taylor Arcade must surely be haunted on this night by the faces it has known—or that we have known and loved—Morris Miller, Don Bregenzer, Hart Crane. Our own candle is lit at 11 Charles Street, in the heart of Greenwich Village, New York City. We know (yet we shall not be there!), that from Brooklyn, the line of buildings over in New York, is like a shimmer of gems....

Lights—lights everywhere! And wherever it blows or wherever it snows, to everyone in all this wide and wonderful world—A MERRY CHRISTMAS AND A HAPPY NEW YEAR.

An Unedited Anthology

Once upon a time, we determined the accomplishment of an anthology. Not your ordinary anthology, but something so precisely different and of such incalculable dimensions, that it was to partake not only of the hugeness, but the pity, joy, tragedy and exaltation of this our existence. Lines, incidents prose and poetic snatches, color, music, ribaldry and cacophony, were all to be involved in the pattern. We were to direct it as one might direct a symphony such as the Ninth of Beethoven, and of equal dimensions. Yet we shall never do this anthology. It remains a fragment, though we took a few notes for the major motif—

"One faint, eternal eventide of gems."

These were to have been the recensions:
The last hour of Socrates, with the blue, Athenian midday stream-

ing over the heads of his stricken disciples; the slaying of the children of Jason by their mother, Medea, intoned from the veiled Chorus outside; the death of Christopher Marlowe in a tavern of riot and wastrels, imbued with a more profound significance than the merely violent altercation over an Elizabethan trull; John Brown of Ossawatamie, face to face with eternity, on his way to the gallows; Emily Brontë, so weak that it required all her strength to walk alone to the window and observe the rain streaming across her beloved moors, the brown grass on the undulating heath turn to green, in the first, wild gale of Spring; Hardy's Tess, in the silence of the night, baptizing her illegitimate child; Schopenhauer writing his diatribe against women, with his housekeeper snugly cradled in the hollow of his arm; Mr. Barkis's classic demise in "David Copperfield"—"People can't die along the coast, except when the tide's pretty nigh out. They can't be born, unless it's pretty nigh in . . . He's going out with the tide;" The death of Flavian in Pater's "Marius," faint thunder detonating in the Roman hills, the suffused, violet evening, a flicker of light in those lucent eyes so soon to be extinguished by pagan death: Bierce's last letter to a young friend—"This is only to say goodbye. I am going away to South America and have not the faintest notion when I shall return. May you prosper and be happy"; Melville's Ahab, in his final drive against the portentous and overwhelmingly occult Moby Dick—"He peered down into its depths, he profoundly saw a white, living spot . . . It was Moby Dick's open mouth and scrolled jaw, his vast, shadowed bulk still half blending with the blue of the sea. The glittering mouth yawned"; Frank Harris apostrophizing the goddess Liberty, before an audience composed of rapt but scandalized business men, in Cleveland, Ohio; Duse dying in a lonely hotel-room in Pittsburgh; Isadora Duncan dancing all evening—a miracle, a slender and foot-loose enchantment—to the silver music of Gluck's "Iphigenia in Tauris"; Ellen Terry on a lecture tour in old age, stumbling over the lines that had made her so famous—"There's rosemary, that's for remembrance, pray love, remember"; Robert Ross, himself, reaching down into Wilde's grave, to pluck what remained of the poor body for transference into the cemetery of Pere Lachaise; the once-ecstatic Fanny Burney, grown old and tired in life-long service to a witless king; the episode of Mme. Verdurin's party for the curious protege of M. de Charlus, in Marcel Proust; the Marquisa de Montmayer in the "Bridge of San Luis Rey," submitting herself to utter degradation in beseeching the pardon of Camila, the prostitute and actress—"You and she are great women . . . I am only foolish . . . a stupid woman. Let me kiss your feet. I am impossible . . ."

It was on a long and winding road in the Ramapos, that this idea first came to us. Larks fluttered in the zenith. The mountains shone and receded, moth-veined in the clear and opal flame of day. We put it aside for a week, a month, a year, when, with the transmutation of time, came the transubstantiation of values, and the change had already begun to solidify within ourself. We shall never do this anthology.

Books That Talk

In the silence of the night, the books began to talk. Boswell's Johnson opened conversation, and his voice boomed out deep and stentorian, drowning the whistles and sirens of boats in the harbor, the bells and buoys in the pale offing.

"Sir," he roared, and he seemed to address an invisible Boswell, "there are altogether too many books in existence. I asseverate—"

"You could do nothing else," declared a voice that clearly came from the "Indicator" of Leigh Hunt.

"I asseverate," repeated the Doctor with grieved but insistent dignity, "that were I to assume dictatorship (shrill cries of 'Heaven forbid!'), only such publications as contribute to the ideality of youth and the reality of their elders, should find place on the shelves of our institutions. An over-abundance of foppery in the present civilization demands it!"

"All my years," began a sweet and drowsy voice with an archaic inflection, "I longed for an escape from life and from the bondage of gold. So I betook me on board a wine-colored galley manned by Cretan sailors, to an island set midmost a thousand leagues from Greece, in the blue sea. I loved but one love and I sang but one song . . ."

"What was that? Who the deuce are you?" queried an unforgettable voice, unmistakably from the "Essays" of Hazlitt.

"My dear chap," interposed still another, "he hardly knows himself, but if curiosity proves strong enough, you will find his exquisite four-line poem in one of the lesser books of the Greek Anthology. What he said there, was said a thousand times before and a million times since, yet never so perfectly as then. But royal irony! He doesn't know what or why he sang, nor even who he was—much as one who bends down to Lethe to drink to forget—and forgets (in stooping) why he bends down to drink!"

"Sophistry!" ejaculated Hazlitt. "By what right, sir," he continued, "do you set yourself up as chief plenipotentiary in the cause of forgotten literature? In my day, the scoundrels on 'Blackwood's' and the 'Quarterly,' did singular service in obliterating the nonentities that were parasitical to the Muse. I myself, if I may so add, have chastened pretence and catechised mediocrity with no illiberal hand. But who are you, sir?"

"Author of a 'Ballad Written in Reading Gaol,'" came the modulated answer. "In my purple period—the Nineties, Mr. Hazlitt—we did ourselves honor to acclaim you as the one person worthy of standing side by side and rank to rank, with glorious Charles Lamb. The eighteenth century, that period of Alexander Pope and Dr. Johnson, was then as dead as a series of stark exhumations of Etruscan sarcophagi. We worshipped the return of sheer, binding Beauty, and knelt submissively before a carven altar in the white Temple of Youth!"

"Unmitigable nonsense," roared again the voice of Boswell's Johnson. "Who are all these usurpers and pretenders to a literature that has had for six hundred years its basis of substance and standing in only the solidest good sense and the most expert discrimination of breeding?" There was a murmur of dissent that became positively violent—a strain of negation that arose by degrees into a gale. "Silence!" he raged again, "this is neither the time nor the place to discuss matters of such great import. We'll to the 'Mitre.' Francis!—my cloak, my stick, and a light! It begins to snow outdoors."

There was a deft turn of a key in the lock, and the darkened room was flooded and bright. A real voice began to talk. "Funny smell—queer feeling, like something out of the remote past—right here in this room. Br-r-rh! Turn on the radio—what izzit—ah, there we are: "Benny Goodman, Ladies and Gentlemen—broadcasting at such-and-such a time from such-and-such a place, in New York City!"

Where Do They Go To?

What happens in our favorite characters in our best-beloved books, when the Author (so to speak) rings down the curtain and dims lights, when the prompter ceases to guide his brilliantly painted and manipulated mannikins, the call boy and the door man have departed, when the old house creaks and settles itself to long rest—a month a year or possibly forever. Admittedly, any Author's "they lived happily forever," doesn't completely satisfy us. We know that Thackeray, greater realist than even our boldest are prone to conjecture, gave the lovely Beatrix of "Henry Esmond" back to us once again in the person of the aged Baroness de Bernstein—she, whom we had known as "haughty, rapid, imperious," with a beauty, "such as that of the famous antique statue of the huntress Diana"—made into the hard and folly-stricken woman of advanced years. Her portrait is inexorable. We read it once more, with an ache in the heart and a thickening of the throat.

Again we are not quite certain that Miss Austen's outspoken "Emma Weston," comfortably ensconced after an escapade with the dumb but Adonis-like Frank Churchill, did not lead the irrefrangibly sedate and middle-aged Mr. Knightley the devil of a life. She had, beneath the rosy candor of her English face, the temper of a harridan. Of the various characters in Miss Jewett's great "Country of the Pointed Firs," we are reasonably certain. What their Author stipulates, actually happened to them. Those delicate casuistries that make the existences of her ancient men and women so inextricably and permanent a portion of the light and color of the tides, render their own personalities rigid and intractable. We should question the solubility of Hawthorne's "Hester Prynne," were it not that the brain which fashioned and the cunning that cajoled her into the crystal orientation of a self-made prison, also ceded the rights to her escape. On the other hand we find ourselves creditably certain that Fielding's scoundrel, "Tom Jones," betrayed his trusting and not so sophisticated "Sophia" as often as opportunity presented itself: while the "Heathcliff" of Emily Brontë's miraculous "Wuthering Heights," after a life of fairly indecent deviltry, simmered and mellowed down to an irascible, elderly gentleman with a penchant for telling stories of terror and an unquenchable thirst for innumerable glasses of grog. Concerning John Loveday, hero of Hardy's loveliest novel, we satisfied ourselves long ago. If he actually did go off to Spain to blow his martial trumpet and perish for love of the fair but fickle Anne Garland, he was a fool. We know, however, that he did nothing of the sort.

Life, as a media for natural experiences, disapproves of the Storyteller's faculty for pulling into pieces or ticketing his puppets. Nature, herself, continues to be a consistently shrewd and imperturbable pastmaster in the art of mortal disposition. To her advancement retrogression and extinction become as natural a process as the flicker of bright sun and pale shadow, on the least of her summer flowers. Where then do they go to—the men and women we love in books? For the wisest and greatest novelists, this is as open and easy as the secret of Nature herself. To the perfection of their knowledge we owe "Pere Goriot," "Madame Bovary," "The Brothers Karamazoff," and in the almighty realm of Poetry, the entirely stupendous "King Lear."

A Holiday Party

It began to snow thick and heavy in the late afternoon. Then, I remembered a legend of the miraculous, honey-colored Bird of Paradise; so beautiful was it, that all the tints and hues of a chromatic prism shone on its brilliant plumage, as it circled over an evergreen valley in the heart of Tibet. Midday it became bronze, vermilion, citron and saffron; by moonlight the feathers began to fall intensely but delicately in crimson; as they fell they turned to silver, then to quiet gray, and last to purest, blanched white.

Against the Manhattan shore a veil of snow fell sheer and imponderable; lights glittered, waned and were lost; whistles and sirens drifted disconsolately over the opaque harbor as I turned away. Books lined the yellow walls; an Etruscan mask caught the deft light into its arched, cavernous eyes, that bespoke a leaping ecstasy. There was a stirring, a scraping at the wide window. The snow sifted aimlessly and continued to fall.

"Who is there?" I asked. "All of us," came the reply. "All of you?" I queried. "Yes, all of us," it continued "we want to come in. You must let us in. It's such a long way to go." "From where?" I queried. "From everywhere," it answered "only let us in!" The voice was like a running, golden rhythm I had once heard among the giant pines of Georgia, in a storm over Stone Mountain at twilight.

I did just what anyone else would have done under the circumstance and opened the window. There was a clear gust of wind and a sparkle of flakes, that blew in about as strange an assortment of elfin guests, as one could assemble in a lifetime ... men and women, old and young; ugly, fair, exquisite, misshapen and perfect; some so odd that their appearance might have been incredible; others that were tragic, fierce, pathetic, lovable and even mild. The small room seemed all too tiny to hold them, yet seemingly they entered flocking in rank and file, adjusting themselves with the infinite grace and transparency of autumn gossamer.

"Why, I don't know you," I remonstrated. "O, *yes* you do!" they replied in unison, "look a little closer." I did—and marvels of marvels—recognition was there. As fast as the percussive names came to my lips, I called them aloud: Tom Pinch, Lorna Doone, Huckleberry Finn, Emma Woodhouse, Mrs. Leeks and Mrs. Aleshine, Rhoda Fleming, Little Nell, Mr. Micawber, Effie Deans, Mr. Pickwick, Becky Thatcher, Tom Jones, Hester Prynne, Kentuck . . . hundreds, literally hundreds.

"I know you!" I cried with arms outstretched, "I know you all and love you! I've lived among you and with you, ever since I can remember—oh, such a long time ago!" "But which of us do you love *best?*" was asked. I pondered and stared; a faint but unwavering intermezzo of music had just begun. "I don't see *her* here?" I vouchsafed resolutely. "Who is it? Come, tell us who it is," was the insistent demand. "Mrs. Sairey Gamp," I avowed firmly. "Sairey Gamp—where is Sairey Gamp?" was re-echoed, until the room became a vast sounding-board. A fragrance as of a multitude of vineyards in full bloom, was borne into the room. I knew now, that it was none other than Mrs. Gamp herself.

"Dear, sweet creeturs!" she crooned. "Here I am again to draw the breath of freedom after Mrs. Harris's last being safely delivered, and Poll Sweedlepipes, *drat* the rascal, settin' my luggage ten, tejus miles from the proper coach, this fine and snowy Christmas Eve! I say, *drat* the orkard rascal!"

I seemed to be alone. The lights on the New York side shone tier on tier against a malachite sky. "Stay with me this Christmas Eve, Mrs. Gamp," I pleaded suddenly. "We shall have a flask of true Chianti, and—if it so please you—a tender fowl. My invitation (need I add?) is extended not only to yourself, but to charming Betsy Prig and to dear, dear Mrs. Harris. Come now, Mrs. Gamp, be a good sport and stay!"

"Young man," was the firm answer, "I must denige myself the privilege as well as the pleasure; my place is by the side of Mrs. Harris." Her voice alone remained. "Merry Christmas!" it rang out hoarsely but jovially: "Merry Christmas to you, young man, and a Happy New Year!"

AND TO YOU ALL

A MERRY CHRISTMAS AND A HAPPY NEW YEAR!

Forgotten Books

If you have loved English Literature, you will observe in all its length and breadth of area, on starred hills and in its ill-starred abysses, that there are books and for that matter, authors of books, engulfed in what our old friend, Sir Thomas Browne, has called "the oblivion of the Poppy"—perfect books, poetry, novels—work that has fallen by the infrequented wayside, or failed, for a reason we find not quite tangible. We could enumerate a dozen without hesitation—actual volumes of prose or poetry—so authentic in their manifestation as great literature that the near-annihilation that has overtaken them, is positively dismaying. What we are most confirmed in, is the fact that even in the success of such a certain masterpiece as "South Wind," the early elements of its discovery were originally so tenuous or slim that the knowledge of its later existence could have been confined to only the esoteric few. There are also others that had their brilliant day, folded their hands quietly and fell into a long sleep.

How few of us, for instance, know one of the greatest scandal-autobiographies ever written—"The Memoirs of Captain Peter Drake?" Privately Printed in 1755 for its Author's handful of subscribers, it was properly squelched by the impecunious and elderly Captain's numerous relatives, and is now as rare, though not nearly so valuable, as a First Folio Shakespeare. For a life of endless intrigue, wine-bibbing, food-gourmandizing, weariless adventure, and a succession of consummate amours, commend us to Peter Drake. You will find nothing else exactly like this book. That the ladies he favored eventually worsted him, is not at all to the point. He lived, and what is more, he loved. His gusto in that undeviating, unspiritual direction would have won him the acid acclaim and admiration of Hazlitt or Casanova. As a matter of fact, we have decided to call him "The Irish Casanova." Rightly publicised, Peter would make a fortune for his modern publisher.

We have still one more instance to recall. This is none other than "Vikram and the Vampire" a forgotten book by Sir Richard Burton. It professes to be a translation from the Hindu but is actually an original work, built with such a wonder of wit, brave diablerie and mordant suavity, that we place it beside the best of "The Arabian Nights." In its impact of horror, lies the derelict of all lost things, while on the side of artistic inevitability we find it written in prose that marches and sings like music.

Why We Read

To the old Apple Woman in George Borrow's "Lavengro," there existed only one book in the wide world—"Moll Flanders." "I am poor," Borrow had persuasively urged her, "but I will give you two silver crowns for your volume." "No, dear," was her reply, "I will not sell my volume for two silver crowns; no, nor for the golden one in the king's tower down there; without my book I should mope and pine, and perhaps fling myself into the river . . . No, dear, I won't sell my book!"

Some, be it affirmed, read only to be drugged or narcotized. In the mesh of verbal glitter or the coil of involute imagery, any actuality that life fails to afford them, is there entirely realized. Such a one was our dear friend, M. M., dead in his youth for nearly twenty years, whose Keatsian face grew alight on the subject of books. "I can't read the big things—the cosmic entities in literature," he would say, "but the lesser ones: Pater, Dowson, Crackanthorpe, Amy Levy and Wilde—footlessly exquisite and radiant all of them—I love those best." Hart Crane, however, was a striking instance of the reader who reads altogether for content. Unfailingly and tenaciously, the assertive embodiment of mentality that was Crane's, literally tore the heart out of his books. We remember his first immediate assimilation of the "Ulysses" of James Joyce—read, re-read and consumed in the heat of intense reading—only to pass into the recessional finality of the poet's rich, volcanic mind. Our friend, William Sommer, of Macedonia, Ohio, least exploited but one of the greatest painter-geniuses since Vincent Van Gogh, kept a book recording the various disturbing transmigrations of nomenclature during his reading of "The Brothers Karamazov"; while his conversation about books, music and art, must always recall to his friends, the sort of naked and omniscient spirituality that is usually associated with the rapt, personal utterances of William Blake.

So, bit by bit, we revert to our own self; what we read, and why our preferences—discordant enough with much that finds modern publication—afford us the greatest pleasure, the deepest and clearest source of permanency and relief. We read, because in a world rocking with gigantic disaster in a civilization seemingly gone utterly and hopelessly insane, we find the greatest wisdom, the highest possible ideals in utterances among peoples of the past. Turn to Richard De Bury and hear him say: "You, only, O Books, are liberal and Independent. You give to all who ask, and enfranchise all who serve you assiduously. You are golden urns in which manna is laid up, rocks flowing with honey, or rather honeycombs; the four-streamed river of Paradise, where the human mind is fed, and the arid intellect moistened and watered; fruitful olives, vines of Engaddi, fig-trees knowing no sterility; burning lamps to be ever held in the hand."

Charles Dickens and Christmas

Out of an unrecorded night in the Hartz Mountains, to the fall of snow, to the thunder and fury of wind, to the cry of troll and kobold in the heart of the hills, came the sound of bells ever so long ago. The peal of bells on bells—soft and thick and golden, piercing sweet and mistily remote—we know now that it must have been the first sound that hailed to our forebears what we since cherish as Christmas.

English writers have always loved Christmas. Curl yourself in an armchair when the lights are low, with a wintry world draped and sheeted white before you, and begin to read Dickens. Forget the scene without, forget the mechanism of an iron civilization, forget the cry and clamor of the city—then read him as though nothing else in the world ever mattered. But be quick, lest he elude you, for the heart of Youth grows old....

Ebenezer Scrooge will sit blinking in the evil, yellow light of his counting-house awaiting final redemption; you shall be shyly hailed by Mr. Pickwick at the curved doorway of the oldest English Inn, when field and hedgerow are filled with roses and the scent of thyme and blowing lavender permeates the green lanes; Mrs. Sairey Gamp, arms akimbo, leaning tenably out of an open window of her balmy London domicile, will confide the most intimate utterances of her insolubly mysterious friend Mrs. 'Arris; Miss Fanny Squeers, late of Dotheboys and best-loved of the Master's comics, may insistently and openly set her cap at the astute and none too clever Nicholas, brightly brazen and undenuded to your gracious laughter and kindly eyes. But the Cricket—ah, the Cricket on the Hearth—listen close, and you must hear it sing as magically and ecstatically as it sang when you first read Dickens, with the charming Mrs. Peerybingle sitting and musing before her sea-coal fire: "He's coming, coming, coming!"

For Dickens, as we have so often been assured, is Christmas. The seal and signet of its vast, meridian festivity, its lighted and flickering, wintry grace, is set forever on the least of his pages. Has life dealt hardly with you? A pity, truly, but Dickens will not have it so. Take up your "Pickwick." Can you conceive a happier ending—the glitter of a well-waxed parlor floor, the mistletoe overhead, the Fat Boy stuffed to contagion in the kitchen-pantry ("young boa-constrictor," he is called)—with the Old Lady and Sam Weller in a corner, furtively nudging and tee-heeing at one another in an active participation of risibilities over the immortal, the ever-blooming Mr. Pickwick?

Read your Charles Dickens and you will know that the end is good. If it isn't, close your tired eyes and love life and the joys that life must have given you, for Old Age—affirms Dickens—is rosy. With it, one must needs grow fat and rubicund and well-content (but not stodgy), with the easiest seat in an ingle, a pipe and flask with a book at one's side, and a roaring fire up the old fire-place into the wide chimney.

Howard Phillips Lovecraft

American literature has produced three great writers of terror fiction: Edgar Allan Poe, Ambrose Bierce and Howard Phillips Lovecraft. It has been my good fortune—certainly, no inconsiderable one—to have been on intimate terms with two of these: Ambrose Bierce and Howard Phillips Lovecraft.

It is now nearly thirty years ago that I received a letter, fantastically worded and written in an obsolete style that simulated the early 1700's, with meticulously-rounded sentences that made me hover (as I read) between sheer envy and downright laughter. I remember the inscription at the close: "I remain, dear Sir, your Most Humble, Obedient Servant, Howard Phillips Lovecraft, Esquire." The gist of the letter was this: the writer had long been an admirer of my poetry, and its appearance had, from time to time, excited his admiration to such a degree that he had made bold to institute inquiries as to my whereabouts. He had, he asserted, practically given up any hope of finding me, when a clue to my location was indicated. Hence, his letter of inquiry: was I alive or dead? Would I write to him if I were still in the land of the living? I had always been a legend to him—could I, or rather would I, remove his doubts?

I removed them. Letters were exchanged and flew back and forth between us. I have never been a good letter-writer and the demands that Lovecraft made upon his correspondents were prodigious as well as extraordinary. A letter of a single page on one side, could (and usually did) evoke an answer of from forty to fifty closely-written pages. They were wonderful letters—marvelously readable, astonishingly erudite, incredibly human. Their range of subjects was monumental: Astronomy, Sorcery, Witchcraft, Archeology, English Literature, Cabalism, Dutch New York, 18th Century Poetry, Alexander Pope, Roman Sculpture, Greek Vases, Decadence of the Alexandrian Period, Baths of Caracalla, T. S. Eliot, Hart Crane—heaven alone could enumerate their infinite range and breath-taking variety! They were written with a verbal abundance and a feeling for prose construction, that the best of us might well envy. Lovecraft was a stickler for grammar and syntax.

The upshot of it was that we arranged to meet in New York, to visit the very beautiful woman who was later to become Howard's wife. She was (let this be affirmed for once and for all) the very soul of loyalty, graciousness and lavish generosity. We occupied her apartment near Prospect Park in Brooklyn, while she removed herself nightly to sleep in a neighbor's rooms on the same floor. The long evenings of conversation between the three of us, the endless discussions as to what was and was not permissible in good writing, the timelessness of everything, are phases of my visit that I keenly recollect—with a little shiver over the passing of years—it seems all so long ago. Howard's conversation was without boundaries, on any subject. I have never known him to hold the slightest resentment against any one; I have never known a human being to secrete less envy, malice, morbidity and intolerance, than did Howard. Toward the worst of rascals or scoundrels, there was not a single line of remonstrance. "Only another arrangement of chemical molecules," he was wont to ascribe to any persons malingering in the long and particularly fine range of his lifelong friendships or acquaintances. His sense of irony, as well as his projection of quiet humor with an occasional jet of ambient and satirical badinage, was complete.

He visited me in Cleveland, where I procured a room for him close to where I lived. There were wonderful walks at night and a marvellously brilliant but solid exchange of conversation. I had, in Cleveland, become the friend of Hart Crane, and it is one of the singular occurrences among not a few in my life, that these two men of genius met on a personal basis. Neither cared for the other. Crane demoded Lovecraft as old-fashioned and the soul of pedantry; Lovecraft, on the other hand, sardonically and not without mimicry, disparaged Crane's modernity as well as his morality. Both settled with tolerance for one another, during an entire evening devoted to a coruscating glorification of the heavenly cosmogony; Lovecraft's knowledge of astronomy was phenomenal. It was in Cleveland that Howard confided to me that he had long since visited the battlefield at Lexington, in company with our friend, James Ferdinand Morton, Jr., grandson of the composer of "My Country 'Tis of Thee."

"Were you stirred to patriotism over your visit to this hallowed spot?" I asked.

"Yes," he responded, "I was—but not in the direction that you would imagine. When James Ferdinand and I stood before the grave of the Revolutionary soldier who had been the first to fall on this memorable and lamentable occasion, I bared and bowed my head. 'So perish all enemies and traitors to his Majesty, King George the Third!' I cried."

"Rubbish!" I commented. "Did you really feel that way?"

"I did, and most profoundly," he announced with fervor. "Our severance from the British Dominion has been the head of a long line of cataclysmic disasters. I am a Tory, sir! I still declare my everlasting and loyal allegiance to England, God bless her!" He meant it.

Lovecraft's stay in New York, after the separation from his wife (a tragedy to those who knew the inside of the affair), was one of complete rebellion against everything that the huge city had to offer. He hated the noise, the interminable rudeness of the inhabitants, the rowdy and rancid slums. He confided to me a way that he had found of reaching the New York Public Library at the corner of 42nd Street and Fifth Avenue (his favorite haunt)—without so much as exposing himself or walking more than a dozen feet, up the marble library steps from the subway nearby. He declaimed with flushed cheeks and a rising voice against (so he called it) "the mixed mongrel population—the very scum and dregs of Europe and the Near East," that filled and permeated the area of the entire city. He anticipated with a heart-breaking intensity and longing that only his closest friends knew—a liberation and return to New England—back to his beloved Providence with its antique gables and narrow streets, to the Colonial reconstruction of what is now known to the readers of his weird fiction as "Arkham country."

It was only at night that Lovecraft actually began to live. Then it was that we had long walks together, in and out of the dusky thoroughfares of lower New York, ending up in a state of somnolent and dreamy contentment, on a park-bench in leafy Washington Square. Howard's faculty for searching and ferreting out old houses that had originally been Colonial in spite of the multiplicity of their modern architectural alterations was truly amazing. He loved every line, every angle of the 17th and 18th centuries. A visit we made to Salem, Marblehead and Boston, remains indelibly fixed in my memory. Salem we did at sunset, and the memory of a pause in our long tramp, lingering for a few moments at the foot of Witch Hill, while Lovecraft conjured up—across a black sky streaked with sinister scarlet—the row of imaginary gibbets and the fury of the demoniacal populace silhouetted across the horizon, are unforgettable. Marblehead he knew and loved. For the fortunate companion who accompanied him to Boston, it may be affirmed that he became a veritable guide-book.

These few, slight notes would be sadly incomplete without some scattered references to Howard's procedure and method in his process of weird-story writing. He wrote rapidly and without effort. "The Shunned House," of which I have the original manuscript, tells the tale of easy, fluent writing. His own work he spoke of lightly and even disparagingly, without the slightest conception of its lasting quality. The ego that stimulates many of us to write or create, was—in his instance—entirely absent. "Much that I have written, I have dreamed," he once confided to me. "'The Statement of Randolph Carter' was altogether a dream. You," he said to me, "were 'Harley Warren' in that story. I dreamed of a huge and ancient graveyard filled with tombs, and the marble graves as old as eternity, with crawling ivy underfoot, and each mouldering slab covered by a growth of green moss and evil lichen. And as I strolled through those ominous precincts, I became aware of a voice that called me. Impelled by fear and urged through sheer horror, I made my way to the one grave that seemed to open and yawn with flaring, blinding lights before me, the voice—your voice—calling—calling.... I descended and followed the voice, the voice that was yours, into the hollow obscurity of that unspeakable grave!"

A visit to Providence and a walk at midnight to the scene of "The Shunned House" near his own home with Lovecraft, still brings the thrill that it brought to me so many years ago. "You shall see it," he announced, after we had decided to visit the spot of his finest creation in terror. "It isn't so far off," he continued. "Directly across is the little graveyard where Sarah Helen Whitman walked with Edgar Allan Poe, which adjoins the house she lived in. He courted her in that uncanny but romantic place." So shortly after midnight we sallied forth (the phrase seems apropos) and made our way by brilliant moonlight to Howard's original of "The Shunned House." "It is owned by a retired, wealthy bachelor," he confided, "who no longer lives in it." "And this place," I queried, "held the incredible, intolerable horror of your tale?" "Unquestionably," he replied humorously. "There are those," he added with a sinister intonation, "who say *the end is not yet!*" I stood and surveyed the solid, frame building, opaquely silent, with windows barred and shuttered, the old roof flooded with clear moonlight, "And now," he announced, "we must walk down into the graveyard where Sarah Helen Whitman became affianced to Edgar Allan Poe." I followed with no little misgiving. The path was devious, rugged and winding. It slipped down the dark hill where Providence lay like a cup of silver in the vague and misty valley below. "Anything could happen here," I muttered with some misgiving. Howard jeered at me not unkindly. "Nothing ever does," he replied rapidly with emphasis. "The conjurations that the brain has given forth, have bred all the misbegotten superstition and errant bigotry of witchcraft and miracle-mongering down the long and dusty ages. Science is true and irrefutable. Look at the stars above you!" He began to talk astronomy. It had become freezing cold and the stars continued to glitter like so many diamonds, as we ascended the hill to the house where Lovecraft lived. He was in high humor, demurring over what he considered the early hour we were forced to retire. At five the next morning we left for Boston.

Lovecraft as Conversationalist

At a certain gathering which Lovecraft attended, a remark was made and later printed: "And there was Howard Phillips Lovecraft a-talking just like a book!"

I have in my possession some 500 folio pages of his letters, generally in his handwriting and one running to as much as sixty pages. Now, what has frequently characterized great letter-writers of any period has always been their congenial ease, the fluidity and, occasionally, the enchanting gossip that permeates their writing—Madame de Sévigné, Horace Walpole, Thomas Gray, James Boswell, Charles Lamb, Edward FitzGerald, and even Oscar Wilde. Premising future publication, the letters of Lovecraft would require an enormous amount of pruning and selection. Whatever their topical interest may have been at the time of writing, much appears resolved into a laborious surplusage of words, words, words. Things that are permissible and even add to the flavor of his fiction, freeze into an attitude in his letters. And yet, even while one is prone to condemn their verbal vomit, one must admit that sound editing, and the process of still sounder omission, should free and add to the Lovecraft legend, and deliver him to posterity as he actually was—a charming companion, a wonderful human being and a loyal friend.

But the conversation of Lovecraft—ah, the conversation! For a matter of three years and more I was actually in daily association with him—years of plenitude and literary activity; years of happiness. I can safely assert that Lovecraft's conversation takes its place among the masters of that brilliant but difficult art. The texture of his voice was uncomfortably high and when the element of satire or irony entered into his subject, could rise even higher. Yet, it was not, as has been asserted of Shelley, strident like "the cry of a peacock"—but capable by the merest intonation into a twist of sarcasm and of devastating confutation.

His pity for the peccadilloes of his friends or acquaintances was unswerving. I remember a specific instance where one of our friends whose predominating characteristic was that of insincerity, became involved in an incriminating, ghastly episode. Lovecraft's remark, made with a negative gesture of both hands: "Well, only another collection of molecules!" Adding: "I pass no judgments on anyone. I take no one too seriously. Disillusion has its disadvantages, but therein lies safety."

His appearance was frequently a shock to those who met him for the first time—the long, lean face, the extended jaw, the deadly pallor of his skin (except when it became flushed with excitement) caused him much silent embarrassment. "My one desire," he had confided to me in a subway train when a young woman steadily "gave him the eye," "is to remain inconspicuous and unnoticed. If I could render myself invisible, I would gladly do so. I avoid the ordinary run of human beings and have imbibed much of the philosophy of good old Bishop Berkeley, who denied the existence of matter and even the actuality of life itself. Nothing really exists for me. Dreams provide me with a solution to the fantastic ambiguity that we choose to call life. I begin to live only when I pass through the embroidery of dream. You, Samuelus, (meaning me) place too much stress and importance on human beings and, since this is so, you suffer. Make yourself impersonal and impervious to the mob. Deny not only contact with them, but with their existence. Books and old Colonial houses are safest; they hold well their sinister and mysterious secrets. Mistrust everything except the past or antiquity."

I heard Lovecraft utter profanity on only one occasion. That was in my apartment on Columbia Heights in Brooklyn—and how he loved the lighted tier upon tier that constituted the fabulous skyline of New York! Some nondescript person had engaged him in a heated and deliberately antagonistic argument, with insistence on his own point of view. Howard's reply was succinct and was blurted out like a blast of dynamite: "That's a lot of *****!" I gasped. His antagonist colored. There was, for an instant, an ominous silence in the room. Then the conversation proceeded without interruption.

My roommate, Pat McGrath, who shared the apartment and privately called Howard a "ghoul," decided on a certain New Year's Eve celebration and, so, some twenty-five of our friends were invited. Included were Mrs. Grace Crane (Hart Crane's mother), who was properly appalled at the unconventional conversation of some of our guests, and Howard P. Lovecraft. Drinks were served and, to Lovecraft, who never even remotely tasted hard liquor, ginger-ale. Pat beckoned me into the kitchen. "Have you noticed how talkative Howard has very suddenly become?" I hadn't, but, as we entered the room where the guests were assembled, there was Lovecraft, the very life of the party, talking, gesticulating, radiating smiles and laughter, rolling his verbal gymnastics with witticisms and even indulging in a spirited aria from Gilbert and Sullivan's "Mikado"—a display of exhilarating pyrotechnics that I had never seen or heard him indulge in before. Pat whispered mirthfully into my ear, "I SPIKED HIS DRINK!"

I should say that, conversationally, Lovecraft was at his best with men, rather than with women. A certain restraint and progressive hollowness entered into his addresses with the female sex. I may be mistaken, but the deferential and overwhelming politeness that he conveyed seemed always strained and faintly artificial.

Introduction [to *Dead Letters Sent and Other Poems*]

This is a first book of poems by Maurice Kenny who is still in his twenties, and for a first book it holds its own with many well-known American and English contemporary poets. Here is the very spring and savour of youth ... the timeless and perfumed joy of winds, stars, flowers, birds, natural scenery ... the disembodied ecstasy that fades and hardens with the passing of years. Kenny is one of the few poets who have sprung full-blown from the loins of golden Apollo. Perfection is present in these poems from the very beginning, and whoever searches for crudity or immaturity, will find himself sadly disappointed. Traces of Dylan Thomas and Robert Frost there are ... of the former a reserved but flowing lyricism, and in the instance of Frost, a lovely evanescent charm. Kenny's poetry is akin to that of John Clare, who allied himself so closely to Nature that to find him one must search for him among the microscopic growing things that spring from the pulsating earth.

There are poems in this volume that could only have been written by a major poet. This, for instance, from "Grandeur and the Subtle Pain":

> Reach for the rose of sunset in the bleating gold

or this from "Noon":

> What a world with peacocks in the berries
> And broken children in despair;
> What a world without the midnight fairies
> To blow their magic across the Spring air.

the pathos and tragedy in "Ezra Pound":

> Ezra, and do you breakfast at six,
> Every morning, every
> Morning, every morning; time fixed;
> Time in, time out, time come and came.
> Time—time, the blasted time the same?

the Sapphic heart-break of:

> I will learn to bear the sting of fire
> As I have learned to bear the scent of flowers:
> A blaze of fire

>Is nothing
>Compared to love.

There are at least a half-dozen poems among the twenty-three, that will take you with a catch in your throat, while for a balance of pity and sheer grief there is also the turbulence and Bacchic movement of sheer joy. Only Ezra Pound or Hart Crane could have given us in their fixity of purpose and integrity of writing, the four lines from Kenny's "Four: In The Chinese Manner," with their burning import and clear imagism:

>The wind pounds the clouds.
>But no one will believe the poet
>That the things of Summer
>Have their evil way.

This is the door and here is Maurice Kenny, who holds it wide open for you to enter. Let us hope that those who scan the horizon for a new poet, will find him here.

New York City, 1958

From a Diary

In 1932, during a pilgrimage to the Whitman house on Mickle Street in Camden, New Jersey, I ascertained that there were over 60 letters written by Walt Whitman to his mother, that were being offered for sale. This entire episode, in arranging for their eventual purchase, involved me in as strange an experience as I have ever had. These letters, purporting to be unpublished, were later found to have been already included in the collected edition of Walt Whitman's works, but the daughter of Thomas Harned—Whitman's friend and executor—who owned them, knew nothing of this. I was invited by the young curator of the place, who wrote poetry in the approved Japanese Hokku style, to stay there over-night—so over-night I stayed in the very room that Whitman died in on the upper floor (and for all I know in the very same bed). The curator, with whom I shared the bed, confided to me that the identical bedpan used by Whitman—a giant affair—lay preserved under the bed, and after opening the window in a room that was already freezing on one of the coldest and bitterest nights I can remember, we lay down in the wide four-poster, where, after a curious conversation, with my teeth chattering and my body shivering from the onslaught of a cold that had developed, we both turned on our several sides and fell asleep.

This, however, was only the beginning. I was informed that we were both invited the following evening to the home of one of the actual survivors of the Whitman circle—Harry Fritzinger, brother of Warren ("Warry") Fritzinger, Whitman's male nurse and the stepson of Mrs. Mary Davis, Whitman's housekeeper and factotum in the Mickle Street establishment. Fritzinger lived in a modest frame house with his wife, not far from Mickle Street, and there I was welcomed simply but sincerely during an entire evening devoted to more anecdotes of Whitman and Mrs. Davis than I can comfortably remember.

"I was still pretty young when I came back from the sea," said Fritzinger. "My mother embraced me and greeted me—she was a quiet woman who never spoke out—saying: 'Harry, go right upstairs and meet Mr. Whitman. This is his house.' Well, I went up the one flight of stairs as fast as my legs could carry me, and there was old Walt with his rumpled gray beard in a night-gown, sitting propped up against a pillow in his big bed, writing away on a sheet of paper, with a lot of other papers and books scattered all about him. He held out his hand to shake mine, and said: 'Harry, I heard you were coming back; I'm glad to know you; make yourself right at home.' I sat alongside his bed; the old man breathed hard and looked pretty tired out. 'Now, Harry,' he continued, 'if you will bend down low enough you will find a bottle of prime Scotch whiskey tucked away under the bed. That's it! Take the glass tumbler on yonder table and pour yourself a good, stiff drink.' I did so, and man—after the rotten grog I had swilled on shipboard and in odd ports—it tasted better than anything else in the whole world. It loosened me up so that I felt like a human being once again. 'Now tell me all about the ships, the sailors and the sea,' said Walt, and so, every day I came punctually up to the old man's room. Hell! I wasn't interested in his poetry that he read to me occasionally, but what I mostly coveted and always got, was a good, deep swig from that bottle of whiskey under Walt's bed. The old gentleman asked me more questions than would ever fill a book—all about my sea-life, whether the sailors were real pals with one another, what they did on shore-leave, their girl-friends, the different ship-watches, the grub, names of the spars and riggings, a description of various parts of the boat. We became first-rate friends and I got to like the old man more than I can tell you. He had a soft, pleasant way about him that never riled one; just like a father! He would ask me to bend down so that he could kiss me; I obliged him. When my brother "Warry" was on leave, I took care of him and used to trundle him in his wheel-chair down to the Camden docks so that he could see the ships coming and going, and talk to the roustabouts who loafed in the vicinity. He was easy-going and seemed to be like one of them. Yes sir, I named my son after him—Walt Whitman Fritzinger, and Walt held him in his arms—a tiny tyke—when he was being baptised." Harry fixed his blue eyes on me long and soberly. "I'll tell you something else. When he died, I was the one who carried him in my own arms down the stairs and helped to lay him out in the front parlor. He was so thin and wasted that he weighed little better than a youngster. You can still see the marks on the floor by the front window, where he used to pound his cane every time he shouted for 'Warry.'"

"It was a shame," broke in Mrs. Fritzinger, "the way his three executors threw Mrs. Davis out after the old man died. She hardly had time to pack her things before they ordered her to move." "Human nature is human nature," commented Harry Fritzinger philosophically. "They had their own ideas about the place."

"She came to live with us," continued Mrs. Fritzinger. "I took as good care of her as though she were my own dear mother. She didn't talk much and she never asked favors from anybody; she seemed to have something on her mind. My own opinion is that she loved the old man, who must have been pretty set and selfish in his ways." "He *was* set," corroborated Harry Fritzinger emphatically.

"As the years went by," she continued, "Mrs. Davis became quieter and quieter, until we could hardly get a word out of her. We just knew that there was something that preyed on her mind. She took sick in the same, quiet way. Then, one day, I found her burning papers—stacks of them in the fireplace—scrap by scrap, letter by letter. We never knew what they were, but I've always had a suspicion and would wager they had something directly to do with Walt Whitman."

"My brother 'Warry,' died of consumption," mused Harry. "His widow remarried and lives in Detroit, Michigan. We never hear from her. She had a son by 'Warry.'"

******

There was really an incredible creative group that we had, meeting and functioning together in Cleveland over forty years ago. The focal center was the bookstore of Richard Laukhuff in the Taylor Arcade, where introductions were made, friendships were formed and future meetings arranged. Laukhuff, a fine and dominant personality, the friend of Sherwood Anderson, Randolph Bourne, Charles Burchfield, and many others of like celebrity, served as a sort of semi-tyrannical impresario—a master of ceremonies. A weekly event was a luncheon participated in by the entire ensemble every Saturday afternoon at Klein's Hungarian Restaurant on Prospect Avenue. Here, Hart's boisterous and unmorbid streak of humor would free itself from the restraint at home into a personality quite different from the paranoiac presentation of him in Mr. Morton's facile biography. Nor had he then begun to drink as he did later; he loved good food, and conversationally delivered himself with an incessant, roaming and ever-widening variation over the literary field. Our group consisted of William Sommer, the artist, whom I introduced to Hart; Willy Lescaze, a young Swiss, who has since become a famous New York architect; Katharine Kinney, Hart's brilliant and jovial girl-friend; Charles Baldwin, writer and journalist, who knew everyone and had interviewed everybody of consequence in the American literary scene; Dudley Carroll, from Nashville, a lawyer and government-employee of great affability who wrote stories à la Dreiser, and had a Southern accent that defied reproduction—and myself. It was at Laukhuff's then, in 1919, just after my release from the army, that I first met Hart Crane. We were introduced together by Laukhuff as I was leaving, with his accustomed semi-satirical geniality: "Mr. Loveman, meet Hart Crane, Cleveland's great modern poet. You are two literary men who certainly should know one another." There was a desultory conversation in the doorway, with a tactless remark by Hart: "Most people try to make my acquaintance because I am the son of Clarence Crane, the millionaire candy-manufacturer!" I assured myself that this would never be so on my part, but an invitation was cordially tendered and before I knew what had actually happened, I found myself committed to a visit for the following Monday evening. Hart had then taken temporary living-quarters at the still-extant Hotel Del Prado on Euclid Avenue, while his mother and grandmother were sojourning in their cottage on the Isle of Pines. It is difficult now to realize that with this chance meeting and introduction, I was to be flung as a literal participant in a tragedy as profoundly true to type and characteristic in essence, as anything in the Greek dramas. I know of only two other analogies in life, at all comparable to the Crane debacle—the American Edgar Allan Poe and the French Arthur Rimbaud. I came at the appointed time and my welcome was as open as it was assured and unhesitating. Hart's practically instantaneous divulgence of himself as an active homosexual was as surprising as the fact that he could actually be one—since there were no indications of it on the surface. He confided to me shortly after that he had so practiced the art of camouflaging and hiding anything that might possibly be construed as feminine in his makeup—the long and somewhat ponderous, swaggering stride, his inveterate cigar-smoking, the Whitmanesque habit of wearing expensive but extremely comfortable and easy "crash" clothes—that what had once been assumed actually became a part of him. A subject that never seemed to evade Hart for very long, was his inborn predilection—homosexuality. He read letters to me from a socialite friend in New York, and from a poet of Washington, D. C., who wrote eighteen-ninety-ish poetry. I met him; he was a fantastic chalk-faced man of middle-age, with an extremely deliberate and artificial manner of speech. The letters to Hart from these two men were of an outrageously suggestive nature in a jargon that bore largely on the enormous sexual activities in their lives. I was fascinated as well as horrified. It was a milieu that I now heard of for the first time at first-hand. Hart had originally met the poet in Washington, where he became extensively involved in the progressive activities of a well-defined circle of inverts—the commerce being mostly between wartime male government civilians and sailors. Here it was that Hart's histrionic, well-known proclivities for the navy were first bred and fostered. The evening was a long one, and I staggered dizzily out at two in the morning. Hart was as fresh as daybreak. By the time my visit came to an end I had heard readings of T. S. Eliot ("Prufrock"); Edward Thomas (for whom I still retain the greatest admiration); Robert Frost, and Hart's own poetry besides an inordinate amount of fascinating gossip that awaits impatiently to be retold. He showed me a letter—an unbelievably rude one—written to him by Ezra Pound. Terse and impudent, unflinchingly brittle—it had advised him to gather whatever poetry he had composed and to throw it into the nearest toilet, adding a peremptory injunction to be sure and flush it after doing so. Hart read it to me with great thumping glee and explosions of loud laughter. This was my first of many visits to follow. I remember them nostalgically.

******

There are stories about Hart Crane that could not possibly be told except through a more unorthodox channel than this. The peak of his career undoubtedly took place at 190 Columbia Heights. His basement apartment was gaily hung with stray colored prints, mementoes and funny decorations from the five and ten cent stores (Hart loved to shop in them). Here, I once met Marsden Hartley, who was just departing as I made my appearance. "Marsden, meet Sam Loveman," called out Hart in his vigorous, easy fashion, and I turned to face a mousy little man of an indeterminate age, who took my hand and shook it with a shy, shrinking gesture that could only indicate utter defeatism. I found it difficult to reconcile the painter of those brawny and boldly modern canvasses that we have become accustomed to associate with Marsden Hartley; it remains a riddle. And here too, I met Katharine Ann Porter, then without the reputation that was to descend on her later, and with whom Hart was to conduct a feud in Mexico (they both bore Guggenheim scholarships). She was thin, pale and quietly composed as she sat conversing with him in a low-voiced, pronounced Southern accent on the various phases, personalities and evocations of contemporary literature. I fancy that Hart was entirely at fault in their difficulty with one another.

******

Grace Hart Crane, Hart's mother, died 31 August 1947, at a little Catholic Hospital in New Jersey. It was the only one that would accept her as a patient without money. She had cirrhosis of the liver; the young and extremely pleasant physician in charge said that she could not possibly live. I went to see her several times within the week before her death, and only once did she emerge from her coma. Then it was to tell me that she was dying. I said: "Nonsense, Grace, you will outlive me!" "I know what I am saying," she insisted. She called me "Doctor," and when I corrected her, "this is your old friend, Sam," she answered: "I know, I know." The young nurse asked me who she was. I said: "The mother of a very great American poet, Hart Crane." Mrs. Crane, with a flash of her old intelligence and curiosity, snapped out of her oncoming coma, and queried: "What did you say about me?" I repeated what I had said. "Poor boy—poor boy," she murmured, relapsing again into unconsciousness. The nuns at the hospital phoned me of her death. In the interim after Hart's suicide, she had done housekeeping, scrubbed floors, taken care of invalids and children, or subsisted precariously on grudging pittance from others. I thought of my first visit to the Crane home during her absence from Cleveland, to visit Hart, and her photograph on his desk. "My mother," he had said with lighted eyes, "isn't she beautiful?" She looked 90 as she lay a charity patient—white and wasted under a gray coverlet, on her hospital bed. I had her cremated and about two weeks later on a beautiful and blazingly blue autumnal Saturday at noon, a few of us—three woman-friends, Pell, the publisher of Hart's poems (Liveright), Brom Weber the author of a book on Hart, a young New York poet, and myself—took her ashes in a little box to the center of Brooklyn Bridge (very quietly and almost secretly, because the authorities had refused us permission, advising us to consult the Aeronautic Commission!). An occult prayer was uttered by one of Grace's woman friends, and the ashes were slowly scattered from the bridge accompanied by roses into the river below, to rejoin symbolically Hart in the Caribbean seas. And so, the career of a much-misunderstood but courageous woman—once the mistress of a fortune (the Cranes had been rated at a million dollars), came to an untimely end. Vain and mettlesome, kind but high-tempered, literally a daughter of the gods and in many ways a replica of Hart Crane, she was reduced to insecurity and poverty. She had exactly $46.00 and a check from social security in her handbag when she died.

******

I witnessed Isadora Duncan dance an entire evening to the enchanting music of Ritter Gluck's "Iphigenia," played by an orchestra directed by Walter Damrosch. There was nothing in all the world to compare with it, unless one remembers the Greek vases of the best period—for here they were transfixed again in life, presented with marvelous, moving plasticity. Emerging, I went out into a world made hideous by machinery and voltage, ugly buildings and the crass blare of sound and color. With that memory in mind, I wrote my long Bacchanalian poem, "The Hermaphrodite." I saw Isadora once again, years later after her return from Russia, during her nearly final phase. She appeared before 7000 people in the huge public hall of Cleveland, Ohio, to an audience who hissed and hooted and threw objects at her on the stage. Thousands left the hall during her performance. Her lover, Serge Yessenin, peered handsome and white-faced from the wings. She danced as no one else has danced before or since—nearly static but radiantly beautiful—with a vast red scarf alternately flourished or draped around her—that alternately enraged or antagonized the audience almost to the point of violence. She danced the vision of a world revolution which must come as all things eventually come, as a means of purgation and spiritual renewal. In her, I saw something great and biblical—prophesying and forecasting everything that she herself most certainly believed—the ruin and demolition of an old order and the delivery of a new one, but with the maintainance of eternal, protective beauty. The handful of people who waited to the end to hear her talk, clustered around the stage. She spoke clearly and faultlessly at great length, with a strange, transfigured ardent light in her eyes. Hart Crane was present with me at this performance.

******

To Columbia Heights, Brooklyn, to take a last look at what remains of this once enchanted street that faces the New York skyline and bay. The scene of desolation there, reminds one of Dante's "Inferno." Huge steam-shovels are roaring and pouring out the earth that has remained unscathed and unmolested for over a century. All the buildings that occupied half the west side of the street have been demolished. The esplanade at the foot of Montagu Street is covered by a mountain of rubbish and resurrected dirt. The old stone house to the right—really a palace—still stands untenanted, but the stairs that once descended, ruined but picturesque, to "nothingness" (a phrase I made that delighted Howard Lovecraft), have been cruelly ripped away. Hart Crane's last residence with his "basinette" apartment as he called it, at 196 Columbia Heights, is still there. I peered in and saw the same door through which he had come and gone, drunken or sober—so many times—but the sinister, gray old negress who had guarded the entry and who was so dreaded by him, no longer sat as a sentinel in the hallway; the windows were covered by heavy green baise curtains. Number 130, where I had rented the top floor and where Hart later occupied the apartment below, is utterly demolished. He lived there for nearly a year. Here it was that he was occasionally robbed and beaten up by the sailors and their affiliates to whom he offered his generous drunken congeniality, sponsored by a young wharf-rat he called the "pimp boy." Here too, was held the celebrated party that he tendered to Harry and Caresse Crosby, and to which every notable of the young modern group attended—Matthew and Hannah Josephson, e. e. Cummings, Isadore Schneider, William Slater Brown, Waldo Frank. I was invited but could not come, yet when I passed the door of his apartment after midnight, on my way up to mine, and heard the voices, the muffled laughter and soft shuffling of feet, I knew that all was well. "I had a wonderful time," Hart announced joyfully the next morning, "I DIDN'T THROW A SINGLE PERSON OUT!" A bullet that he found on the floor after the party, caused him considerable concern. Oddly enough, he placed its ownership to Harry Crosby, who—strangely prophetic—committed suicide less than a week after. Further down the street, Number 110 is also gone, and gone are the wonderful old houses owned by a curious and eccentric millionaire art-connoisseur. It was here that Hart conceived his idea of what was to be a vast monolithic poem, "The Bridge," now really existing as a printed fragment, and here he wrote his "Voyages." I have elsewhere written concerning this tiny, lovely room with its amazing frontage of water—the same room from which Washington Roebling, a helpless paralytic, watched the material construction of his gigantic dream, Brooklyn Bridge. I occupied the room for a month, pending placement, after which Hart took over. He loved it. Here, for a while, he lived with the young sailor-friend to whom he dedicated and for whom he wrote, his "Voyages," until the latter's departure because of a neurotic quarrel between the two. At No. 110 also lived John Dos Passos and the artist Kunyoshi. The walls of the rooms were covered with fabulous Japanese color-prints, rare tapestries and stylized paintings, all at one time in the collection of the millionaire-owner, Hart had told me that, sunken in the roofs of the buildings below, was the owner's palatial apartment with a spacious pool, where his guests were offered entertainment not unbefitting the splendor and decadence of the later Roman Emperors. These too, have been scooped out. A little further down the street, Number 78 is gone. Here I first occupied a room when I came to New York, with an overwhelming view. The building was owned and occupied by four elderly spinster sisters. It was a wonderful four-story brownstone, so quiet that even a footfall sounded out of place. Joseph Pennell, who lived at the Hotel Margaret directly across the street, could be seen almost any morning striding along and cursing at heaven knows what under his gin-soaked breath. Or Thomas Wolfe, who also lived nearby, a huge ton of a man with a not unkindly stare, and whom one would have liked to talk to. Here at 110, Hart Crane had once lived until discarded by the quartette of landladies, but both he and Howard Lovecraft made frequent visits there to see me. The old ladies lived on to a tremendous age. One who survived, fell periodically down the stairs. Another—the strong-minded and youngest one—who had taught for 40 years in a school for delinquent boys, became senile, wandering about the house until early morning in a nightgown à la Lady Macbeth—with a lighted candle in her hand. One of her sisters confided to me that she had been romantically jilted in her girlhood. I listened to her anecdotes without flinching, and finally moved to New York. But the bay and the scene directly across, which Joseph Pennell once called "the most beautiful thing in the whole world," still survives, and remains unchanged and changeless as anything in this incredible city. Against it, at night, one can see the boats and tugs and steamers, pass and repass with colored lights and silhouetted spars in the fathomless blue space; and when the mists hang veiled and heavy, one can hear the organ music of the horns and whistles, with the somber low tones and a diapason of the harbor-buoys and water-murmurs out in the vast pale offing.

PREFACE [TO *THE HART CRANE VOYAGES*]

Although much has been written about the series of poems by Hart Crane known as "Voyages," little is available concerning their origin. The incident is tragic and literally left an indelible mark on Hart's brief life and his career as a poet.

I was still living in Cleveland in 1924, out of work and clearly at odds with an environment and conditions that were stultified by the boring backwash and hopelessness of establishing a career in that city. I was, however, deep in the composition of writing poetry, much of it on a long poem later to be published when I came to New York.

Hart had returned temporarily to Cleveland, filled with the enchantment that only New York could provide, much of which is now gone and relegated to studies of a period in American literature known as the golden "Nineteen Twenties." This is a phase that has utterly and completely vanished. The sordid shambles of what we still call Washington Square, now a place of squalor and disrepute, was surrounded by the homes and lodgings of poets, writers and artists, who were then busy in carving careers that were later to make them famous.... Eugene O'Neil, Willa Cather, Dos Passos, Waldo Frank, E. E. Cummings, W. Slater Brown and hosts of the equally celebrated.

Hart's return to Cleveland was to be of only brief duration. We were together much of the time. His mother, who wailed and deeply deplored his permanent departure, could not shake him in his determination to leave the beautiful old house on East 115th Street. He urged me to come to New York. "I want you to live near me," he said, "Brooklyn Heights is one of the loveliest places in the whole world. Imagine, the panorama incessantly before one's eyes—a glorification of beauty with the New York skyline always before one, Brooklyn Bridge, ships that come and go by day and night—and sailors. You will never care to live elsewhere, and wherever I may be, I shall always return to you."

He continued to disclose his own happiness. "I have met a young man, a seaman, at Fitzi's (Eleanor Fitzgerald, director of the Provincetown Playhouse), and I realize for the first time what love must have meant to the Greeks when one reads Plato. He's a Scandinavian and extremely handsome, yellow-haired and blue-eyed—a real human being. I believe my love is returned. He's at sea now; you must meet him when his voyage is over. I'll never come back to Cleveland. If Mother wants to see me let her visit me in New York. For the first time in my life I'm utterly free from the ghastly family bondage and the infernal squabbles between Mother and Father. Their divorce seems to have made no difference. Money and me seem to be the sole crux of their dissension. I'll be out of it for good."

I met Hart's "Greek" ideal on his return from the voyage, and he answered his description—an extremely well-coordinated and attractive youngster, certainly prepossessing but outwardly unemotional, and since Hart was inwardly a veritable caldron of conflict, I felt that this balance in their friendship was sufficiently warranted. I continued to see him day after day; his later acceleration in drinking was not then present and his sexual promiscuity apparently absent. He had acquired what he claimed to be the first copy of "Ulysses" ever to reach America, smuggled in by a friend, and bored me interminably by his insistence on reading it to me a loud. Spirited and certainly assertive on occasions of ordinary conversation, Hart's recitals abutted into a kind of clergical drone. He, on his part, assailed my own way of reading.

Then, the inevitable happened. His friend returning unexpectedly one evening to their apartment at 110 Columbia Heights, encountered Hart's stupid betrayal. There was no explosion, except Hart's ineffectual hammering protestations and attempt at an explanation—then silence. The friendship was resumed; their love never.

Yet in this fulmination of love and disaster, there emerged the creation of Hart's "Voyages"—poetry as passionately authentic as any love-poetry in literature. Whether it be addressed to normal or abnormal sexuality, matters little. There is nothing to be compared with it, excepting possibly, in the pitifully extant fragments of Sappho, the Sonnets of Shakespeare, John Donne's love-poems, or Emily Brontë's burning exhortations to an unknown lover. Compared with it, Mrs. Browning's much-belauded saccharine and over-burdened "Portuguese" Sonnets, are sentimental valentines. In his "Voyages," stripped of the verbiage that emphasised so much of Hart's poetry at its weakest, and which is transparently present in many passages of "The Bridge," the poet of "Voyages" becomes blazingly clairvoyant and achieves an astonishing profundity. "Voyages" is a classic in English literature.

Out of this extraordinary series of poems, Hunce Voelcker has fashioned his inspired and splendid study of the "Voyages." Phrase by phrase, passage by passage, all pass under the scrutiny of his magic, microscopic lens. So completely does he discover the genetic essence and spirituality of the "Voyages," that we would hesitate to read any further digression or elucidation of the poems. Actually, this book is not a study but should be read as one would read minutely and poetically into the superb symbolism of the "Prophetic Books" by William Blake. Both have the same artistry and the same extra-sensory perception. In Voelcker's book, as in Blake, we are confronted by a blinding light as well as by a deep shadow, much as one can visualize in the great but completely forgotten mezzotint plates by the great but completely forgotten John Martin in his illustrations to Milton's "Paradise Lost." Voelcker's magnificent prose and his equally magnificent analysis of Crane's "Voyages," deserve the highest placement in modern creative literature. I believe it should.

Of Gold and Sawdust

I came to New York City in 1924, worked nine months for a Jewish-Hungarian louse in his book establishment on Fourth Avenue, and when I found out he was releasing me for the summer, I quit. Before returning to Cleveland, I took up quarters in H.P.L.'s rooming house at 169 Clinton Street, Brooklyn.

The landlady seemed refined but had seen better days; the house was run down in a slattern way. Lodgers seemed to come and go. In May, 1925, I stayed there about two weeks. The front of the building was remodeled even in my day. I don't remember what the structure was made of—certainly not wood. You ought to take a trip to see this ghoul-haunted edifice. These were happy days when I believed H.P.L. was pure gold—not sawdust!

To the best of my recollection we lived on the first floor in separate rooms. Due to skin trouble, H.P.L.'s toilet took at least two hours. His nights were practically sleepless.

After Howard and I were robbed—he of most of his clothes and I of my radio—I went back temporarily to Cleveland.

During this period in Brooklyn, and even before, H.P.L., Rheinhart Kleiner, and myself (and probably a fourth person) used to meet regularly at a Scotch bakery and restaurant in the immediate neighborhood. The toughs (and I mean *toughs*) from Red Hook used to congregate there nightly. We listened to them recounting their marauding and robberies in the choicest and vulgarist Brooklynese slang; it was an unforgettable experience. Howard was enthralled. His mimicry of their conversations, at which he was so adept, went to the final writing of his masterpiece of a story—"The Horror at Red Hook."

There you have it! During that period I believed Howard was a saint. Of course, he wasn't. What I did not realize (or know) was that he was an arrant anti-Semite who concealed his smouldering hatred of me because of my taint of Jewish ancestry. It would be impossible for me to describe the smug, cloaked hypocrisy of H.P.L. The one last letter of his I have fills the bill, and a hundredfold more! It advocates the extinction of the Jews and their exclusion from colleges. The letter was written to a partner of W. Paul Cook, who published my books, "The Sphinx" and "The Hermaphrodite."

Lovecraft had a hypocritical streak to him that few were able to recognize. Sonia, his wife, was indubitably his innocent victim. Her love for him blinded her to many things. Among the things he said to her was, "Too bad Loveman's a Jew; he's such a nice guy."

I was, in the early phase of our friendship, an easy mark. He was, however, loyal in his appreciation of me as a poet.

Sonia was one of the most beautiful women I ever met, and the kindest. Her treatment by H.P.L. was, whether consciously or unconsciously, cruel. His anti-Semitism formed the basis for their eventual divorce. Howard's monomania about race was about as close to insanity as anything I can think of.

APPENDIX

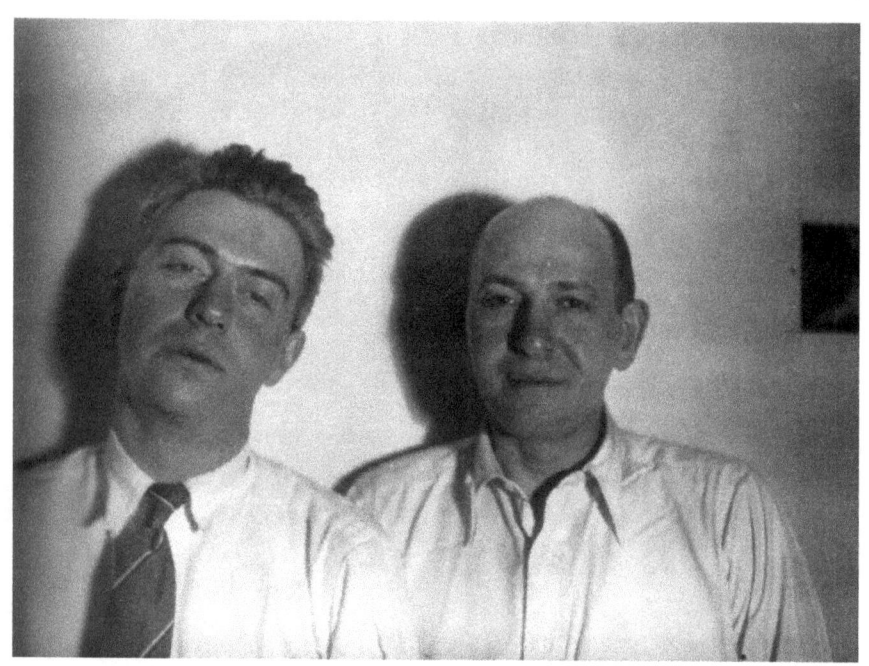

Hart Crane and Samuel Loveman, 1929, by Walker Evans

Interview with Sam Loveman

John Unterecker
New York City, 4 August 1962

JU: Let's start talking about Hart and then go back and talk about some of the others. You first met him about 1919, right?

SL: I met Hart in the winter of 1919, January of 1919. [probably Jan. 1920]

JU: That was in Cleveland, wasn't it?

SL: That was in Cleveland at Laukhuff's bookstore.

JU: Tell me about Laukhuff first.

SL: He had an element of the German in him that was a little disconcerting, but when you got to know him he could be very genuine, very warm, and rather dominating, I must confess. In the beginning there he knew very little about American and English literature, and he depended a great deal upon two or three of us who used to come in and give him advice as to what to buy and what to put into his stock. And we did that very eagerly. He knew nothing about people like Pater or the 1890 group, and bit by bit we had him assemble quite a few things that were really worthwhile. And then he began to function. People began to drop in—people like Hart and myself and there were some other people who were regular visitors—and he made it a point of introducing everybody who did come in.

JU: He had a section in the back with some chairs—was that right?

SL: He had finally confined himself to one chair that was a favorite. And, for instance, if I came in, he would immediately replace the person who sat in that big easy chair by myself. And as time went on, when I was permanently in Cleveland at that period, I sat there nearly every day for an hour, and then I could see he got a little bored, so I bade him goodbye. This was the daily program.

JU: Where were you working then?

SL: I wasn't. It was very difficult to get work in Cleveland. That's why I came to New York. But I met Hart at Laukhuff's during this period, and I was invited up to the Del Prado Hotel where he functioned while his mother and grandmother were in the Isle of Pines. And I must say that there were many people in literature that I was unacquainted with or knew only in a cursory sort of way. Hart had to a certain degree an amazingly broad knowledge of modern literature.

JU: Where had he begun to pick that up? He must have been as well read as anyone in the early days, don't you think?

SL: I recollect one in particular—Edward Thames, who was a friend of Frost's, a protégé of Frost's; I think did better poetry than Frost ever could write, who was killed during the First World War. And Hart read an extract of him to me and I liked it so much that I went out and got a copy and I've had it ever since.

He did not know the earlier people. Anything earlier than what we call the modern period, he didn't know. Later on he became conversant with it. I recollect that when he read Ben Jonson, he—what I once termed "tore the heart out of him." He read everything eagerly. But he miscalculated the person that he used to converse with about him. He would assume that because it was a discovery of his, that everybody else had known nothing about him before that. But I knew the Elizabethans, and I knew the Restoration people, and I knew the eighteenth century, and certainly I knew the Keats–Shelley period. And I think that outside of knowing a few poems of these people, Hart had no knowledge of their literary history or what they really meant in relation to the period they functioned in.

JU: Did he have much of an interest in painting then in 1919 when you first knew him?

SL: Yes, he did. He knew about Picasso. I did, too. There were a little series of books published in Germany that had all of the people that we now call the moderns, like Paul Klee, and Picasso, and Braque and Matisse. They were little slim books with the text in German, but Hart knew of them in a definite way—yes.

JU: I always feel that his interest in painting is very important in the poetry. I think, for instance, that Sommer and even Carl Schmidt were very important to him in giving him ideas about the shape of a poem.

SL: Well, Carl Schmidt was academic, definitely.

JU: Did you know Schmidt at all well?

SL: I had a letter from him, a beautiful letter. I don't know what became of it. Maybe it's with the letters up at Columbia.

JU: Maybe it is. He was Zel Demming's friend, right?

SL: I didn't know that.

JU: She had sent him to Europe.

SL: Well there is a painting in the collection up there done by him. I think it's a pastel-like painting.

JU: It's a Cleveland scene. He'd sold a painting to Hart's father once named "Olga."

SL: Well, there is a painting in that collection—a very Whistlerian painting, an amazing painting in oils—done when he was nine years old. They had it very elaborately framed. You must have seen that.

JU: I've seen that. He did quite a number of drawings.

SL: He was a good graphic artist, a very good one. The one at Columbia, have you seen that of me? It's a good one; it looks like me. He did it very hastily. He just sat down and drew. And his lines were excellent. He knew just what to do and what to make. And he made a likeness.

JU: When did he meet Sommer?

SL: He met Sommer through me. He met Sommer, he met Nelson, and many other people through me. He met [   ] through me. Sommer he must have met shortly after I became acquainted with him, because Bill and I had been friends for quite a while.

Samuel Loveman, as drawn by Hart Crane

JU: Bill was then at Otis Lithography, right?

LS: Yes, a wonderful companion except when he was at home where the lines were very rigidly laid down as to his behavior. Well, that's a story I suppose one shouldn't retell out of bounds.

JU: He was an enthusiastic painter, wasn't he? I mean he painted every time he could get a scrap of paper.

SL: Wonderful, wonderful. I think if he had been properly managed, he would be as well known as the French artists are today. There's no doubt about it. It needs someone to rediscover him.

JU: Well, of course, Hart thought he had discovered him, didn't he?

SL: Well, Hart had a very curious way of believing that he was the prime instigator in any movement. For instance, when we went to see Isadora Duncan on that amazing night when she appeared at the Great Hall in Cleveland, she was hissed, she was hooted, she was booted, they threw things at her, and left the hall. There were a few hundred people who stayed. Well, now, Hart claimed that his hand-clapping had forced the acclamation that was heard by the few hundred that remained, which was not true. I'm sure that it took more than Hart's hand-clapping.

JU: He went out to Sommer's place, didn't he, at Brandywine?

SL: We went out together, yes. That is a place you should go to see. You've never been there?

JU: I'm not sure if it's still there.

SL: It is there. So far as I know, the studio has been converted, owned by someone who bought the place. It's an amazingly beautiful place, amazing. There was at the time the old mill down there, which was still there, ruined, and there was the lapping water over the mill, and this wonderful vista of farm land and hills from the farm that Bill occupied. Bill's farm and the old studio and house, which was just like a Dürer drawing, occupied an ascendancy. And there were trees. I always thought that the landscape had some comparison to a poem by Sappho, the one about the apple on top of the topmost bough; the pluckers forgot to ... and so forth.

JU: Hart liked his apples, too.

SL: Yes, "the apples, Bill, the apples. . . ."

JU: Was Bill as devoted to apples and cider as Hart makes a him out to be? Or just hard cider?

SL: I don't know just what Bill's drinking amounted to. I know that toward the end he became terribly, terribly obsessed with it.

JU: His son said that when prohibition came, he stopped drinking; and he started as soon as prohibition ended. Is that true?

SL: That's not true. He had marital difficulties, and then when his wife died, I think that in spite of the difficulties between them, he loved her. Apart they couldn't live and together they couldn't live. And so it was just a case of everything going to pot. I think the children resented his actions, and it was very typical, very characteristic of an artist—I think a great artist.

JU: Was he a quick artist?

SL: Extremely quick. His lines—they seemed to start from nowhere and spring into life in a sort of an abundance that you couldn't guess would materialize when he began his drawing or his painting—his drawing especially.

JU: At about that time, was that when Hart met Jake Falstaff (Herman Fetzer) or was that later?

SL: Did he meet him?

JU: He knew him a little, yes.

SL: I don't think they were overly friendly. They may have been friendly in Akron, which I didn't know very much about. I used to hear about Hart's Akron days. I must confess, I wasn't especially interested in that phase of his. I was interested in him as a companion during the period that we were together.

JU: In those days his mother and grandmother were in and out, weren't they, regularly? I mean, they would be down at the Isle of Pines or back?

SL: They were only away once at the beginning. Later on, I don't recollect that they left him. The grandmother was an adorable human being. She bad this wrinkled face, a sort of a wry smile, that would make you think, "Well, now, she may not be so friendly," and yet she was so warm, such a compulsive person, and she adored Hart.

JU: You told me about her baking cherry pies and leaving them on the window sill.

SL: Wonderful. She used to tell me anecdotes about her early life. She said that when Lincoln was assassinated they set him out on the Public Square in Cleveland, and she and her husband—she was then a young bride—rode horseback to Cleveland where they viewed the remains. A tremendous number of years to look back to, isn't it?

JU: In those days when Hart was first in Cleveland, was Grace as nervous as . . . ?

SL: She was spoiled. She was always a spoiled child. She studied to be a singer. She wanted to be an opera singer. She was very handsome

JU: Did you ever hear her sing?

SL: No, never.

JU: I'd love to know somebody who . . .

SL: But she told me. She was a very commanding person, tall, and, as I said in this other little interview, imperious, which is an old-fashioned word, but she was kind. They took to me immediately. I think Grace had social ambitions which she never realized. I went there every day. There was no feeling that I was imposing on them. They loved to have me. And I think that they felt that I was a good influence on Hart, if one can claim that honor.

JU: What was Hart doing in those days? Was he then working for his father?

SL: Originally. Early. He left because, as he claimed, the old man tried to dominate him, treated him as though he were an underling and he resented it. The old man had this old-fashioned idea that to gain anything, to become anybody, one had to start at the lowest rung of the ladder, and Hart certainly did that. It was an imposition because the other employees, instead of accepting him in the right way, looked down on him, and resented it.

JU: I suppose one of those was Ed Morgan.

SL: No, Ed Morgan was not affiliated with him then. I think he was a free-lance who did work later on for the old man.

JU: Oh, I thought he was working for him.

SL: No, no. He wasn't there steady. No, not at all.

JU: McHugh mentioned him, too.

SL: Did McHugh mention him? I wish I'd taken McHugh's address. When I get to Cleveland again, if I do . . .

JU: I'll give it to you.

SL: Yes, I'd like to have it.

JU: He's very different now.

SL: Well, he was a shy, very quiet person. Of course . . .

JU: Were you with him when he and Hart and he said somebody else—he couldn't remember who—went to hear Mary Garden sing?

SL: No, I wasn't with him. Hart must have invited him then, and Hart—I had the anecdote about that—he introduced himself to Mary Garden, and, of course, Mary Garden had permitted her name to become . . .

JU: The Mary Garden chocolate . . .

SL: ... the Mary Garden chocolate queen. But Hart had a deep reverence for Mary Garden's voice. I loved her type of singing, because it was ostensibly French, and I love French singing even if it does have a sort of nasal quality to it. When I had a gallery she came up there one day . . .

JU: Did she? I didn't know that.

SL: She was over eighty then, and I didn't go up to her but I saw her from the distance and she was waltzing around on the floor there as though she were a youngster. I hear she's been very ill recently. But an amazing woman.

JU: Did you ever see Grace dance?

SL: Never.

JU: Because she was, you know, a would-be dancer, too.

SL: No, but Hart loved to dance. The minute Hart became intoxicated he wanted to do mazurkas. Mazurkas were his favorite form of the dance.

JU: Did he learn the dance steps from Potapovitch, do you?

SL: I imagine.

JU: I thought he must have.

SL: I imagine.

JU: Everyone, of course, remembers it, but I wondered where he'd learned it.

SL: Well, was Potapovitch—did you inquire or find out whether he was connected with any ballet group?

JU: With the Russian ballet, yes.

SL: Oh, he was with the Russian ballet. Well, I saw Nijinsky in Cleveland. It was an unforgettable performance. I may have gone with Hart.

JU: Hart liked the theater, didn't he? and the dance?

SL: Yes, he loved the dance. He loved symphony concerts. He and Bill Sommer and I went to hear a concert given by Hoffman, and Bill, who had not seen Hoffman since he was a boy prodigy, was quite excited. When this tiny figure, with the huge head and the long white hair, come out on the platform, Bill turned to me and said in German, "Look, the winter has come."

Hart and I went once and heard the Dvorak *New World Symphony*. Then Hart laughed, cackled, I should say, over Oscar Wilde's statement in one of his dialogues in the *Book of Intentions*. He said, "Oh, let us hear some mad scarlet thing by Dvorak." He said to me "Fancy, Sam, anything, mad and scarlet by Dvorak."

JU: How was Hart as a piano player—good?

SL: He was very efficient. I did a poem called "The Chopin-Player." It was done during a rainy evening, when he played Chopin. He would offer to play and I would sit there very quietly and listen. Too, he loved to play the old-fashioned 1880 or 1890 waltzes. I would say he was excellent. But he gave it up entirely. He never alluded to it later on. I never heard him play after he left Cleveland. Never.

JU: He must have sometimes because Lorna Deitz remembered him playing one song that she associates with him, a jazz tune. I've forgotten now. I suppose he learned that from his Aunt Alice. She was a music teacher, wasn't she?

SL: She was a music teacher? I didn't knew that.

JU: Did you know his other aunts?

SL: I knew none of them. I never met them. And there was a sort of a feud I think at that time between Hart and them. He always alluded to them in a not uncomplimentary but desultory sort of way.

JU: Did you know Charles Brooks?

SL: Yes, I met him. Hart introduced him to me. He did a fancy sketch . . .

JU: I've seen it.

SL: Yes, it's very condescending. Hart introduced him to me . . .

JU: What did Hart think of that?

SL: He laughed. There was really no malice in Hart except when it came to people like Yvor Winters, when he got very angry at him. Even then, it took a good case of drunkenness to bring out his anger. I think he resented Tate very much toward the end.

JU: He never really resented Waldo Frank at all.

SL: No. There was a very deep friendship there. They went to the Isle of Pines together. As a matter of fact, he looked up to Waldo, something that Hart rarely did to anybody.

JU: How well did he know other people in that little Cleveland circle—people like Charles Harris?

SL: Well, very well—[   ]—he loved Charlotte. Charlotte was a real . . .

JU: Tell me about Charlotte.

SL: Charlotte? Well, Charlotte was a wonderful companion. Her husband was very stolid and quiet; Hart liked him. But Charlotte was the real person. They used to love to dance together. Charlotte had a long plum-colored or deep velvet robe that she would put on and they would cavort around the room, you know. One of Charlotte's friends—he used to be there—was the man, the Czech composer who did *The Village Blacksmith* and something else. He was there. And then Charlotte's mother was there at the time. She died later. I think she sent back to Prague.

JU: James Daly was also, of course, there. . . .

SL: Daly is dead, you know.

JU: I know that.

SL: He's dead. Yes, he was a good poet. I have his book of poems; there's a poem to Hart in it.

JU: I didn't—yes, I did know that.

SL: He was very quiet. He married. And I think the marriage was not overly successful. I think they were divorced. I was surprised to learn about three, four years ago that he had died. I thought he was still alive.

JU: You weren't involved in that game of charades that Harris remembered at Jim Daly's house?

SL: No, I never went to Jim Daly's house.

JU: Hart and I think Charlotte played charades together, very elaborate dress-up kind of game of charades.

SL: No, that I didn't know of. I introduced Hart to the Rychtariks.

JU: He was working with the Cleveland Playhouse then?

SL: Who—Hart?

JU: No, Rychtarik.

SL: Yes. Well, he was connected with the Glidden Oil and Varnish Company. He did occasional scenery for the Cleveland Playhouse. He did some of it.

JU: Brooks was . . .

SL: Brooks was one of the big factors there. Brooks was the moneyed man. The Drurys there had left a lot of money to the Playhouse, which still functions as a very very good, profitable organization.

JL: Was Crane a friend of Brook's or was Mrs. Crane?

SL: No, I think it was Hart. They were not friends. Hart made funny, snide remarks about Brooks and about his social prestige. Brooks was not a bad writer, as a matter of fact. He did very good academic travel sketches, and the sort of thing one would like to read around a log fire when the wind is howling outside and you recollect that you've been to Italy and you think of the olive trees and [   ] and so forth.

JL: Was there anybody else in that group in Cleveland? I've been trying to think of Daley and Harris and Lescaze—you knew him, too?

SL: Yes, I'd rather not discuss him.

JU: Okay. When did you begin work on Saltus, because that was one of the first things that Crane talks about in his letters when he talks about meeting you.

SL: Well, I was working for a book store in Cleveland, owned by a man who got very angry if you foisted any sales that were concerning books of an intellectual order, when he would rather have sold Zane Grey. At that time George Kirk and I were very friendly and I worked nights, and George used to come there at night and wait on trade while I turned out so many pages of this book on Saltus—night after night. I did it completely impromptu. George had introduced me to the books of Saltus, who is still, so far as my own feelings are concerned, an amazing writer. He was a friend of Oscar Wilde's. He knew French literature. His books were extremely sophisticated. Finally I contacted Mrs. Saltus, who wanted the book to be published. The book was accepted by the press that functioned in Philadelphia. There were broadsides mailed to various booksellers; then they went broke, and it was never published, and it remains unpublished. But I knew Mrs. Saltus, who is now dead and who became an occultist. She was a friend of Rex Ingram out in California, the big movie man, whom I corresponded with. She was an odd person. She once proposed to me. But I didn't want to be the second Mr. Saltus. She was wealthy. She came from a very good family. Saltus had a daughter, who is probably still alive.

JU: Have you written her or talked with her?

SL: Oh, I visited her. I met her twice—a very beautiful woman, a society woman.

JU: Does she have any sense at all that her father as a writer?

SL: Yes, she had all of his books, all of his manuscripts—many of them she had purchased from booksellers—and she had a very definite reverence for him.

JU: What was George Kirk like? Did he do any writing at all?

SL: George didn't do any writing. In the early days, I would say, he had a wonderful feeling for good things in literature, a natural instinct. He became part of the circle . . .

JU: And was Kay Kenney part of that circle?

SL: Yes, yes, yes!

JU: Tell me about Kay Kenney.

SL: A wonderful girl—big, fat, jolly, with a laugh that was infectious.

JU: Hazel Hutchinson said she was such a good cook.

SL: Well, she may have been. We used to meet every Saturday and go to a restaurant on Prospect Street—a Hungarian restaurant, Klein's. And we'd sit there for two hours, three hours, till the middle of the afternoon and then disperse. And there was no dominating figure. I wouldn't say that Hart was dominating figure. But everybody conversed, and everybody was happy. These things are very common in periods of creative activity, where a group springs up like a mushroom out of nothing.. Take the Keats–Shelley period, Lamb, Leigh Hunt. They function for a certain amount of time, and then, like these natives that are born in the South Sea, simply die of malnutrition. They disperse.

JU: Was Kay Kenny writing much then?

SL: She wasn't writing at all.

JU: Later she did.

SL: Yes she did. She wrote monologues for Sheila Barrett, who recently reappeared in New York and was dreadfully panned. She had become dated.

JU: Lescaze said that some of the meetings were also in a roof garden. Do you remember that?

SL: That I don't recollect.

JU: This may have been just a little later.

SL: It may have been once or twice.

JU: He remembered it as the roof of a hotel . . .

SL: Well, he confused it with Klein's, which was not a roof. It had palms.

JU: That's what he was talking about.

SL: Yes: It was on Prospect Street. It's probably occupied by a radio store now.

JU: How about when you got down to New York? Did you and Hart come down about the same time?

SL: He came down first, then returned to get some of his possessions and told me that my best bet was to come to New York. I was always out of work in Cleveland. I couldn't get employment there. I had friends who had good positions in the business. I never mentioned Don Bregenzer to you, did I?

JU: No.

SL: Well, we formed the Colophon Club, Don and I, and everybody of note was a member—but not Hart. I don't know where Hart was. Maybe he was in California at the time. But Don knew Hart very well. His sister was alive up until a few years ago. I tried to find her once in the telephone book, but apparently she's dead. And there may have been others. . . .

JU: Well, then, you came down to New York about when?

SL: I came in November of 1924. Hart gave up his room to me.

JU: Which room was that?

SL: The room at 110 facing the river. That was the room where Roebling had watched the building of the Brooklyn Bridge after his paralytic stroke.

JL: And Hart was already working on *The Bridge* at that time.

SL: Yes, I think so. It had been occupied by Emile's father, who had gone to the hospital to die. It was a beautiful room and I loved it, but of course it was Hart's and I gave it back to him.

JU: What floor was it on?

SL: The third floor.

JU: At the back, wasn't it?

SL: At the back facing the entire bay. It was a scene that was dominated by New York, by the Statue of Liberty and Brooklyn Bridge—so beautiful

JU: I think Rychtarik had a photograph of it, looking out toward the window.

SL: Oh, that's wonderful.

JU: I think so. I'm not sure it's the right room. I want to show it to you.

SL: I visited him once with his second wife, but they never kept in touch with me. I felt all that was gone.

JU: Did you know Emile at all well?

SL: I didn't know him well. I saw a good deal of him.

JU: He was, of course, in and out during this period.

SL: He was in and out, and he was not very articulate. I don't think he's articulate even now.

JU: No, he isn't.

SL: But I knew him and liked him. You know that when you come to a new city there are so many attractions and there's so much—it's almost like a kaleidoscope. You just can't take in everything.

JU: Did Hart introduce you to Gorham [Munson]?

SL: I met Gorham in Cleveland.

JU: Oh, when Hart brought him out there?

SL: Yes, he as doing a book on Waldo. By the way, Munson did the first book on Robert Frost, too. I'd like to get a copy of it.

JU: I didn't know that. I knew about his book on Waldo Frank.

SL: I suppose it's heresy to say so. Maybe the Kennedys are overhearing me. But I think that Frost is terribly over-rated. And I think that his last book, which has sold into the hundreds of thousands, is just a lot of junk.

JU: Yes. Yes.

SL: And if it hadn't been for the publicity, this man, who seems to have assumed the robe of Tiresias, would be no great shakes at all.

JU: Did you know Jimmy Light at all?

SL: I met him. I visited him with Hart. Yes, a very fine person. Light had just finished doing for the Provincetown Playhouse *The Rhyme of the Ancient Mariner* with masques. And the masques were all suspended from the walls in his apartment—the garments and the masques. Yes, he was a very fine person

JU: Rychtarik has that masque that he gave Hart.

SL That Light gave Hart?

JU: Yes.

SL: How did Rychtarik get it?

JU: I think Hart gave it to him. Somewhere in here Lovecraft comes in, doesn't he?

SL: Yes, that *was* a feud. Hart took a dislike to him, and Lovecraft, who, as I said a few minutes ago, was a prig and prissy in his choice of language—you would imagine that the vocabulary of the Queen's English had been manufactured for him for his sole use. I could see where Hart disliked him.

JU: That was in Cleveland where he first met him.

SL: Yes. Then they came together one evening at my apartment on Columbia Heights with that miraculous view the river and New York, and they began to talk astronomy. Lovecraft was very conversant with the subject, had been writing for years a weekly diatribe on the austere heavens. He discussed it with Hart and Hart listened to him, and I thought to myself, "Well, this should do a lot to cement an acquaintanceship, certainly not a friendship."

Well, after they left, separately each said to me that both were amazed at one another. I don't know whether Hart's attacks on Howard Lovecraft were before or after this incident, as the letters convey in the Brom Weber book, but he certainly attacks him.

JU: Yes, he does. Well, Lovecraft didn't have any great affection for Crane.

SL: No, no.

JU: But that first time in Cleveland, Lovecraft did seem to like Crane. Was it Lovecraft and you and someone else ... Galpin ... went down to hear....

SL: Another prig.

JU: You went to bear a concert of music by Bloch, wasn't it?

SL: Oh, did I? Well, I've forgotten that.

JU: At least there's a letter that says that you and Galpin and Lovecraft and Hart went to hear this concert.

SL: That has escaped me. You see, that is what seventy-six years does.

JU: Bloch was one of the persons, too, in Cleveland, who . . .

SL: Yes, he knew Bloch. He knew Ivan Bloch, who was out in the Northwest, or was last, and Bloch was an amazing little man—a genius.

JU: Did you know Bloch at all?

SL: I didn't meet him, although I sat in the streetcar right next to him and his family. He was like a little jumping jack. But I know of a very amusing anecdote. We had an orchestra conductor in Cleveland at that time named Boris Sokalaff. And Sokalaff was socially very prominent. So, of course, Bloch, who was the antithesis or liking anybody of that sort was once asked what he would like to be if he weren't a musician. He said "Sokalaff!" I mentioned it to Ivan, Bloch's son, who said, "That's just like my dad. I believe it's true."

JU: How about Walker Evans? When did you meet him?

SL: I met Walker Evans on Columbia Heights when Hart was living at 110 below me.

JU: Hart was down below at that point?

SL: Yes, I had my troubles with him.

JU: With whom—Hart?

SL: With Hart. He would come up drunk and try to smash things and then he was being continually robbed. He would bring in sailors, and before had brought them to his rooms, he would hide everything, and then forget that he had hidden them and so throw the sailors out. This process went on interminably.

JU: When did he begin drinking heavily?

SL: When he came to New York—not immediately, but I would say shortly after. He was away from the austerity of his mother—that is, the dominating austerity. And he began. I would say that *The Bridge* was written completely under a state of drunkenness, then revised in sobriety. The manuscripts show less of wine and possibly tears. Hart wept under the stress of an emotion.

JU: Did he talk much about Mrs. Simpson?

SL: Yes, he loved her. She replaced his mother. She disliked Mrs. Crane and Mrs. Crane disliked her. I think there was jealousy—maternal jealousy—there. But he refers to her in one of his poems—I think "The Lonely Woman." A wonderful old lady.

JU: And did he talk much about the woman up at Patterson that he stayed with—Mrs. Abbey Turner?

SL: Oh, goodness, that poor woman was in a state of fright half the time over Hart's antics. Yes! Yes! My God, after he had been on a toot of some sort, she would say, "Why, Mr. Crane, really, you must be quiet and behave yourself." Hart would mimic her, you know, and laugh.

JU: You were saying that he had a habit of slapping his thigh.

SL: He slapped the knee or leg above his knee with a resounding thwack every time something struck him as being spectacularly funny.

JU: Did he work very closely with Walker Evans on *The Bridge* or . . . ?

SL: No. Walker and Hart were very friendly, for a while. Hart proclaimed to everyone that he and Walker had discovered a new dimension. Now, I don't know how many dimensions there are, but Hart's favorite word was "mystical." I don't think that Hart as a mystic. I never did think so. He wasn't a materialist, but he was not a mystic. I think he got a lot of that from Waldo Frank who inculcated the idea of mysticism into him. But Walker and he worked on this project. Walker took some wonderful photographs of him and one of me, which Hart called "Flight." I had my hand this way on my forehead and Hart said, "Flight."

Finally it got—as it did in many cases—to the point where Hart in his period of drunkenness would bombard Walker Evans' residence, ring his doorbell, wake him up by telephoning him at three or four in the morning. I think Walker couldn't take it. I myself always had one recourse. I would numb my doorbell. As a matter of fact, he wrote a little note that I have: "Sam, you scoundrel, you've once again numbed your doorbell!"

JU: Tell me about that Peggy Joyce business. The dance.

SL: He said one afternoon, "Well, I've just come back from a wonderful afternoon. I've been to a cocktail party given by Liveright (Horace Liveright) in honor of Peggy Hopkins Joyce's new book, her autobiography." He added, "I danced with her."

I said, "Do tell."

And he said, "Yes. I danced and danced until finally she said that she had to turn to some of the others and do the courtesy act." He said, "I proposed to her."

I laughed. I said, "What did she say?"

"'Well,' she said, 'Mr. Crane, there are at least two ahead of you. I hope you will have the patience to wait.'"

JU: Tell me about Bobby Thompson.

SL: He's dead.

JU: I know he's dead. I just know nothing about him and everyone has mentioned him as in a way almost everybody's friend.

SL: He was a natural writer who never could bring himself to putting much down on paper. He wrote one story which I published in my magazine called *Trend*, called "The Dehydrated Wife." He became a drunkard, and when he drank, he had tendencies that were criminal. He descended lower and lower, became a vagabond, a bowery bum, just like Walter Edwin Peck whom I knew, and finally ended up in Bellevue. He had been to the Kings County Hospital as an incurable dipsomaniac but I think he died in Bellevue. I don't know of what—I got a letter from his woman friend telling me about it.

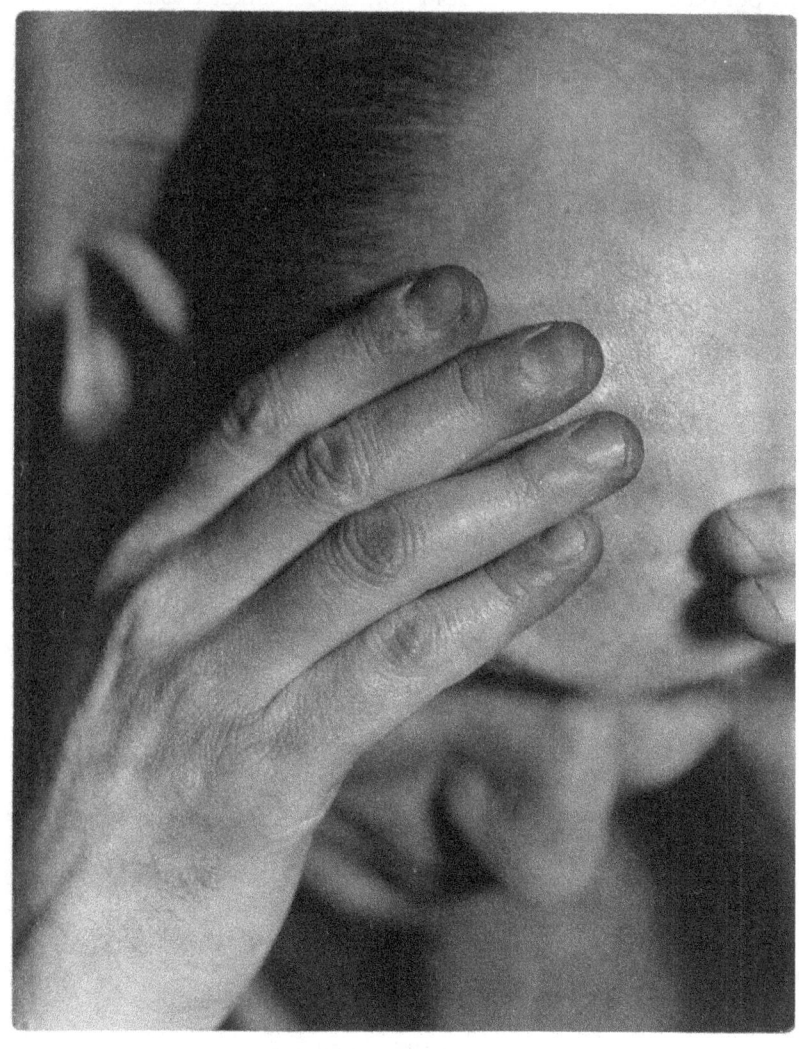

Samuel Loveman, c. 1929, ("Flight")
by Walker Evans

JU: You have no records of him and yet so many people remember him—Slater Brown remembered him. . . .

SL: Yes. He stayed with the Crosbys when he went to France, and he visited Roy Campbell.

JU: He wrote an awfully nice letter to Mrs. Crane, you know, after Hart's death.

SL: There were a series of letters written by Hart to Bobby. I never found out what became of them.

JU: All but one of his have disappeared, and I suppose Mrs. Crane threw them out.

SL: No, what I'm thinking of is Hart's letters to him.

JU: I know.

SL: Horton used them. Now, whether he returned them or not, I don't know. But they must have been very much on the fringe of being unpublishable.

JU: You told me a wonderful story once about a night that Hart spent in jail and came out laughing.

SL: He would come to Dauber and Pine, where I worked, laughing first thing in the morning, saying that he had spent the night in jail.

JU: Did you know him just after he met Charlie Chaplin?

SL: Yes, that was after. He said that he was living at the Grove Street house. Was that Fitzie's?

JU: Yes, that was Fitzie's house.

SL: A beautiful old house. It's still there. I think it should be. You must look it up. It's a beautiful place—long-halled, with wonderful staircase and high ceilings.

There was a knock at about eleven o'clock. Hart was reading or writing. He went to the door and in walked Waldo Frank and Charlie Chaplin. Both invited him out to walk the streets of New York. They were going to spend all night walking. So he went out with them, and he said he had never spent such a wonderful evening before. As they walked., Chaplin recounted his marital woes and the fact that he had been so unsuccessful—I don't think one ought to mention the cause— but he seemed to be a very unhappy man. And of him, Hart said, "Just like a figure out of William Blake."

JU: Hmmm. I hadn't heard that. Did Hart like to walk much? Was he much of a walker?

SL: Oh, not bad. He used to walk a good deal.

JU: He wrote about you, you know, that you were always walking.

SL: I love to walk. I can't walk much now. This damn physical condition. Well, I'll wait. I can walk in heaven. Yes we walked—on Sundays. It was wonderful to be with him because certainly I was never bored. He may have been bored by me. He never made any manifestation of it. And riding on the subway was just one holocaust of laughter because he saw double meanings in all the ads, and usually obscene meanings. He claimed that most of them had some sexual or phallic undercurrent of meaning. I doubted that, although very frequently he was right or seemed to be right. He didn't have a pornographic mind, though. He was one of the cleanest human beings I have ever met in that sense. No matter what his life was, he was a very clean human being and completely wholesome. I said that in this truncated interview with this beastly WBAI. You can erase that if you want to.

JU: No. Why? It'll be a nice part of the record. When did you know Bierce? Was that before you knew Hart?

SL: I wrote to Bierce when I was a kid. Well, I don't know. I wrote to him around 1908. I sent him a poem, and he wrote me back how much he liked it. And he said he had read many of my poems in various magazines, so I immediately wrote back and said, "You must be mistaken.

That's a cousin of mine down in Georgia known as the Georgia poet, Robert Loveman." Then I said, "I'm only sixteen," or seventeen. He said he would like to do something for the poem. And he did. He sent it around everywhere. Previously to that I had sent the poem to William Dean Howells, who turned it over to *Harper's* magazine, who told me they liked my poem very much and would I give them a selection that they could pick from. I never did, of course. That's my fatal fault.

Bierce went to work and did a great deal. He was unable to place the poem. He sent me the entire list of correspondence where they turned it down. He thought it was a very good poem. It was called, "In Pierrot's Garden."

JU: Oh, I've seen that, haven't I?

SL: I think you have.

JU: Was that in *The Hermaphrodite*?

SL: Yes.

JU: I think that's where I read it then.

SL: Yes, it is. I did that when I was fifteen or sixteen. It was published by Edwin Markham in *The Younger Choir*, his anthology. George Sterling was in that book; Louis Untermeyer, Ludwig Lewisohn, Joyce Kilmer all made their early appearance there. I was man with a very bright future behind him.

JU: You kept up a correspondence then with Bierce until his death.

SL: Yes. Just before he left the *Cosmopolitan*, he wrote an entire article about me, and then unfortunately he had a row with Hearst, whom he hated, despised, and left him. Well, I visited Bierce in 1913, a few months before he left this country. I had a very interesting evening with him. I have the entire interview with him written out. It's never been published. He had been out to California. I was supposed to meet him and George Sterling out there in Yosemite, and I bought a ticket to go out there, and being under age, my father forced me to return the railroad ticket, so I never went. But wherever he went he wrote me. And he wrote me one of the two or three last letters he wrote to people saying he was going to South America and didn't know whether he ever would return, but he wished me good luck. That was the last. But after his passing, I discovered that this article—or something akin to it—is in his Collected Works, and it's called "Poetry and Feeling." It is about me.

George Sterling, incidentally, wrote a review of my long poem "The Hermaphrodite," completed it two days before his suicide, and Robertson Jeffers sent it to me with some very complimentary remarks. He didn't even read proof on it.

JU: Maybe we could just say a little bit about Hart's personality.

SL: He had a devastating sense of humor when he was sober. When he was drunk he lost it. I've never met anybody who was as quick in taking over a comic situation as Hart was. The Horton book is factually an excellent book, but it completely avoids or seems to be oblivious of the fact that Hart was not a morbid human being—except, as I said, under the influence of drink or possibly anxiety—and that when you were with him, there was no time limit to what you wanted to say. Conversation went very easily. He was not contradictory. He had very decided opinions about literature. I never attempted to confute what he felt about certain books or about certain styles or modes of poetry because I realized that this was his way and my way was different. In the letters, I think he becomes rather condescending when he refers to me. He refers to me as being a sort of an academic human being. Well, the fact is that I never was academic. And when I became cognizant of the new trend in poetry—providing it was poetry and not prose attempting to deform itself into poetry—I accepted it and made it a part or my reading. And this has been the same way with me all my life. In painting, in music, and in poetry. I hate discordances. I think many of Picasso's things are deliberately ugly, and I think many of them belong to the greatest painting that was ever consummated in what we know as modern painting. Hart was prone to accept certain discordances in poetry and in painting as a part of his own feeling about the subject.

JU: You once told me something about the intensity of his friendship that I always remembered and that was that he would almost grab you as a friend.

SL: He held onto you. I had one quarrel with him and that was entirely possibly due to my quick temper. He spoke in a derogative manner concerning the poetry of Ernest Nelson. Now, he was completely right. Ernest Nelson's poetry was very academic. His drawings were very academic. But he was of such a sweet nature that I couldn't permit anybody to offer an open introduction against anything that he did. And I went up there one evening and out of the blue there began an argument. He said something in a very derogative way about Ernest's work and I proceeded to deny it and one word led to another and there were plenty of words. And I walked away from the porch where he was standing and went out of his life, so to speak. Well, the next morning I received a letter saying, "If I have said harsh words to you, you have said harsher words to me." I didn't answer him. But many, many weeks—probably six months later—later I met him at George Kirk's and it was as though nothing had happened. We shook hands and there was never again any friction, except once on Columbia Heights when he became drunk and came up to my apartment and tried to smash things. I got him out, shut the door on him; he hammered at the door, and at intervals came up and then downstairs I heard the opening and the closing of the door all night long. I couldn't sleep. I was very upset.

Well, in the morning I went downstairs. I knocked at the door. He lets me in and he sat in a chair exhausted. I was very angry. And I said, "You bastard, don't you ever try to do what you did last night." He didn't seem to realize it. He had forgotten it. He didn't answer me. He just sat there with the sweat pouring from him. Then he accused me of having let him alone to the mercy of the people who had come in and robbed him that night. I denied it. He said it was my fault; I should have taken care of him. I said, "I'm not your nursemaid."

I felt very sorry. I thought he was very pitiful. Finally I bent down and I kissed his forehead and shook hands with him, and that was the only quarrel I ever had with him after the first occasion.

JU: You told me once a sort of sweet story of him reading his poetry to a sailor.

SL: Well, we were invited . . . He was friendly with a rich Scandinavian who manufactured tiles or something for roofs. You possibly know all about him. Well, he had a boat on the Hudson. And Hart would occasionally invite some of his sailor friends up there. I leave the purposes to your imagination. And I came in one day and there he was sitting on the bed reading passages of *The Bridge*, or was it *Moby-Dick*—I forget what, to a stoker, a stocky, rough stoker I think from the battleship *Wyoming*. And I looked down at the stoker who was listening with rapt attention and couldn't understand a word, of course, while Hart went right on after saying hello. I noticed that the stoker's fingers were grimy from the coal. He hadn't been able to cleanse his hands completely.

Well, Hart invited me to accompany both of them to this yacht on the Hudson. We went up there and the Scandinavian cruised around and Hart introduced him. I don't think Hart liked him, but he found an abundance of drink there and an abundance of entertainment because this man had people coming and going all the time. And so it was a very pleasant afternoon. I left alone. I left Hart on the boat. I wanted to get away. The atmosphere confused and somewhat disheartened me.

JU: You told me also about his once telling you that he deliberately schooled himself to appear masculine.

SL: He told me once . . . Now, Hart was a very masculine person. He smoked cigars. He chewed tobacco—I thought an abominable vice, a filthy vice—and spat, and it was revolting. But he had a stride, a very masculine stride. So he told me that he deliberately, as you say, schooled himself to adopt this to avoid any feeling of resentment against him on the score of masculinity or non-masculinity. I knew of one incident where a poet came there—I shan't mention his name; I met him in later years; I met him in Harlem. He wrote; he wrote well. He came in there one day and flung his clothes off and began to dance naked around the room. And Hart got very angry, very offended, and put him out. He told me of the occurrence later and said he couldn't tolerate it. He could not tolerate feminine people. There was a young fellow who used to come up to my place. I became acquainted with him . . . He belonged to high society. He wrote poetry, and the poetry was not bad. Well, he was rather on the borderline. I never interrogated him. I wasn't interested. I was interested in revising his poetry. He asked me to revise it. So he would come up there once a week. And it so happened that Hart came into the apartment on one of those occasions and I introduced him. And I noticed that Hart was rather nervous and presently he simply departed. Well, the next day I saw him. He told me that he did not like to see people of that type visiting me. Well, I said to him, "I don't know anything about him." He was writing good poetry under a sort of semi-tutelage that I gave him. I wasn't being paid for it. And that was all. "Well," he said, "after all, that may be right, but I don't like it." And that ended it.

JU: But most of the time he was a very outgoing sort or person, wasn't he?

SL: What do you mean?

JU: Oh, affectionate and joking and . . .

SL: Completely, completely. When you walked with him his hands had the Whitmanian gesture of one arm on your shoulder, which I didn't like so well. It impeded my walk. But there was certainly no semblance of what people have inferred against him.

JU: And there wasn't much of a picture of him as a tragic character, was there?

SL: I wouldn't say so. The left-wing have made him a victim of the social system, as you probably know. But he really wasn't. He really wasn't. He didn't blame . . . He was not political in any sense. I honestly never heard him utter a word on politics. He did get terribly sick of this country—what was going on here, the juggling of the intellectuals, you know, who finally were forced to go to Europe to find what they couldn't find here, and had to come back because of the hard times in 1929. But otherwise he was perfectly acquiescent to everything.

JU: Tell about Hart's cat.

SL: Oh, yes, a little vagrant kitten appeared on the scene—black like pitch, dark like midnight. And I said, "Well, what are you going to call her?"
    He thought for a minute and he said, "Agrippina."

I said, "That's a wonderful name." She was a sinister sort of person. I hope that your dachshund has a much better moral character than Agrippina had, who used to pick out the gladiators and make them her consort.

He said, "She looks very nice. She or he."

A few days later I said, "How's your cat?"

"Oh well," he said, "I'm not going to call her Agrippina. She's a male. I'm going to call her Agripenis."

Conversations with Sam

Thomas J. Hubschman

Introduction

I met Sam Loveman in 1963 at a party in a mutual friend's apartment. Ron and his wife lived in a walk-up on Hicks Street in what was then still known as South Brooklyn, taking its orientation not from its position in the borough but by its geographical relation to the erstwhile City of Brooklyn just to the north. Ron's building had an exterior stairwell, and on the landing of each story you had an ascending view of New York Bay, a lovely vista especially at sunset. The building was supposed to have been modeled on a design of Leonardo da Vinci. Not bad for fifty or sixty dollars a month, a reasonable rent even in those days.

Ron was a playwright, a very prolific one. He once showed me a closet that was stacked to the ceiling with manuscripts. In those days I was still devoted exclusively to the short story form and wrote at an agonizingly slow pace, though that year, the one following my graduation from Fordham College, I did have a burst out of which I produced four or five in succession—a kind of celebration of my liberation from academic life. Ron and I had met on campus the year before when I was living out of a shared apartment on Webster Avenue just off campus. He invited me to see where he lived in Brooklyn, a place I had never been to. What I found there that mild spring evening was a piece of Italy: pasticcerias, greengrocers, Italian restaurants, and as much Italian spoken as English. Plus, a "big sky," as Ron put it, something that can be at a premium in a city as vertical as New York, even in parts of the so-called outer boroughs. I fell in love with that neighborhood and resolved to move there myself, which I did after my new wife and I, having tried to make a living in Washington, D.C., were forced back into the city where we both had roots, she as a native, I as an migrant from nearby New Jersey.

Sam Loveman was easily the oldest guest at that party, in his mid-seventies. The only other "older" person was someone named Tony, a painter in his late thirties or early forties, the man who had introduced Ron to Sam. I remember Sam sitting as if in state—his age according him that position; there was nothing imperious about his attitude, which was always welcoming and gentle—receiving introductions to other guests, myself included. He immediately asked how I knew Ron, which in turn led to my confessing my own literary predilection (the sort of ornate phrase Sam liked to use). Ordinarily at a loss for words in circumstances like this, I found it easy to talk to Sam—or, rather, Sam made it easy to talk. Before our conversation was over, we had made a date to meet for dinner—his treat—the following weekend.

Sam ate most of his meals out and knew where the best buys were, though he probably took most of his dinners in the diner near his fourth-story walk-up on Second Avenue between 77th and 78th Street in Manhattan. The venue he chose for us was Paddy's Clam Broth House on West 34th Street, a big, no-nonsense establishment that served tasty fresh fish with gigantic boiled potatoes, nothing garnished, let alone seasoned. Sam loved good food—he especially enjoyed my wife's cooking, which was also tasty but not heavily seasoned. It may have been the same sort of fare his mother had prepared for him back in Cleveland. I remember how his eyes lit up when Susan put a bowl of small boiled potatoes on the table and he cried, "New potatoes!" raising his arms in a kind of hosanna.

After that first meeting in Ron's apartment my courtship and subsequent marriage interrupted my relationship with Sam for more than a year. When it resumed I began seeing him regularly, usually at his apartment, where I subsequently lugged a friend's heavy reel-to-reel Grundig "portable" recorder to make the tapes from which the transcript that follows was produced. We continued seeing each other that way for a couple years, with side visits to my apartment in Brooklyn, to poetry readings at St. Mark's in the Bowery (where Sam introduced me to Alan Ginsburg, who ignored me but greeted Sam with teasing banter), to the old Gotham Book Mart on 8th Street in Greenwich Village, or just to join Sam at his latest eatery—always good, always reasonably priced.

There's a persistent background noise on the tapes—an old floor fan Sam kept running to mitigate the summer heat. Along with the heavy recorder I lugged on the subway from Brooklyn most Saturday evenings, I also arrived with a large bottle of Cott soda, raspberry or black cherry, Sam's favorites, that I picked up at a deli near his place. We sat, I on the only chair, an old straight-backed wooden affair, Sam perched on the edge of a cot in what under other circumstances, with a very different sort of tenant, would have been the living room. Around us were stacked towers of books, old books, new books. The book towers were replicated in the adjoining middle room and in the back room behind that. The floors were wide bare wood planks, the varnish long since worn away.

I had no specific purpose in recording Sam apart from the depressing prospect of his rich memories of Hart Crane and other luminaries he had known being lost to posterity. It was during this time that Louis Untermeyer's biography of Crane, *Voyager*, came out. Sam spoke of it now and then, with some gratification I only realized in retrospect because the author had interviewed Sam in depth and drew liberally on his memories of Crane for it. Other scholars and literary lights also used Sam as a resource for Crane or H. P. Lovecraft, who was just then being revived.

I was no fan of Hart Crane, at least not as a human being. Indeed, I confess to remaining ignorant of his work throughout my relationship with Sam because Crane came across in Sam's anecdotes as an insufferable egotist. For his friends Sam had played the role of counselor, confidant, and best friend, always self-effacing and always available, even for the most outrageous demands. The tapes were my way, I suppose, of putting Sam into the spotlight for a change, making him the main character of his own life, from its beginnings in a nineteenth-century Ohio family of Jewish origin to his life when I knew him as mail-order bookseller and go-to source for scholars looking to make their reputations off the careers of dead poets and other scribblers Sam had known.

And whom hadn't he known? He had corresponded with Swinburne, whose "Go down to Kew in lilac time" still echoed in me from the pages of my high school English text. Sam had himself been "discovered" as a significant new poet by the author of "An Occurrence at Owl Creek Bridge," a writer whom I in my callow youth thought of as far removed in time as Keats or Poe. A great-uncle had described to a young Sam Loveman Napoleon's army marching through Bohemia on its way to Russia in 1814. For the first time in my life I felt connected to a past beyond that of my parents' generation, well beyond, a deep past rich with famous people with whom my friend had had personal, sometimes intimate relationships.

I also felt that Sam the poet had gotten the short end of the stick by an unfortunate twist of history. He had come of age just before the great shift from nineteenth-century expression into the more vernacular speech of Ezra Pound and T. S. Eliot. Sam's only published books, *The Hermaphrodite* and *The Hermaphrodite and Other Poems*, appeared after Pound and other moderns had already made their marks. Sam told me Hart Crane congratulated him on the appearance of *The Hermaphrodite*, recognizing the genuine accomplishment of that slim volume and doing so, it seemed to me some forty years later, with uncharacteristic lack of ego. But recognition of the kind Crane and even lesser talents were accorded never came for Sam. The language he employed in his poetry automatically made him irrelevant and passé in the eyes of critics who fear being out of date more than they do of missing real talent when it crosses their paths.

I find it gratifying that Sam's achievements as a poet are now receiving some degree of appreciation, largely thanks to the Internet, though still to a large extent because of his association with people like Crane and Lovecraft. After several decades I find his poems to be even better than I did when he first recited them to me. Back then I, too, found his language dated, though I nevertheless felt the remarkable impact of many of those poems. Mere print cannot convey the rich Middle-Western speech I heard in person, but its qualities of sincerity, keen insight and, perhaps most of all, genuine compassion for the lot of those he held dear and indeed for humanity itself are clearly present.

On Poetry

TH: Sam, I wonder if you would say something about your theory of poetry in general. The philosophy of composition behind your poems.

SL: Well, I believe that much of the modern poetry, and I have read a great deal of the avant-garde, so-called, which is really not poetry but conversational, has not the slightest approach to what poetry really is and should be. Poetry should have a definitely lyrical quality. It must have it. [. . .] An epic, of course, necessarily wouldn't have it, because it is a solid structure very much like Milton's *Paradise Lost* and even his *Samson Ago-*

nistes. But suppose we take as an instance the lyrics of Heine, which are more or less extremely difficult to translate. In a prefatory note to my translations of a few of the Heine poems, I said this. I quote briefly: "With Heine, poetry was mostly a matter of passionately exalted lyricism. But his translators, new and old, seem to have divined something vastly and variously different. Louis Untermeyer, for instance, approaches him with all the gigantic conception of a Ulyssean galleymaker. The dawn is blue and radiant, the material is chryselephantine. True enough. But his restive craft will not reach Ithaca. Hardly. In his hands the marvelous music of the Lotus flower, a thing of opal and iris, becomes unreal and metronymic. It is not thus that great poets are translated. Nor is it thus that great poetry is ever written. More than one translator and his translations have foundered under the too-liberal interpretation of literalism."

People like Robert Lowell, who has been panned [*sic*] to high heaven for his so-called translations, did not even attempt to make a translation. You can make a translation and not be too literal, but it should be poetry. But in the hands of Robert Lowell it simply becomes the medium of his own definite technique for writing poetry. And I don't believe that Robert Lowell is the great poet—he is supposed to precede all the others—that the critics, some of the critics, have represented him to be. If you read the Jean Stafford ... No, she didn't do that; someone else did it lately in one of the scholarly magazines.... A good critic, I think a professor at college, and he tore him to pieces, just as though he were an animal that he had caught. And he was right. He was right. Now, when I translated the Heine poems, I altered, I altered, but they had the essence of Heine.

TH: Rather than try to define what you mean by lyric, what would you cite as paramount examples of lyric poems?

SL: Define a lyric poem?

TH: No, rather than try to define it in philosophical terms, what would you cite as the lyric poems par excellence that you hold up as the standard of lyricism? In other words, when you say "lyric" you're thinking of a certain type of poem as opposed to another type. Now, would you be thinking of ...?

SL: Well, I don't necessarily mean that a lyric should be, as so many of mine are, composed of eight lines. [...] It can be a long poem and yet have the lyrical swing to it, or the surge that you want to embody into a poem. It should sing.

TH: For instance, would you say that Alexander Pope had this quality in his poems?

SL: I think he was a great poet. You can't compare Pope, or you can't define Pope, as a lyrical poet.

TH: No.

SL: Some of the lesser ones did. People like Matthew Prior. Chatterton did one ballad, called "The Ballad of Charity," that is one of the great poems in the English language. And it's written in his synthetic, archaic style, but it's wonderful.

TH: Well, let me take it from a different angle. Would you say that a true poem, which means that it contains a touch of lyricism at least, according to what you said before, would always have a certain kind of, maybe you could call it an exalted diction, as opposed to a very mundane type of diction, which is characteristic of the very modern, or at least the contemporary poetry we read now?

SL: You want me to define a lyric. And I must confess it's a very difficult thing to do.

TH: But would you agree that it has a certain type of diction which is more exalted than ordinary conversation?

SL: Yes. Oh, yes, yes. Yes, yes.

TH: And contemporary poetry tends to copy ordinary conversation deliberately, doesn't it?

SL: Yes, yes. I've been reading many of the so-called better poetry magazines like the *Beloit Poetry Magazine* [sic]. *Poetry*, which is the last word in poetry that isn't poetry. I don't know who is the editor of the *New York*

Times editorial page poem that is in there every day. Rarely if ever are they poems. [. . .] Someone once said a sonnet is a moment's monument. A lyric should have that pervasive, instance crash appeal to you.

TH: These people that we speak of disparagingly right now would probably disdain the use of the word *lyric* at all, though, wouldn't they? They wouldn't accept the idea.

SL: They would resent it. They would resent it. The St. Mark's school of corruption . . .

TH: [laughter]

SL: . . . and I think they're the most odious gang in the world. They're one for all and all for one. I noticed that Anne Waldman, the little boy-girl, and her husband, the softie, both have poems in the current *Poetry* magazine in Chicago.

TH: Oh, really?

SL: Yes. Even Harriet Monroe would get up from her grave.

TH: They're no good at all?

SL: They're no good at all.

TH: I wonder how they got in.

SL: Well, occasionally they have good poems. Or rather poets. You see, some of these people have an approach. My definition of what actual poetry is doesn't fit in with theirs. But people like Michael McClure, Robert Duncan, are very likely poets. In the sense that the avant-garde could be called poetry. They're super-intelligent in their manipulation of words. Frequently the so-called sophistication is simply meaningless, because they use words very frequently without any link to what they're trying to say. You don't get it.

TH: I think that one of the great successes of your lyric poems is that they combine, without seeming to be a combination, a certain poetic diction with ordinary speech which seems to gild ordinary speech rather than . . .

SL: Maybe.

TH: . . . writing in an artificial way. In other words, a great many poems, for instance, the poems that are included in [F. Scott] Fitzgerald's first novel, which he had written at an earlier age, seem to me very pseudo-romantic in their diction, and nobody could possibly have spoken that way. And yet your poetry tends, as I say, to be very current usage, and yet at the same time it infuses a poetic touch which exalts the diction.

SL: This is possible.

TH: And I suppose you would say, making it conscious this way, you would say this is the standard of poetry, wouldn't you?

SL: Well, I was always very sensitive to the usage of words welded into thought. In other words, you can take . . . oh, I want to give you before you leave tonight—have you ever read . . . I had it in my last catalog, it didn't sell—Thompson's, Francis Thompson's essay on Shelley?

TH: No.

SL: I may have catalogued it. But if I haven't I'll give it to you. Well, he says that certain words outwear the use, or not the use, but the—how I shall express it?—well, they become trite, they become faded, they're words that at one time had a definite poetic quality. You'll find them in people like Thomas Gray—and only the extreme talent of a man like Thomas Gray saves the "Elegy Written in a [Country] Churchyard" from being devastatingly dull. He had a contemporary, I don't know if whether you've read him, William Collins. There was a touch of insanity in William Collins. And some of his lyrics, in spite of their usage of the eighteenth-century verbiage, are incomparable, because he knew how to keep it fresh. You must keep your language fresh. And conversational poetry—and I call that whole school the St. Mark's school, for want of something better to call it—is just an outworn attempt to confer the term poetry onto prose. I think at certain intervals Ginsburg has the really—and I don't say this because I like him personally—but I think he really has it way over the people who are around him. Way over them. There's a man named Clifford Eschelman who read. He has done a great deal of translations of the Spanish poetry and so forth, a very, very intelligent and fine human being who's also a poet, in spite of the fact that he confers much of this conversational tone to his poetry. That can even be overcome, but it can only be overcome if the people who utilize it have talent.

TH: Well, you've given me about five questions while you talked. Let me start with this one. While you were talking it occurred to me that, I was wondering what you would say about some of the later poems of W. H. Auden. I'm thinking more of the less successful ones. He tends to be a very conversational poet, everybody agrees, in the sense that John Donne was perhaps too. But I wonder if you would agree that what is lacking in some of his less successful poems is this...

SL: The recent ones?

TH: Yeah, well, since the war, say. Or many of the ones before the war.

SL: What is lacking?

TH: Yeah.

SL: Juice. They're so dry that if you applied a match to them they'd become a torrential conflagration.

TH: Would you say that a synonym for what you call "juice" would be this so-called exalted diction that I spoke of before? In other words, that he doesn't use rhetoric in the traditional sense of rhetoric, that he doesn't exalt the language without being artificial about it. In other words, what I said about your poems was that the language of your lyrics, without being artificial in any way, immediately uplifts the tone of the language in the poem, and immediately you're in a poetic level, and that in the less successful poems of Auden, only as an example, or perhaps you would say Robert Lowell too, but in general when a poem isn't successful, especially when it's trying to be conversational, would you say it's this lack of poetic diction which maybe modern people tend to be more shy of? That's really what I'm getting around to. I think that we almost apologize for saying something poetically rather than in a mundane manner, for some reason now, don't we?

SL: I think they've lost their foothold on what poets like to call the Ladder of Parnassus.

TH: I don't think they'd accept that term either. But I remember that you once told me that before Hart Crane left, the last time you saw him, he told you that he was depressed because he thought he was writing rhetoric only. And by rhetoric he meant something. He said that disparagingly. But when I say rhetoric I mean you can say that at its worst it's just a tricky way of using language to move other people, but at its best it can be the most poetic use of language. But in a contrived way—without meaning that in a disparaging way either.

SL: That's right.

TH: And really when you said, when you mentioned prose as opposed to poetry before—I don't want to put words in your mouth—but I would just want to get your opinion on this view of mine, that there really is no distinction between poetry and prose, that a successful work of art will contain poetry and if it doesn't contain the poetic it won't be successful, particularly short pieces.

SL: Well, I'll cite you an instance. There are huge gobs of prose in Thomas Wolfe's books that all you need is to break them up and you have modern poems. He knew it. Someone has already done it, has taken some of these things and converted them into poems just by . . .

TH: Verse.

SL: Yes, yes.

TH: But I mean, for instance, in Katherine Anne Porter, or in any other prose writers that I respect, like F. Scott Fitzgerald, or in the early Hemingway, what appeals certainly to me, and I think what appeals to people in general, is the same element in the works as would appeal in your lyric poetry, despite the difference in form. In other words, the difference between poetry and prose, if you're going to make it good and bad, is not form but rather lack of quality. In other words, prosaic means "not poetic," not really just the form in which it's written. Do you think so?

SL: I think you're right.

TH: I would like to in that connection read you a paragraph out of the introduction to [Katherine Anne Porter's] *Flowering Judas*, and it bears on what you were saying before, since she's more or less a contemporary. I'd like to get your opinion on it.

She was writing about the period in which she wrote these stories. And she said, "We none of us flourished in those times, artists or not, for art like the human life of which it is the truest voice thrives best by daylight in a green and growing world. For myself, and I was not alone, all the conscious and recollected years of my life have been lived to this day under the heavy threat of world catastrophe, and most of the energies of my mind and spirit have been spent in the effort to grasp the meaning of those threats, to trace them to their sources and to understand the logic of this majestic and terrible failure of the life of man in the Western world. In the face of such shape and weight of present misfortune, the voice of the individual artist may perhaps seem of no more consequence than the worrying of a cricket in the grass, but the arts do live continuously and they live literally by faith. Their names and their shapes and their uses and their basic meanings survive unchanged in all that matters through times of interruption, diminishment, with neglect. They outlive governments and creeds in the societies, even the very civilizations that produce them."

And she goes on and concludes by saying, "And even the smallest and most incomplete offering at this time can be a proud act in the defense of that faith."

Her use of the word *faith* in reference to art at this particular—well, this was twenty years ago she wrote this—indicates to me that it was on her mind and that in general she sensed the lack of faith which to me parallels the lack of exaltation in the diction of both the poets and the prose writers of the time. And you were around when she, in the period she's referring to, and I wasn't. I'm very curious for you to say whatever you, whether you disagree with that or whether . . .

SL: No, I think she's right. I think she's right. There's another element that must be present in writing poetry that is poetry. No matter how sad a poet can be, there should be an element of exaltation to it. It's gotta have it. This young fellow who, from California, as I read some of the poems, I didn't take as much anything like that. Well, he said they're all so sad. Well, I said, they reflect whatever I felt, and if I were to, I say this to you, if I were to yelp out the old pirate ballad, "Yo-ho-ho, and a bottle of rum," with a shout and sort of festive feeling, it would be utterly false. But she is absolutely right.

I'm not sticking to what you were talking about.

TH: She also writes stories which are sad. Very frequently. Sad endings. And what this young man said to you is not an unusual opinion. I remember when one of the first things Pope Paul VI did when he took office was . . .

SL: Who?

TH: The current pope.

SL: Oh, yes.

TH: . . . was to make a plea to the writers and artists of the world not to write so many books with sad endings. Now, that may be a reactionary view, yet I think many people who don't have a great familiarity with poetry or with literature in general feel that there is a contradiction somehow between the very tragic statement which much poetry makes and yet the expression of it in the first place, why the man should bother to say it and what good it does. What good does it do to say that life is bad, because everybody knows it? And why harp on the subject? Now, a lot of people, certainly a lot of people in my generation, would write poetry off because, certainly a man like Robert Kennedy, I think, would tend not to be a great advocate of poetry, because he sees the world as something that needs to be changed. And you don't sit around and talk about how bad it is. You're supposed to get up and do something about it. Now, what do you say to people who feel that way?

SL: Well, I would say that the world is divided into, as far as I'm concerned, two [kinds of] people: the people who look forward and the people who look backward. And that doesn't mean that I, how shall I say, simply haven't advanced. It's just my feeling. This man, Bob Kennedy, who is not a poetic person, I doubt it. I think the brother was . . .

TH: I use him as an example because it's kind of obvious to me there. But I think that people in general aren't devotees of poetry, and it's not an integral part of their life the way it is of yours . . .

SL: Well, they want joy, they want whatever, whatever joy means to them.

TH: I think they also feel that it's almost, it's almost a sinful act to give in to poetry and to these kinds of moods because the world won't be better for it. That you'll prolong misery rather than do something about it.

In other words, they don't know anything about poetry to start with. What I'm trying to get you to say is what you see the function of poetry to be.

SL: Well, I think the greatest poetry has been tragic poetry. The greatest. Look at it, whatever you want. Think of it in terms of Walter Savage Landor's exquisite little gem of a poem, "Rose Elmer." I think six or eight lines, maybe eight lines. This was a girl he knew who died young, and apparently had a deep feeling for. And it ends up, I can't give you the whole thing, "a night of memory and sighs, I consecrate to thee." You couldn't say anything else. You couldn't. You couldn't.

I think from the Greek tragic writers, from the people who wrote the epitaphs that are collected in *The Greek Anthology*—Sappho, Emily Dickinson, Emily Brontë, this wonderful creature Nora May French, there's nothing, there's not what you'd call salutary joy about it. Their perception leads them to realize that sooner or later, after everything goes, after youth, after appearances, after everything, and sometimes even talent, if one has anything, you're left with the shell. And if you can express that in a poem, while the feasibility of expressing it is present, then you have a poem. You have it in people like Housman, A. E. Housman, not his brother who was manufacturing, of course. But, that's it. That's it.

Before Swinburne became nuts about babies, he wrote very great tragic poetry. Do you know his *Garden of Proserpine?* Would you like to hear a couple of verses?

> Here, where the world is quiet;
> > Here, where all trouble seems
> Dead winds' and spent waves' riot,
> > In doubtful dreams of dreams;
> I watch the green corn growing
> For reaping folk and sowing,
> For harvest-time and mowing,
> > A sleepy world of streams.

Then he describes Proserpine.

> Pale, beyond porch and portal,
> > Crowned with calm leaves, she stands
> Who gathers all things mortal
> > With cold immortal hands;
> Her languid lips are sweeter
> Than love's who fears to greet her
> To men who mix and meet her
> > In many times and lands.

That's tragic poetry. Because even at the age of twenty-three or twenty-four he realized it. There's only one answer: the greatest poetry is tragic poetry.

TH: *Tragic* meaning a dim view . . .

SL: . . . of life. And of the ultimate prospective end to it.

TH: I presume you would see a direct conflict between this type of attitude and the attitude expressed by most of the great religions?

SL: Yes. Because . . . not in the Hebraic religion.

TH: I was going to exclude that myself.

SL: Not in the Hebraic. No. And if you take the gospel of Jesus without the decorations of some of his apostles and some of the primitive schoolmen who annotated him and repeated ad nauseam all the myths and legends, I think that Jesus was essentially a very, very tragic figure. And he realized it. He realized it.

TH: But he didn't, granting that the evangelists represented him more or less the way he was, he preached a salvation which certainly Sophocles didn't admit of and many of the so-called Christian, tragedians perhaps didn't admit of either. In other words, there was a salvation from this tragic view of life which you see to be the essence of poetry.

Do you agree with that or don't you accept that . . .

SL: You may be right, partly. But I think he himself, if you would divest even the Sermon on Mount of some of the . . . if one could read it as he spoke it directly in the Aramaic—I think he spoke in the Aramaic language—you might find that it isn't, it isn't all goo or honey. He was, it was essentially tragic. I see it in him.

TH: In what he said as well as his life?

SL: Hmm?

TH: In what he preached as well?

SL: I think much of that had the substratum tragedy to it. Yes. Yes. Now, remember this, that so much of what he talks about the Kingdom of Heaven may be just the embroidery of what I call the schoolmen, or the people who surrounded him or wrote about him. And Christianity has suffered the indignity of a fanatic like Paul who did more harm to Christianity than even the Borgias.

TH: But what about the notion of salvation? Does that seem acceptable to you in any sense?

SL: That was not essentially a Hebraic element, because the Hebraic element does not preach hope or joy. People like Jeremiah and all the great prophets, they are pretty grim figures. And even if you take what little hope they offer you, it's not too much.

TH: What about the Messiah? Isn't he a hope, isn't he a savior? Isn't he supposed to be the Savior? In the prophets.

SL: I think that's a side issue. I think too much has been made of that. [. . .] My father gave one Seder, they call it, for Purim [*sic*]. My father knew Hebrew very well. My mother knew it. And I remember very distinctly he put a chair, an empty chair, beside me. And I said, "What's that for?" All he said was, "He may come." But even that, I think in people like my father, was semi-materialistic, you see. I don't believe there was the extreme vision that people like William Blake had in Judaism. I don't think it's present now. And maybe that's the saving grace of the Jews.

We've wandered far from the lyric.

TH: Well, when I was in college, one of the things on the minds of a lot of people at the time was whether it was possible, or whether it had already occurred, for a Christian tragedy, in other words something which is a tragedy and yet Christian at the same time, to be possible. And I used as a reference—remember I told you about the priest who had written that book called *Apollo and Christ*? And that type of man, I think, would say that a Christian tragedy was a contradiction in terms, because Christ came to do away with tragedy, because he brings the great hope, the happy ending. I think this is all relevant to what we started out talking about, but I want to get your opinion on that before we returned full circle.

SL: Well, that would be in conflict with what I actually believe. In other words, I think that Christ was, apart from the crucifixion—forget that—was a very, very tragic, dramatic figure. Don't think of the crucifixion. Don't think of the fact that he himself felt it was going to happen, but the isolation of this human being, this man who probably, with the exception of John, had no close affinity with any other person. Mary may have been an extremely astute person who realized that she had a son who had the elements of the old prophets. One can't tell. I don't believe for a moment in all this business of the virgin birth or anything like that. I believe that if you could divest the New Testament of all the sanctimonious, miraculous element in it, you'd have something very realistic. Just as you have when they unearthed . . . they're finding in Israel all the things that coincide with the battles and everything else in the

Old Testament. Absolutely. Because the Jews, basically, except where corruption might have crept in in the text, did not believe in the miraculous element. The Jews are a very materialistic race. I think one of the wonderful things about Jesus was he was devoid of this materialistic element and that may have made him the visionary that he was.

TH: Well, then, getting back to what I read before, that a major author in the twentieth century should speak of her art as an act of faith, using the traditionally religious word . . .

SL: Yes. She's absolutely right.

TH: That's the greatest possible vision into things, then, you think, the artistic experience.

SL: This is something that is a priceless possession, if you have it.

TH: Do you think that the lack of belief in this by, I would say, most people . . . I mean, from my experience most people certainly would not let anybody talk about works of art in terms of religious experience, would you think this accounts for the lack of exaltation in the so-called poetry that they write, because they can't think in terms of words like faith when they apply it to art?

SL: They just don't have the inner—call it urge or whatever you want to call it. They don't have it! They're mediocre people who have the itch to write and to publish, and they have a terrific amount of fecundity in being able to pour it out, which I never had. Hart [Crane] didn't have it either. Hart wrote with great difficulty.

TH: Well, the difference between my generation and your generation when it was my age, would you say that there was a kind of a creeping secularism that's come into poetry and a general loss of faith in the, well, whatever you want to call it?

SL: In the poetic values? Would you want to use that?

TH: Yes, for lack of something else.

SL: Yes.

TH: In other words, the world has crushed them. The world has snuffed out this instinct.

SL: Snuffed it out. Snuffed it out. You couldn't have a Francis Thompson now. You couldn't.

TH: Or a John Keats either? I think he had greater faith than Francis Thompson.

SL: You couldn't have a Keats. I've been looking into this new book on Keats. It's incredibly good. It beats any of the two other ones. Because of its factualism.

TH: Which one is this? Who wrote this one?

SL: Giddings. Robert Giddings. Just come out. I had to buy it. I couldn't sleep without it.

TH: Keats has always impressed me as a man of great faith. As you have, in many ways.

SL: I have that. Yes. In spite of my complete disbelief in, well, you know, what should I call it . . . For instance, right now I'm going through a dreadful scare. I'm frightened to death. These horrible attacks have made me realize how close the boundary line now is, and all I can say is what my mother said just before she died. She said, "I don't want to die." Because the desire to live, the desire even to create, could still be very strong in me. If I didn't have to worry a little about money and so forth, I could probably sing my song just as I did, in a different way.

    I think that going—I know I'm divagating—going to the St. Mark's did me a lot of good. Because I felt myself reconstituted, just as they reconstitute lemon juice. And every time I went there I didn't lessen my stature within myself. I have no ego, really. I'd say the amount of ego in my makeup is less than twenty-five percent. I have to have some to be able to live, you now, to be able to exist. But it's less than that. Now a youngster like this creature that Mrs. Lovecraft writes me the letter about must have a ton of ego. I don't have that.

TH: Do you sense as I do that many people today trying to get into the arts or practicing them tend to equate ego with talent? In other words they feel that if they are going to . . .

SL: Yes. Oh, definitely. Definitely.

TH: You don't think that's true, though. That there is any reason to believe that an overbearing personality . . .

SL: Some great writers have been possessed of talent or genius and ego at the same time.

TH: I wouldn't think, for instance, of John Keats as an egotistical person, though.

SL: No. You haven't read the letters.

TH: Some of them.

SL: You haven't [read] the collected. I have to get those for you. I know where there's a copy. Yes, without being sententious, Keats was able to define all the technique that he used in his life and in his writing. Is that clear, what I'm trying to say?

TH: By technique you mean . . . ?

SL: He was able to give a definition of what he was doing, what his procedure was in his relation to other people. One of the things he did before he died was to write two letters to Fannie Keats, his sister. And they were letters pertaining to the Christian doctrine. They were religious. Openly. Giving her advice about the life to lead and so forth and Christianity. And they're amazing. Because they're the only—I think there are two of them—the only two letters by Keats in which he ever converted the element that was absent in his poetry and in his daily life. He never talks about going to church or anything like that. Except there's that little medieval fragment. It's like a stained-glass window in one of his poems. *The Eve of St. Agnes* or something. It isn't a fragment. But there is a fragment similar to it.

TH: But you don't see any contradiction in this final attitude of his to what he had written in his poetry.

SL: No. No. Except, like many people, their religion was conventional and they took it as they would take a medication or something like that. It was part of it. He had been brought up into it. Now, the Jewish religion, barring my love for the Bible, isn't a part of me, isn't a part of me. Couldn't be. Couldn't be.

TH: For what reason?

SL: Well, my complete disbelief in anything except my racial heritage. I think I owe a great deal to that. A good deal of my nature has probably an Oriental derivation. Of course, it's liable to have faded away in eighty-two years.

Now, ask your questions. We've wandered a great way from lyricism.

TH: Well, in a way we have. And in a way we haven't. Because you've expressed yourself in a kind of at times defensive attitude about your lyrics. Whether they were relevant anymore, in a way. "Relevant" wasn't the word you used, but I think maybe that's what you meant. We're to the point now where we have to justify lyric poetry, and it's a sad state of affairs, I would agree. But there is certainly a difference between the kind of attitude you had toward it, which can't merely be called old-fashioned just because it's old . . .

SL: Well, I can tell you this. Do you remember Andre who worked for the . . . I came in one evening, and he complimented me. He had heard me read at the Folklore Center. That's a good place to go to when they open up. The people are completely different. There's none of this snobbery. And Israel Young who runs it . . . I'm going to read there again, if I'm alive, this year. He wants me to. Now, what was I saying? When I ramble I lose my train of thought. Oh. Andre, when I came into the Eighth Street Book Shop, he complimented me. And I said, "Well, it's old-fashioned. My poetry is old-fashioned." And he said, "That's just it, it isn't. It's very modern." And that sort of heartened me.

TH: It's very modern in spirit.

SL: Yeah. That's what he meant.

TH: I think you yourself have put too much emphasis on this notion of free verse as opposed to meter and rhyme. I think you've drawn the lines a little too thickly.

SL: Now, even Hart now would be old-fashioned, you know, in relation to the . . .

TH: What would make him old-fashioned, though? Would that really be his technique or his spirit?

SL: No. [. . .] Nothing is old-fashioned if it's not commonplace, it's not old-fashioned. It couldn't be.

TH: Do you think that whatever is written in the present time, at the present moment, has a relevance, even if it's not done well, that something perhaps that's better, written in a previous generation, doesn't have? Which might explain the great favor certain authors have in their lifetime, and then . . .

SL: Well, modern poetry, the avant-garde, is based on the flowering of many things. It's based on people like [Tristan] Corbière, Jules Laforgue who began the epidemic. They were amazing. They were amazing. And if you want to see how far this gang has drifted from these people . . . People like Eliot owe everything to Jules Laforgue. Everything. And even people like the man, the genius who wrote [as] the Count de Lautréamont—you've never read that—well, it's advanced. Rimbaud. They all began with these precursors and then drifted into this stupid display of the commonplace that they call poetry. It isn't poetry.

TH: Do you see in this, though, an attempt to express the contemporary world?

SL: You mean that is their attempt to express . . . ?

TH: Do you think they're sincere in their attempt to express reality as they find it.

SL: I question their sincerity. There may be some. There are some.

TH: Well, you say nothing is old, nothing is old-fashioned in poetry. Do you think it's necessary for each generation, though, to strive to . . .

SL: Yes.

TH: In what sense? Mere competition or . . . ?

SL: Yes. If you are really, if you really have the—what do you call it—the divine afflatus, whatever makes for great writing. Yes. Because every generation revives itself, and out of all of this manure pile of writing, tons of it, tons . . . look at the stack I had in back there. Only insanity could have led me to collect all of it. They are pouring it out. It's like diarrhea. People like Ted Berrigan, Ron Padgett. I elicited something—are you comfortable?—very amusing.

I resented Bob's putting *Ubu Roi* by [Alfred] Jarry, the surrealistic or Dadaistic play that was done in the 1890s. A translation, a new translation by Ron Padgett, one of the gang, who writes generally in partnership with Ted Berrigan, who is a lousy poet. He is also in *Poetry* magazine this month. That high-class poetry magazine has gotten down to the point where they print these people. And it's no excuse.

This is a preface that was printed to my translation of Baudelaire and Verlaine. And it applies more or less not so much to the so-called avant-garde now, not at all, but to what was coming, what was coming. It was written in March—and printed—in March of 1922. Forty-six years ago. I gave a copy of it to Hart, at a bar where he was drinking. And he said, "Really, Sam, you mustn't." It's called "Modern Poetry: An Exorcism":

> We are told with something approaching portentous significance, that the new era in Poetry has dawned, and from the remotest gutterhole and sewer-trap in Greenwich Village, to the heroic skyline on Michigan Boulevard, vers-libre squalls and moans with the gusto of something newly-created, resolved to announce itself at the very outset as the one thing worthwhile and permanent in literature. Magazines with strange names, geometric illustrations, and Euclidean contributors, spring up overnight with as determined a plea for existence as do enchanted mushrooms by moonlight. Emotion and duty, the pity and the tragedy, the loneliness and oppression of life and humanity—are all to

> no purpose or concern in a movement that seems to have discovered itself originally within the chaste and holy precincts of a Parisian latrine, take third-class passage on a freighter laden with hogs across the Atlantic, and brought its corporal and personal characteristics to the vicinities of Hester Street or Coney Island with a pomp and dignity not unbefitting mightier artistic influences.

I must just put a little parenthetical statement here. It's written with my tongue in my cheek.

> A cube, a straight line or a circle asseverates these plastically-minded folk, are as capable of performing or perpetuating a direct emotion, as any of the tremendous passages in King Lear. Life, in a word, consists of three or four dimensions solely....
>
> And so, the movement wags as it will and increases with vehement and widening rapidity. The few who steadfastly remain aloof, find themselves as steadfastly ostracized or outmoded. Already is Walt Whitman a legend of a colossus, but the flowers at his feet of clay are those planted by other than his fervent disciples. Ezra Pound gathers the clouds upon his aureoled head even as the earliest of the Nietzscheans, Moses on Mount Sinai. T. S. Eliot acclaims with the precision of a bronze gong the discovery of literary genius among the Elizabethans. The Sandburgs and the Kreymborgs shriek and display their meticulous wares and chromatic stalls in the market. Mr. Frost, not inconsistent with his desire for the peace that is not of this world, turns freezingly a brilliant eye on the aridity of New England plowshares.... In the meantime, the endless, metallic lines fizz and splutter, minus all capitalization and punctuation, in their endless periodicals; fragments of glass in the clear sheen of silks are assembled by Miss Lowell and charted into lines with the consummation of dexterity that would have set the Chinese heart old Po Chü-i afire with envy ... and the end is not yet.
>
> Brethren, let us pray.

TH: It's very pertinent to what we said, yes.

SL: As you say, this is pregnant with what we've discussed. Although the monomania or the disease has grown much further than I even dreamed of here. But I saw it coming. This is, of course, written with my tongue in my cheek.

TH: In your poetry, in the shorter poems, what function do you think now rhyme and meter had, and has, in them?

SL: I don't get that.

TH: What function do you think now that rhyme and meter had in your lyric poems? When you wrote them.

SL: Well, according to the present mode it would not have a place.

TH: According to you. What in your opinion?

SL: According to me. Yes.

TH: It doesn't have a place in the poems you wrote or in the sentiments that you felt? Or in this period? What do you mean?

SL: Oh. It has its place there because I knew of nothing else. [...] For instance, I gave Ann Waldman for her *World* magazine, you know the poem "Stevie." Now, that is not a bad poem. It was written some time ago, later than some of the earlier ones. [...]

She asked me for some love poems for an issue that would have so-called love poems. So I gave her three or four, including "I shall walk to Dover when the blackbirds fly" [i.e., "Transience"]. And "Stevie." And I gave her "Times Square." Sort of acrid and wry twist-of-the-mouth in answer to her request for a love poem. Properly, they were. And of course she turned everything down. She's never returned the others to me.

Now, Bob Brotherson has a poem in there, a satire on Dadaism, under an assumed name called R. Mutt. It's a satire. But he is capable of writing in the new mode very, very fine poetry. I like it. He has a friend, a woman friend in California, who's a superb poet. Writes in the avant-garde manner. Bob doesn't write, let's say, oh ... "As I was going down such and such a street, I noticed someone looking at my pants. And, looking down, I found that my fly was open," or something like that. And that's the sort of stuff that these people write. I state that because I forgot to button my fly this evening, and the first thing someone said—I forget who it was—"Oh, Sam. You forgot to button your zipper, put your zipper up."

TH: I don't quite understand. Do you repudiate the form that you wrote the lyric poems in?

SL: Oh, I don't repudiate them. Except, I'm not sure that I could write that way. The Jason poem would be in free verse.

TH: Why?

SL: Because I couldn't do it and be honest with myself.

TH: What's changed your technique, though? I don't understand. Do you really think that rhyme has no function in the present day, or it never had any function?

SL: Well, I think Robert Lowell—not Robert Lowell—Auden published his poems with rhymes too. Right now.
   I might. I'm not sure. I'm not sure.

TH: Is it just a question of fashion with you?

SL: Possibly.

TH: My own personal opinion is that it has a very integral part in poetry. I write most of my poetry in rhyme and meter. And I don't feel I'm old-fashioned or out of tune in the least. I think it's one of the techniques that poetry uses. Not the only one. But to discard any technique is to give yourself less tools to work with.

SL: Well, apparently, I was successful in the "Times Square" poem. I have a poem in here that's in free verse that I did a long time ago. "Fragment." The Jason poem would be in free verse. Maybe part of that is due to the fact that I might find it more difficult and that I might revert to a sort of sing-song without the barb that I had in the old days. You know?
   No, I don't feel that there would be a reversion. I just think that possibly the changes happen, and I've accepted it. I don't know. It would depend on just how I was writing.

TH: Let's look at it this way. When Robert Frost was asked about this problem, he said that writing poetry without . . . meter, I think, was like playing tennis without a net.

SL: I never heard that, but it's very good.

TH: Well, at least what he wasn't saying was that meter was something that is relevant in some periods and not relevant in other periods of time. He seemed to think that meter had a relevance to poetry that was eternal.

SL: Maybe. Maybe. He's probably right.

I was thinking of Yeats. Well, before I proceed, I think Dylan Thomas, there's too much sing-song there. He wrote some things, I think that he was at his best when he didn't try to chant in his poetry. For instance, I told you that he has one poem called "The Boys of Summer." It's one of the most beautiful things I ever read. I don't know why. I don't know why. But it's beautiful. Well, Yeats, in his early poems, was not the great poet that he was toward the end. At the end he had become as hard as a diamond. [. . .] There was music! But there was no longer the chanting. Like "The Fiddler of Dooney." Do you remember that poem? Or "The Lake Isle of Innisfree," you know. There was no longer that. It was hard, it was bound with steel. You could feel the sinews in the poem. And that was it.

Frost had a disciple named Edward Thomas. I knew nothing about Edward Thomas until I came up to see Hart the first time at Hotel del Prado. And he read and showed me some of his poems. They're beautiful. I have his book. [. . .] They're modern, they're Georgian. That's the only way to describe it. That school. But they're wonderful. And in many ways they beat Robert Frost at his own game. Now, Robert Frost is accepted by most of the moderns. Isn't he? I don't know whether he's accepted by the avant-garde. I don't know. But even in his rhyme he had the modern, he had the modern feel to it.

TH: Nothing about you mystifies me more than this attitude you have about meter and rhyme. I don't understand what's behind it at all.

SL: That what?

TH: I don't understand why you feel the way you do about meter and rhyme.

SL: Well, it's a very sincere feeling. Maybe basically I should say that I don't have the faith in the way I wrote now as I had then. Maybe that's possible. Deep down.

TH: I doubt very much that you could have written that way without that form, that you could have achieved that, without that, you could have expressed yourself without that form. I don't think it would've been possible. I think that there are ... A lot of the traditional poets used rhyme, like Tennyson. It doesn't help them, it doesn't make any more poetic what they're saying, it's just a convention they use.

SL: Yeah. It's a convention.

TH: That's a defect in them. But the people who use meter and rhyme, the other great poets, it's not a defect and certainly it's not a convention, it's an integral part of what they're doing and they would have been appalled at the use of free verse exclusive of the use of meter and rhyme. It would have made no sense to them, I think. I don't think that Keats wrote in meter and rhyme because it was merely conventional. I think it was because it was part of poetry.

SL: Well, after *Endymion*, the poetry that Keats wrote was miraculous. Nothing like it. Now, one critic—because there were quite a few professional critics who ... I don't even have the reviews anymore; my publishers use to send them to me, of *The Hermaphrodite*—said that I had used an invention, or words to this effect, in taking care of the meter, so that there were diverse ways of accentuating the line, you know, the words. You'll notice that it isn't tum *tum*, tum *tum*, tum *tum*, tum *tum*. It isn't that way.

TH: But in *The Hermaphrodite*, it seems to me that both the meter and the rhyme serve a different purpose than it does in the lyrics.

SL: They're different.

TH: In the lyrics it's absolutely integral. You couldn't possibly have the meaning without the form. In *The Hermaphrodite* the form is a vehicle for the meaning, but it's not as integral. Do you know what I mean?

SL: Yeah.

TH: But in either case the poems would not have existed, either the long poem or the short poems, without the form they were in. And yet the spirit, as everybody's pointing out to you all the time, is very modern, very contemporary, not old-fashioned.

SL: Howard Lovecraft once told me that if he were offered a collection of poems, he could immediately pick out my own. Because of their characteristics.

Here I am, here I am talking about technique and poetry and being devastatingly . . .

On Hart Crane

SL: I knew little about the subject [homosexuality] except possibly in a classical sense, and that made no difference to Hart. He proceeded to tell me about all of his escapades in Washington during the war. And there was a vicious circle of homosexuals there who battened themselves on the men in the Army and in the Navy, and Hart became sort of a figurehead among them. In particular he related the man who kept open house there, who had an extremely funny appellation which I forbear to register on tape.

He varied the evening with talks about poetry. He asked me what I was writing. I told him I was writing *The Hermaphrodite*. He said, "You won't dare to get published." "Well," I said, "I will." Possibly he was right, because there is a stigma attached to the name that vulgarity has practically erased the beauty of the figure. Anyway, I said, "I will get it published." I was deep in it then. Completed it later when I came to New York.

Well, that evening was followed up by meetings, usually at his house. With Hart every meeting meant a new seduction. That I obviated, very frankly. And of course he apostrophized me as a creature of frustration. I let it pass. When his mother and grandmother returned, I met them. I liked her. She [his mother] was very beautiful, blond, took wonderful care of her physical self. She had just recovered from the divorce. She had a breakdown. According to Hart she was neurotic and probably, he assumed, sexually cold. The elder Crane must have been a full-blooded person. I saw him only once. He was a duplication of what Hart would have been now—gray-haired, white-haired—and I never met him personally. I really had no desire to.

But my visits to Hart's home were frequent. We were together practically every day. As soon as he wrote a poem he gave me a copy of it. Signed it. And I introduced him to William Sommer, the Cleveland artist. I introduced him to a whole circle of people I knew who were not of his ilk, but they were wonderful people. And we met frequently at Laukhuff's, talked. Every Saturday there was a meeting at a Hungarian restaurant on Prospect Avenue, where discussions went on. The one woman who was present was a girlfriend of Hart's, who is still alive but I understand not in very good condition. She was a socialite. She came to New York. She was involved in the theater later on.

And at one time I had a quarrel with Hart. I left in a huff. And I didn't see him for six months. We met at a mutual friend's whom I had introduced him to. And we made up. And there was clear sailing after that.

The mother was very solicitous about Hart. He was the one person in her life that meant anything. And usually the assignations that he made were done in his top-story room in the tower they had. It was a lovely place. A lot of light, a lot of air. And it opened into the attic. But every few minutes Mrs. Crane would yell out the stairway, "Harold? I'd like to talk to you." And Hart would say, "I'll come." And he'd say to me, "Oh, I wish she would let me alone for a while." The woman was lonely, and she felt that Hart was the one human being in her life that meant anything to her.

Our friendship ripened. I must say this, that in later years Hart's behavior toward her was vindictive, miserable, and in a certain sense evil. There was someone who maligned Mrs. Crane to Hart. And Hart took it literally. Mrs. Crane became the victim of a great deal of gossip, that she led an immoral life. Which was not true. She was extremely puritanical. I know that. Because what she told me about the malignity that had been fostered onto Hart. She said to me, "You know me, Sam. You know what a puritan I really am at heart."

Hart went out to California with a very rich man who was related to a big publisher in New York, a millionaire. And this man had a retinue with him. Of course, Hart proceeded to seduce as many of the people that were there as he could. Mrs. Crane was out there too, with his grandmother. She was an adorable lady. She told me that when she was first married she rode on horseback, I think from the small town where Hart was born, to the public square in 1865 where Lincoln was laid out in his coffin, and she saw Lincoln, as a corpse. She liked me. She had a curious, wry smile. Dry, but with a wonderful sense of humor, and so completely American! One wonders whether the type has vanished since then.

The smash-up between Hart and his mother came when they were both in California. She had rented a little house there, and she had a lot of difficulty, financial. Her money was running out. Someone that she seemingly accused to me had stolen a $5,000 diamond ring. She went out and tended to a lace curtain, and when she got back the ring was stolen. And it was stolen by one of her guests. She was very open about the accusation. But it was during this stay in California—Hart stayed with her for a while—and he divulged his predilection to her. And she was aghast. He told me that to escape her he had propped a ladder against the upper story and fled from her. She sent me a lengthy telegram begging me to give her his address. He forbade me to do that. I don't know what became of the telegram. I wish I had it.

I must tell you that before that she had married a socialite in Cleveland, a second husband. I was present with Hart at the wedding breakfast. This man was an oculist. I forget his name. He was present. And when he left the table for a moment, she said to me, "I really shouldn't have married him. I love Hart too much." And that of course was the gist of the whole battle between the mother and son.

But the real battle was concerning money. She wanted a part of the money that had been left him by his grandmother. The family had been wealthy [unintelligible]. And he was already becoming hardened to her. I was present during the telephone call when he refused to send her the money. It's inconceivable, and it's incredible to me that he should have done that. But I think Hart was in the opening stages of the paranoid state. All this led to the final suicide and death, because when he dispatched his relationship with his mother, that was the time when he began to go downhill. He proceeded to dissipate to an extremity, night after night, day after day. How he stood it I don't know. I don't know. Certainly, it must have had an effect on his writing later on, because he could not write.

I must say this, that I never sided with Hart in his antagonism toward his mother. I felt that he had wronged her and that what he did was beyond anything that any human being could do toward anybody who had given him birth and fostered him as she did. [Philip] Horton, who did the book on Hart, turned against her. I tried to stop her from giving the book to Horton. She blamed me later for introducing him to her. She held me responsible for the fact that the book had been published.

Horton was not very ethical with me about the book. I was supposed to do it with him, and he accepted a contract from Norton who published it [in 1937]. Came up to my apartment and told me that the book was to be done by himself alone. I was very angry, and I told him to get out of the apartment in no uncertain terms.

I think factually the book is a good book. I think it'll be replaced by Unterecker's, although why eight hundred pages should be devoted to Hart is something that I can't understand. That is what the size of the book will be. It will be a good seller, but I think it's too long. After all, what can one say? So much can be said, and after that the rest is silence. Who said that? Hamlet? [Laughter.]

My friendship with Hart, however, remained fixed and stable. I knew everything, and I say that, everything, concerning his sultry, insane sexual life. He had to have someone to divulge it to, and I seem to have been the person. None of the rest of the clan, [Malcolm] Cowley, and so forth, Slater Brown, knew as much about it as I did. Because whatever happened the night before was told me the next day.

He told me that I was the one person who never irritated him, and I think he said "bored" him. He said the relationship was very satisfactory to him. We had dinner frequently. We had breakfast together, and there was no hitch to it. I doubt, in spite of all my feelings against him—and I have very definite feelings against him—that there was ever a friendship as well balanced as that. It was not a literary friendship. I made up my mind at the beginning that I *would not* permit him to see my work, because he was very cruel and I would say somewhat off-balance in his criticism of other people's work. Except he had a penchant for being attracted to people who were already famous, like Waldo Frank, e. e. cummings, and so forth.

So I made up my mind at a very early stage that I was not going to let this be a literary friendship. I think I may have shown him one of my lyrics, I'm not sure. I showed him *The Hermaphrodite*. He asked for it. He asked for a copy, and later told me that he thought it was one of the most beautiful poems he had ever read and timeless. And that ended it. He never referred to it again. It was *fini*. And knowing as I did what his nature was, I never tried to sound him on anything. He read *The Sphinx*, but he didn't like it. I knew why. I knew why. And possibly I condoned his dislike for it.

I would like later on to read an account, an anecdote, an account of a horrible sexual affair that Hart had. I don't mince words. I don't want it to be lost to posterity. I've written it out *in extenso*, and I think it should be taped. Maybe I'll change my mind before the taping is over. But we'll see.

He went to Mexico, made no further effort except occasional references to his mother's so-called immorality to me. When he came back, for the second time, we spent two weeks together in Cleveland. He did not want to go back to Mexico. He was lonely and adrift. He called me up—I was with him the night before with Gervaise Butler—and he told me that he was through with the crowd. They were all gossiping about him. They were all talking about him. Everybody was repeating anecdotes concerning his licentiousness. And Hart knew it, and yet he kept talking, telling people. He had the "Ancient Mariner" complex. He had to relieve himself, or he used most people as Catholics do the confessional, as a relief.

In Cleveland he told me that unless he could attach himself to someone, he faced spiritual annihilation. And he had known someone in Paris, someone named Peter. I think Peter was a Norwegian who used to send him provocative photographs of himself. He was a gigolo. And Hart asked me, he said he would like to send him passage money to have come and live with him. And he would attach himself to him, and he would stop all the philandering that had been going on. He said he thought he could send him about a hundred and forty dollars. So I said it was a wonderful idea.

He sent him the money. He waited, and he waited. Finally a letter came from the boy, saying he had spent the money and attached himself to someone with whom he was very happy and would not come to New York. And that was that.

So Hart went back to Mexico. He was very angry with me. He called me up just before he boarded the boat and wanted me to come down and see him off. I didn't, for one reason: The night before, I started to tell you, we had been together and he had said he was through with this gang. And as we were walking away from dinner to spend the evening on Columbia Heights with him, four members of this gang, these friends, came along and there was this hurried conversation and he turned to me and he said, "You won't mind, Sam, if I go with them?" I said, "Not at all, Hart."

So that when he called me up the next morning, I said, "No, I'm at work, I can't come." And that was the last time I ever saw him. I had letters from him, very beautiful letters. There was no recrimination. He couldn't be angry at me, because I think I was certainly one of the most loyal friends he ever had.

I was working in New York in a bookstore, and I used to go to a restaurant every morning at Borough Hall, and I had a copy of the *New York Times* and I saw this terrific headline: "AMERICAN POET COMMITS SUICIDE." Well, all the reporters descended on me. I was in every interview. Somehow they found out about me. And that was that.

Then she [Mrs. Crane] came to New York, completely on her uppers. She had very little money. She had some wealthy friends who helped her out. She took a room in a tenement hotel on upper Broadway. I saw her very frequently. And every Saturday night she would sally out—I usually was with her on Saturday night—sally out and get the *Times* for the advertisements. And she got a job with Towne House at a very good salary. She was there for quite a while. She was very efficient. She was a wonderful business woman. I think a great deal of her husband's prosperity was occasioned by the fact that she took care of his business affairs, in the candy business.

When the boat landed she took care of all his effects. She was afraid that the third Mrs. Crane would take it, attach it. But it was really hers legally. Hart liked the third Mrs. Crane.

I'd better not say anything more.

I think there should be some justification in erasing the popular image of Mrs. Crane. She was conventional. She told me that when Hart first divulged his homosexuality to her, she was shocked. She said she had never come in contact with things of that sort, and that a son of hers should be afflicted with it was simply indescribable. Then she said, "I began to think about it. I read about it." And she added, "Do you know, Sam, I really don't think it's as bad as I thought it was, and it really doesn't matter how it's done."

The result of course was that she had suspicions, as so many people after that. I knew that. I felt that. She possibly may have thought that the friends of Hart who constituted his circle were mostly of the same gender. But there was never anything said to me, and I simply let it slide.

I saw her at least once a week. She had difficulty at the hotel. There was a manager there that she felt very maternal toward. She told me he reminded her of Hart. She saw him after hours. They would talk together. It was a replacement. I knew the man. He was nice. He was quiet. He had a strange phobia—he collected rats. Tamed them. Or tamed rats. They were odious to her, as they are to me. I saw them. He kept them in cages.

Well, then she found out about *him*. I think her tongue began to wag, and it finally led to her leaving the place. I used to take dinner with her there. She was very hospitable. I was a sort of, how shall I say, relic of something that had happened before the flood.

And the same thing was true of Hart's grandmother. Grace was not very patient with the old lady. In her old age—she lived to [be] over ninety—they lived in a very expensive apartment house in Cleveland, and I imagine that the grandmother, being a very intelligent woman, wished it were all over.

Then Grace's marriage was not happy. There was a time when Crane, the first husband, made overtures to her again. I don't know what happened. He took her out. I thought there would be a resumption of the marriage, but it fell through.

The letters that Crane senior wrote to Hart belie his hardheadedness. They're very affectionate. But he didn't understand, he couldn't understand. I doubt that even now, with all the fame that Hart has had assembled, whether the father would understand why. And finally the gossip about Hart reached him. Hart blamed it on his mother. There is a passage in *The Bridge* which has never been explained called "Birthright by Blackmail." In other words, he felt that the mother in one of her angry moods had told the father about it. I don't believe that.

I knew someone who was a good friend of mine, incidentally, an artist, who was Crane's advertising artist. He told me this story that the elder Crane had found it out through other sources. So Grace was really innocent of any harm-doing toward Hart. I doubt whether anything like that ever happened.

SL (reading): "There is an anecdote concerning Hart Crane that belongs properly in its utter degradation to the sultry pages of Suetonius. Anything in the lives of Verlaine, Villon, Baudelaire, or Rimbaud are beggared by it. How is one to transmit the extent and abasement that drove him night after night into the hell of drunkenness and homosexual promiscuity? An urge that was unceasing in its endless mechanistic repetition.

"There were several occasions when he came into the bookshop where I worked after his release from a night in jail, hilarious with laughter over the jape of his arrest and the moralistic admonitions of the presiding judge. His eyes, beautiful eyes, and pathetic—I have called them 'smoldering'—could only too well tell the tale of any inner hopelessness and his inability to bring to an end what Keats in the throes of his own agony had called 'my posthumous existence.'

"To me Hart had once confided, 'Unless I can find someone that I can attach myself to and love without recourse to male prostitution, I face spiritual annihilation.' But this was never to be.

"We had been together on an evening, one of the few Saturday nights Hart was completely himself and sober, and his conversation was one of singular gravity. After an excellent dinner in a quiet Village bistro, during which he had abstemiously drunk only one glass of Chianti, he remarked, 'I'm tired as all hell. I want to correct proofs for *The Bridge* that have just arrived from Paris. I'll go straight to bed when we reach Brooklyn.'

"I left him at the door of 190 Columbia Heights, his 'bassinet apartment,' he called it, which still stands in spite of the indecent massacre of most of the beautiful old brownstone mansions that were sacrificed to make way for the stupid luxury apartments and the open, roaring freeway that faces the spectacular East River with its magnificent New York skyline far below.

"I arrived punctually at nine that Sunday morning. 'Come in,' came the voice of Hart through the closed door. I entered. He stood before me with a dishcloth in his hands, wiping the bed, the furniture, the door knob, practically everything available, moaning all the while. 'I'm doomed, I tell you. I'm completely doomed. I shall never get over this. Never. This is the end.'

"'What's it all about?" I asked.

"His hysterics slackened. 'When you left me last night,' he began, 'I told you that I was really going to give myself a rest. One can't actually create and carry on as I do every night. I fully intended to hit the hay as soon as I got home. I did so, but was awakened by gravel thrown against my window. By a hammering on the pane and a loud hallooing that took me out of a deep sleep—it must have been around two o'clock—I looked out and in the moonlight recognized a sailor with whom I had had a torrid affair a couple of nights before. There was a woman with him. The sailor was young and handsome. She wasn't. The three of us got into bed together. I don't propose to bore you with the details. It was all too disgusting. One has no sense of proportion in matters of this sort.

"In the early-morning half-light the sailor hopped out of bed, saying he had to hurry and rejoin his ship. 'Rules are rules in the Navy,' he commented. 'Both he and the woman stood before me stark naked. I looked at her as she proceeded to dress. She was thirtyish, and, Sam, by all that's holy, believe me, I don't exaggerate when I tell you that one half of her side was eaten away by syphilis.'

"He broke off and began to moan again and cry aloud. I left him to take breakfast by myself."

I have interpolated this as an example of one night in Hart Crane's life. Strangely enough, he recovered during the daytime. Most of *The Bridge* was written during a stage of incipient drunkenness and corrected in the daytime. Many corrections. Pages and pages of the same passages. The worksheets at Columbia University should show that, if they ever confide them to someone who would to do a real work on Hart. Just as something of that sort has been done with Fitzgerald. On one of his books, I forget which one.

I think Hart wrote with great difficulty. I think the difficulty with much of his work is that it was not, to use a word that many people use in poetry, inspired. It was hammered out. And Hart knew that. I must relate another anecdote. And by the way, I've had this printed, and I might as well give it once again.

We had been to the Village in a little restaurant on Waverly Place. We ate very early. There was only another man there who sat in a far corner. Hart knew him. Dudley Diggs, the famous Theatre Guild actor. And Hart was already a little high. He waltzed me over to Dudley Diggs, introduced me and did a couple of mazurkas and came back again. And we ate. And he drank. He was in a very good mood. After we had eaten, the usual formula went on. He hailed a cab. He searched for the money in his pocket. He didn't have it. I paid for the cab. Under no circumstances would he have paid more than two dollars to go to Brooklyn. Imagine anybody going to Brooklyn now for two dollars in a cab. We were very jovial. I don't drink. So that I was completely myself. Except it irked me to have to pay for the cab fare. I hate cabs, because I think they're greedy for the money that one really doesn't have to spend.

When we got to Brooklyn, through an error we landed at the Williamsburg Bridge. That's some distance from Columbia Heights. Hart was still in this wonderful mood. He got off, he went to one of the pillars and proceeded to urinate against it. I don't know whether that was a sacrificial rite or whether it was simply a matter of relieving himself.

Anyway, we began to walk across to Brooklyn Heights. And as we neared—I forget the street that runs off of Henry Street—we saw a big truck in front. In front of an old apartment house, which I think is still there. There were four legs and four feet sticking out and a sign against it. They were truckers going to the early market. "We are not bums. Kindly do not disturb." And Hart laughed and laughed, and his mood was so completely disenfranchised from any worry that I was amazed.

But as we neared 110 the paranoid element in him entered and became obvious. He broke away from me, ran up four flights of stairs—three flights and a ladder—and I followed him. I did it—then. And followed him to the roof, and he jumped over with his head pointing into space down below, hundreds and hundreds of feet. I grabbed his leg just as he was about to fling himself over, and I pulled him away.

And I said, "You son of a bitch. Don't ever play a trick like that on me again."

So he said, "Well, I might as well. I'm only writing rhetoric."

So I said, "Come on, let's go down."

We went downstairs. He poured himself a glass of dago red, Italian wine. Turned on the radio—not the radio, no—there were no radios [. . .]. It was a Victrola. I think he was writing *The Bridge*, and he was playing interminably, as soon as it ran off he wound it up again and played Ravel's *Daphnis and Chloe*. He was hipped on that.

I left him—and I knew he was safe—and went home. I worried a great deal about him. When I saw the lights lit up there, the shades drawn, if I passed by—because I worked frequently till ten at night, at this bookstore—I felt easy because I knew . . . One night I saw the light lit—he had been entertaining cummings. They were very good friends. I think cummings respected him, and liked him, and understood the homosexuality apart. And it takes, really, it takes an artist, as cummings was, to understand a thing like that and condone it. Not everyone did. I think Malcolm Cowley did. Slater Brown did. These were really the loyal friends of Hart. He had others, but they were people who were adjuncts. They came, they went. He never lost real friends. That was the amazing thing about Hart. And much of that trait was in his mother too.

I would like to write not a rambling sort of dissertation, as this is, about her. I think she needs a defense against the villainy of Hart's spreading gossip. Horton certainly didn't give it. She told me that she made Horton rewrite a good portion of the opening because of his vilification of her, or rather, let's say—how shall I express it?—the fact that he didn't like her. I know that. He wrote me a letter once attacking her. It was all superficial, because when you first met Grace you met the grand lady. Now, it was not all grand lady. The Cranes always had a desire to be socialites. They came from a small town. They never achieved the stellar position that the real notables in New York or Cleveland—Cleveland had a real social colony, the elegant people, the people who were millionaires—and somehow Grace, I think, felt deep down that she was not accepted and would have liked to have been accepted as such, instead of [as] the wife of a very wealthy businessman.

Hart Crane had one human being that he loved. He was never successful with this person. This was a boy named Bob Stewart. I am not sure, but I think he was on the battleship *Wyoming*. I came into Hart's apartment one evening and there were two sailors there. One of them was Bob Stewart, a very handsome kid, I think from Alabama. He had the real Southern accent. And his buddy, a sort of kind of wizened, diminutive boy from Philadelphia.

Hart introduced him to me, and I could see that he was terribly attracted to Bob. When ten o'clock rolled around, he said, "Will you take so-and-so"—the younger, or the wizened boy—"up to your apartment and let him stay there overnight?"

Well, reluctantly I did, because I don't like . . . I like to sleep alone. Now, there was absolutely—whatever may have been expected—there was absolutely nothing that happened.

In the morning I went down. They were both still there. He left. He asked me for some money. I gave him in a dollar. He slept. I slept. That was the beginning of Hart's friendship with Bob Stewart. This boy had a quality for friendship that matched Hart's. He was a normal boy who happened to fall into Hart's clutches. And he took a terrific amount of mistreatment from Hart. Because when Hart was drunk he was not pleasant. Very few people are, as a matter of fact.

So one morning—or was it one evening?—I came in there from work and I heard this screaming and yelling. And I open the door, and they were both sitting on Hart. Hart was in the last stages of hysteria. And he began to yell and say, "Call the police!"

The portières were down. One of the doors was ripped from the hinges. The telephone had been torn loose. He said, "They're trying to murder me! They're trying to rob me and murder me!"

So I said to the two boys, "Get up from him." And Hart sat there on the floor, and I said to Bob, "What's the trouble?"

He turned to me and he put his head against my chest. And he said, "Sam, I love Hart like a brother. But I can't stand what he's doing to me anymore."

Hart sat there in a sort of maudlin state. Finally I said, "You'd better go."

That didn't end it. They remained friends. When Hart committed suicide, he left everything to this boy. He couldn't be found. Mrs. Crane I think destroyed every vestige of Hart's homosexual affair. Only one escaped [her]. And that was because of me. I'll tell you about that. Unterecker has spent any amount of money trying to find him. He has never found him. He had advertised. He sought records. He's never found him. There is one reference to "Lee" [?] in a letter at Columbia, in which he says, "Hart, give my affectionate regards to Sam." Only one. After that, silence.

But this was the one human being that Hart really loved and whose love he abused. He didn't take it.

I believe I ought to say something about Grace Hart Crane's last days. Her demise.

She disappeared after she lost her job. Brom Webber found her at the Sutton Hotel. How she managed to live there—probably by borrowing money; she had wealthy friends in Chicago. Very much herself. She had been doing laboring work as a hired servant, if you can imagine it, during her absence, I don't know where. Scrubbing floors. This beautiful woman. Still very much herself. And I went to see her and we resumed our friendship. Kenneth Patchen when he heard about it from me, wanted to have organized a big concert of literary people and so forth to donate her money. And she refused to let me give my consent.

It so happened I had to go out of town. She was ill. She had yellow jaundice which finally turned into cirrhosis of the liver. Now, that doesn't mean that she drank to excess. I heard later that it could come from anything. Just as diabetes can come from anything.

But when I came back I got a telephone call saying that she was in a little Catholic hospital in Teaneck, New Jersey. She had been taking care of two brats, as she calls them, of a New Jersey woman who paid her fifteen dollars a month and board to take care of these bad children. And they hauled her off to the hospital. And when I got the phone call from the hospital, they said, "Mrs. Crane is in very bad shape."

So, I went over to Teaneck. She was in a coma. She lay there. The nuns took care of her. And I always feel that if one is poverty-stricken, if one has no money, that as a surety the Catholics will take care of anybody, no denomination necessary. I felt that then. I feel it now.

And she lay back on the pillow, hair no longer coiffured, streaming against the pillow, white hair. No cosmetics on her face. Pale lips. She was seventy. She looked ninety.

There was a French doctor there, who was very fine. He told me her case was hopeless, that she had cirrhosis of the liver. And as I sat by the bed all of a sudden she snapped out of her coma. And she said, "Doctor, I want some coffee and they won't give it to me." So I said, "Grace, this is not your doctor. This is your friend, Sam." "Well," she said, "I call everybody doctor here. But I would like coffee."

I think the truth was she could no longer hold it.

So a nun brought her coffee. She sipped it and she said, "I'm strong for coffee."

Then she said to me, "I'm dying."

"Oh," I said, "nonsense."

"Oh, "she said, "I know. I'm not a fool. I'm dying." Then she said, "I want to give you directions where I have all my effects." She had them in three places. Which meant that she wanted me to take care of them. One place all the manuscripts, one place her jewelry—she had no ... it was costume jewelry. She had one exquisite jade thing that was given to her by her second husband. Jeweled jade pendant.

I gave the costume jewelry, I had to dispose of it, to my sister. The jade thing I kept. The dresses and things I gave to charity. Then the question arose ... I consulted [Arthur] Pell of Liveright, who's a very dear friend of mine, I must call him up. What to do? Well, we decided to have her cremated. So her remains were sent out of town to be cremated and brought back to this Amsterdam Funeral Parlor—it's still there. And when she came back we decided that we would throw the ashes into the river from Brooklyn Bridge to rejoin Hart.

First of all, we consulted the city authorities. And they said you have to see the Aeronautic Authority. Joke. So we decided to take the law in our own hands, and on this Saturday morning, a brilliant Saturday morning, a group of us, Pell of Liveright, Brom Webber and his wife, a young poet and a young woman who was a friend of Grace's—she was a friend of Sir Cedric Hardwick, she was an actress—and two women, one was Mrs. Bates who remained a dear friend of mine, she was the mother of millionaire Ted Bates who has a big advertising agency, and her friend who was a boarding housekeeper, they were both occultists.

The remains were carried by Brom Webber. I looked at them. They were ashes, bones that were pink. One of the women brought roses along and uttered a prayer, an occult prayer, for Grace. And the roses and the ashes were thrown from Brooklyn Bridge to rejoin Hart. Brom Webber became violently ill after the event.

And that was the end of Grace. That was the end.

I mustn't be misconstrued in my attitude toward Hart, because his influence on me in a literary way was great. I realized somehow that poetry must eventually depart from the sing-song and become harder. For instance, Yeats—his earlier poetry is quoted and quoted. Now, Hart knew that Yeats was a far greater poet in his last phase, or last phases, than he had been. For instance, during the writing of the "Innisfree" poem, which everybody knows, everybody quotes, or "The Fiddler of Dooney," if I get that correctly. Later on, his poetry began to have a metallic quality plus the emotion. And by a "metallic" I don't mean that it was artificial. It wasn't. It wasn't. But there was no longer the melodic essence that you will find in his early Irish poems, where everything is lyrical and everything is secure in its complete poetic quality. Sometimes he sacrifices lyricism to boldness. Poetry that almost precipitately stumbles into prose, but never does. He was too great a poet for that. Any number of things like that.

Then Hart was a great admirer of Pound. He was a great, great admirer of Joyce, although when he read parts of the *Work in Progress*, now called *Finnegans Wake*, and when I told him I couldn't understand it, he would say to me, "Well, we must wait until it's completed." Well, I still don't understand it. I still don't get it. To me *Ulysses* is an open book. The short stories are open, and so forth. Hart read too little to be able to be a good critic. He read . . . I remember when he was reading *Bartholomew Fair*, by Ben Jonson. And everybody had to share the discovery. The fact that ever since I had been about fifteen or sixteen I knew Ben Jonson meant nothing to Hart. This was his discovery. He was the first to burst into that unchartered sea.

He made me acquainted with a poet whom I reverence and love who was a disciple of Robert Frost—I think a far greater poet than Robert Frost—Edward Thomas, who was killed during the first world war. Edward Thomas was everything—a prose writer, a journalist, everything, a nature writer. His poetry is wonderful. The first night I visited Hart he had Thomas's little book of poems and he read things to me, and I loved it. I have them now. I still have them. To me they're much less colloquial than Frost—he was a very close friend of Frost—but they have the British, how shall I say, continuity of being able to sustain a poetic passage, which Frost doesn't always have. He has to build fences, and he has to do this, and finally he comes to the end of the poem and you have the spark that ignites the entire poem into something that is poetry.

He loved Gerard Manley Hopkins. So much so that he borrowed a copy from a friend, and the book was very scarce at that time, and confided to me, "I'm going to steal this. I must have this." He never once mentioned Robert Bridges, who was Gerard Manley Hopkins's editor and closest friend. I have a great admiration for Robert Bridges. He's academic. Hopkins is supposed to belong to the new order of poets. But there are times when he's a bit chaotic, when his verbal onslaught makes your teeth grit against one another. That's a quality that bothers me in poetry, especially the modern poetry. I don't know what Hart would've thought of the modern poets, the extremely modern poets. People like Ginsburg, Michael McClure, Robert Duncan, and the whole raft of people. Diane di Prima. They might have overwhelmed him by their anarchism in writing poetry. If you have written conventional poetry ... And Hart's poems, remember this, are now a part of the conventional technique. They're no longer innovations. No longer. That's all been cast aside. But there was enough sustenance of the new order of things in Hart's poetry that might have contributed to what really has made him, I suppose, a great poet. Sort of rock-bound. Not vulnerable to just melody. I think sheer melody alone won't pull the poem.

Among Hart's manuscripts at Columbia on yellow paper was an amazing poem completely Swinburnean. So that he must have known Swinburne. That has disappeared. No one seems to know where it is. I think due to the original access to much of the material up there, some of it may have been stolen. I mentioned this to Professor Unterecker, but he didn't think so. In the meantime, they have taken care of everything, arranged it and so forth, and probably it's safe. But nothing really professorially is done with this mass of material. There are five hundred letters. All the versions of the poems. Everything is there. Everything. And there it is.

When I confided the material to Columbia, they had just gotten in—this is a curious instance—all the manuscript material published and unpublished of Stephen Crane's work. In cartons. Carton after carton. And it seemed strange that the two Cranes finally found their resting place at Columbia. Some of it is at Princeton. There is, I think, some material in the Morgan Library. Some in the University of Virginia. All over, it's scattered. Some people have retained them. I know some people who still have them.

I keep wondering whether Hart's fame will last. I'm not altogether certain, but I think there are people who feel that the legend of this young man and his poetry are inseparable. And that may keep it flowering from generation to generation.

Dylan Thomas has never held me the way some of Hart's poetry has. For instance, I think that some of the passages in *The Bridge*, for instance, the Poe passage. Do you remember that? Don't you? Where in the subway he encounters the image of Poe. Oh, it's horrible and wonderful.

I always think of another occasion when I think of that. I was returning to Brooklyn one evening with Pat [McGrath], who lived with me, and he said, "Look who's on the . . . !" The old-fashioned subway had an entry, a little lobby before you came into the—the door was shut—lobby, one could stand outside. "There's Hart!" And I looked, and there was Hart reading a copy of *White Buildings* and smiling to himself. So I didn't bother him for a while. Just before we came to Columbia Heights, to the station, St. George Hotel, I said, "Hi! Hart!" He looked up. "Oh!" Very jovial. And he said, "I'm going to Borough Hall." So we got off. I knew where he was going. He was going to Sand Street, the sailor neighborhood, and I left him.

But our relationship had no strain to it. He irritated me when he was drunk. And I think I irritated him when I wouldn't see him. I have a little note among the manuscripts, the few that I still retain, and this is the way it reads: "Sam, you scoundrel, you've been deafening your doorbell again." He knew. Because he could very easily tire you out. And I tire very easily if there's a strain between me and the person with whom I'm talking. There seems to be a sort of a rhythm.

But on the whole we got along. We saw one another especially during weekends, and every evening. There was no time limit. And if he wanted to see me here, he saw me. In Cleveland I was out of work, and I saw him all the time.

He gave a wonderful party once when his mother and grandmother were away. They went on a trip somewhere. And they had a vast garden in back. Beautiful place. And he invited at least twenty, twenty-five people to the party. After it was over I stayed, and he said to me, "Did you enjoy yourself?" I said, "Very much." "Well," he said, "so did I."

There's another occasion I must mention. When we lived on Columbia Heights, he gave a party. I'll never forgive myself, I had an engagement that evening. I don't know what it was, but I didn't attend. He invited me. Everybody was there. Everybody. Caresse Crosby and her husband. Later on Hart found a bullet on the floor, and he attributed it to Harry Crosby, who committed suicide a few days later, as the owner.

But when I came home I heard this soft murmur of voices. It was at 78 Columbia Heights. No, it was 110. I lived upstairs, and he lived downstairs. I heard the shuffling of feet, and I went upstairs to bed. Slept the sleep of the just. And in the morning I knocked at the door, and he opened the door and he said, "Sam, I wish you'd been here. I had a wonderful time. I didn't throw a single person out." And that was that.

Later he became a little different. I still claim that if Hart had lived he would have become a complete paranoid. I think there was the making of that there. His memory was going. He no longer knew what he did drunk when he became sober. As I have repeatedly said, much of *The Bridge* was written when he was intoxicated. And the verbal flow was like a gush of oil. It came rich and, as it were, filled with flaws. He would correct it the next day. He did that. He was very meticulous. He was a consummate workman. He borrowed. He was not ethical in borrowing material. The [Samuel] Greenberg material, for instance, which he never mentioned to me, and for good reason. He was worried about it. He was conscience-stricken. The man who gave him the material is a man named Fisher, who is still here, spends his summers elsewhere and his winter here in New York. I've never met him. I've wanted to meet him. But I've never met him. But he was the one who consigned the Greenberg material from which Hart peculated many phrases and embodied in a poem called "Emblems of Conduct." Hart tried to suppress that poem, but he was unable to do it. So it exists as his own poetry.

Well, that is done frequently. For instance, Dreiser plagiarized in one of his books, a book of poems, a complete poem by Sherwood Anderson, without reference to Sherwood Anderson, and used it as his own. There are other instances where people have used material like that.

Now, I was thinking of another instance. A very famous one ... Well, I have a book here by Mary Miles Patrick, who taught in the American-Greek University in Athens, a book on Sappho, in which she has taken two pages from John Addington Symonds's book on the Greek poets and utilized them in her book on Sappho of Lesbos, without quotation marks. These things are done. Shakespeare did it. Shakespeare did it in his historical plays. *Antony and Cleopatra*. He used Plutarch, the translation of Sir Thomas North.

And then I had a copy of the Elizabethan translation of Pliny's *Natural History*. I found any number of phrases that Shakespeare had used in one of them in particular, in *King Lear*, where he takes a phrase translated from Plutarch by Sir Thomas North—no, not Plutarch, it was Pliny. "Poor, pelting villages." It's in *King Lear*. You'll find it there, and you'll also find it in Pliny's *Natural History*.

TH: I wanted to ask you, Sam, about the first poem following *The Hermaphrodite*—"River Pattern." About the Mississippi. It seems a little bit different in subject matter from your usual poetry. I wonder if you could tell me . . .

SL: It was to be a part of a long poem devoted to the American scene. And there were to be eight or ten portions to it. One of them, I recollect, was the execution of John Brown. Another was the funeral of Billy Leonard, the soft-shoe dancer whom I adored. He was a black-faced comedian. And various other things, not of the especially grandiose type, but something that would elaborate my whole feeling. It would have no approach to anything like Hart Crane's *The Bridge*. Not at all. But it would have various portions. Sometimes I still dream of doing it. It would be done in the same type of versifying as "The Mississippi." And that poem was drawn from my recollection when I had to take a dead man who had died of typhoid fever before he could be inoculated. I had accompanied his casket to Kansas. And I recollect looking out of the window and seeing this broad expanse of water, and this was a recollection of it.

But this was to be part of, really, an epic. And that's why you sense a difference between this in the other material.

TH: How many other parts have you conceived of it?

SL: I hadn't done anything.

TH: But you conceived of several other parts, at great length.

SL: I hadn't written them.

TH: No, no.

SL: No. But I had them down on a piece of paper. They were to be different. You see, Crane's long poem, that was thematic, but it had sort of a grandiose or grandiloquent feeling about it. And probably mine would've been more emotional and less synthetic than I think that *The Bridge* is, in part.

TH: The other poem that I wanted to ask you about in the collected one [*sic*] is the one on Oscar Wilde. When was that written, first of all? Do you remember?

SL: I don't remember. It was written, must have been written quite early, fairly early, at about the same time that I wrote things like the John Clare and the poem I dedicated to Howard Lovecraft, "Bacchanal," about the same time. Oh, at least forty years ago. At least forty years ago, when I was filled with the Greek, the spirit of Greek literature. I think I still am. And if I can go across, if I'm permitted to live a little longer, there are two or three places I'd love to see. I'd love to go of course to Europe, Italy, France. I'd love to go to Greece. I have a woman friend there who would probably fall dead if she could see me. She lives on the island of Keros, and she once invited me to spend an entire summer there. She's Greek, but she has an American citizenship. I owe her a letter for several years. I used to see her religiously. Every week here. Every week. Go to dinner with her. She left. She hasn't come back. She may be in ill health. She must be seventy-six now. I'm gonna try and find out about her. I know a way.

I told you the other evening my affection for Wilde was very deep. He is a very, very real living person to me. The tragedy that involved him is something that could involve anybody. Anybody. With bad luck.

TH: I sense a certain disillusionment in his life about the end of your poem there. About the reference to dust. Did you . . .

SL: Well, that has troubled me because there may be a slight moral tag to it, but it really didn't resolve itself into moralistic diatribe, or snap of the whip, in the last couple of lines. What I really meant was just simply a sort of a fatalistic ending.

TH: When you read through the poems, there is, I presume, a restaurant that keeps popping up in different poems—called Andre's. What was Andre's? Was that a famous restaurant?

SL: Andre's was a restaurant that is now devoted to a sort of a nightclub, at the corner of Fourth Street and McDougal. Right next to the, right by the Provincetown Theater. I went there every night. The meals were superb. They were of the French order. The fee was a dollar. I think I mentioned to you that the cashier was Andre's mistress, a young woman named Sophie. She had been accredited by Einstein to be the greatest woman mathematician that he had ever met. The guests, or rather the clientele, were seated all around the room, against the walls.

A group of us went there night after night, met and after that we distributed ourselves to our various errands or things that we were gonna do for the evening. But the food was excellent. Excellent.

I understand Cabell used to come there. I was introduced to [George] Eastman, the head of the Kodak concern who later committed suicide, a very affable and quiet man who later took Andre in tow. He was a musician, a violinist. He led the Eastman orchestra later on, gave up the restaurant.

But there were several places like that. There was another place that was run by a sculptress, a very mannish ... she wore mannish clothes. And again the fee was a dollar. The rooms were in an old house. The restaurant room had been gilded over with pure gold leaf. She supervised the cooking of the food. Excellent. Excellent. Food like that would now cost ten, fifteen dollars.

It no longer exists.

TH: Were Howard Lovecraft and Hart Crane in that group, at Andre's?

SL: No.

TH: I remember you once told me that you met somewhere, and frequently you wrote a poem a night after ...

SL: Well, that was on, I think ... Double-R it was called. It was backed by the Roosevelts. It was a South American, Brazilian restaurant. The Lovecraft crowd went there. That was night after night. We'd sit ...

Tables were in close proximity so that you could talk. Usually we sat there and most of us did poetry. I used to do a poem a night there. Many of them are probably lost or heaven knows where they are, because I never took good care of the things I wrote.

There was another place where Lovecraft and the crew used to meet when we lived in Brooklyn. It was a Scottish bakery and restaurant. One of the members was of course George Kirk. Rheinhart Kleiner. There may have been others. Myself. That was where the story by Lovecraft called "The Horror at Red Hook" was evolved. Where he imagined that underneath Red Hook there was a whole civilization, just as in the story by the English writer [John] Collier who imagined... I think Howard's came much earlier. Collier wrote this story about the people who inhabited Macy's and came out only after the place was closed and conducted their animosities, their amorous affairs and everything else ["Evening Primrose," 1940].

TH: Each time I read through the volume of poems I'm struck by the simplicity of the language, the elegant simplicity of the language which seems not so much modern or old-fashioned as timeless, but very much not of the period—the way I think of the period in which they were written. For instance, Wallace Stevens's or Crane's poetry or Eliot's, the language is so tortured. Before that it seems it was very Victorian. But yours seems to be more Grecian in its simplicity. I wonder if it ever struck you and how you account for it, if you've thought about it.

SL: Well, I can only say that I'm incapable of being involved when I sit down to write. I think, for instance, that element is becoming worse and worse. Because what they did was to evolve from people like Laforgue—Jules Laforgue—Tristan Corbière, and many of the others. I think I was incapable of writing except to state my terms very explicitly, whatever there was to be stated.

It is just possible that someone will rediscover me. I know exactly where I stand. I'm perfectly aware of the quantity of work I've done and, all persiflage aside, no human being who writes and writes from within "outwardly"—I think that's the way to phrase it—can be skeptical about that point. Somewhere, somehow, what I've done will be known.

I think Hart exists for two reasons, not discounting the fact that he was a very fine poet. Maybe a great poet. Maybe. He was a discovery to himself, just as any true poet is. But Hart is associated with, first of all, the legend of a young man who died just when he might have gone completely gaga in writing. Because there is every sign of it in the few fragments that are left that are deposited at Columbia. There's an epic started there on the Mexican tribal gods that is absolutely worthless. When he did "The Broken Tower" he knew he had shot his wad.

Secondly, there is also his proximity to the homosexuals to whom he has become a sort of a fetish or a symbol of what can be done by a person with the predilection that he had. Now, he was very tactful in writing. "The Voyages" are masterful. And they're masterful for several reasons. He was able to dissociate himself from the sexual element of homosexuality and to bring out the more rarefied feeling that not even Whitman was always able to do, because Whitman can be pretty vulgar when he deals with his sexual instincts.

And, when I wrote, my mind was uncluttered. It may still be.

TH: Getting back to your own poetry, you told me once that you were a great fan of *The Greek Anthology* when you were young. This element, this quality of simplicity, reminds me of some of the poets that I studied in Greek in school where the great element and the great power in it was its very brevity and its simplicity of structure. I wonder if that's . . .

SL: I didn't discover that until many years later. Many years later. In the Loeb Classics. Many years later. There is a translation of them by [J. W.] Mackail that I may have read, but I don't believe, I don't believe that they were influenced. They were just influenced by a terrifying love for everything that was Greek. Well, many people who wrote on the subject like John Addington Symonds derived it not second-hand or third-hand the way I did, but they derived it from a wonderful knowledge of Greek literature.

TH: Your affinity for the spirit is so obvious. I don't know that much about poetry, really, historically, but it seems to me that it was not fashionable at the time either, that type of diction. Would you say? It seems as if the Renaissance was the big thing and the Italian authors and Shakespeare as always.

SL: Well, you know a very strange thing, I was so completely isolated in my writing that, barring the things I read, [my poems] were just something that were an evocation of the feeling I had. It's hard to tell because so many years have gone. It's hard to revitalize how I felt, why I wrote. Now it seems to me that, outside of the inspirational quality that I may have had, I can't understand how I did it or why I did it.

TH: You once told me too that you hadn't read Pound or any of the so-called moderns until you were in your thirties, I think.

SL: No, no. Oh, later. Well, the only poem I read of Pound was when I was corresponding with Bierce and he sent me a copy of "The Ballad of the Goodly Fere." Do you know it? It's a great poem. Well, I found that in a copy of the *Literary Digest*. They use to have a poetry résumé every week. I liked it, and Bierce sent me a copy of it and wrote me that Pound had asked him to do something about it. I think that was the gist of the letter. So I wrote him back then I knew the poem and I liked it very much.

But I didn't know Pound. I knew nothing about Eliot. I did, through Bill Sommer, know a good deal about the people that are acclaimed now, like Klee, Cézanne, Rousseau, Matisse, from the little German brochures that I used to find at Laukhuff's bookstore, and bought them. They came in boards, they were very slim, the reproductions were very bad. I bought them and read them assiduously in the German at the time.

But I was uninfluenced by anybody. I owe to Hart my love for Edward Thomas's poetry, who was a very close friend of Robert Frost, when Frost lived in England. He told me, he read portions of them to me when I first visited him, and I immediately got a copy of his book of poems, the collected poems. I have it. I think he strikes the bell far oftener than Frost himself did. He wrote of nature, and he wrote in a very easy way, almost colloquial. But much less strained than Frost in his attempt to be realistic in writing poetry. A very fine poet. But I heard a great deal that first night when I visited Hart about these people, Pound, so forth, T. S. Eliot. I knew nothing about them really. Nothing.

TH: And even after you did know something about them they had no influence apparently on your own . . .

SL: They had no influence. None at all. None at all. Heine had an influence on me. People like Walter Savage Landor had an influence on me. Swinburne. In the very early poems. Later on the terrific barrage of adjectives sort of weaned me off of him. But the assonantal music remained with me. Someone has said, it's Bob Brotherson, that I had an amazing ear for music in writing poetry. Well, that's true, because much of the modern poetry, the rhymes bother me—not the rhymes, no, I don't mean that—the corrosion between the vowels and the consonants bother me. Because I think, necessarily, poetry, one should be able to read poetry aloud. And unless we can, your . . . For instance, I can't read Carlyle, and I know he's a great writer. But I can't stand the Germanic verbalism that he employed. It's just as though you were translating literally something from the German. Because that's his style of writing.

TH: Do you think poetry in the future will follow more or less the course it has for the last thirty or forty years, or do you think we'll get a turning back to this more simpler . . .

SL: There doesn't seem to be any sign of it. There's a book of poems just come out by Allen Ginsberg. It's a very slim book bound in wrappers that are really boards. It's just been published. It's called *TV Baby Poems*. I haven't read it yet. But it sounds to me as though it's going still further into the jungle of incoherence.

TH: Do you think the educational level has something to do with this? You call it lack of coherence, but really there's at least a façade of intellectuality about it, isn't there? Of ideas as opposed to images.

SL: I don't think that most of them have any idea of what they're doing.

This reminds me, I had a very good friend who was an excellent sculptor, maybe a great one. And he turned to painting—now, what is it, objective painting?—I forget, they have a name for it. I used to go there of an evening to see his paintings. He now lives somewhere in New Jersey. I haven't kept up my correspondence with him. The last letter I got from him was, "You son of a bitch, why don't you write to me?" But we used to come there and he would take something that he had... He was very avid. He wanted to know your opinion. The colors were beautiful. There may have been even a trace of figures or landscapes in it, but he'd turn it around and he'd say, "Now, which way does it look better? This way or that way?" Well, invariably, I would be right. It would look better in a certain way. But these people had no definition either in poetry or in painting.

I think the most coherent work that is done now may possibly be done in prose.

TH: Despite the egotism which seems to be involved in much of the production of this poetry, do you sense, as I seem to, that there's really a lack of personality, of true personality, which somehow you're... it almost seems that your lack of education, your lack of exposure to the so-called world of ideas, allowed you to develop more so? Your poetry bristles with your own personality. I wonder if you sense that about it, or if it's just something peculiar to me?

SL: No, I don't, because... I don't know, I think I once told you, sometimes I feel very much like an abstraction myself. I don't even realize that I am I. I think there's a complete lack of egotism in me.

TH: Well, I'm contrasting mere egotism with what I called true personality...

SL: I wouldn't be able to tell you, Tom, because...

TH: Do you feel that about these poets that you don't like now, that you feel are incoherent? Do you sense that there's any individual personality in the poems?

SL: No. No.

TH: I don't either, and I was just wondering... There seems to be an effort almost to deny the individual personality despite the egotism which is in it. If I'm not being too...

SL: Well, it's completely verbal. There was a review in the *Times* recently of a book by Robert Duncan. I have it somewhere. I haven't read it. They head the review "Pure Poetry." Well, Duncan is one of the better people who write. Much better. Duncan, Ginsberg, and there are others. There are people like Clayton Eshleman, who has done a lot of translations from the South American people.

One should not downgrade these people. I'm certain of that. But at the same time their ways are not my ways. If I write again it will not be in rhyme. It will not be in rhyme. It would be more modern, but it would be poetry. I couldn't do it otherwise.

TH: Would you say that poetry, whether or not you want to define poetry, that there is such a thing, and that despite the difference in styles and difference in ages, that it's recognizable?

SL: Immediately.

TH: There is such a thing as a standard, then. Even though it's not something that you can express or define rationally. Or maybe you can when . . .

SL: I once started a definition of poetry. I said it is the unmoral and responsive recollection of a vigorous and assertive intelligence. And so on. I went on. I don't believe I could recollect the rest of it.

But I still have a feeling that poetry should be non-synthetic, that it should be something that simply pours out of you, just as the rhapsode makers used to do in the old times. I don't doubt in the least but the big Homeric poems were written like that. The miracle of their having been rescued from complete oblivion doesn't deter me from feeling that. That they were outpouring, outpouring . . . I don't know how it was done. I can't imagine. Just as I don't know how, when I wrote, why I wrote and how I wrote it. But it came . . . and went.

TH: I wanted to ask you about the very last poem in the book. I think it's the very last one. "Terminus." I wonder if there's a story behind that poem.

SL: That was written as a recollection of one person who in the early days was more or less associated with much of my writing. You write under the dictation of friendships. And I mean friendships. Nothing but.

Just as when Hart was writing, what he did the night before I got the day after. I'm sorry the manuscripts have disappeared. But everything he wrote he handed to me the next day. It's just possible that I may have been some influence to him.

But this person was much younger than I am. Later on, he went the way of all flesh. Which was not my way. But many things were written so that I could show them to him. And they were ... I knew him during the Lovecraft period. Hart Crane knew him. Hart liked him. He's dead. I have a picture of him, a drawing I did of him. When I get back I'll show it to you, if I can find it. A pencil drawing.

I had photographs of him. But he was directly responsible for the Saltus book, of whom I knew nothing. He had, later on, I think, it all disappeared. That's one of the tragedies in life. It's that people change, and it takes something extraordinary to maintain the same reservation for emotions and to keep a certain rigidity in life without discarding it. But he couldn't. My recollections of him simply went blah. I think of him now without any—he was younger than I am—I think of him now simply as nonexistent. The woman he married who is an editor—she must be close to seventy now; the magazine was devoted to children—was a hard-core journalist. I introduced her to him. That was it.

But this poem tells a story in eight lines.

Somehow, he liked the things I liked. I was friendless in Cleveland, until Hart came along. I worked in complete isolation. When anybody like that came along, it was welcome. That's it.

TH: Did you frequently write with a specific reader in mind?

SL: No. No. Don't be misled. This is not false emotion. But I think that everyone who writes, everyone who continues to write poetry, more or less enacts a dramatic scene which may not even be posturing but be very sincere. But nevertheless ... Someone said—pardon me for interrupting myself—someone said that when Thomas Hardy stopped writing novels due to the complete antagonism against *Jude the Obscure*, because of its alleged obscenity and open disclosure of sexuality among certain types of the English, that his poetry, each poem, contains a novel within itself, a dramatic ... something that could be a cynosure for a novel. And that's true.

I don't say that I had all this in mind when I wrote. Just as I never did what Poe did. After he had written "The Raven" he wrote this lengthy essay, which was fiction to the nth degree, how he came to write "The Raven" and what he thought and how he felt when he wrote it. Which was pure fiction. He wrote it!

TH: Do you feel that that compactness that you were describing in Hardy's poetry is in your poetry too? I think that the poem you just read is an example of a novel in brief.

SL: Well, it has that element, because ... in your relationship with people, and I refer even to my relationship with people like Hart and others who have disappeared over the horizon, there was no dramatization at the time. The drama follows later when it goes through the spectrum of your brain.

TH: But it seems as if that kind of compactness in short poems has gone out of vogue starting as early as maybe Eliot or ... certainly Crane's poems seem to run long ...

SL: Eliot has some of it in his early poems.

TH: Yeah?

SL: I have a great respect for Eliot. I have to a certain degree for Pound. Pound of course started out as an adherent to Robert Browning. Had the same sort of roughness that Browning used in writing poetry. Of course the *Cantos*, I must agree, may be very, very great poetry. But I don't think they're coherent. I don't think that the relationship follows. There may be. There will be elucidations after he dies, or after he's finished. He hasn't finished them yet. He's still writing them. I have one or two magazines within the past two or three years where he's contributed more of them.

Poetry should be all of one piece.

TH: What I was trying to point out, and you know more about this than I do, poems tend to be longer now and in a way say less, say less in more words. Do you feel that? Do you think that it's more ... It seems to be a style as well as a temperamental thing.

SL: I would like to write a long poem, longer poem. I had meant for *The Hermaphrodite* to be longer. But I felt that I'd reached the end of it and there was nothing to do but to finish it. But I would like to ... For instance, the American poem, the long American poem. That would've been a long poem. But I've always been beset by economics. I've had to work and I've had to burn my brain out on this horrible catalog writing. Hart did a little catalog work and finally gave it up. He couldn't do it. He couldn't stand it. I wasn't strong enough to obviate the lure of the little money I've ever made—and I haven't made much. So I kept going and going.

TH: I was wondering if it ever occurred to you to write something, probably in prose, that would incorporate your experience with books. It's been very extensive, and it hasn't been merely a business with you, it's been a love.

SL: Well, I did for money. I dictated it to Venable Herndon, a complete book on book collecting—autographs, everything, everything in the collecting line. Prints. It was done for someone who paid me, and I divided it up with Herndon. It was done completely from dictation. All he had to change was occasionally to substitute a word that I couldn't think of. We worked together. I think it took us about three weeks.

But he never published it. He gave us three hundred dollars and that was all. It seemed to me it was a good . . .

TH: What ever became of it?

SL: I don't know. I saw him at an auction sale recently. He's moved to the country.

TH: Herndon?

SL: No. This bookseller who commissioned it. No, Herndon is here. I ought to see him.

TH: What is the bookseller's name?

SL: Gould. Raphael Gould. His father started the business. Calls himself American Library Service. Nothing was ever done with it.

But it was purely ... And I dictated a catalog for the Harlem Book Company once, to a girl. Just as I am talking to you now.

TH: Did you ever write a poem about books?

SL: Yes. Yes. There is one written for George Kirk's bookshop on 14th or 15th Street in Chelsea. When I get back I'll be glad to show it to you.

In one of the numbers of Irving MacDonald SinClair's magazine that I contributed so many of my early poems—called *Cartoons*, is the magazine—he did an article on my room in Cleveland. An article embodying a lot of my conversation. It was when I was very much under the influence of Charles Lamb and writing prose. I used to write letters that were very much in the way of Charles Lamb, whimsical letters, you know. Heaven knows what became of them. I hope they don't exist.

This was written shortly after my experience in Georgia during the first world war. It's called "Memoralia."

> Here in the room as darkness falls
> Faces are pressed against the pane
> The night without is shrill with calls
> And, oh, the boys are back again.
> "Open the door, we've come," they cry
> Some that are scarcely dust and light
> And they that fared so brave to die
> Pass in from the tempestuous night.
> Tucker and Osborne, blithe as gold
> Miller with Keats-like radiant face
> And suddenly the room grows cold
> Shadows are these that take their place
> For phantom are the eyes that shine
> Hands I would clasp, souls I would keep
> If this immortal hour is mine
> That takes them from eternal sleep.

Tucker and Osborne ... Tucker I think I have a photograph of. He was a blazing redhead from Memphis, Tennessee. Osborne was from either Iowa or Indiana.

I came back, I had very little to say to him. I came back one day after lunch. The barracks was empty, and in a corner Osborne sat there crying with his head on his knees. So I went up to him and I said, "Why are you crying?" He said, "I can't stand this any longer." So I comforted him. He left the next day. He clasped my hand. He wrote me a beautiful letter. He went across. I have the letter somewhere, I'm sure. There was no more. I don't know.

Miller was Morris Miller who did not die of a wound. But he died of—what do they call this—fit?

TH: Epilepsy?

SL: Epilepsy . . . that he must of had before, because he was a couple of times before he came from Cincinnati to Cleveland. George Kirk's first wife was engaged to Miller.

TH: That's where I remember him.

SL: Miller had a face like Keats. He had very rich brown hair, not the ordinary. Like waves, very thick. Beautiful face. Maybe a little shorter than I am. Occasionally he'd get a little high. I have a series of letters from him that are very good. Very good.

This is "Understanding." I used to go down to the shore, to the lake, and sit there and just think. I didn't write. I sat there and just thought. I was very alone. My whole life, younger years, were very lonely. I was very shy. I sat . . . it must've been a log or, I don't know what it was . . . a seat. And a young Negro came and sat next to me.

I don't know, I'm incapable of analyzing, but he seemed to be attracted to me. He was very good-looking, tall. He followed the horses. After thinking of him, I certainly shouldn't have the prejudice I have.

TH: To somebody who was born in 1941, the way I was, it seems that your memory must contain an incredible richness about the world that happened before. I'd like to bring out what I could from you about what was like just to be alive.

SL: Completely different from what it is now. Corruption hadn't advanced to what it is now. The element that came up here from the

South and from Puerto Rico were not here. They were not present. They hadn't come up here in the hordes and droves that they did. Necessarily, when they did come up here they caused trouble, because they had never had it in the South ... My cousin, who is still alive, who fostered much of whatever talent I have, I visited [in] Chattanooga and stayed with them. My aunt was a wonderful woman. She had a cottage in the back of the house and it was tenanted by a Negress, usually. She always had a Negress wait on the table and so forth. There was always a sort of condescension on her part toward the Negroes. She claimed when I was there one day—she had another woman there, who lived there—that they didn't like her. And this woman was off one day, and she went into the cottage and she found any number of things that the Negress had stolen. She came back. She made light of it. They didn't do into anything heated about it. The whites tolerated the Negroes just as they would tolerate pieces of furniture. Of course, that's all changed now.

But what I started to say was, it was a different world. It was nothing like it is now. In the 1920s, let's say, in particular, there was incandescence about people and about places. The landmarks hadn't been torn down. Washington Square was still surrounded by a group of houses that had been there during colonial times, and a little later gabled houses, you know, all that is gone.

I must say I had a great deal of pleasure being with Lovecraft. He was a wonderful companion. The racial element hadn't, I was not cognizant of, which seemed to have been hidden from me. He was richly antagonistic toward the Jews. So there was constant companionship. George Kirk was on tap, he hadn't married. There was a group that used to meet in George Kirk's bookshop. Night after night. I usually used to leave about midnight. But they stayed till three and four in the morning. Time had no relationship to any problem. You lived, if you wanted to work, write, you wrote. And that was it. There was no interruption.

In 1929, the escapees who had gone to Europe came back, everything went up the spout. The banks failed. People lost fortunes, their annuities. People who had sent their sons to Paris to study or to live the life had to come back, and the city was flooded with them. And they were wonderful people. People like William Carlos Williams had come back, cummings, they were all, all of them came back. Of course people like T. S. Eliot made their exit very early and became victims of Anglophobia. And stayed.

TH: The war didn't make that big a dent on things, then. The war wasn't a great disillusionment, then, for most people. They still had their esprit, apparently . . .

SL: I was in Cleveland during the war. I was working for a big manufacturing concern—it was an odious place—when I received a call to go down to the examining board. When I finally left I left on about sixteen hours' notice. I was in service close to a year. Well, I came here much later. I could not get work in Cleveland. It was impossible. I had these friends there like [Don Bregenzer] with whom I did the James Branch Cabell book. And there were others. And I could not get work. I wanted work the worst way. I would go to an employment agency and they would say, What is your race? What is your . . . I forget how they phrased it. So I would say, I'm an American. Oh, we know that. But what . . .? Well, I'd say, My people are Jewish. That would be the end of it. Employment agencies, the YMCA was the same way. Rigid. And I understand that a good deal of that demarcation still exists there. It doesn't here in New York. All you have to do is think of today, with a city like a desert. Yom Kippur.

But during that period there was a very rich young man whom I had known in Cleveland, alienated from his family and made much of by an aunt who lived in a cottage on the lot where they lived. They had a magnificent old house. His father was a very rich insurance man. His name was Gordon Hatfield. Gordon is still alive in Florida. And a sister. In Cleveland every once in a while [he'd come] to the door and say, "Come out and ride with me." And I'd go out and ride with him.

He was one of the troisième sex, but he absolutely never approached me and never referred to it. But I knew what was going on. There was a group. And when he came to Cleveland he took an apartment in what is now fabulous Radio City, which had apartment houses, old houses. He took an entire floor. That's where I met my friend Hazel. He told me about her.

Hart knew him. Hart disliked him, he disliked Hart. Because he didn't like Hart's action when he was drunk. Hart was boisterous, and since many of these people were like porcelain figures, Hart was like a bull in a china shop when he came there. He grabbed. There was no end to it.

For instance, when Noel Coward's group came here, Gordon entertained the whole group up in his apartment.

And I was invited carte blanche anytime I wanted to come there. I'd come there, I'd sit very quietly. Listen. And go my way. He lived later on Washington Square. That's torn down.

And night after night we'd go to Andre's. He and someone else that he lived with, they broke up. But Gordon liked me, liked my company because he sought it. He was completely different from Hart. He was a composer. We were going to do a story, a medieval story, into an opera. Some of his things were published. He set some of my things to music. I think the Chinese . . . Something. Or one of the . . . three or four of the lyrics. He gave them at a recital too. But I did the opening part of it, I still have it, one scene. It was a murder drama, murder opera. I sent it to Cabell and he liked it very much. Gordon did the opening of it, and then all of a sudden he would do no more. And he never wrote again. But Cabell liked it. Incidentally, Cabell liked *The Sphinx*. I sent him a copy.

And there was this group, night after night. We went to Andre's. There was the son of a millionaire, I don't know whether he mingled with Gordon, or came later. Thomas Carlisle, who was a fantastic person, had been living in England—I think I showed you his picture, blond. I saw a good deal of him. There was no difficulty. You made friends, and you met . . . The wonderful thing about it was these people met for dinner, usually. Later on we used to meet in a serve-self on, I think, 46th Street, or 40 . . . or 50th Street. It was run by a woman, and the cashier was the butt of . . . she was lovely. Her name was Dorothy. She was middle-aged and grayish. She knew nothing about the sophistication of this group that used to meet there. Because there were many of them, you know, on the outer fringe. And this was night after night. We'd meet, eat, then part. Go our way.

There were so many, many of these wonderful restaurants. They were kept usually by people who did home cooking. There was one in the village that I used eat, on 9th Street, run by a Negress. The food was admirable. You served yourself. I went there all the time. She was forced to give it up. She went on a vacation, and when she came back they moved all her things out. And everybody went there night after night. Including myself. These things . . .

So the only place now is the Times restaurant, which is so-so. Not too bad, and certainly not too good.

But there was an exuberance, and there was a brilliance. There was a feeling in the air that no longer exists. It's as dead as Mr. Humphrey.

TH: What kind of feeling? How would you, how would you describe that feeling? How would you describe that feeling?

SL: Oh, it was spiritual rather than concrete. It was something that existed. If you were creative it came out like a flood of water from the faucet. You couldn't stop it. And if you went to Washington Square, the corner that I liked the most, it's at the corner of where you come in from Eighth Street, you know, McDougal, McDougal, where the Hotel Earl is, well, that was where the literary people sat. They met night after night. Some of them still do, but not much. And you'd see Joe Gould who has become a legend of non-productivity. And Maxwell Bodenheim, who hadn't entered into the final phase of degradation. Always with a pad. People walked up to him and talked to him, and he kept on writing, writing, writing. Night after night.

TH: And it all changed in '29, you think?

SL: Well, the change was probably gradual, not so perceptive [*sic*].

TH: Was that a big . . . that wasn't as big a blow to you, the Depression. I mean that, the crash, as it was to some . . .

SL: No, I never had any money then. I was working for thirty-five dollars a week when I came here. No.

TH: Did you have a job all through that period?

SL: When I what?

TH: Did you have a job all through that period? Or were you out of work due to the . . .

SL: I had a job, yes. I worked for, when I came here, for Harry Stone. And I got a job with Dauber & Pine. And then I opened up my own establishment.

TH: So the Depression didn't hit you too hard.

SL: No, because the Depression only hits people who have money. If you don't have it you don't feel it. That's why, as little as I have, and probably will have to the end of my life, it never . . . it bothers me, but not too much.

TH: Yeah. It can be a burden, I guess, too.

SL: What?

TH: I guess it can be a burden too, money as well . . .

SL: It can be a burden. Well, the only advantage that I had was that I had an unholy knowledge of books acquired or sensitized [sic], and I was able to say something about them in cataloguing.

TH: You didn't save all those old catalogs, though? You haven't collected your old catalogs.

SL: Yeah, I have.

TH: You do?

SL: Many of them, bound together.

TH: Oh, that would be nice to see. I'd like to see them.

SL: Yes. I think they must be packed up. I discovered one the other day.

For Samuel Loveman

Thomas J. Hubschman

A star
Two galaxies away
Ignites our sun
Supports terrestrial respiration
Its song is light.

A voice
Gives perfect pitch
Strikes a tuning fork
To mute creation
Its light is song.

The hand
That underwrites creation
Plays it on a lacquered pipe
In Eden
On Parnassus
In Pierrot's Garden.

The lips
Your lips
Sound music through the light-years
Of your verse:
Creation
Is its resonance.

The poem
Once sung
Suffices.
The song
Is every thing
And everything
Is song.

Samuel Loveman

Harry Edwin Martin

Samuel Loveman is the premier poet of organized amateur journalism. In quality, as recognized by critics and laureate judges, his exquisitely lyric and highly imaginative verse has placed him at the head of the list during practically all the years of his activity in amateurdom. Back in 1908, Edwin Markham named Loveman poet laureate of the National Amateur Press Association, giving the verse of the late Brainerd Prescott Emory, a leader of the literati, honorable mention. In awarding the honor to Loveman, Markham said, "It (In Pierrot's Garden) carries poetic atmosphere, and shows feeling for the unique word and the fresh phrase."

In 1907 the Clevelander's "Arcady" won from him honorable mention.

In 1918 the judge of verse named Loveman poet laureate of the National. This was also true in 1919. This year he received a triple honor. He and Miss Edna Hyde were jointly named poets laureate; he received honorable mention for a prose sketch; and he won the poet laureateship in the United, according to the decision of Lord Dunsany, judge. Honorable mention was bestowed upon Loveman by the latter organization in 1919.

This Ohio poet entered amateur journalism in 1902, became inactive early in 1910, and reentered the fold at the beginning of the writer's presidency of the National in 1917.

Professionally, Sam, as his friends call him, is a cost accountant. He might readily be a successful professional journalist or writer, but he has always fled from the temptation to prostitute his artistic genius for the mere coin of the land. Many of his friends, however, would like to see him devote all his energies· to the world of letters because they believe his pen would add something worthy to this age of much literary effervescence and froth.

Loveman naturally has a fondness for all the literary masters and near masters of all times and all nations, and his collection of first editions, rare letters and original manuscripts in value and size is an eye opener, to the bibliophile. A peep into his library and an evening's visit with him supply a rich delight to the book lover.

My Friend, Samuel Loveman

Rheinhart Kleiner

In the early 1920's, I was a frequent visitor at the apartment of the Houtains, at 1128 Bedford Avenue, Brooklyn. A little room beside the parlor was George Houtain's study, and here, where we sat so often in all seasons, I used to notice a framed photograph on the wall.

My host informed me that this was a picture of Samuel Loveman, the Cleveland bard. I knew of Loveman's poetic fame, having, on my first entry into the National, read some of Maurice W. Moe's references to him. Later on, I had even read one or two of his poems. Lovecraft's letters had frequently contained laudatory comments on his work, combined with speculations as to what might have befallen him. So it was with no ordinary interest that I scanned the features of this individual in a gray suit—this man whose brow gave just a suggestion of thinning hair, and whose forehead and eyes showed the vaguest, most elusive touch, of something other-worldly.

Among the poems I had seen was one on the death of Thomas Dermody, and another may have been a paraphrase of some Chinese verses. I recall that the lines on Dermody—the exact title of which escapes me—had been read at a Blue Pencil meeting, and I was among those who had been much impressed. There was an antique touch to the lines, a classic undertone, as it were, which seemed to speak sadly of verities long neglected.

It was probably about this time that Lovecraft wrote me enthusiastically that Loveman had been found—employed, then, in some commercial house. Loveman, it appeared, was just about to make a connection with one of Cleveland's well-known bookstores. It proved to be this establishment, in fact, which started him on his long and successful career as a bibliophile.

As an illustration of how Loveman's name and fame persisted through the years, I remember a little paragraph in *Invictus*, published by that sterling amateur, Paul J. Campbell. It was to the effect that Samuel P. Lovecraft was returning to activity. This particular item really referred to H. P. Lovecraft. Not until a few years later did Samuel Loveman really make a brief return.

While on the subject, I might add that Samuel has even been conspicuously confused with his cousin Robert. Alfred Kreymborg, in his history of American poetry called "Our Singing Strength," makes a general statement about "the verse of Van Dyke, George Edward Woodberry, Samuel Loveman, Frank Dempster Sherman," and winds up with this: "Loveman is remembered for the lilting English lyric, 'It isn't raining rain to me, It's raining violets'." Needless to say, our Samuel Loveman is remembered for other and equally notable achievements.

It was sometime in 1925 that Loveman finally came to New York. He had previously become Chairman of the Critical Bureau of the N. A. P. A., and his articles duly appeared in the *National Amateur*.

Under what conditions I met him, I cannot now recall, but the Kalem Club drew us quite closely together in a short time. In appearance, at least, Loveman had not changed much from that pictorial representation of him in Houtain's room. He was a little older than myself, having contributed mature work to amateur publications while I was still a schoolboy, but, as in the case of many bachelors, he seemed to carry the aura of youth with him, as he does to this day. I have more than overtaken him, in appearance. I found him very shy, very sensitive as to opinions held of him by others, but not at all given to malice, or to the cherishing of grudges. There was an air of frankness and friendliness about him which must have been enough to place everyone worthy of it on his mettle.

Loveman had been a student and booklover for years, and while, so far as I know, he brought no books with him, his little apartment on Brooklyn Heights was soon sufficiently furnished and adorned. Among his newly acquired treasures, I recall a number of Nonesuch Press editions—among them being Burton's "Anatomy of Melancholy," Milton's "Paradise Lost," and one or two similar editions of lesser known bards. There were other books, of course, one of them being a large. substantial edition of Boswell's "Johnson," edited either by Croker or Malone. There was a much begrimed painting on the wall, found in some old curio shop, which we regarded with respectful awe but did not examine too closely. It was Loveman's landlady who discovered it to be a nude, and who raised some objections to having it there. Among various Buddhas, of different attitudes and periods, was to be seen a fine clay mask of the features of John Keats. It had been taken right from the face of the subject, and was really more satisfactory than a photograph would have been, had it been possible to take one at that time. On one occasion, some irreverent person in the group placed a cap, at a "tough" angle, on that classic brow, and tied a colored cloth around the neck. The bard looked most convincingly like a Parisian Apache; but, at this point, Loveman's outraged feelings asserted themselves, and the disguise was swept away.

It was during this time, while browsing around in O'Malley's uptown bookstore, that I found a copy of Edwin Markham's long forgotten anthology "Our Younger American Poets." The very last poem in the book was by Samuel Loveman, "In Pierrot's Garden." This was the poem which had so impressed Ambrose Bierce, to whom Loveman had sent a manuscript copy of it, that he spent months trying to sell it to one of the standard magazines of the day. He was not successful, but thirty-five years ago was a period of peculiar aridity, not to say ossification, in the entire literary scene. Editors of magazines like *Harper's*, *Century*, and *Scribner's*, could hardly have been expected to realize that all they stood for, and all they were earnestly trying to perpetuate, had already been condemned and was on the way to oblivion.

The letters of Bierce to Loveman, on the subject of "In Pierrot's Garden," and the general state of poetry at that time, were published by George Kirk in Cleveland very shortly before he, too, came to New York. And to satisfy any reasonable curiosity that may be felt by the reader as to the actual poem, here is the first section of "In Pierrot's Garden":

> This is the way the moon comes up
> From under the glimmering fallow fields;
> First but the rim of a silver cup,
> Where the farthest twilight primrose yields
> Its earthly beauty up;
> And now where the deep light winks abrim
> You can see it flutter and fail for breath,
> And a single star falls rapt and dim—
> I call it Death.

The second section consists of two stanzas, and the third of three. Amateur journalists may be interested to know that the above lines have been copied from the July 1919 issue of W. Paul Cook's *National Amateur*, which contains practically all the laureate and honorably mentioned poetry of the N. A. P. A., from 1877 to 1917. It is nothing less than a treasure-house to the student or historian seeking information about this particular phase of amateur activity. It is the list of laureates, with dates and names of poems, in this same issue, which tells me that Samuel Loveman won the honorable mention in 1907 with "Arcady," while Richard Braunstein came in first with a poem called "November." Knowing what I do about Braunstein's later exposure as a plagiarist by A. M. Adams, I have just spent a little time trying to find his poem—with, possibly, some more famous name attached as author!—in one of my anthologies. No luck, however. In 1908 Loveman won the title with "In Pierrot's Garden," and Brainerd Prescott Emery achieved honorable mention with "Love's Triumph."

I may be pardoned for mentioning Loveman's acquaintance with Hart Crane, who lived nearby on the Heights, and who had won considerable recognition as a poet in professional circles. They had become acquainted in Cleveland, but Crane's social exploits in New York were of a sort to repel and alarm Loveman. He came to see Loveman one night while I was there; and, a few evenings later, Loveman took me with him on a return visit to Crane. He lived on the same side of the Heights, with back windows overlooking the East River, which lay some distance below. We found him working on his poem, "The Bridge," and through the window behind him, could discern many of the details of that spectacular view, with the very bridge, itself, duly in evidence at the extreme right. Only a few years later, Hart Crane committed suicide by leaping from the deck of a steamer at sea, and I recall that a reporter from the *Evening Post* called on Loveman for some personal details regarding the dead poet. I have no doubt that he was all compassion and sorrow, for, as George Kirk once remarked, "If a poet is young, and commits suicide, he is Sam's man!" Loveman had more than one occasion to feel sorry during the time I knew him—but George Sterling of California, who also died by his own hand, is the only one who occurs to me now.

In recent years, as opportunity has arisen, I have called at Loveman's office in lower Fifth Avenue, New York. In two rooms, on one of the upper floors of an office building, he conducts a mail-order book business called "The Bodley Book Shop." He issues catalogues at frequent intervals, and has built up an excellent business. The last time I saw him, he had just received proofs of "The Sphinx" from W. Paul Cook, and sat contemplating them with something like amazement. It was Cook's redemption of an old promise to H. P. Lovecraft, that he would one day publish this work of Samuel Loveman's.

A Scene for "King Lear" by Way of Introduction
Harry Edwin Martin

Lovers of "King Lear" well remember that poignant moment in the last scene when, after the old king has tottered upon the stage with the dead Cordelia in his arms, and after he has failed to recognize certainly his late servant and former lord Kent, he cries out in grief-stricken madness:

> And my poor fool is hang'd No, no, no life!
> Why should a dog, a horse, a rat have life,
> And thou no breath at all? Thou'lt come no more,
> Never, never, never, never, never!
> Pray you, undo this button, Thank you, sir,
> Do you see this? Look on her, look, her lips,
> Look there, look there! (Dies.)

Most modern critics hold that "my poor fool" refers to Cordelia, who, we are told in the scene, was hanged before her father succeeded in rescuing her from the hangman. This view is taken because this term was not uncommon as one of endearment in Elizabethan times, and because of the lines that follow. Sir Joshua Reynolds, Algernon Swinburne, and others maintain, however, that the mad king thinks here of the fool. And Swinburne goes so far as to conjecture that the two editors of the First Folio excised the scene of Cordelia's and the fool's hanging.

Sensing the possibilities of such a scene, and loving Shakespeare profoundly, Samuel Loveman has attempted to dramatize the situation, He has, in doing this, utilized his wide knowledge of Elizabethan English; his appreciative study of Shakespeare's method and manner; and his insight into the characters of King Lear and the babbling fool, whose "wits are set a-dancing by grief."

How near he has come to a reproduction of the lost scene, if ever one existed, no one knows. But the reader who knows his Shakespeare will discern the resemblance and will praise the new artist's dramatic and poetic power.

Editor's Note to "A Scene for Macbeth"

H. P. Lovecraft

The ensuing suppositious scene, designed for the tragedy of Macbeth, displays anew the almost uncanny genius of Samuel Loveman in the field of Elizabethan scholarship. Shakespearian students will find in these lines an identification of the author and his chosen period which constitutes a notable achievement in the annals of archaic imitation, and will marvel at the depth of insight which makes possible a reflection not only of the form but of the spirit of a literature three centuries behind us.

This is the second of Mr. Loveman's Shakespearian scenes to appear in the amateur press, the first having been published in *The Sprite* for August 1917. We are here given an important dramatic moment missing from all existing texts of Macbeth: the death of Lady Macbeth, oppressed by fear and conscience, and with a mind haunted by remorseful images, chiefly of the murdered wife and children of Macduff. Herself a mother, she suffers most of all from the memory of the helpless children slain by her husband's men: a thought embodied and phrased with supreme skill by Mr. Loveman in her brief utterance:

> "Here's where it hurts!
> O little baby hands that pluck me close,
> Poor wandering atoms in this night of pitch—
> Fordone, fordone, fordone!"

The death itself is poignantly realistic, revealing the author as always an artist even when most an archaist.

We now approach the scene, which may be taken as following Scene III of the fifth Act, in which Macbeth has asked the Doctor of Physic:

> "Canst thou not minister to a mind diseas'd:
> Pluck from the memory a rooted sorrow:
> Raze out the written troubles of the brain;
> And, with some sweet oblivious antidote,
> Cleanse the stuff'd bosom of that perilous matter
> Which weighs upon the heart?"

Rhymes and Reactions

George Sterling

Long Island is the terminal moraine of the great glacier of the last Ice Age, and on some of its eastern beaches one may find beautifully lucid quartz crystal, eternal dews that the sun and wind of Time have not effaced.

Thinking of them, I am reminded of a remarkable poem that has just reached me, "The Hermaphrodite," by the young poet Samuel Loveman.* It is from The Recluse Press of Athol, Mass., which has printed three hundred and fifty copies of the small book—in a true civilization thirty-five million would be required.

If you expect to find in it any tale of erotic aberration or stimulus, you would better leave this splendid poem unread. It has none of that: it is "only" poetry, pure poetry of as marvelous a translucence as any crystal polished by the sand and waves of lonely beaches. Here indeed Mr. Loveman has taken all the loveliness and tragedy of the great Past, and distilled from them his necklace of immutable dews. The poem is coherent and mournfully beautiful, and the lament of the hermaphrodite over the perished splendor of old years is, as De Casseres points out in his all-too-brief preface, of "a magic as authentic as Keats and a contained and sustained lyrical frenzy for the 'Supreme Loveliness' that sets it apart from all other fads, fancies and transparent fakery that are yawled and yawped abroad as the 'ultra modern note.'"

One can more than echo all that De Casseres says in praise of the poem. Reading his preface I feared that it must prove extravagant, but the lyric outburst in the pages that followed gave rest to my apprehensions. Here is an unforgettable and almost perfect poem, as authentically the work of genius as "The Eve of St. Agnes." Whether or not Mr. Loveman can follow it up with others of the same amazing quality I do not know. Even if he fail to, his fame should be assured by this single triumph of sheer art and inspiration. No reader of "The Hermaphrodite" will forget it, for

"Beautiful was this god and tender,
 Whose footfall loosed Olympian splendour,

---

*The typographer misspelled Loveman's name as *Tweman* throughout, and *footfall* as *football*.

Where on the golden hair were set
Wind flower for a coronet."

Preface [to *The Hermaphrodite*]

Benjamin De Casseres

Maybe it was more than a coincidence, for there is a profound courage in certain forms of credulity. And so, on second thought, I will call it literary, or psychic magnetism.

I was deep in a second reading, after a quarter of century, of Balzac's "Seraphita," that amazing imaginative flight of the French writer into the realms of the occult. Seraphita–Seraphitus, the hero–heroine of Balzac's book, is a hermaphrodite, a mysterious and divinely beautiful boy–girl of the Norse Mountains, who is loved by both a girl and a man. She is an epiphany, an incarnation, the final evolution of the human being before its evanescence into a super-dimension, where male and female are one, a union in one body of eternal mates lost to one another for kalpas of time before the Fall into duality, a myth that is universal and which is the basis of profoundest mystical thought.

It was while deeply absorbed in the philosophy of "Seraphita" that Samuel Loveman, a poet whom I knew only vaguely by name, brought to my house casually a poem called "The Hermaphrodite." I had not read the first four lines of it when I was completely under the spell of Loveman's magic—for there is in this poem a magic as authentic as Keats and a contained and sustained lyrical frenzy for the "Supreme Loveliness" that sets it apart from all other poetic fads, fancies and transparent fakery that is yowled and yawped abroad as the "Ultra-Modern note."

No, there is quite another "note" in Loveman's "The Hermaphrodite." It is the note of the Eternal. There is in his work the breath of Ineffable Beauty that soars and shudders and flashes and blazes in the souls of Spencer, Herrick, Marlowe, Keats, Swinburne, Baudelaire, Poe and Verlaine. The footprints of the phantom Helena are in every line of "The Hermaphrodite."

Passion, sensuousness and spontaneity are inherent in this poem. In art there cannot be illusion without spontaneity. It is implicit. Because of this spontaneousness—this unfettered parade of vision and image from brain to paper—I received this rare blessing (rare in poetry nowadays) of perfect illusion. Samuel Loveman is Prospero.

His style is simple and chaste. One can easily see he is not a poet by profession. He is a poet by election, "whose footfall loosed Olympian splendour."

[Review of *The Hermaphrodite and Other Poems*]
Ernest A. Edkins

The Hermaphrodite, And Other Poems, by Samuel Loveman: Caxton Printers, Caldwell, Idaho, 1936. $2.00.

The Parnassian enclave wherein Mr. Loveman chooses to dwell is curiously remote from his own times. If one were to cast about for some illuminating phrase with which to epitomize the delicate spirit of his poetry, one might well linger over "Kalokagathia,"—beauty-and-goodness,—"that solemn word in which even the gods take delight." Here is a poet who broods only on "the glory that was Greece"; a poet for whom the modern scene is merely a bewildering phantasmagoria of madness. Heart-sick for the happiness of some dimly divined anterior life, he turns from the forbidding proscenia of the present to a nobler *mise-en-scène*,—the Æschylean stage of an antique world,—whereon he wanders, half distraught, a wistful Pierrot searching in vain for the phantom which is Beauty and for the illusion which is Love. If anything a more pronounced Hellenophile than Keats, he invokes every mood of the Hellenic tradition except, perhaps, the mood of pagan laughter. Beauty lures and eludes him, Love abides only in unavailing dreams, and if among these vanishing apparitions he occasionally sees the backward glance, the enticing smile of some kindlier vision, it is

> "Joy, whose hand is ever at his lips,
> Bidding adieu."

It might be pleasant, though perhaps unprofitable, to examine those inevitable questions relating to the province of poetry which must occur to one sits down to read *The Hermaphrodite*, and who arises perplexed. To the lover of beautiful language these poems are sheer enchantment; to the reader seeking some interpretation of life's enigmas, they are almost a revelation of spiritual bankruptcy. Let me say at once that the poet's integrity is beyond question; the testimony of what he thinks he sees, and of what he thinks he thinks, is absolutely sincere, as far as it goes,—nor could he write in any other fashion and be true to himself. There remains, however, the question of whether (to borrow Arnold's somewhat threadbare phrase) he sees life clearly and sees it whole? Does he, indeed? Alas, do any of us? Poetry is a by-product of mental and sensory reactions to emotional stimuli,—a very small utterance of what is largely inexpressible. Of these excitements, which are the most compelling? The choice is debatable, but I would say Grief and Joy; Love, of course, is a fusion of both. Grief comes first, because life involves more sorrow than happiness. But here a point should be noted; the poets to whom we return again and again are those who endeavour to find something joyous and inspiring in life itself, apart from its tribulations and despite the universal burden of doom and despair. Milton was profoundly right; "what though the field be lost, all is not lost." There still remains *courage*. And what though the blight of an ineluctable caducity rests on man, nature, love itself? There is always the promise of better days, fairer Springs, lovelier vistas beyond the blue hills; or even otherwise, for God's sake let us die like gentlemen, fighting to the last stand, snatching the sweetness of the moment, gathering our roses while we may and perishing if we must with a song on our lips. We know, without the assurances of Loveman or of Leopardi, that life is an affliction; but the brave man makes the best of it and goes down to ultimate defeat, laughing at the fates and flinging his defiance in the very teeth of the dark gods. This unyielding spirit is not often found in the poet who confesses that

> "Sorrow comes ever with delight
> And finds no better haven,"

or who asks,

> "What should one who tries
> To dream the world away,
> But to close his eyes
> For a better day?"

The dominant note is one of nostalgia; the jewelled beads on this poet's rosary are the crystallized tears of renunciation, of love forsworn, of an all-pervading melancholia; the repetitious theme, woven through wistful variations, is that of a stricken soul lost in an alien world. Happiness is considered in the past tense,—something to be remembered, but only remembered in sorrow. If Mr. Loveman still draws strength and inspiration from the indomitable heart of man, from the fair face of nature, from the spiritual victories no less than from the disasters that invest the drama of existence with such tremendous significance, he seldom reveals these qualities in his poetry. Here, of course, it must be recognized that we tread on delicate ground; if the poet prefers threnodies to paeans, who shall gainsay him? Yet the too insistent note of mourning, the unremitting lamentation for "the days that are no more," cannot escape unfortunate repercussions, and there comes a time when grief ceases to be sad, and begins to be lugubrious. Callous wretches that we are, we not only resent our own sorrows, but grow impatient with the sorrows of others. Life despoils us of everything,—our youth, our illusions, our hair, our friends,—but still we must live on, and once the dead are decently buried, we hasten to forget. It may be going too far to say that a poet's obligations include definite responsibilities to his readers, or that he is under any moral compulsion (by reason of his high vocation) to administer to man's happiness; but certainly this much seems implicit, that he should not pander to despair. Beauty did not vanish from the world when the old gods were overthrown; it still lives with us, imperishably, and though Mr. Loveman proclaims the fact, it does not seem to relieve his dolour. Courage, honor and joy are still our heritage; life, in spite of all hell, is still sweet and desirable. The sense of loss should inspire something nobler than a personal defeatism, and from the very grave of our lost loves we should be able to pluck some flower of fortitude, some shred of resolution with which to face whatever is yet to come. Mr. Loveman is still young enough, I think, to outgrow his present disillusionment, and to achieve both a clearer vision and a less bitter philosophy. There is a recurrent disclosure of fatalistic resignation in his verses, slightly suggestive of the decadent school. He is "a lonely, unsought thing," a harp "broken and jangled," his song merely stirs "the perfumed darkness around oblivion," he finds himself one "who could not scale those lonelier peaks of blue," from him "the winged voice took flight, but not the old despair," and by way of completing the picture he admits that he is "a withered chaff tossed by the wind." It is difficult to pin this feeling down with isolated quotations, and the method itself is not quite fair, but the impression still lingers, of a painful sense of personal unworthiness, quite unjustified by the high quality of the work. I prefer to think that many of these poems were composed in Mr. Loveman's early youth, in spite of their technical perfection, since they reveal most unmistakably both the *morbidezza* and the melancholy of precocious adolescence.

In the long poem from which the book takes its title, there is much to justify the rather exuberant panegyrics of Benjamin De Casseres, who contributes. a graceful introduction. "The Hermaphrodite" is a poem of overpowering loveliness; to linger amongst its exquisite verbal felicities is to experience an intoxicating assault on the senses not unlike the swooning fragrance of an orange grove in full bloom. Its infinite elaboration of *décor* almost conceals the structure. Like some of Swinburne's complicated orchestrations, its interfluent harmonies are easier to chant than to understand, but the reader, adrift on this swift tide of passionate song, is too entranced to wonder or to care whither he is being carried away. Hermaphroditus, the incarnation of Ideal Beauty, is buried alive, and resurrected, and doomed to a frozen death-in-life for countless ages; the story is beautifully told in somewhat obscure but supremely musical lines, so that from the dusky *penetralia* of Mr. Loveman's hieratic legend you may emerge with whatever interpretation you like. The narrative is immaterial; the poet's aesthetics are unimportant; but here is a temple lovelier than that "where Alph, the sacred river, ran," a temple to Beauty, built with beautiful words,—and like the Taj Mahal, sufficient unto itself, without need of further explanation. If I were in a hypercritical mood, I might possibly deplore such a phrase as "that crocus-coloured brow," or even fancy something more than a mere echo of Tennyson in

> "One face alone, that drew
> Mine, as the sunlight drinketh dew,"

but these piddling exceptions would only serve to accentuate the tremendous technical distinction of the work as a whole.

I have not allowed myself space in which to quote or to discuss Mr. Loveman's shorter lyrics; nor, upon reflection, do I care to deprive my readers of that first pleasurable shock to which they are entitled when they conduct their own exploration of these "realms of gold,"—an emotion which I am sure will remind them of the thrill which Keats experienced when he opened the pages of Chapman's Homer. If I were to nominate my favorite where choice is so difficult, it would be a poem that I first encountered in an amateur paper, many years ago, entitled "In Pierrot's Garden." The faery-like delicacy of this little song, in which the divinely young and tender yearning of a bewildered Pierrot is indicated by the subtlest effects of an almost artless simplicity, tempts me to indulge in extravagant language. Much as I reprehend that tendency toward hyperbole which now and then makes amateur criticism faintly ridiculous, I am bound to confess that these lilting lines have haunted me ever since I first came across them. Escaping by the narrowest of margins those pitfalls of preciosity for which Mr. Loveman's muse has a perilous predilection (what an alarming lot of p's!) the poem in effect creates an absolutely authentic atmosphere of innocent wonderment. Some of its stanzas, I like to think, are precisely the sort of verse that a very lovely, sensitive and brooding child might compose,—if such a child knew how to write, as well as dream, poetry. The lines are fairly saturated with the misty magic of a twilight garden,—colour, perfume and glamour distilled in a drowsy brew from the glimmering dusk,— where Pierrot, fathoms deep in some elfin abstraction, whispers his amazing phantasies. Was it not Wordsworth who said, "the tall cataract haunts me like a passion"? Though we are all subject to these queer, irrational obsessions, I expect few to agree with me; but I regard "In Pierrot's Garden" as one of the most delectable short poems, of its kind, in English literature.

I would like to dwell at length on Mr. Loveman's splendid verses to Apollo and to Dionysus, on the strength and nobility of "River Pattern," on the quiet drama of "Understanding." But since I have purposely refrained from analysing the few unimportant things that displease me, so must I also forego the pleasure of quoting the many passages in which I find an enduring delight. There are only a few strings to this poet's lyre, and his appeal is mainly to other poets, rather than to casual readers; but how moving is that appeal! In this drab and mechanistic age Mr. Loveman has performed a miracle and fulfilled a promise:

> "But come, I have never grown old, and if you but harken,
> My song shall bring you release;

Far, far from these faces, these eyes that shiver and darken,
I can take you back to Greece."

[Review of *The Hermaphrodite and Other Poems*]

William Rose Benét

[T]hough "The Hermaphrodite" by Samuel Loveman (Caxton Printers, Caldwell, Idaho) is introduced with a flourish by Benjamin De Casseres, (even Sir Edmund Gosse has called the title poem vivid and accomplished, and this poet has received plenty of encomia elsewhere,) I consider Mr. Loveman merely a pleasing poet and no more.

Loveman's bookplate

BIBLIOGRAPHY

Dedication. [Chapbook with two poems, "David, King of Israel" and "The Witch of Endor," July 1905.] Not seen, possibly a one-shot magazine by SL.

Poems. Cleveland: Published for the Author, 1911. 24 pp. *Contains:* In Pierrot's Garden; Ode to Dionysus; Ode to Ceres; Fra Angelico; Song; Dirge; To. P. G.; Lines; A Twenty-second Birthday; From Heine [6 poems]; Oedipus at Colonus.

Twenty-one Letters of Ambrose Bierce. Cleveland: George Kirk, 1922. Norwood, PA: Norwood Editions, 1976. West Warwick, RI: Necronomicon Press, 1991 [adds Introduction by Donald R. Burleson]. The preface ("A Note") is quoted in part in H. P. Lovecraft's "Supernatural Horror in Literature."

A Round-Table in Poictesme: A Symposium (co-edited with Don [Marshall] Bregenzer). Cleveland: Colophon Club, 1924 [774 copies]. New York: Gordian Press, 1975.

The Hermaphrodite: A Poem. Athol, MA: Published by W. Paul Cook, The Recluse Press, [July] 1926 [350 copies]. Preface by Benjamin De Casseres. 33 pp.

The Hermaphrodite and Other Poems. Caldwell, ID: Caxton Printers, [January] 1936. *Contains:* Preface by Benjamin De Casseres; The Hermaphrodite; River Pattern; Will o' the Wisp; Steener Haakonson Dances; Dream Song; Heckscher Building; Euphorion; Agathon; Arcesilaus; Lineage; For a Book of Poems; Ascension; Thomas Holley Chivers; The Ramapos; Oscar Wilde; John Clare in a Madhouse; The Minstrel; The Chopin-Player; A Dedication; Vice; Transience; Dolore; Bacchanale; To Simone's; Ad Fratrem; Isolation; Remonstrance; Proteus; A Voyage; Legend; The Return; Memoralia; Forest of Rhododendron; Understanding; Ecce Homo; Ariel; Visitor; Inarticulate; Madison Square; Contrast; Invocation; Song; Harbour; Admonition; Foes; Limbo; Interlude; Gates Mills; Wasteland; Amy Levy; Forest Hill; Andenkung; Dream of Spring; Finis; A Georgia Garden; Palingenesis; Belated Love; Nostalgia; Becalmed; Mutation; Dirge; To Dionysus; To Apollo; Quatrains; In Pierrot's Garden; A Chinese Pavilion; Ben De

Casseres in Camden; Terminus. [H] Dedicated to Howard and Geraldine Wolf and Philip Gordon.

The Sphinx: A Conversation. [North Montpelier, VT]: Published by W. Paul Cook, 1944 [150 copies].

"Hart Crane": A Conversation with Samuel Loveman. New York: Interim Books, 1964 [500 copies]. Transcript of an original tape recording at Brown University.

Lovecraft's New York Circle: The Kalem Club, 1924–1927. Edited by Mara Kirk Hart and S. T. Joshi. New York: Hippocampus Press, 2006. [NYC]

Three unpublished poems (The Bowery; Illicit; [Prologue to *Circe*]) narrated by Loveman were taken from in "Conversations with Sam" by Thomas Hubschman. [TH]

POEMS

"The Abyss." TMs. found in book inscribed by SL to Mrs. E. B. H. Bates, 12 March 1947.

"Ad Fratrem." *H.*

"Admonition." *United Amateur* 25, No. 3 (July 1926): 5. *H.* In *NYC* 196.

"An Admonition to the Ladies." Unpublished.

"Adventure." *United Amateur* 21, No. 4 (March 1922): 42. ["Epilogue" unpublished.]

"Aftermath." *Californian* 3, No. 1 (Summer 1935): 7. *H* [under heading "Quatrains"].

"Agathon." *Pegasus* (October 1924): 47. *H. L'Alouette* 13, No. 2 (Summer 1936): 71.

"Amy Levy." *Saturnian* 1, No. 3 (March 1922): 16. *H.*

"Andenkung." *H.* In *The William Sommer Memorial Exhibition.* Cleveland: Cleveland Museum of Art, 1950. [2].

"Antenor." Unpublished, incomplete.

"Arcady." *Cartoons* 2, No. 4 (November 1906): 31–37. *National Amateur* 30, No. 4 (March 1908): 58. *National Amateur* 41, No. 6 (July 1919): 231–32.

"Arcesilaus." *H.* In *NYC* 198.

"Ariel." *Clevelander* 1, No. 1 (June 1922): 4. *H.*

"Ascension." *H.*

"Avalon." *Wild Rose* 1, No. 3/4 (January–February 1906): 1–2.

"Bacchanale." *United Amateur* 23, No. 1 (May 1924): [1]. *H.* In Lovecraft's *Writings in the United Amateur 1915–1925*. Ed. Marc A. Michaud. West Warwick, RI: Necronomicon Press, 1976. 141. In *Fear and Other Poems*, ed. Tom Collins (Mailing No. 21 of the Esoteric Order of Dagon Amateur Press Association, 1977). 2. In *Writings in* The United Amateur, *1915–1925*. West Warwick, RI: Necronomicon Press, 1976. 65. In Lovecraft's *Letters to Samuel Loveman & Vincent Starrett*. Ed. S. T. Joshi and David E. Schultz. West Warwick, RI: Necronomicon Press, 1994. 42.

"Be Thou a Jew!" *American Israelite* (2 November 1905): 1. In *The Standard Book of Jewish Verse*, ed. Joseph Friedlander. New York: Dodd, Mead, 1917. 596. In *Poems for Young Judaeans*, ed. [Unsigned]. New York: Young Judaea, 1917 (rev. ed.). 28.

"Becalmed." *H.*

"Belated Love." *H.* In *Masquerade: Queer Poetry in America to the End of World War II*, ed. Jim Elledge. Bloomington: Indiana University Press, 2004. [160].

"Belshazzar" [verse drama]. *Monitor* 2, No. 8 (March 1906): [1–4].

"Ben De Casseres in Camden." *Trend* 1, No. 2 (June–July–August 1932): 49–50. *H.*

"Birth of Fear." *Southerner* 2, No. 6 (15 October 1905): 12.

"Birth of Poesy." *Illinoian* 1, No. 1 (April 1906): 9.

"The Bowery." TH. See "The Faithful."

"A Burden." *Sprite* 9, No. 1 (March 1919): [3] (under heading "Five Poems").

"Catullus" [translation of Catullus 101 and 85; as "Caullus"]. *National Times* No. 1 (June 1921): [3].

"A Chinese Pavilion." *Sprite* 10, No. 2 (May 1920): 6–8. *Cygnet: A Quarterly Journal of Arts and Letters* 1, No. 3 (July 1920): 6. *Clevelander* 2, No. 1 (April 1923): 8 (as "Six Chinese Poems"). *H.*

"The Chopin-Player." *National Tribute* (February 1922): 4 (untitled; as one of "Three Poems"). *H.*

"Christmas—1923." Unpublished.

"Contemporary Verse" [10 poems: "Dream Song"; "Foes"; "To a Child"; "Simeon Solomon"; "Music"; "The Dead King"; "God's Work (After Rainer Maria Rilke)"; "Kin"; "Episode"; "Madison Square"]. *Californian* 3, No. 1 (Summer 1935): 14–15.

"Contrast." *Californian* 3, No. 1 (Summer 1935): 36 (under heading "Five Short Poems"; as "A Contrast"). *H*.

"David, King of Israel." *Dedication* (1905).

"David Gray." *Mite* 3, No. 1 (Summer 1907): 1.

"De Profundis." *Cartoons* 1, No. 5 [1907]: 16–17.

"The Dead King." *Californian* 3, No. 1 (Summer 1935): 15 (under heading "Contemporary Verse").

"Debs in Prison." Unpublished. [Probably written 1918–21.]

"A Dedication." *H*.

"A Departure." *Sprite* 10, No. 2 (May 1920): 13 (under heading "Five More Poems").

"Dirge." *Cartoons* 2, No. 4 ([December] 1907): [11]. *Poems. H*.

"Dolore." *Bacon's Essays* 1, No. 1 (Summer 1927): 8. *National Amateur* 50, No. 5–6 (May–July 1928): 7. *H*.

"Dowager." *Works: A Quarterly of Writing* 1, No. 1 (Autumn 1967): 47.

"Dream of Spring." *H*.

"Dream Song." *Californian* 3, No. 1 (Summer 1935): 14 (under heading "Contemporary Verse"). *H*.

"Ecce Homo." *Sprite* 9, No. 1 (March 1919): [3] (under heading "Five Poems"). *H*.

"Episode." *Californian* 3, No. 1 (Summer 1935): 15 (under heading "Contemporary Verse").

"An Epitaph." *Cartoons* 2, No. 4 ([December] 1907): [10].

"Ernest Nelson." *Clevelander* 1, No. 1 (June 1922): 8.

"Euphorion." *Saturnian* 1, No. 3 (March 1922): 17. *H*.

"Euthanasia." *Sprite* 9, No. 1 (March 1919): [2–3] (under heading "Five Poems").

"Eventide." *Sprite* 2, No. 3 (October 1906): [n.p.].

"The Faithful." TMS. Alternate title: "The Bowery."

"Finis." *Clevelander* 2, No. 1 (April 1923): 5. *H*.

"Five More Poems" [5 poems: "The Return"; "Isolation"; "A Georgia Garden"; "A Departure"; "W. E."]. *Sprite* 10, No. 2 (May 1920): 12–14.

"Five Poems" [5 poems: "Resurgam"; "Shadow-Love"; "Euthanasia"; "Ecce Homo"; "A Burden"]. *Sprite* 9, No. 1 (March 1919): [2–3].

"Five Short Poems" [5 poems: "Rescue"; "The Ramapos"; "Transit"; "A Contrast"; "Night Piece (Forest Hill)"]. *Californian* 3, No. 1 (Summer 1935): 36.

"Foes." *Californian* 3, No. 1 (Summer 1935): 14 (under heading "Contemporary Verse"). *H*.
"For a Book." TH. See "Two Poems for Book Marks."
"For a Book of Poems." *National Amateur* 50, No. 5–6 (May–July 1928): 7 (as "In a Book of Dreams"). *H*. In *NYC* 196.
"For the Chelsea Book-Shop" ["Walk into Chelsea where each street"]. Broadside, bookmark, n.d. In *NYC* 195.
"For the Chelsea Book Shop" ["The night is over Chelsea Town"]. Previously unpublished. In *NYC* 195.
"Forest Hill." *National Amateur* 44, No. 5 (May 1922): 51. *H*.
"Forest of Rhododendron." *H*.
"Fragment." Nonextant?
"The Forgotten Poets." See "Quatrains."
"Fra Angelico: 1387–1455." *Cartoons* 2, No. 5 (May 1908): [n.p.]. *Poems*.
"From Heine" [six poems]. *Cartoons* 4, No. 1 (September 1910): 11–13 (as by "Caviare"). *Poems*.
"Gates Mills." *H*.
"Genesis." *United Amateur* 25, No. 2 (May 1926): 2. In *NYC* 197–98.
"A Georgia Garden." *Sprite* 10, No. 2 (May 1920): 13 (under heading "Five More Poems"). *H*.
"The Goal." *National Amateur* 50, No. 4 (March 1928): 4.
"God's Work (After Rainer Maria Rilke)." *Californian* 3, No. 1 (Summer 1935): 15 (under heading "Contemporary Verse"). A translation of Rilke's "Werkleute sind wir."
"Harbour." *H*.
"Heckscher Building." *H*.
"Heldenleben" [= "Heroes live]. *Clevelander* 2, No. 2 (June 1923): 8. In *Fear and Other Poems*, ed. Tom Collins (Mailing No. 21 of the Esoteric Order of Dagon Amateur Press Association, 1977). 7.
The Hermaphrodite. The Hermaphrodite (1926). *H*.
"Hope." *Wild Rose* 1, nos. 3 & 4 (January–February 1906): 3.
"Illicit." TH.
"In Pierrot's Garden." *Cartoons* 2, No. 3 (November 1907): [18–19] [3 stanzas]. *Cartoons* 2, No. 5 (May 1908): [78] [stanza IV only]. *National Amateur* 31, No. 3 (January 1909): 33 [3 stanzas]. *Poems* [5 stanzas]. In *Mon Ami Pierrot: Songs and Fantasies*, ed. Kendall Banning. Chicago: Brothers of the Book, 1917. 59. In *The Younger Choir*, ed. Edwin

Markham. New York: Moods Publishing Company, 1910. 61–62 [3 stanzas]. *National Amateur* 41, No. 6 (July 1919): 232–33 [3 stanzas]. In *Twenty-one Letters to Ambrose Bierce* [in all editions] [4 stanzas]. *L'Alouette* 1, No. 1 (January 1924): 16–17 [3 stanzas]. *H* [4 stanzas]. In *Threads in Tapestry*, ed. Charles A. A. Parker, Rachel Hall, and Marcia A. Taylor. Medford, MA: C. A. A. Parker, 1935. 90–91 [stanzas II, III, and V; numbered as I, II, and III]. In *The Ancient Wood and Other Poems*. Ysleta, TX: Edwin B. Hill, 1942. [12–13] [omits stanza I, renumbering the remaining stanzas].

"In Sepulcretis." *Saturnian* 1, No. 3 (March 1922): 16.

"Inarticulate." *H*.

"Interlude." *L'Alouette* 1, No. 2 (March 1924): 48. *H*.

"Invocation." *H*.

"Isolation." *Sprite* 10, No. 2 (May 1920): 12 (under heading "Five More Poems"). *H*.

"John Clare in a Madhouse." *Sprite* 8, No. 1 (January 1917): [1–2]. *United Amateur* 20, No. 1 (September 1920): [1]. *H*.

"John Clare in 1864." Previously unpublished. In *NYC* 198.

"Kin." *Californian* 3, No. 1 (Summer 1935): 15 (under heading "Contemporary Verse").

"Legend." *Bacon's Essays* 2, No. 2 (Summer 1929): 7. *H*.

"A Letter to G—— K——." *Rainbow* 2, No. 2 [sic] (May 1922): 15. In *NYC* 193–94. The title refers to George W. Kirk.

"A Lily." *Inland Amateur* 2, nos. 1 & 2 (December 1905): 4.

"Limbo." *United Amateur* 25, No. 3 (July 1926): 8. *H*. In *NYC* 196–97.

"Lineage." *United Co-operative* 1, No. 3 (April 1921): 15. *H*.

"Lines." *Poems. Crypt of Cthulhu* No. 20 (Eastertide 1984): 52 (Part II only; as "To Heine").

"Lost Youth." *Southerner* 3, No. 1 (December 1905): 4.

"Madison Square." *Californian* 3, No. 1 (Summer 1935): 15 (under heading "Contemporary Verse"). *H*.

"Memoralia." *Vagrant* No. 10 (October 1919): 5. *H*.

"Metropolitan Museum." *World* 10 (February 1968): [55].

"Michael Scott's Wooing." *Lucky Dog* 8, No. 3 (April 1910): 46–47.

"The Minstrel." *Clevelander* 2, No. 2 (June 1923): 1. *H*.

"Monolith." *United Amateur* 25, No. 2 (May 1926): 7.

"A Moth's Wings." Unpublished, incomplete.

"Music" [I] [A dream of music in the long, long night;]. *Californian* 3, No. 1 (Summer 1935): 15 (under heading "Contemporary Verse"). *H* (under heading "Quatrains").

"Music" [II] [When I stood in mid-heaven,]. Printed on a card from the Chelsea Book Shop (c. 1926).

"Mutability" [by Heinrich Heine, translated by SL]. *Waste Basket* 4 No. 1 (January 1909): [back cover].

"Mutation." *H.*

"My Tribute." In *In Memoriam Hazel Pratt Adams*, ed. [unsigned]. Brooklyn, NY: Blue Pencil Club, 1927. 29. One TMs. titled "Hazel Adams."

"Narcisse" [verse drama]. *Cartoons* 2, No. 4 ([December] 1907): [12–19].

"Nepenthe." *Crypt of Cthulhu* No. 20 (Eastertide 1984): 16.

"Nero" [verse drama]. *Minnesota Amateur* No. 21 (March 1906): 1–2.

"Night Piece (Forest Hill)." *United Amateur* 25, No. 2 (May 1926): 6. *Californian* 3, No. 1 (Summer 1935): 36 (under heading "Five Short Poems"). [Not identical to "Forest Hill."]

"Nostalgia." *United Amateur* 18, No. 1 (September 1918): 8. *H. Literary Digest* 121 (25 January 1936): 26.

"Ode to Ceres." *Cartoons* 3, No. 1 (October 1909): 12–14. *Poems.*

"Ode to Homer." *Cartoons* [2, No. 2] (July 1907): 13–14.

"Oedipus at Colonus" [verse drama]. *Poems.*

"The Old Cobbler." *Wild Rose* 1, Nos. 3 & 4 (January–February 1906): 3.

"On Lost Friendship." *Sparkler* 2, No. 1 (April 1906): 6.

"On the Passing of Youth." *Sprite* 10, No. 2 (May 1920): 3–6 (as "Ode on the Passing of Youth"). *Saturnian* 1, No. 1 (June–July [1920]): [1–4]. Epigram from *Purgatorio* 32.70–2.

"Oscar Redivivus." Previously unpublished. In *NYC* 196 (as "For a Cat").

"Oscar Wilde." *Saturnian* 1, No. 1 (June–July [1920]): [6–7]. *H.* In *Fear and Other Poems*, ed. Tom Collins (Mailing No. 21 of the Esoteric Order of Dagon Amateur Press Association, 1977). 1.

"Palingenesis." *National Amateur* 50, No. 5–6 (May–July 1928): 7. *H.*

"Peccavi." *Roamer* 1, No. 1 ([1906]): [5].

"Phryne." *Works: A Quarterly of Writing* 1, No. 1 (Autumn 1967): 47.

"Pierced." *American Youth* (November 1905).

"The Plaint of Bygone Loves." *Sylph* (July 1906): [15–16].

"A Poet." *Minnesota Amateur* No. 18 (September 1905): 4.

"Poppies." See "Quatrains."

"Prologue to Arcadia." *Cartoons* 4, No. 7 (November 1910): 14–16 (as by "Caviare").

["Prologue to *Circe*."] TH. *Circe* was a play by SL's friend Hazel Krantz.

"Proteus." *H*.

"Quatrain." *Crypt of Cthulhu* No. 20 (Eastertide 1984): 24.

"Quatrains" [3 poems, untitled; different from below]. *Sprite* 5, No. 1 (Spring 1908): [9].

"Quatrains" [6 poems: "Poppies"; "The Forgotten Poets"; "Space"; "Music"; "Simeon Solomon"; "Aftermath"]. *United Amateur* 17, No. 4 (March 1918): 61. *H* [3 poems: "Poppies"; "The Forgotten Poets"; "Space"].

"The Ramapos." *Californian* 3, No. 1 (Summer 1935): 36 [under heading "Five Short Poems"]. *H*.

"Reliquiae." Unpublished.

"Remonstrance." *National Tribute* (February 1922): 4 (untitled; as one of "Three Poems"). *H*. In *Masquerade: Queer Poetry in America to the End of World War II*, ed. Jim Elledge. Bloomington: Indiana University Press, 2004. 160–61.

"Rescue." *Californian* 3, No. 1 (Summer 1935): 36 (under heading "Five Short Poems").

"Resurgam." *Sprite* 9, No. 1 (March 1919): [2] (under heading "Five Poems").

"The Return." *Sprite* 10, No. 2 (May 1920): 12 (under heading "Five More Poems"). *H*.

"River Pattern." *Trend* 1, No. 1 (March–April–May 1932): 15. *H*.

"Saturday Evening." *Saturnian* 1, No. 3 (March 1922): 17.

"Shadow-Land." *Wild Rose* 1, Nos. 3 & 4 (January–February 1906): 2.

"Shadow-Love." *Sprite* 9, No. 1 (March 1919): [2] (under heading "Five Poems").

"Ship of Dreams." *Kansas Zephyr* 1, No. 2 (February 1906): 1. In *Dreams of Fear: Poetry of Terror and the Supernatural*, ed. S. T. Joshi and Steven J. Mariconda. New York: Hippocampus Press, 2013. 298.

"Simeon Solomon." *Californian* 3, No. 1 (Summer 1935): 14 (under heading "Contemporary Verse"). *H* (under heading "Quatrains").

"Song" [6 lines, beginning "Blossoms, blossoms, pink and white"]. *Poems* (1911).

"Song" [8 lines, beginning "In the Spring of the year, in the silver rain"]. *Conservative* 5, No. 1 (July 1919): 1. *H*. In Lovecraft's *The Conserva-*

tive: Complete. Ed. Marc A. Michaud, West Warwick, RI: Necronomicon Press, 1976.

"A Song of Chamisso's." *Dowdell's Bearcat* 6, No. 18 (December 1919): 5. A translation of one of Albert von Chamisso's "Hochzeitslieder."

"The Song Unsung." *Wild Rose* 1, Nos. 3 & 4 (January–February 1906): 3.

"Sonnet: After Leconte de Lisle." *Clevelander* 2, No. 2 (June 1923): 5. A translation of Leconte de Lisle's "L'Ecclésiaste."

"A Sonnet: Lethe." *Mite* 1, No. 3 (October 1905): 1.

"Space." See "Quatrains."

"Spring at El Retiro." Unpublished.

"Steener Haakonson Dances." *Bacon's Essays* 2, No. 2 (Summer 1929): 7 (as "Steener Haakonsen Dances"). *Akron Beacon Journal* (5 April 1932): 4. H.

"Stevie." Nonextant?

"Talent." *Buckeye* 1, No. 1 (December 1921): 2. *Search-Light* 15, No. 1 (January 1922): [12].

"Terminus." H.

"Thomas Dermody 1775–1802." *Adelphian* 1, No. 2 (September 1917): [4-5]. *National Amateur* 61, No. 4 (March 1919): [121]. In Bodley Book Shop. *A Summer Catalogue of Unusually Desirable Books* . . . No. 30 [July 1939]: [2].

"Thomas Holley Chivers." *Conservative* No. 12 (March 1923): 1. H. In Lovecraft's *The Conservative: Complete.* Ed. Marc A. Michaud. West Warwick, RI: Necronomicon Press, 1976.

"Three Poems" [each poem untitled]. *National Tribute* (February 1922): [2]. For No. 1, see "The Chopin-Player." For No. 2, see "Remonstrance."

"Times Square." *World* 8 (November 1967): [35].

"To a Child." *Californian* 3, No. 1 (Summer 1935): 14 (under heading "Contemporary Verse").

"To Alfred Noyes, Oversea." *Waste Basket* 4, No. 1 (January 1909): 1.

"To Apollo." *Sprite* 8, No. 1 (January 1917): [5] (as "Ode to Apollo"). *Saturnian* 1, No. 1 (June–July [1920]): [4–5]. H. *Yawning Vortex* 3, No. 1 (October–November 1996): 38.

"To Dionysus." *Poems* (1911) (as "Ode to Dionysus"). *Cartoons* 3, No. 1 (October 1909): 10–12 (as "Ode to Dionysus"). *Saturnian* 1, No. 1 (June–July [1920]): [5–6]. H. *Yawning Vortex* 3, No. 2 (July–August 1997): 16.

"To George Kirk on His 27th Birthday." Previously unpublished. In *NYC* 194.

"To M. L. M." Unpublished, incomplete. Ms. JHL. The dedicatee is Morris Longstreet Miller, a friend who died in World War I.

"To Mr. Theobald." *United Amateur* 25, No. 3 (July 1926): 8. In *NYC* 197 (as "To H.P.L."). In *Ave atque Vale: Reminiscences of H. P. Lovecraft*, ed. S. T. Joshi and David E. Schultz. West Warwick, RI: Necronomicon Press, 2018. 470–71 (as "To H.P.L.").

"To P. G." *Poems*. The dedicatee is Philip Gordon.

"To Satan." *Conservative* No. 13 (July 1923): 1–2. *Miskatonic* No. 15 (August 1976): [25–26]. In Lovecraft's *The Conservative: Complete*. Ed. Marc A. Michaud. West Warwick, RI: Necronomicon Press, 1976. In *The Miskatonic: Lovecraft Centenary Edition*, ed. Dirk W. Mosig. Glenview, IL: Moshassuck Press, 1991. In Lovecraft's *Letters to Samuel Loveman & Vincent Starrett*. Ed. S. T. Joshi and David E. Schultz. West Warwick, RI: Necronomicon Press, 1994. 41–42. *Yawning Vortex* 2, No. 1 (July 1995): 13–14.

"To Simone's." *National Amateur* 45, No. 5 (May 1923): 3, as "To Ravioli's." H.

"Transience." *National Amateur* 50, No. 5–6 (May–July 1928): 7 (as "Transcience"). H.

"Transit." *Californian* 3, No. 1 (Summer 1935): 36 (under heading "Five Short Poems").

"Translations from Baudelaire." *Saturnian* 1, No. 3 (March 1922): [3–11] (thirteen poems): "1. La Musique"; "2. Parfum Exotique"; "3. Horreur Sympathique"; "4. De Profundis Clamavi"; "5. La Béauté"; "6. Causerie"; "7. Chant d'Automne"; "8. La Couvercle"; "9. Le Chat"; "10. La Fontaine de Sang"; "11. Sonnet d'Automne"; "12. Ciel Brouillé"; "13. Les Chats."

"Translations from Verlaine." *Saturnian* 1, No. 3 (March 1922): 12–15 (seven poems): "1. Sagesse"; "2. Buxelles"; "3. Romances sans Paroles"; "4. Il Bacio"; "5. La Bonne Chanson"; "6. Vert"; "7. Sappho."

"A Triumph in Eternity." *Rainbow* 1, No. 1 (October 1921): 13. *Bacon's Essays* 2, No. 1 (Spring 1929): 2. *Yawning Vortex* 2, No. 4 (July 1996): 19–20. In *The Rainbow: October 1921*. West Warwick, RI: Necronomicon Press, 1977. 13. Epigram from *Inferno* 4.19–21.

"Twenty Four Translations from Heine." *Saturnian* 1, No. 2 (August–September [1920]): [2–13].

"A Twenty-second Birthday." *Ariel* 1, No. 1 (November 1910): [1] (as "A Twenty-third Birthday"). *Poems.*
"Two Poems for Book Marks." In Bodley Head, *Books Old, Rare and Unusual* No. 29 [May 1939]: [2]. SL recited the first poem for Thomas J. Hubschman as "For a Book."
"Understanding." *H.* In *Masquerade: Queer Poetry in America to the End of World War II*, ed. Jim Elledge. Bloomington: Indiana University Press, 2004. 160.
"Unfulfilled." *United Amateur* 25, No. 3 (July 1926): 3.
"[Untitled]" ("He said: This is the city . . . "). *Buckeye* 1, No. 1 (December 1921): 4.
"[Untitled]" ("I dreamed I had a pocket book,"). Unpublished.
"[Untitled]" ("The lanes are drifted white with snow,"). Unpublished.
"[Untitled] ("Within my little plot of light,"). See "Three Poems."
"Varden." [verse drama] *Cartoons* 2, No. 1 (May 1907): [11–17].
"Versailles." Unpublished.
"Vice." *Clevelander* 1, No. 1 (June 1922): 5. *H.*
"Vigil." *Californian* 3, No. 1 (Summer 1935): 7.
"Visitor." *H.*
"A Voyage." *H.*
"W. E." *Sprite* 10, No. 2 (May 1920): 14 (under heading "Five More Poems").
"Wasteland." *Bacon's Essays* 1, No. 1 (Summer 1927): 8. *H.*
"Will o' the Wisp." *H.*
"Winter." *Clevelander* 2, No. 2 (June 1923): 8. In *Fear and Other Poems*, ed. Tom Collins (Mailing No. 21 of the Esoteric Order of Dagon Amateur Press Association, 1977). 1.
"The Witch of Endor." *Dedication* (1905).

Prose

"Amateur Poetry." *Buckeye* 1, No. 4 (July 1908): [1], 4.
"Antenor" [prose poem]. Unpublished.
"Back to La Mancha." In Bodley Book Shop *Fine, Old and Rare Books* . . . No. 33 [November 1939]: [2].
"Ballads." *Cartoons* 1, No. 5 [1907]: 18–23.
"The Book of Life" [on *Jurgen*]. In *A Round-Table in Poictesme.* 51–53.
"Books in Summer" *Catalogue* No. 153. New York: Dauber & Pine, n.d. 2.

"Books That Talk." In Bodley Book Shop. *A Midwinter Catalogue* . . . No. 44 [February 1941]: [2].

"Boswell Redivivus." In Bodley Book Shop. *Fine and Rare Books* . . . No. 2 [Fall? 1935]: [2].

"The Bureau of Critics." *National Amateur* 43, No. 2 (May–July 1920): 3, 6–7.

"Bureau of Critics." *National Amateur* 45, No. 1 (March 1924): [1].

"Bureau of Critics Comment on Late Amateur Papers." *National Amateur* 46 (i.e., 44), No. 3 (January 1922): [25], 32. [There were two issues of this date and number; one issued by the elected official editor, John Milton Heins, which includes his resignation "Due to the insulting imputations accompanying the President's Message," and another edited by replacement editor William J. Dowdell. The story appears in Dowdell's issue.] The essay is the same as "Official Criticism: Bureau of Critics" (q.v.).

"By the Way." *The Hobo* 1, No. 1 (May 1904): 3–4. As by "Brainy Bowers."

"Charles Dickens and Christmas." In Bodley Book Shop. *A Holiday Catalogue* . . . No. 66 [December 1943?]: [2].

"Charles Lamb." *Cartoons* 2, No. 3 (November 1907): [13–15].

"Christmas-Eve with Sherlock Holmes." In Bodley Book Shop. *A Holiday Catalogue of Books* . . . No 96. New York, [n.d.].

"A Christmas Party." See "A Holiday Party."

"The Cleveland Amateur Press Club Comes to Life." *Buckeye* 2, No. 2 (January 1909): 9, 12.

"Cleveland Club Notes." *National Amateur* 31, No. 3 (January 1909): 52.

"Cleveland Notes." *National Amateur* 29, No. 2 (November 1906): 42.

"The Coast of Bohemia." Catalogue 125: *General Literature with an Addenda* [sic] *of Americana, Sport and Natural History*. New York: Dauber & Pine Bookshops, n.d. n.p. In Bodley Book Shop. *Rare Books* . . . No. 93 [1947?]: [56].

"Collecting Curious Books." *Catalogue 107*. New York: Dauber & Pine, n.d. 25.

"Comment." *Saturnian* 1, No. 1 (June–July [1920]): [7–8]; *Saturnian* 1, No. 2 (August–September [1920]): [13–15]; *Saturnian* 1, No. 3 (March 1922): 18–19.

"A Convention Address." *Hazel Nut* 5, No. 2 (October 1923): 6–7.

"A Conversation with Ambrose Bierce." *Catalogue 121*. New York: Dauber & Pine, n.d. n.p.
"Critic's Letter." *Buckeye* 1, No. 1 (October 1908): [8].
"The Departed" [fiction]. *Toledo Amateur* (May 1920): 4–7.
"The Dog (After the Russian)." Unpublished.
"Edna Hyde—A Preface." In *From Under a Bushel* by Edna Hyde [McDonald]. Saugus, MA: Charles A. A. Parker, 1925. 9–10.
"Ernest Nelson: In Memoriam." *Saturnian* 1, No. 3 (March 1922): 18.
"The Faun" [fiction]. *Vagrant* No. 12 (December 1919): 4–12. *Leaves* No. 2 (1938): 102–6.
"A Feast of Charles Lamb." In Bodley Book Shop. *Books Old, Rare and Unusual* No. 3 [after November 1935]: [2].
"Ferris Thone" [fiction]. *National Amateur* 46 (i.e., 44), No. 3 (January 1922): 26–27. See note at "Bureau of Critics Comment on Late Amateur Papers."
"Foreword." In *Poppies and Mandragora: Poems* by Edgar Saltus; with Twenty-three additional poems by Marie Saltus. New York: Harold Vinal, 1926.
"A Foreword" [with Don Bregenzer]. In *A Round-Table in Poictesme*. ix–xi.
"Forgotten Books." In Bodley Book Shop. *General Literature, Rare Books* . . . No. 65 [November 1943]: [2].
"Forth from La Mancha." In Bodley Book Shop. *General Literature* . . . No. 1 [Summer? 1935]: [2].
"From a Diary." *Magazine* 3 (1965): n.p.
"George Herbert." *Cartoons* [2, No. 2] (July 1907): 22–23.
"George Meredith." *Sprite* 5, No. 1 (Spring 1908): [23–24].
"Hart Crane." See "A Letter on Hart Crane."
"Hart Crane" [letter to the editor]. *New York Times Book Review* (10 August 1969): 22.
"A Holiday Party." In Bodley Book Shop. *A Holiday Catalogue of Fine, Rare and Beautiful Books* . . . No. 51 [December 1941]: [2]. In The Bodley Book Shop. *A Holiday Catalogue of Books* . . . No. 90 [December 1946]: 80 (as "A Christmas Party").
"A Holiday Post-Card." *Catalogue 124*. New York: Dauber & Pine, n.d. [2].
"A Hopeless Love" [fiction]. *National Amateur* 45, No. 6 (July 1923): [1]–3.
"Howard Phillips Lovecraft." *Arkham Sampler* 1, No. 3 (Summer 1948): 32–36; *The Arkham Sampler: A Facsimile Edition*, ed. August Derleth.

Sauk City, WI: Arkham House, 2010. 32–36. In Lovecraft's *Something about Cats and Other Pieces*, ed. August Derleth. Sauk City, WI: Arkham House, 1949. 229–33. In *Vita Privata di H. P. Lovecraft: Documenti e Testimonianze per una Biografia*. Tr. and ed. Claudio De Nardi. Trento: Reverdito Editore, 1987. 51–60. In *Lovecraft Remembered*, ed. Peter Cannon. Sauk City, WI: Arkham House, 1998. 204–8. *Conversations with the Weird Tales Circle*, ed. John Pelan and Jerad Walters. Lakewood, CO: Centipede Press, 2009. 44–47. In *Ave atque Vale: Reminiscences of H. P. Lovecraft*, ed. S. T. Joshi and David E. Schultz. West Warwick, RI: Necronomicon Press, 2018. 89–93.

"Hubert Crackanthorpe: A Realist of the Nineties." *Recluse* No. 1 (1927): 71–75.

"An Impression" [prose poem]. *Clevelander* 2, No. 1 (April 1923): 7.

"Introduction." In *Dead Letters Sent and Other Poems* by Maurice Kenny. New York: Troubador Press, 1958. i–ii.

"A Keats Discovery." *Dial* 63 (19 July 1917): 77–78.

"A Letter on Hart Crane." *Nassau Literary Magazine* 91, No. 6 (June 1933): 19–21. *New English Weekly* 5, No. 16 (2 August 1934): 830 (as "Recollections of Hart Crane"). In The Bodley Book Shop. *Books Old, Rare and Unusual* No. 92 [April? 1947]: [63–64].

"Literature and Dry-Rot" [review of *Expression in America* by Ludwig Lewisohn]. *Trend* 1, No. 2 (June–July–August 1932): 58–59.

"Literature and Life." In Bodley Book Shop. *General Literature* . . . No. 32 [October 1939]: 2.

"Lovecraft as Conversationalist." *Fresco* 8, No. 3 (Spring 1958): 34–36. In *Caverns Measureless to Man: 18 Memoirs of H. P. Lovecraft*, ed. S. T. Joshi. West Warwick, RI: Necronomicon Press, 1996. 45–46. In *Lovecraft Remembered*, ed. Peter Cannon. Sauk City, WI: Arkham House, 1998. 209–11. In *Ave atque Vale: Reminiscences of H. P. Lovecraft*, ed. S. T. Joshi and David E. Schultz. West Warwick, RI: Necronomicon Press, 2018. 240–42.

"Marcel Proust: 'Le Temps Retrouvé'" [review]. *Trend* 1, No. 1 (March–April–May 1932): 8–9.

"Modern Poetry (An Exorcism)." *Saturnian* 1, No. 3 (March 1922): [1]–3.

"Mr. Sterling and Minor Poets" [letter to the editor]. *New York Times Book Review* (4 June 1911): 352.

"New York Dynamics." *Dance Observer* 2, No. 6. (Summer 1935): 65.

"Notes and Review." *Buckeye* 1, No. 1 (October 1908): [1–6]; 2, No. 2 (January 1909): [1]–6. Epigram from Juvenal, *Satires* 6.

"Notes and Reviews." *Buckeye* 1, No. 2 (January 1908): 1–4, 9; 1, No. 3 (April 1908): [1–4]. Epigram from Thomas Herrick's "To His Muse," ll. 7–8.

"Of Gold and Sawdust" [essay]. In *The Occult Lovecraft*, ed. Anthony Raven. Saddle River, NJ: Gerry de la Ree, 1975. 21–22.

"Official Criticism: Bureau of Critics." *National Amateur* 44, No. 2 (November 1921): 29, 33.

"Official Criticism: Bureau of Critics." *National Amateur* 44, No. 3 (January 1922): 29, 33.

"The One Who Did Penance" [fiction]. *San Francisco News Letter* 92, No. 16 (14 October 1916): 6.

"The One Who Found Pity" [fiction]. *United Amateur* 24, No. 1 (July 1925): 5–6.

"Preface." In *The Hart Crane Voyages* by Hunce Voelker. New York: Brownstone Press, 1967.

"Preface." In *The Man from Genoa and Other Poems* by Frank Belknap Long. Athol, MA: W. Paul Cook, 1926. [5]. *National Amateur* 48, No. 5 (May 1926): 51 (as "The Poetry of Frank Belknap Long, Jr."). In Long's *In Mayan Splendor*. Sauk City, WI: Arkham House, 1977. [vii].

"Preface" [dated 24 September 1922]. Unpublished, to a scene, translated by George Borrow, from *Hakon Jarl*, by Adam Gottlob Oelenschläger, which George Kirk intended to print.

"A Preface." In *The Fear* by Philip Spira. Cleveland: Perlmuter Press, 1924. [v].

"A Prefatory Note." *Saturnian* 1, No. 2 (August–September [1920]): [1–2].

"A Ruined Paradise." *Quaker* 3, No. 2 (January 1910): [13]–16. As by Ianthe Brooke.

"Salute!" *Catalogue* No. 164, New York: Dauber & Pine, n.d. [2].

"A Scene for *King Lear*" [prose drama]. *Sprite* 8, No. 3 (August 1917): [2–10]. [Introductory note by Harry Edward Martin, pp. [1–2].]

"A Scene for *Macbeth*" [prose drama]. *United Amateur* 20, No. 2 (November 1920): [17]–19.

"Scene from 'The Duchess Tragedy.'" *Quaker* 3, No. 2 (January 1910): 30–34.

"A Sea-Coal Fire." *Catalogue 157.* New York: Dauber & Pine, October 1934. [2], 48. In Bodley Book Shop. *General Literature and an Unusual Selection of Books.* No. 37 [May 1940]: [2].

The Sphinx [one-act play]. *Ghost* No. 2 (July 1944): 19–41. The speech beginning "Love had crazed him! . . ." is in *Saturnian* 1, No. 3 (March 1922): [1].

"The Theatrical Season" [essay]. *Trend* 1, No. 1 (March–April–May 1932): 23–24.

Thracia Deane [novel]. Nonextant.

"Tips from the Hobo." *The Hobo* 1, No. 1 (May 1904): 1–2.

"Under the Mistletoe." In Bodley Book Shop. *Books Reasonably Priced* . . . No. 34 [December 1939]: [2].

"An Unedited Anthology." In Bodley Book Shop. *Mid-winter Catalogue* . . . No. 35 [January 1940]: [2].

[Untitled description of book by M. R. James, mentioning H. P. Lovecraft.] *Catalogue 135.* New York: Dauber & Pine, [1933]. 30.

"We Break the Silence." In Bodley Book Shop. *Books Fine, Old, Rare* No. 17 [December 1937?]: [2]

"Where Do They Go To?" In Bodley Book Shop *An Early Autumn Catalogue* No. 49 [c. October 1941]): [2].

"A Whittier Discovery." *Catalogue 127.* New York: Dauber & Pine, n.d. n.p.

"Why We Read." [Unsigned]. In Bodley Book Shop. *General Literature, Rare Books* . . . No. 65 [November 1943]: [2].

Loveman also published:

The Hobo 1, No. 1 (May 1904).

Wild Rose [c. 1905–06?] 1, No. 1 [not seen]; 1, No. 2 [not seen]; 1, Nos. 3 and 4 (January–February 1906): Avalon; Shadow-Land; The Old Cobbler; Hope; The Song Unsung.

The Saturnian. Cleveland, Ohio. Three issues published. 1, No. 1 (June–July [1920]): Three Odes: 1. On the Passing of Youth 2. To Apollo 3. To Dionysus; Oscar Wilde; Comment. 1, No. 2 (August–September [1920]): A Prefatory Note; Twenty Four Translations from Heine; Comment. 1, No. 3 (March 1922): Modern Poetry (An Exorcism); Translations from Baudelaire; Translations from Verlaine; Four Poems: Amy Levy; In Sepulcretis; Saturday Evening; Euphorion; Ernest Nelson: In Memoriam; Comment.

The Poetical Works of Jonathan E. Hoag. New York: Privately printed, 1923. Loveman assisted in revising Hoag's poems.

Trend [SL is listed on the editorial board only for 1, No. 1]. Brooklyn, NY. 1–3, No. 1 (March–April–May 1932 through March–April 1935). Suspended July 1933–February 1934. Begun as *Trend: A Quarterly of the Seven Arts;* continued after suspension as *Trend: An Illustrated Bimonthly of the Arts.*

Two Letters by Hart Crane [4 pp.]. Brooklyn Heights, 1934. "Fifty Copies—For the Friends of Jack Birss." [Two letters addressed to SL, 9 December 1928 and 13 April 1932. They are reprinted in part in Brom Weber's edition of Crane's letters.]

As The Bodley Press, in a partnership with David Mann:

Hart Crane: A Biographical and Critical Study by Brom Weber. New York: Bodley Press, 1948.

The Case of Ezra Pound by Charles Norman. New York: Bodley Press, 1948.

The Wound Dresser: Letters Written to His Mother from the Hospitals in Washington During the Civil War by Walt Whitman. New York: Bodley Press, 1949.

The Blood of a Poet by Jean Cocteau, trans. Lily Pons. New York: Bodley Press, 1949.

Other

Benét, William Rose. "The Phoenix Nest," *Saturday Review* (14 March 1936): 22

Crane, Hart. *The Letters of Hart Crane, 1916–1932,* ed. Weber, Brom. Berkeley: University of California Press, 1952.

De Casseres, Benjamin. "Preface [to *The Hermaphrodite*]." H 7–8.

Edkins, Ernest A. [Review of *The Hermaphrodite and Other Poems.*] *Causerie* (June 1936) 2–4.

Kleiner, Rheinhart. "My Friend Samuel Loveman." *Aonian* 3, No. 3 (Autumn 1945): 241–44.

Lovecraft, H. P. Editor's note to "A Scene for Macbeth." *United Amateur* 20, No. 2 (November 1920): [17].

Martin, Harry Edwin. *National Times* No. 1 (June 1921): [3].

———. "A Scene for 'King Lear' by Way of Introduction." *Sprite* 8, No. 3 (August 1917): [1–2].

Sterling, George. "Rhymes and Reactions." *Overland Monthly* 84, No. 12 (December 1926): 395. Contains his review of *The Hermaphrodite*.

Index of Poetry Titles

Abyss, The   140
Ad Fratrem   78
Admonition   85
Admonition to the Ladies, An   142
Adventure   127
Aftermath   94
Agathon   70
Amy Levy   87
Andenkung   88
Arcesilaus   71
Ariel   83
Ascension   72
Avalon   101

Bacchanale   77
Bacio, Il   217
Be Thou a Jew!   100
Beauté, La   211
Becalmed   90
Belated Love   89
Ben De Casseres in Camden   97
Birth of Fear, The   99
Birth of Poesy, The   104
Bonne Chanson, La   217
Bruxelles   216
Burden, A   119

Catullus   208
Causerie   211
Chant d'Automne   212
Chat, Le   213
Chats, Les   215
Chinese Pavilion, A   95
Chopin-Player, The   75
Christmas—1923   133
Ciel Brouillé   215
Contrast   84
Couvercle, Le   213

David Gray   107
De Profundis Clamavi   210
De Profundis   108
Dead King, The   138
Debs in Prison   115
Dedication, A   76
Departure, A   120
Dirge   91
Dolore   77
Dowager   147
Dream of Spring   88
Dream Song   69

Ecce Homo   82
Episode   139
Epitaph, An   109
Ernest Nelson   131
Euphorion   70
Euthanasia   119
Eventide   106

Faithful, The   141
Finis   88
Foes   86
Fontaine de Sang, La   214
For a Book of Poems   71
For the Chelsea Book Shop [I]   142
For the Chelsea Book Shop [II]   143
Forest Hill   88
Forest of Rhododendron   81
Forgotten Poets   94
Fra Angelico   43
Freine   146

Gates Mills   87
Genesis   133
Georgia Garden, A   89
Goal, The   146
God's Work   220

Harbour   85
Heckscher Building   70
Heldenleben   131
Hermaphrodite, The   49

Hope   102
Horreur Sympathique   210
Illicit   147
In Pierrot's Garden   41
In Sepulcretis   128
Inarticulate   83
Interlude   86
Invocation   84
Isolation   78

John Clare in a Madhouse   74
John Clare in 1864   148

Kin   138

Legend   80
Letter to G—— K——, A   129
Lily, A   100
Limbo   86
Lineage   71
Lines   46
Lost Youth   101
Madison Square   84
Memoralia   81
Metropolitan Museum   141
Michael Scott's Wooing   110
Minstrel, The   75
Monolith   134
Music [A dream of music in the long, long night;]   94
Music [When I stood in mid-heaven,]   136
Musique, La   209
Mutation   90

My Tribute   136
Nepenthe   143
Night   107
Night Piece (Forest Hill)   134
Nostalgia   90

Ode to Ceres   42
Ode to Homer   108
Old Cobbler, The   102
On Lost Friendship   104
On the Passing of Youth   121
Oscar Redivivus   134

Oscar Wilde   73
Palingenesis   89
Parfum Exotique   209
Peccavi   105
Pierced   100
Plaint of Bygone Loves, The   105
Poet, A   99
Poppies   93
Prologue to Arcadia   111
[Prologue to *Circe*]   147
Proteus   79

Quatrain   144
Quatrains   109
Quatrains   93

Ramapos, The   73
Reliquiae   144
Remonstrance   79
Rescue   139
Resurgam   118
Return, The   80
River Pattern   67
Romances sans Paroles   217

Sagesse   216
Sappho   218
Saturday Evening   128
Shadow-Land   103
Shadow-Love   119
Ship of Dreams   103
Simeon Solomon   94
Song of Chamisso's, A   197
Song [Blossoms, blossoms, pink and white]   44
Song [In the Spring of the year, in the silver rain,]   85
Song Unsung, The   103
Sonnet: After Leconte de Lisle   219
Sonnet: Lethe, A   99
Sonnet d'Automne   214
Space   94
Spring at El Retiro   145
Steener Haakonson Dances   69
Sunset   106

Talent   126
Terminus   98
Thomas Dermody   114
Thomas Holley Chivers   72
Times Square   140
To a Child   137
To Alfred Noyes, Oversea   110
To Apollo   92
To Dionysus   91
To George Kirk on His 27th Birthday   136
To Mr. Theobald   135
To P. G.   45
To Satan   132
To Simone's   78
Transience   76
Transit   139
Translations from Baudelaire   209
Translations from Verlaine   216
Triumph in Eternity, A   124
Twenty-four Translations from Heine   197
Twenty-second Birthday, A   46
Twilight   107
Two Poems for Book Marks   112

Uncollected Poems   99
Understanding   82
Unfulfilled   135
Unfulfilled [Alternative]   135
[[Untitled] [He said: This is the city . . . . here have we,]   126
[Untitled] [Within my little plot of light,]   126
[Untitled] [I dreamed I had a pocket book,]   145
[Untitled] [The lanes are drifted white with snow,]   146

Versailles   145
Vert   218
Vice   76
Vigil   137
Visitor   83
Voyage, A   79

W. E.   120
Wasteland   87
Will o' The Wisp   68
Winter   131

Index of First Lines

A blossom dropped from God's domain   100
A dream of music in the long, long night;   94
A flagon is filled for the vintage guest,   77
A heaven is over these houses,   216
A little white lady who lived apart,   144
A man is but the Pendulum of Fate,   99
A moth's wing beats the feathered night,   84
A pine stands bare and lonely,   200
A purple mist o'er-shadows all the vale,   106
A star falls out of the heavens,   201
A thousand shadows darken yonder hill,   107
All night the Mississippi on the banks   67
As I sit in this room with half a shiver,   75
As I went through the rain and wind   133
As we came up the little steep street of signs,   78
At Andre's in the soft Spring night,   90
At evening in the moonlight on the regimental street,   120

Back to the fountain runs the flame,   77
Be thou a Jew! Let oppressors scoff   100
Beautiful was the byway,   146
Beauty am I, O mortals, dreamed in stone!   211
Behold the fruits, the flowers, the leaves, the branches,   218
Below were ships and then the bay,   85
Bend close and listen: Long ago,   135
Bend close and listen: long ago,   135
Beneath these pines and lucent skies,   72
Bill, when the eastern moon hangs low,   88
Black hulls, black spars against the darkness lie;   87
Blake, who beheld the stars beyond the sun,   94
Blossoms, blossoms, pink and white   44
Brave, pitiful, loyal, suffering, true,   136
Bronze, in the green, inverted night,   76
Brother and bunkmate, old friend Epe,   120
Brothers, who passed before me, one by one,   94
By a wizard moon in an elfin wood,   198
Byron's soul was mire,   69

Caught in a web of silver hail, then blown   80

Cleis, the daughter of Sappho, she sat by a twilit sea,   119
Close thine eyes, the night is come,   91
Come, Jesus, be this night my guest,   141
Could I but drink a draught, however small,   99
Cupid grasped his bow one day,   100

Dante saw hell, an opal lit with ice,   126
Dawn, shimmering like a boundless rose,   94
Death comes—now I can say with pleasure,   199
Death is the cool sweet night, they say,   201
Deep in the moonlight—Oh, so deep and quiet!   94

Ecclesiastes said: Better a dog that lives   219
Encased in rouge, a rhythm gone astray,   148
Ere half my youth had flowered and broken   110
Ere long we plunge benumbed into the pall;   212
Ere men can pluck you stem by stem,   93
Eurydamus of Crete, with his beaked green ships   79

Fever and heartache, joy and grief,   85
Forth from the deep, the Odyssey in blue   147
Friendship! thou mighty crown of love's devotion!   104
Furious, with sunken eyes and rigid breasts,   218

Gentles and Ladies, and it please you list,   111

Half the world was chaos,   133
He is   99
He lived within a golden house,   73
He said: This is the city . . . . here have we,   126
He, with his dying eyes said: All is well,   88
Heere beneath this marble lyes,   109
Here in this valley blue with mist,   89
Here we are come to a place where Summer ends,   98
Here, in the night, are winds that cry and keep   129
Here, in the room as darkness falls,   81
Here, in the shadows of the creek,   148

I am a dreamer in the world,   74
I am a withered chaff tossed by the wind,   82
I am he who came   121
I am the princess Ilse,   207
I am the surge and the song of the sea where the tides sweep along to their refluent sleep,   108
I can not think it that the souls of all   101

I dreamed I had a pocket book,   145
I hate and love. You ask how this can be?   208
I implore thy pity, Thou, the unique adored,   210
I in the night heard   137
I know no light beyond the night,   46
I lay at last in my resting-place,   119
I saw a dancer dancing on a mesh   69
I shall build a palace with a wall around it,   86
I shall go back to my life of dreams,   78
I shall walk to Dover when the blackbirds fly,   76
I that am Beauty's slave,   79
I was a harp untouched by fingers   75
I was born a singing bird,   83
I was once in fever   90
I would be back in Lesbos when the Spring begins to break,   71
I would make the thing I love,   134
I, who came from a wandering star,   83
If, in the Æschylean night   76
In Florence, under morning skies,   112
In old Versailles the days that fare   145
In Providence at fringèd eve   135
In the Spring of the year, in the silver rain,   85
It seems my blood runs ever on and urges,   214
Ivy grows wild among the hills,   73

Kings of the Nile that lie in painted wood,   86
Kiss! rose-red hollyhock in the garden of caresses!   217

Ladies, when at night you close   142
Leaves shine and flicker on the walk,   84
Li Ho Chan in the sunset's gleam,   95
Lie, lovely cat, the idol of the wise;   213
Life is a pearl that with the sea   144
Little sophist, sweetly-wise,   109
Lo—from the lapping sea, there rose a star,   104
Look for me at dusk when the lights begin to burn,   80
Lord! how they loved in a wanton way   105
Lucent was the twilight   139

Mother, that in the Asian sapphire dawn,   115
Music, that bears me oft times as the sea!   209
My songs, my songs are poison'd,   203

Never again shall I come to you in Spring divinely drunken   71

Night had come, and o'er the moor,   105
O Michael Scott is a-wooing gone   110
O my sweet love, when to the grave   206
O thou, from whose pale brow the vine leaves fall,   91
O to be with gods, to shout the golden tumult   83
Oh, 'tis I that would be a pirate bold,   127
Old remembrances, how sweet?   101
On a day of azure in the golden Spring   90
On her hand a lamp lies gleaming,   198
Once, with the south wind and the swallow,   70
One last sweet look at boyhood's fledgling gleam,   46
One who sought his soul in a life that joyed in faring,   131
Oscar, when your eyes of light   134
Out of my infinite woe   200
Out of the deep, immortal night   49
Out of the night exhaled in sleep and tears   143
Out of this strange and livid shell,   210
Over many lands and many seas I come,   208
Over the silent mere it drifts,   103
Over the western rim it slips,   139

Proteus of Sparta came to Troy to thieve,   79

Rose-colored in its firmament of clay,   141
Roses soon to follow,   197

Shadow-love and shadow-kisses,   199
She was a flash and he was a thief,   205
So bade my brother when he passed away: 78
So still he seemed, so still he lay,   138
Something within her like a fever,   87
Spring comes this way on bud and briar,   145
Starlit and blue   87
Stars splinter the night, the moon rides high,   97
Still do I hear where hillside winds are shaken,   136
Still he sits and pegs away,   102
Such a world of wonder lies,   109
Sweet Mother, saffron-haired and argent-eyed,   42
Sweeter than all the honeyed sweets,   103
Swift to elude and to evade,   89

That fool am I to whom love came,   89
The apple blossoms drift apart   147

The beggars in the night and rain,   128
The boys of Times Square,   140
The boys who did not choose to fight—   131
The flight is pink and green   216
The golden cock in the golden night,   70
The golden visit of the sun   68
The good king Wiswamitra   204
The great immortal poets   84
The lady sleeps in her chamber,   205
The lanes are drifted white with snow,   146
The leaves were silver in the wood   81
The lotus-flower closes   202
The moon climbs over the garden wall,   134
The moon of snow   217
The night is over Chelsea Town,   143
The nightingales that sang in their Asian garden   71
The petals in the soft May wind,   88
The rain came down on Easter Day and Jesus bared His head;   72
The rose is dead, the leaf is sere,   102
The roses bud and blossom,   201
The shadow of trees in the hazy river   217
The stars are adrift in the breathless night,   137
The very dusk seems shrined in silver here,   107
The west wind ere the morning came   119
The wingèd petals of roses,   88
The world is so sweet   201
The yellow leaves are falling,   206
There is a moaning o'er Sicilian ways,   92
There lies a nook in the imminence of night,   45
There on the lonely moor, storm-swept and bleak,   107
There rose from dreaming in a hueless spring,   124
There shall be music in the night,   70
There was a king of olden,   203
There was a moth that took the flame at even   86
There where the azure skies   103
There's a lark that's drunken with the daedal moon,   41
They have brought Lawrence back from France with flowers,   128
They loved one another but neither   200
They say your gaze is of a cloud enthralled;   215
They say, these crystal eyes, so clear and mute: 214
They tortured me with their whimsies,   204

This is a babe Angelico painted,   43
Those fiery loves and they who wisdom carry,   215
Thou art a sky of autumn, clear and rose!   211
Though who dost hold in thine eternal hands   108
Three friends had I, spake Socrates,   139
Three holy Kings came from the East,   199
Thus died the poet Dermody: I, Gray,   114
To toil with fools, to drudge with slaves   46

Under a rain-reflected light   146
Up from the night that rounds earth's sovereign steep,   109

Walk into Chelsea where each street   142
Whatever land be his, in places wan,   213
When I am dust blown by the wind,   118
When I stood in mid-heaven,   136
When you lie below in darkness and in duress   138
When you sit down to read a book,   113
When, in the night on hill and hillside shaken,   131
When, mid the hyacinth deep that girds the sky,   132
When, with eyes closed, a sultry autumn night,   209
Where, in the frore Atlantic, peaked and hurled,   140
With her shadows vast and dreary,   202
Within my breast there sits a woe   204
Within my little plot of light,   126
Workers are we: masters, disciples, pages,   220

You knew this thing as we two sat together,   82

www.ingramcontent.com/pod-product-compliance
Lightning Source LLC
Chambersburg PA
CBHW060102170426
43198CB00010B/743